An Illustrated Encyclopedia of Clematis

An Illustrated Encyclopedia of

CLEMATIS

Mary Toomey
&
Everett Leeds

Photography Editor
Charles Chesshire

Published in association with the
BRITISH CLEMATIS SOCIETY

TIMBER PRESS

TO OUR PARENTS

Frontispiece: *Clematis patens* in the wild.
Photo by J. Lindmark.

Published in 2001 by
Timber Press, Inc.
The Haseltine Building
133 S.W. Second Avenue, Suite 450
Portland, Oregon 97204, U.S.A.
www.timberpress.com

Designed by Susan Applegate
Printed through Colorcraft Ltd., Hong Kong

08 07 06 05   2 3 4 5

Library of Congress Cataloging-in-Publication Data

Toomey, Mary.
    An illustrated encyclopedia of clematis / Mary Toomey and Everett Leeds; photograph editor, Charles Chesshire.
        p. cm.
    Includes bibliographical references (p.).
    ISBN 0-88192-508-X
    1. Clematis. I. Leeds, Everett. II. British Clematis Society.
III. Title.
QK495.R215 T66 2001
583'.34—dc21
                                            2001027155

Contents

Foreword

The gardening world has for too long been without a reliable and substantial source of information or definitive work on the genus *Clematis*, particularly the cultivars. We are fortunate that the authors, the British Clematis Society, and Timber Press were able to come together to create *An Illustrated Encyclopedia of Clematis*. Setting out to provide comprehensive coverage of this topic required considerable planning, dedication, and resources. Mary Toomey, editor of the British Clematis Society journal, and her enthusiastic and dedicated team worked tirelessly to produce a work of the highest standard. Their commitment and skill are reflected in the depth and quality of the information contained within this publication.

The British Clematis Society was formed in 1991 with the principal aims of encouraging, informing, and promoting the growth and enjoyment of clematis in the garden. These aims are embodied in the Society's efforts to educate gardeners on all aspects of clematis. In the decade since the Society was established it has enjoyed a steady increase in membership, this in parallel with its gaining status in Britain as a registered charity. The Society now promotes a wide-ranging programme of events, which are open to the public as well as to its members, and attends gardening shows and exhibitions throughout the United Kingdom. In my capacity as chairman, I am delighted that the Society should be associated with this prestigious publication, the first-ever encyclopedia of clematis.

An Illustrated Encyclopedia of Clematis exceeds any reference work that has been previously published on the subject, both in its coverage of each variety and in the comprehensive size of the production. Great care has also been exercised in ensuring faithful colour reproduction of the extensive photographs. The book is, of course, a highly specialized work in that it covers only one genus. The content, however, is presented in such a practical style as to be easily digestible for the keen gardener of clematis as well as for the nursery professional or amateur grower.

Clematis have enjoyed increasing popularity in the garden in recent years, and, thanks to the endeavours of plant hunters and hybridizers, the selection of plants available to gardeners includes a rising number of new introductions. About 300 *Clematis* species have been recorded, with more surely still to be discovered, and there are hundreds of cultivars. The process of deciding which plants to include or exclude in this encyclopedia was a Herculean task. I am confident, however, of the final selection of more than 550 garden-worthy species and cultivars. Each description includes information about the plant's origin, parentage, height, habit, and pruning requirements. The authors also offer guidance on the selection of varieties for colour and intended planting position, on the impact of potential pests and diseases, and on all aspects of cultivation and propagation from seed, cuttings, and layering. Clematis are perhaps unique amongst plants, as varieties can be found in flower almost every month of the year. This trait, which may also be a main attraction for the many fervent fans of clematis, is amplified by commentary on flowering period, preferred aspects, and hardiness zones.

An Illustrated Encyclopedia of Clematis represents a labour of love for those who were involved in its production. It is an informative summary of the species and cultivars of this popular genus and will surely be a source of enjoyment to all who refer to its pages.

MIKE BROWN
Chairman
British Clematis Society

Preface

The last decade of the twentieth century witnessed not only an unprecedented rise in the popularity of clematis as a garden plant, but also a surge in the number of specialist nurseries offering a wide range of cultivars and species to the more discerning collector and the gardener who wants one, two, or more clematis in the garden. It is not uncommon to hear gardeners with a passion for this genus talk about the number of clematis in their collections and be on the lookout for more and more choice plants. From the shelves of supermarkets to garden centres, from market stalls to annual private garden plant sales, gardeners can pick up a plant or two of even what would have been considered a difficult, rare, or specialist plant when I started gardening with clematis thirty-odd years ago.

It is not surprising that clematis have become hugely popular plants. The genus boasts a staggering range of colour—from Wedgwood blues to bright purples; from matt, shell pinks to satiny, smooth and vibrant reds; from sparkling starry whites to the somewhat gently captivating creams, culminating in soft, unadulterated waxy yellows. Although there is no black clematis flower, the newly opened, juvenile flowers of cultivars such as *Clematis* 'Black Prince', 'Niobe', 'Purple Spider', and 'Royal Velours' among others almost border on a deep shade of black. Add to that astonishing range of colour, the size and shape of the flowers—from the smallest to the widest, from the bell-shaped to the platelike, from the

upward-facing tuliplike to the gently nodding ones—and it becomes apparent why clematis has been justifiably crowned as the queen of climbers.

Clematis are very accommodating garden plants. With their agile vertical and horizontal mobility, they create drama, rhythm, and movement in a garden of any size or shape. With careful selection there can be a clematis in bloom for more or less each month of the year.

While most clematis are well known and widely grown as climbers, the genus also comprises a number of perhaps less familiar shrubby, subshrubby, and herbaceous species and cultivars. They too are beginning to make their way into herbaceous and mixed borders of gardens all over the world.

With the ever-increasing popularity of clematis as decorative garden plants, hybridizers and nurseries have risen to the challenge and have been busy raising and introducing more and more large- and small-flowered cultivars. Also, during the recent past, a great number of books on clematis have become available to inform and educate gardeners about this magical genus; however, not a single, comprehensively illustrated work has been published to serve the needs of passionate gardeners who grow a large number and variety of clematis. Nurseries have often articulated the need for such a volume of work. The British Clematis Society was also anxious to see this void filled, and is delighted to be associated with this publication.

My co-author, a clematis enthusiast and former chairman of the British Clematis Society, Everett Leeds, and I make no apologies to the botanists, taxonomists, clematis specialists, and horticulturists for this work written in everyday language to meet the specific needs of gardeners who grow clematis with great love and enthusiasm. Simply put, here is a book written by gardeners with a lifelong interest in clematis, for gardeners with a passion for these wonderful plants, which have little in the way of competition except perhaps for roses, honeysuckles, and possibly sweet peas. It is encouraging all the same that roses and clematis are splendid companions. I also found, more by accident than by design, that the sweet pea *Lathyrus* 'Painted Lady' and *Clematis* 'Duchess of Albany' proved to be excellent neighbours. It was a lesson in combining colour and creating harmony between these two very different kinds of plants and flowers. Similarly, the flower-laden vines of *Clematis* 'Comtesse de Bouchard' weaving their way into a low-growing *Daphne sericea* in flower, and creating a true vision of beauty in that togetherness, strengthened my belief in growing clematis with, through, up, and over other suitable garden plants.

This long-awaited book is laid out in two main sections. The first is mainly devoted to the care and cultivation of clematis while the second one deals with an A to Z of clematis. *The RHS Plant Finder* (1999–2000 edition) lists more than 800 *Clematis* species and cultivars, but we have restricted our entries to 550 based on their garden worthiness. Most of these clematis have been growing in our gardens for a long time and are tried and tested varieties. The newcomers, particularly those from Poland, Estonia, Latvia, and Russia, are enchanting too—grow them all with confidence. We appreciate that not all clematis listed in this book are readily available everywhere; however, we have appended a list of nurseries including those which specialize in mail order, nationally and internationally. We trust this will assist gardeners to acquire their favourite plants. We have also given an overview of the different groups of clematis based on the gardener's classification of clematis outlined in chapter one. There are separate lists of clematis, which belong to the different groups in appendix 1. Additionally, appendix 2 carries information on clematis by colour. Both sets of information we hope will prove useful to gardeners in choosing a clematis by name or colour and visiting the plant entry in the directory for all the necessary information.

In writing this book our aim was to help and encourage you, the gardener, to enjoy selecting and growing clematis. It really does not matter how you pronounce the word *clematis* or the name of a cultivar or species. What is really important is the pleasure you derive from gardening with clematis. We should like, however, to issue a *caveat emptor*: growing and collecting clematis can easily become a happy and healthy obsession!

Mary K. Toomey
Editor, *The Clematis*
Journal of the British Clematis Society
May 2000

Acknowledgements

We would like to thank our families, particularly Aoife, Barry, and Carol, for their unflagging love, fortitude, support, encouragement, understanding, and consideration during the long months it took to finish this work.

The photograph editor, Charles Chesshire, would like to convey his special thanks to his wife, Anne de Charmant, for her patience and support, and to his brother Michael and to all the staff at Treasures for their enthusiasm.

The endorsement of this project by the British Clematis Society gave us access to sources of knowledge and expertise that might not otherwise have been available.

Special thanks must go to Catherine Sweeney, Barry Toomey, and Russell Goodwyn, whose computer expertise enabled us to complete this enterprise in a timely manner.

Our gratitude also goes to Robin Savill, who gave generously of his vast knowledge in the areas of history, nomenclature, and cultivation of clematis; Jan Lindmark, who not only made his extensive slide library available to us but also gave us invaluable advice on photographic matters; and Ron Kirkman of the British Clematis Society, who was unfailingly enthusiastic about this project, shared his photographic talent with us, and also helped in every conceivable way.

We cannot forget Maurice Horn and Linda Beutler for their transatlantic aid or leave out the many others who helped in ways too numerous to mention but without whose support and assistance we would have been lost. Chief among these are Professor M. A. Beskaravainaja, Denis Bradshaw, Sheila Chapman, Vince and Sylvia Denny, Peter and Ron Evans, Pamela Gauntlett, the Gibbison family, Ruth and Jon Gooch, staff of the Guernsey Clematis Nursery, Peter Herbert, John and Maureen Hudson, Josie Hulbert, Anita Jean, Patricia Kennedy, Erika Mahhov, Brian Mathew (editor, *Curtis's Botanical Magazine*), Victoria Matthews (International Clematis Registrar), Todd Miles, Nancy Nesathurai, Úna and Paddy Ó Callanáin, Joan and Brian Reilly, staff of the Royal Horticultural Society Library at Wisley, staff at the Royal Horticultural Society Lindley Library, Justina Susla, Monika Svensson, Hiroshi Takeuchi (president, Japan Clematis Society), Marilyn Ward (illustrations curator, library, Royal Botanic Gardens, Kew), Judith A. Warnement (librarian, Harvard University Botany Libraries), and Ken Woolfenden (slide librarian, British Clematis Society).

For use of their photographs we thank Yoshiaki Aihara; M. A. Beskaravainaja; Linda Beutler; Tony Bowran; Maurice Bracher; Denis Bradshaw; the British Clematis Society Slide Library; Mike Brown; Vince Denny; Jack Elliott; Keith Fair; Pamela Gauntlett; John Glover; Anne Green-Armytage; Nicholas Hall; Hamlyn Publishers; David Harding; Jerry Harpur; Marcus Harpur; Peter Herbert; Ingmar Holmåsen; John Hudson; Michael Humphries; Merv Jerard; Ron Kirkman; Satomi Kuriyama; Jan Lindmark; Brian Mathew; Veijo Miettinen; Notcutts Nurseries; Roy Nunn; Pennell and Sons nursery; James S. Pringle; Ken Pyne; Ron Ratko; Royal Botanic Gardens, Kew; Royal Horticultural Society; Chris Sanders; Robin Savill; Jane Sterndale-Bennett; Kozo Sugimoto; Richard Surman; Thorncroft Clematis Nursery; and John Treasure.

To all the people mentioned above and to anyone whom we may have inadvertently omitted, we offer a heartfelt "thank you."

How to Use This Book

We have taken every care to make this book gardener-friendly and have endeavoured to describe the many cultivars and few species under categories such as synonyms; origin; parentage and year; growth habit; plant height; shape, colour, and size of flowers; pruning group; flowering period; cultivation tips; recommended uses; and U.S. Department of Agriculture hardiness zone.

Cultivar names and cultivar groups

At the time of writing this book, *The International Clematis Register* was not published; however, we have, insofar as possible, checked every name and, where necessary, sought and received help from the International Clematis Registrar. In addition, instead of following the conventional method of presenting the cultivar names with the species name, we have simply listed the cultivar name with the relevant group name to which it belongs, where necessary, while omitting the species name. This method is most predominantly used for the Atragene, Heracleifolia, Integrifolia, Montana, and Viticella Groups. For example, *Clematis alpina* 'Ruby' is listed as *C.* 'Ruby' (Atragene Group), with *C. alpina* 'Ruby' as its synonym. Similarly *C. montana* 'Freda' is listed as *C.* 'Freda' (Montana Group) with *C. montana* 'Freda' as its synonym. This format eliminates the confusion of appending a cultivar name to that of the species and makes the alphabetized plant directory easier to use. On the other hand, a species name is rarely appended to a large-flowered cultivar, which makes it less problematic. Never-

theless, large-flowered cultivars also belong to different cultivar groups, but to minimize confusion and maximize ease of reference, these cultivar groups have been excluded totally. Chapter eight provides an overview of the different groups of clematis, and a list of them can be found in appendix 1.

Trade names (selling names) and Plant Breeders' Rights

Plants granted protection under Plant Breeders' Rights (PBR) are often given a code or contrived name for purposes of registration. Under the rules of the *International Code of Nomenclature for Cultivated Plants* (1995), such a name is considered the correct cultivar name for the plant. Furthermore, when a cultivar name is translated into a language other than that in which it was published, the translated name is also regarded as a trade name in the same way as the PBR selling name. The trade and translated names appear in small capital letters after the appropriate entry. For example *Clematis* 'Kugotia' is sold under the trade name of GOLDEN TIARA. In the plant directory it is listed as *C.* 'Kugotia' (GOLDEN TIARA™). Similarly, *C.* 'Kacper' has a translated name and is listed in the plant directory as *C.* 'Kacper' (CASPAR™). All the names by which a given clematis is known are included in the index at the back of the book, with cross references to the correct plant name. Appendix 3 lists cultivar names with their appropriate trade and translated names.

Where plants are protected under Plant Breeders' Rights, that information is included under "Origin." Propagation of such plants under any circumstances is prohibited without a licence from the rights holder. In effect it is a plant patent.

Synonyms

All known synonyms and either translation of some Polish, Estonian, Russian, Latvian, and Japanese names of cultivars or their meanings are included. The name in its original language is the correct cultivar name. Where the species have common names, they are also recorded.

Origin, parentage, and year

Where these details are known, they are given, and with a brief summary of any interesting story behind the origin. Wherever possible, the year the seed was sown or the cultivar was selected, named, and introduced is also recorded.

Habit

Growth habit includes information on whether a plant is a climber, shrub, subshrub, or herbaceous, and whether it is deciduous or evergreen (winter green). Additionally, the vigour of the plant is recorded as not too vigorous, vigorous, moderately vigorous, very vigorous, strong or weak growing, or compact, as the case may be.

Height

Here we have stated the average height of the plant but have refrained from recording spread for each entry for the simple reason most clematis are climbers. Their growth habit precludes any definite method for ascertaining that measurement, especially when they are grown with other garden plants such as trees, shrubs, and climbers.

Flower colour and size

Colour is a very tricky topic. In many cultivars of clematis (particularly those which boast flowers in many different shades of blue and purple), the colour depends on a number of factors including flowering time, composition of soil, aspect (light or shade), and temperature. In some very early flowering cultivars, especially those with white flowers, the tepals turn green. While the description of colour is subjective, photographs seldom lie, although blues and purples can often be challenging to the photographer. Every effort has been taken to ensure the true colour of the flower was captured by the photographers at the height of flowering season (main display) of each cultivar or species. Where necessary, a group of flowers (especially the pinks) is shown in the photographs to demonstrate the variation in the colouring. Another difficulty with clematis flowers is the gradual colour change, as a juvenile flower graduates to maturity; alas, it is a simple truth of young and old. Appendix 2 lists clematis by flower colour.

The size of flowers is also governed by a number of factors including soil, climate, and regular feeding and watering. We have given the average size of blooms of plants grown with great love and care. While most entries give the diameter of flowers, where necessary we have also recorded the average length of tepals.

Pruning

Whether a clematis belongs to pruning group 1, 2, or 3 is stated clearly for each entry. We ask the reader to refer to chapter four for detailed information on pruning.

Flowering period

The flowering times for each entry are indicated according to seasons, which are divided into early, mid, or late. Some clematis, particularly the double-flowering cultivars, flower twice (early double and late single or double at both times) during the same year; where appropriate this information is recorded as well.

Awards

Of the four main awards mentioned in this book, three are given by the Royal Horticultural Society. The Award of Merit (AM) is given to meritorious plants exhibited at the Society's shows including the Chelsea Flower Show. The First Class Certificate (FCC) is more prestigious than the AM and is only given to plants which are outstanding at exhibition. The Award of Garden Merit (AGM), reinstituted in 1992, is presented to plants of outstanding excellence and is of practical value for the gardener. The fourth award, given by the British Clematis Society, is the Certificate of Merit awarded to exceptional cultivars from the Society's trial grounds.

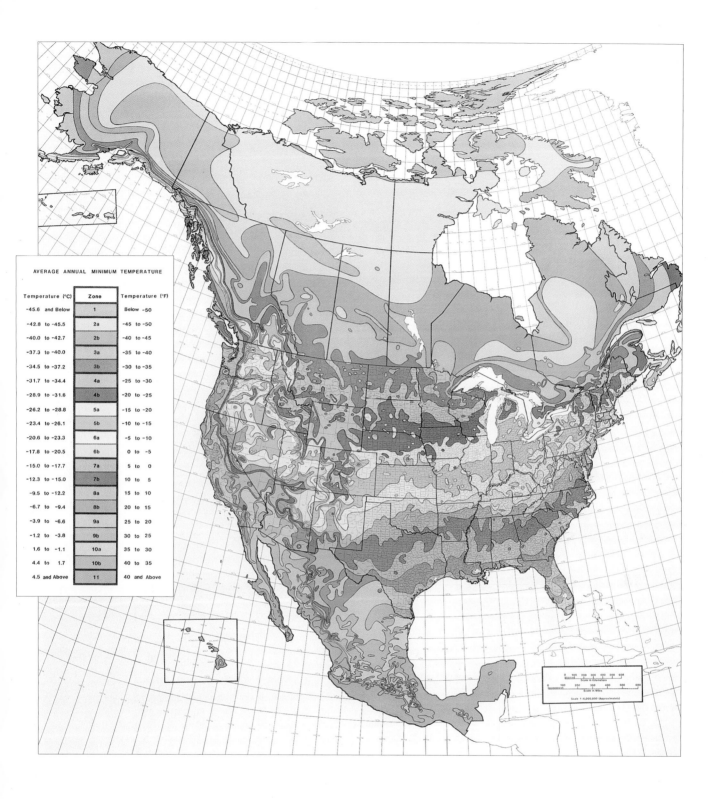

AVERAGE ANNUAL MINIMUM TEMPERATURE

Temperature (°C)	Zone	Temperature (°F)
-45.6 and Below	1	Below -50
-42.8 to -45.5	2a	-45 to -50
-40.0 to -42.7	2b	-40 to -45
-37.3 to -40.0	3a	-35 to -40
-34.5 to -37.2	3b	-30 to -35
-31.7 to -34.4	4a	-25 to -30
-28.9 to -31.6	4b	-20 to -25
-26.2 to -28.8	5a	-15 to -20
-23.4 to -26.1	5b	-10 to -15
-20.6 to -23.3	6a	-5 to -10
-17.8 to -20.5	6b	0 to -5
-15.0 to -17.7	7a	5 to 0
-12.3 to -15.0	7b	10 to 5
-9.5 to -12.2	8a	15 to 10
-6.7 to -9.4	8b	20 to 15
-3.9 to -6.6	9a	25 to 20
-1.2 to -3.8	9b	30 to 25
1.6 to -1.1	10a	35 to 30
4.4 to 1.7	10b	40 to 35
4.5 and Above	11	40 and Above

Scale in Kilometers
Scale in Miles
Scale 1:6,200,000 (Approximately)

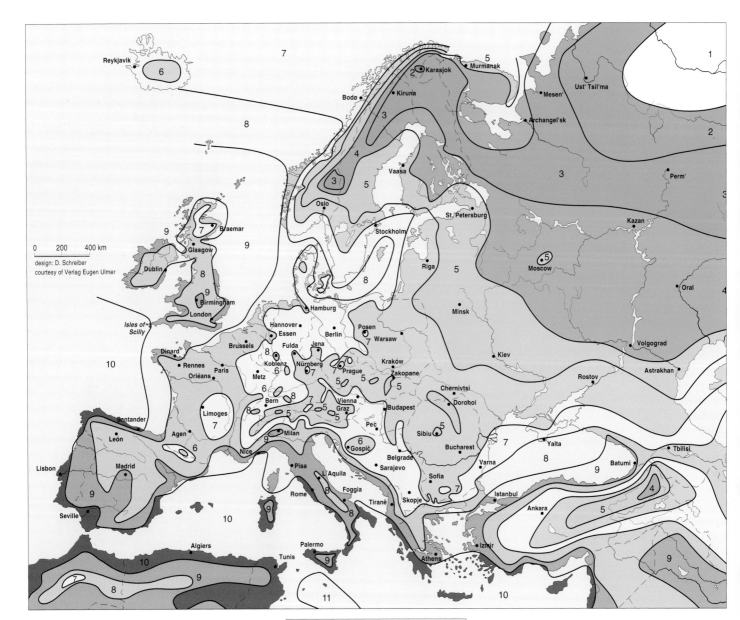

AVERAGE ANNUAL MINIMUM TEMPERATURE		
Temperature (°C)	Zone	Temperature (°F)
-45.6 and Below	1	Below -50
-45.5 to -40.0	2	-50 to -40
-40.0 to -34.5	3	-40 to -30
-34.4 to -28.9	4	-30 to -20
-28.8 to -23.4	5	-20 to -10
-23.3 to -17.8	6	-10 to 0
-17.7 to -12.3	7	0 to 10
-12.2 to -6.7	8	10 to 20
-6.6 to -1.2	9	20 to 30
-1.1 to 4.4	10	30 to 40
4.5 and Above	11	40 and Above

PART I

Clematis 'Tetrarose' finds support on *Pinus nigra*. Photo by C. Chesshire.

CHAPTER ONE

History and Botany of Clematis

The genus *Clematis* has in excess of 1000 species and cultivars, but interest in these plants is a relatively modern phenomenon. There are no written references before the mid-sixteenth century, and even by the end of that century only European species were known in Britain. The work of dedicated plant hunters and the growth of trade in the eighteenth century saw introductions from China and the New World happily coinciding with an interest in the study of botany so that by 1872 more than 200 species had been recorded.

History

Clematis (from the Greek word *klema*, meaning a "vine branch") as a flower, unlike the romantic rose, did not feature a great deal in ancient prose or poetry. It is possible, however, to trace its botanical and horticultural history from about the sixteenth century. *Clematis vitalba*, famously referred to as the old man's beard because of its fluffy white seedheads in autumn, was mentioned as the hedge-vine by William Turner in 1548 in *The Names of Herbes*. It was also called by other names in many different languages, the most common English names being beggar's plant, devil's guts, gypsy's bacca, and traveller's joy.

Introductions of the sixteenth to nineteenth centuries

From a gardener's point of view the clematis came into its own as far back as 1569 when the first species, *Clematis viticella* from southeastern Europe, was introduced into Britain, followed closely by *C. integrifolia, C. cirrhosa*, and *C. flammula* in 1596 and *C. recta* in 1597, from southern and eastern Europe. All four of these species are in cultivation today. After a flurry of activity, there was a long pause of almost a century before the North American species joined the Europeans in Britain. *Clematis crispa* was introduced in 1726, followed by the leather flower, *C. viorna*, in 1730. Neither of these American species played a role in future hybridization programmes, which gave rise to a number of excellent colourful cultivars. Soon afterwards, in 1731, *C. orientalis* arrived from northern Asia.

The second half of the eighteenth century ushered in a very important Chinese species, *Clematis florida*, a native of Hubei province in western China. It is mentioned frequently in the annals of *Clematis*. Barry Fretwell (1989) wrote, "Over the years, many writers have made reference to it, obviously with second-hand knowledge only, as no European has seen a plant in living memory." Fretwell described this rare species, supported by an excellent photograph of the flowers, in his book *Clematis*, first published in 1989, having grown a plant sent to him by a friend who collected it in its native habitat, "an area not open to foreigners." *Clematis florida*, however, did not become established in gardens and seems to have been lost to cultivation (Evison 1998). Other newcomers were *C. cirrhosa* var. *balearica* from the Balearic Islands, and *C. alpina* from northeast Asia and central Europe, which arrived on the scene in 1783 and 1792, respectively.

Of all the *Clematis* species introduced into Europe during the eighteenth century, *C. florida* appears to have caused the greatest flutter. It was believed for a long time that Carl Peter Thunberg introduced it into Sweden from Japan in 1776; however, according to Raymond Evison, author of *The Gardener's Guide to Growing Clematis* (1998), and Magnus Johnson, a distinguished Swedish clematarian and author of *Släktet Klematis* (1996), the herbarium specimen held in the University of Uppsala is not typical of *C. florida* but bears close resemblance to an unnamed poor form of *C.* 'Sieboldii', also known in the past as *C. florida* 'Sieboldiana' and *C. florida* 'Bicolor'. *Clematis* 'Sieboldii' was introduced into the Leiden Botanic Garden in the Netherlands in 1837, by its director, Philipp von Siebold. Soon after its introduction, *C.* 'Sieboldii' sported to produce another double-flowered cultivar, *C.* 'Plena', also known as *C. florida* 'Alba Plena'. Both *C.* 'Sieboldii' and *C.* 'Plena' were introduced from the Netherlands into the British Isles in 1836.

The nineteenth century was an exciting era in the history and development of clematis, with many more valuable foreign species being added to the list of earlier arrivals. Two large-flowered species from China—*Clematis patens* (also found in Japan), introduced by Philipp von Siebold in 1836, and *C. lanuginosa*, introduced by Robert Fortune around 1850—proved to be of particular value, and along with the previously introduced *C. florida* and *C. viticella* opened the channels for future hybridization. Speculation abounds regarding *C. lanuginosa*. Some reports of its discovery suggest that it was found growing in a churchyard, leading to the conclusion that it may have been an early cultivar or even a sport from *C. patens*, rather than a naturally occurring species (Evison 1998).

In spite of all the excitement following the introduction of *Clematis florida*, it was the arrival of *C. patens*, *C. lanuginosa*, and the early Japanese cultivars *C.* 'Fortunei' and *C.* 'Standishii' which offered the greatest potential to future breeding. The latter two cultivars were introduced by Robert Fortune, although there appears to be a difference of opinion on the actual years of introduction. According to Christopher Lloyd (Lloyd and Bennett 1989), *C.* 'Fortunei' was introduced in the 1830s or '40s

and *C.* 'Standishii' in 1861, while Thomas Moore and George Jackman (1872) and Raymond Evison (1998) claimed that both were introduced in 1863.

By the time Moore and Jackman wrote *The Clematis as a Garden Flower* in 1872, about 230 *Clematis* species had been identified and scientifically recorded. The wide geographical distribution of the genus is evident from the data: 17 species from southern and eastern Europe, 43 from India, 9 from Java, 30 from China and Japan, 11 from Siberia, 2 from the Fiji Islands, 24 from South America, 9 from Central America and the West Indies, 35 from North America, 14 from tropical Africa, 4 from South Africa, 6 from the Mascarene Islands and Madagascar, 15 from Australia, and 5 from New Zealand. By the year 2000, there were about 297 recorded species (Grey-Wilson 2000), of which at least 120 are native to China. About 150 species are in cultivation now.

The first hybrids

The nineteenth century can also be rightly considered a very exciting and rewarding period in the history of clematis hybridization. The challenge of breeding new, large, and spectacular cultivars began in earnest, and in a matter of 30 years between 1860 and 1890 "more new varieties of clematis were raised than at any time in the history of clematis" (Fretwell 1989).

The credit for raising and introducing in 1835 the earliest known hybrid, *Clematis* 'Hendersoni' (*C. viticella* × *C. integrifolia*), is usually given to Mr. Henderson of the Pineapple Nursery, London, England. It appears, however, that *C.* 'Eriostemon', also the result of a cross between *C. viticella* and *C. integrifolia*, was the first cultivar to be bred in either Belgium or the Netherlands in 1830 (Evison 1998).

Irrespective of which hybrid appeared first, many British and European nurseries embarked on extensive hybridization programmes to produce some fine clematis. One of them, *Clematis* 'Hendersoni', was later to play a part in the production of a cultivar destined to remain in great demand for more than 100 years. In 1858 George Jackman crossed this cultivar with *C. lanuginosa* and *C. viticella* 'Atrorubens' to produce the magnificent *C.* 'Jackmanii'. This free-flowering, deep purple clematis was the result of careful selection from the resulting batch of 300 seedlings. Its continued popularity is testament not only to its quality, but also to the hard work and vision of

Jackmans of Woking. When describing *C.* 'Jackmanii', Moore and Jackman (1872) wrote, "a wonderfully fine acquisition, and up to the present time stands in the foremost rank as to merit." This quotation remains as accurate today as it was at the time it was written.

As a result of the dedicated work of Jackmans of Woking, Thomas Cripps and Son of Tunbridge Wells, Charles Noble of Sunningdale, Francisque Morel and Bonamy Frères of Lyon, Victor Lemoine of Nancy, and many others, modern gardeners have a great choice of large- and small-flowered hybrids. A number of outstanding old clematis varieties are still in cultivation and are very popular. Unfortunately with the onset of clematis wilt around 1880, interest in clematis amongst nurserymen and -women and gardeners alike simply diminished.

George Jackman II. Reproduced by kind permission of P. Gauntlett.

Charles Noble of Sunningdale with his own introduction of *C.* 'Jackmanii Alba'. Reproduced by kind permission of the Royal Horticultural Society.

Victor Lemoine of Nancy, France, was responsible for delightful cultivars such as *C.* 'Venosa Violacea' and *C.* 'Etoile Rose' among others. Reproduced with permission of the trustees of the Royal Botanic Gardens, Kew.

Clematis in the twentieth century

During the first quarter of the twentieth century William Robinson and Ernest Markham of Gravetye Manor fame (West Sussex, England), through their own efforts and their collaboration with Francisque Morel of Lyon, revived the interest in clematis. Many excellent cultivars resulted, including *Clematis tangutica* 'Gravetye', the beautiful *C. texensis* 'Gravetye Beauty', *C.* 'Huldine', and several cultivars of *C. viticella*, including 'Little Nell', 'Minuet', and 'Royal Velours'. William Robinson, having derived great pleasure from the cultivation of clematis in his own garden, published a small monograph in 1912, *The Virgin's Bower*, in which he made a strong plea for growing clematis through trees and shrubs—the natural way—as seen in the wild. Later on, Ernest Markham, head gardener at Gravetye Manor, cultivated and bred some beautiful clematis, and as a recognized authority on the subject published his book *Clematis* in 1935.

Many plant collectors also were very busy at least until the First World War, and some exciting new species notably from China, such as *Clematis armandii*, *C. chrysocoma*, *C. montana* var. *rubens*, and *C. rehderiana* amongst others, were introduced into cultivation. There was a renewed interest in growing clematis in the British Isles followed by a global revival in its popularity as a garden plant in the 1950s. Hybridization continued with great vigour during the second half of the twentieth century, resulting in some excellent cultivars.

Testament to the popularity and success of clematis as a very versatile garden plant is the founding of the International Clematis Society in 1984 and the British Clematis Society in 1991 to promote the cultivation and preservation of clematis. The last decade of the twentieth century certainly belonged to the genus *Clematis*, which includes versatile climbers and choice herbaceous and subshrubby plants. New and exciting cultivars from all over the world continue to arrive on the scene and are widely available to gardeners.

William Robinson. Etching by Francis Dodd. Reproduced by kind permission of P. Herbert.

Ernest Markham. Photographer unknown. Reproduced by kind permission of P. Herbert.

Botany and Nomenclature

Before discussing the classification of clematis, it is helpful to define a few terms. A scientific species name has two components. The first, the name of the genus (plural, genera), denotes a group of related but distinct species of plants, and the second, the specific epithet, refers to a group of related plants with a number of common features. Examples of species (singular and plural) names are *Clematis alpina*, *C. texensis*, and *C. viticella*.

Cultivars (cultivated varieties) are forms of plants selected for a particular characteristic or combination of characteristics and propagated by layering, cutting, division, or other vegetative methods to maintain them in cultivation. Cultivars do not necessarily breed true if propagated from seed. The name of a cultivar is usually enclosed in single quotes. Examples of cultivar names are *Clematis* 'Belle of Woking', *C.* 'Jadwiga Teresa', *C.* 'Pink Fantasy', and so on.

Hybrids are the result of cross-pollination and fertilization (sexual union) between two species or cultivars of the same genus. Hybrids may occur naturally in the wild or in the garden, although they are more commonly man-made—deliberate crosses. Examples include *Clematis* 'Hendersoni', the result of crossing *C. viticella* with *C. integrifolia*, or *C.* 'Lawsoniana', a cross of *C. patens* with *C.* 'Lanuginosa'. Since the hybrids *C.* 'Hendersoni' and *C.* 'Lawsoniana' were raised in cultivation, they are also cultivars. It is worthwhile noting that not all hybrids are cultivars, and not all cultivars are hybrids because cultivars may be the result of deliberate planned breeding with known parentage or accidental hybridization in cultivation in gardens (parentage unknown). A cultivar may even be a selection from an already existing cultivated stock of plants, or a selected plant from variants found within plants growing in their native habitats and brought into cultivation. Whatever their source, cultivars are maintained in cultivation solely by vegetative propagation.

A Gardener's Classification of Clematis

The genus *Clematis* shares a number of characteristics with other very popular garden plants such as species of *Anemone*, *Aquilegia*, *Caltha*, *Delphinium*, *Helleborus*, *Nigella*, *Pulsatilla*, and *Ranunculus*. All these genera belong to one botanical family of plants known as Ranunculaceae. The family derives its name from the Latin *rana*, meaning "frog," because many of the plants prefer growing in damp sites.

The family Ranunculaceae comprises about 48 genera of mostly herbaceous perennials. The main characteristics of the plants are as follows: leaves generally opposite; flowers generally solitary but occasionally in groups or clusters and mostly bisexual; sepals usually five, and may be petal-like when there are no petals; petals usually five, but may be deformed, small, or absent; stamens indefinite, usually numerous; pistils several to many; and fruit almost always a head of achenes or follicles. *Clematis* is the only genus in the family that includes a large number of semi-woody to woody climbers.

General characteristics of *Clematis*

Clematis species may be deciduous or evergreen, semi-woody to woody climbers or woody-based, erect to sprawling perennials. The leaves are generally opposite, sometimes alternate, simple or compound (ternate or pinnate) with entire, toothed, lobed or irregular margins. The petioles or leaf stalks are often modified to twist and clasp or coil around convenient supports. The flowers may be solitary or in fascicles (bundles) or panicles (clusters). They may be unisexual or bisexual, bell shaped (campanulate) or circular, and flattened like a disc (discoid). Sepals may vary from four to eight and may be petaloid (petal-like). Petals are absent. Staminodes or sterile stamens are sometimes petaloid. Stamens are numerous. Pistils are many, with long, plumose (plumelike), hairy styles. Fruit is a head of achenes with long, persistent, and often plumose styles. The seedheads of some clematis are spectacular and remain on the plant for a long time until they are fully ripened and ready for dispersal or collection.

Clematis groups

With so many different species and cultivars available to modern gardeners, the task of selecting suitable clematis for the garden may not be easy. Botanists and some gardeners who specialize in clematis are primarily concerned with all the detailed botanical characteristics of plants, be they species or cultivars. On the other hand, most gardeners are interested in choosing the right plants for their gardens according to growth habit; height; flowering times; colour, shape, and size of flow-

Leaf arrangements: (*top row, left to right*) simple, ternate, biternate; (*middle row*) triternate, pinnate, bipinnate; (*bottom row*) trifoliate, three lobed. Drawing by E. Leeds.

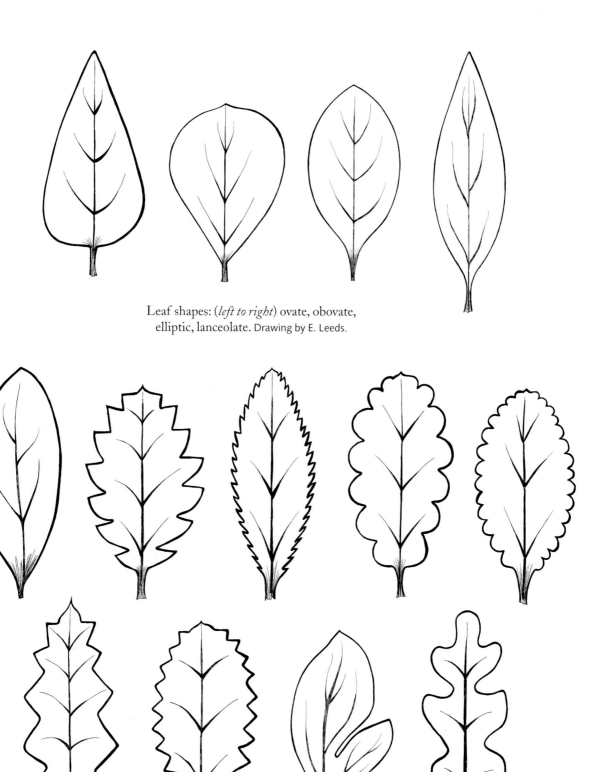

Leaf shapes: (*left to right*) ovate, obovate, elliptic, lanceolate. Drawing by E. Leeds.

Leaf margins: (*upper row, left to right*) entire (uninterrupted), serrate, serrulate, crenate, crenulate; (*bottom row*) dentate, denticulate, single lobed, multilobed. Drawing by E. Leeds.

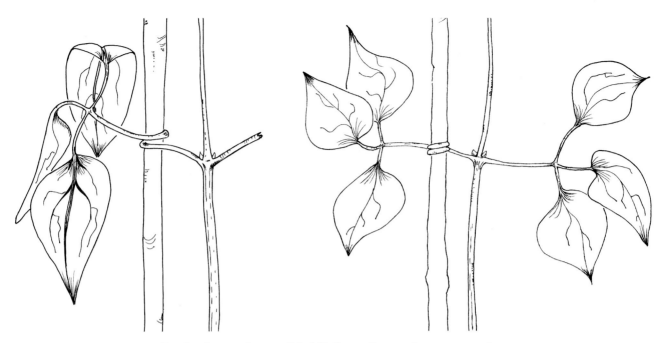

Leaf stalks are often modified (*left*) to coil around a support, and the coils (*right*) may be single, double, or many. Drawing by E. Leeds.

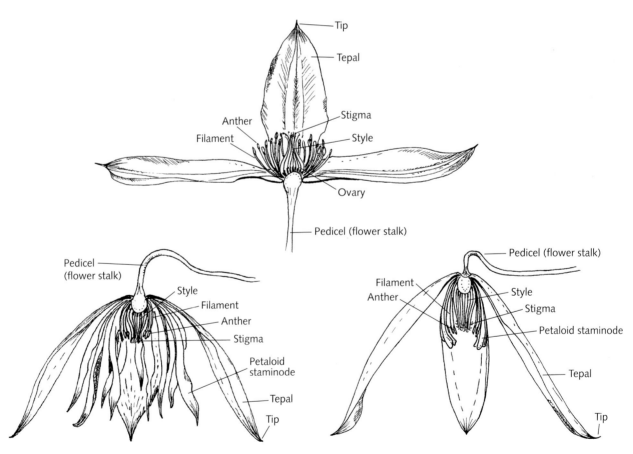

Flower vertical section: (*top*) a typical flower, (*bottom left*) *C. macropetala*, and (*bottom right*) *C.* 'Tage Lundell'. Drawing by E. Leeds.

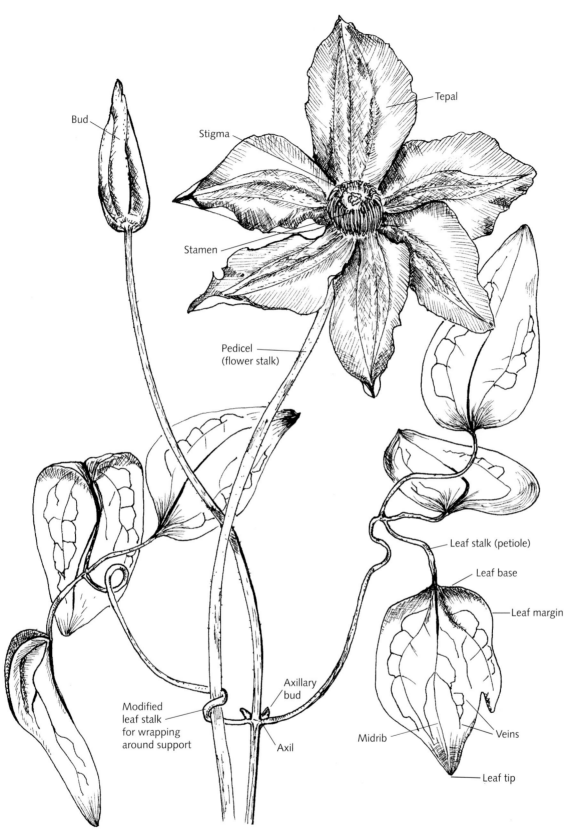

Bud

Stigma

Tepal

Stamen

Pedicel
(flower stalk)

Leaf stalk (petiole)

Leaf base

Leaf margin

Modified
leaf stalk
for wrapping
around support

Axillary
bud

Axil

Midrib

Veins

Leaf tip

Parts of a typical clematis flower stem.
Drawing by E. Leeds.

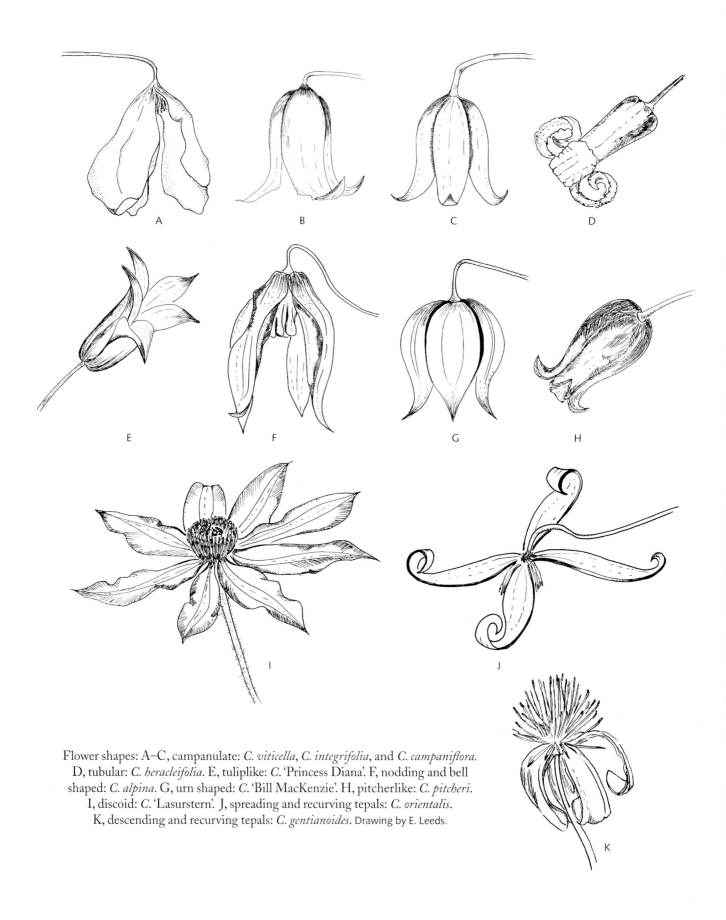

Flower shapes: A–C, campanulate: *C. viticella*, *C. integrifolia*, and *C. campaniflora*. D, tubular: *C. heracleifolia*. E, tuliplike: *C.* 'Princess Diana'. F, nodding and bell shaped: *C. alpina*. G, urn shaped: *C.* 'Bill MacKenzie'. H, pitcherlike: *C. pitcheri*. I, discoid: *C.* 'Lasurstern'. J, spreading and recurving tepals: *C. orientalis*. K, descending and recurving tepals: *C. gentianoides*. Drawing by E. Leeds.

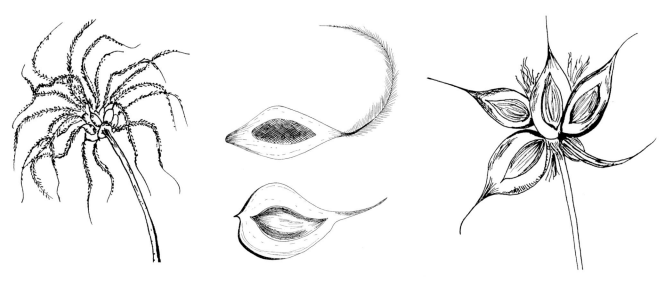

Seedheads: (*from left to right*) *C. ispahanica*, an achene with a persistent plumose style and a single seed, an achene without a plumose style and *C. viticella*. Drawing by E. Leeds.

ers; and uses in the garden. They also want to know how well the selected clematis grows with other garden plants. Therefore, to make the most of clematis as garden plants, it would be helpful to have a knowledge of the different groups of clematis.

For a long time clematis were grouped according to their pruning requirements. While this system is very helpful for indicating how and when to prune the plants, it fails to inform gardeners fully about the characteristics of clematis plants. Therefore, the grouping of clematis in this work is based on "A Gardener's Classification of Clematis" put forward by John Howells (1992, p. 34), former editor of *The Clematis*, journal of the British Clematis Society.

Clematis grown in gardens can be broadly divided into two groups. Large-flowered clematis (cultivars) have lace or spaghetti-like roots and large flowers, are rarely scented, and can suffer from clematis wilt. Small-flowered clematis (species and cultivars) have fibrous (thin and fine) roots, carry numerous small flowers that are often scented, and seldom suffer from wilt.

Large-flowered clematis

The large-flowered cultivars can be further subdivided into early flowering and late-flowering groups. As a rule the early flowering cultivars flower on old wood, that is, on ripened wood made during the previous year(s).

Therefore they require little or no pruning in early spring. Examples are *Clematis* 'Doctor Ruppel', *C.* 'Miss Bateman', and *C.* 'Nelly Moser'. If these clematis are pruned severely, they lose their flowers, although the plants may be tidied up by removing weak growths or dead wood immediately after the flowering period is over. The late-flowering cultivars flower on growths made during the current season and should be pruned hard in early spring to encourage the plants to produce strong new shoots and flower later in the season. Examples are *C.* 'Gipsy Queen', *C.* 'Hagley Hybrid', *C.* 'Jackmanii', and *C.* 'Lady Betty Balfour'.

Small-flowered clematis

Unlike the large-flowered clematis, which can be conveniently placed into two main groups according to their flowering times, the small-flowered species and cultivars are best placed in nine different groups, taking into account their flowering times—early or late.

The early small-flowered clematis are subdivided into four groups. The Evergreen Group includes plants from the Armandii, Cirrhosa, and Forsteri Groups, such as *Clematis armandii*, *C. cirrhosa*, *C.* 'Joe', and *C. marmoraria*. The Alpina Group is represented by *C. alpina*, *C.* 'Ruby', and *C.* 'Willy', and the Macropetala Group by *C. macropetala* and *C.* 'Maidwell Hall'. Clematis belonging to these two groups are also known as the Atragene Group.

The fourth subdivision, the Montana Group, includes *C.* 'Freda', *C.* 'Marjorie, and *C. montana.*

The late small-flowered clematis are subdivided into five groups. The Herbaceous Group includes species and cultivars from the Integrifolia and Heracleifolia Groups, such as *Clematis* 'Durandii', *C. heracleifolia*, and *C. integrifolia*. The Viticella Group is composed of two species, *C. campaniflora* and *C. viticella* and cultivars such as *C.* 'Abundance', *C.* 'Etoile Violette', and *C.* 'Venosa Vio-

lacea'. The Texensis-Viorna Group includes plants such as *C.* 'Etoile Rose', *C. texensis*, and *C. viorna*. The Tangutica Group (yellow-flowered clematis) is represented by *C.* 'Bill MacKenzie', *C.* 'Kugotia' (GOLDEN TIARA™), *C. orientalis*, and *C. tangutica*. The fifth group is made up of other late-flowering species and cultivars, such as *C. flammula*, *C. grata*, and *C.* 'Western Virgin'.

The following chart shows the relationship of these groups to each other.

Opposite page: *Anemone nemorosa* 'Leeds Variety', photo by E. Leeds. *Aquilegia* sp., photo by E. Leeds. *Delphinium* 'Nobility', photo by J. Lindmark. *Helleborus* sp., photo by E. Leeds. *Pulsatilla vulgaris*, photo by M. Toomey. *Ranunculus* sp., photo by E. Leeds. *Clematis* 'Jackmanii Superba', photo by E. Leeds.

A Gardener's Classification of Clematis

Selected Genera of the
Family Ranunculaceae

Genus
Anemone

Genus
Aquilegia

Genus
Delphinium

Genus
Helleborus

Genus
Pulsatilla

Genus
Ranunculus

Genus
Clematis

Large-flowered
Cultivars

Small-flowered
Species and Cultivars

EARLY
Flowers on old wood
Pruning group 2
Examples:
C. 'Asao', C. 'Belle of
Woking', C. 'Guernsey
Cream', C. 'Miss Bate-
man', C. 'Proteus'

LATE
Flowers on new wood
Pruning group 3
Examples:
C. 'Hagley Hybrid',
C. 'Perle d'Azur',
C. 'Prince Charles'

EARLY
Flowers on old wood
Pruning group 1
Evergreens
Examples: C. armandii,
C. cirrhosa, C. 'Joe'
Alpinas
Examples: C. 'Colum-
bine', C. 'Helsingborg'
Macropetalas
Examples: C. 'Ballet
Skirt', C. 'Jan Lindmark'
Montanas
Examples: C. 'Marjorie',
C. 'Mayleen'

LATE
Flowers on new wood
Pruning group 3
Herbaceous and subshrubs
Examples: C. 'Alionushka',
C. integrifolia, C. 'New Love'
Viticellas
Examples: C. 'Elvan', C. 'Etoile
Violette', C. 'Little Nell'
Tanguticas
Examples: C. 'Aureolin', C. 'Bill
MacKenzie', C. orientalis
Texensis-Viorna
Examples: C. 'Princess Diana',
C. 'Etoile Rose', C. texensis
Other late species
Examples: C. flammula, C. vitalba

CHAPTER TWO

Clematis in the Garden Landscape

Clematis, especially those with climbing habit, demand suitable supports to climb on and show off their flowers. With careful planning, they can be grown in many different ways to add to the design, elegance, and beauty of any garden. Supports may be natural and living, such as trees, shrubs, conifers, and roses or other climbing plants, or they may be artificial (man-made), such as a wall, fence, pergola, arch, arbour, trellis, obelisk, pillar, pole, post, bamboo cane, and so on.

Natural and Living Supports

Not all garden plants are suitable partners for clematis; however, many trees, shrubs, conifers, and roses, in particular, make excellent living supports for clematis. Before planting clematis with other garden plants which will act as supports, take into account the vigour, flowering times, and pruning requirements of both the supporting plants and the clematis. It is not prudent to pair a very vigorous clematis with a valuable, handsome, moderate or less vigorous tree, shrub, or other garden plant. Equally, it is not advisable to pair a compact and not-so-vigorous clematis with a large and vigorous garden plant. It is best not to pair an evergreen clematis or one that does not require hard pruning with another shrub or climbing plant, or even another clematis, requiring regular annual pruning. Finally, it is unwise to allow a clematis whether it requires pruning or not to roam into a hedge which needs regular clipping and maintenance throughout the growing season. Keeping these basic pairing rules in mind may help to avoid unnecessary mistakes.

Clematis and roses

Roses and clematis are natural companions. Their cultural requirements are very similar and therefore, with careful choice of species and cultivars of both genera of plants, some rewarding and exciting ways of growing them can be achieved. By choosing plants with similar annual pruning requirements, the amount of labour in the garden is also minimized.

When a clematis from pruning group 2 (as discussed in chapter four) is grown with a rose that needs pruning, the clematis can be pruned following the procedures for pruning group 3 (as discussed in chapter four). The early clematis flowers will be lost, but there will be a display later in the season.

The ultimate aim of partnering clematis with roses should be to enjoy the flowers of both plants individually and together. The basic pairing rules outlined for other garden plants also apply to clematis and rose partnership; however, the flower colour and flowering times of both clematis and roses should be taken into careful consideration if the goal is to have them in flower at the same time. Popular climbing roses such as 'Albertine', 'Compassion', 'Galway Bay', 'Golden Showers', 'Handel', 'Iceberg', 'Maigold', 'New Dawn', and 'School Girl' make excellent partners for clematis. Personal tastes will dictate the clematis-rose associations. There is a wealth of

Clematis 'Floralia' trained on the trunk of a mature juniper. Photo by J. Lindmark.

Clematis 'Lisboa' and *C.* 'Alionushka' supported by a sturdy wooden tripod. Photo by E. Leeds.

Clematis 'Madame Julia Correvon' growing on a pergola made of rustic poles. Photo by M. Toomey.

Clematis 'Jackmanii' and perennial sweet pea (*Lathyrus latifolius*) make excellent companions. Photo by M. Harpur.

Clematis 'Royal Velours' on a wooden obelisk. Photo by J. Glover.

Clematis 'Sieboldii' weaving its way through a medium-sized shrub of *Indigofera heterantha*. Photo by M. Toomey.

Clematis 'Warszawska Nike' growing through the ornamental pear *Pyrus salcifolia* 'Pendula'.
Photo courtesy Thorncroft Clematis Nursery.

Clematis tangutica and *Eccremocarpus scaber* make an ideal combination. Photo by J. Glover.

An unusual support. The deceptive erect shoots of *C.* 'Purpurea' supported by the gnarled old wood of a juniper. Photo by J. Lindmark.

Clematis 'Henryi' and *Rosa* 'Iceberg'. Photo by J. Harpur.

Clematis intricata and *Rosa* 'Flammentanz'. Photo by J. Lindmark.

Clematis 'Comtesse de Bouchaud' and *Rosa* 'Pink Bells'. Photo by R. Surman.

species and cultivars in both groups of plants from which any gardener can make a choice.

Man-made Supports

Some gardeners prefer to grow their clematis on man-made structures. These make excellent supports, and many clever ways of using them can be picked up by visiting private and public gardens; however, supporting structures and clematis must be chosen to fit the garden design and planting.

Walls are wonderful assets in any garden on which to grow clematis, but require additional structures such as a trellis or lengths of plastic-coated strong wire around which the modified leaf stalks of clematis can wrap themselves and grow away. Fences also make good supports but need vertical and horizontal wires which the clematis can clasp and climb. In the absence of garden walls or fences, free-standing structures, carefully erected or placed in the garden, are suitable alternatives. The ultimate aim is to enable the clematis to make their vertical journey with ease and to show off their flowers.

Passing showers of rain seldom reach the base of a wall, where the soil can be very dry and not conducive for healthy growth of clematis. Therefore, it is advisable to plant the clematis at least 30–45 cm (12–18 in.) away from the base of the wall and to enrich the planting hole with as much organic matter as possible. Regular water

Clematis tibetana subsp. *vernayi* spilling over a pergola. Photo by M. Toomey.

Clematis armandii on boundary railings. Photo by C. Chesshire.

supply and heavy mulch to conserve moisture are essential for healthy growth of clematis planted against a wall.

It is also wise to plant suitable shrubs or other climbers with clematis trained to grow on walls. The companion plants may be evergreen or deciduous, and preferably a combination of both. These serve to clothe the wall along with the clematis and at the same time ensure that the naked stems of deciduous clematis during winter months are not altogether an unpleasant sight.

Hardwood or plastic trellises are available in different shapes and sizes. One that gives a three-dimensional effect is most attractive when mounted on a wall. Choosing a trellis is a matter of personal taste, but if a wood trellis is preferred to plastic, it is advisable to invest in one made of heavy-duty hardwood. When hanging a trellis on the wall, do not place it flat against the wall. Allow a space of at least 2.5 cm (1 in.) between the wall and trellis by attaching blocks of wood to the wall and fastening the trellis to the blocks with rustproof screws. Such a method of hanging the trellis on the wall ensures

enough room for air circulation, thus preventing the plants from being attacked by mildew. Furthermore, new growths are also able to scramble up the space behind the trellis, enabling the leaf stalks to coil around it, as well as making it easy for the gardener to tie-in the new and old growths as necessary.

It is not unusual to find some early flowering, vigorous clematis, for example, *Clematis alpina*, *C. macropetala*, and their cultivars as well as some evergreen clematis, planted against spacious walls becoming unmanageable thickets of wood after a few years of planting. Therefore it is recommended that once the plants have become well and truly established and a handsome framework achieved, a certain amount of old wood is either removed or pruned back immediately after the flowering period is over. In fact it is highly desirable to thin out the plants annually once they have established a good framework. Remember to undertake this pruning immediately after flowering if the clematis belong to pruning group 1.

Clematis 'Purpurea Plena Elegans' carefully trained on a wooden arch. Photo by M. Toomey.

Clematis 'Guernsey Cream' supported on a trellis.
Photo by M. Toomey.

Clematis 'Prince Charles' makes its way up a trellised wall.
Photo courtesy Thorncroft Clematis Nursery.

A wall of clematis. Photo courtesy Thorncroft Clematis Nursery.

Clematis 'Albina Plena' on a low stone wall of a bridge. Photo by M. Toomey.

Clematis as Ground Cover

Many *Clematis* species and cultivars may also be grown as groundcover plants or trained along the ground. Space permitting, 'Hagley Hybrid', 'Jackmanii Rubra', 'Niobe', 'Pink Fantasy', and 'Westerplatte', and cultivars of *C. texensis* with their tuliplike flowers, for example, 'Duchess of Albany' and 'Gravetye Beauty', carefully trained along the ground make a spectacular display. Some choice and compact clematis, grown horizontally along the ground, demand extra care and attention. Plant these in the usual way and route the stems horizontally. Hairpins made from lengths of sturdy wire can be used to hold the stems in place on the ground. It is also essential to keep an eye on pests such as snails and slugs to ensure they do not destroy the new and old shoots. Strong-growing clematis, for example, *C. montana* and its cultivars (early flowering) and *C.* 'Jouiniana Praecox' (late-flowering), may also be grown as groundcover plants, provided adequate garden space is available.

Clematis as Container Plants

Some clematis, notably the not-so-vigorous and compact species and cultivars, make excellent container plants. See chapter three for more information.

Clematis 'Hagley Hybrid' grown horizontally as ground cover in a nursery display garden.
Photo courtesy Thorncroft Clematis Nursery.

Clematis 'Jouiniana Praecox' can be grown as a groundcover plant provided there is ample space in a garden. Photo by E. Leeds.

Clematis koreana var. *lutea* trailing along the ground and showing off its pendulous flowers. Photo by J. Lindmark.

Clematis 'Comtesse de Bouchaud' in a large urn. Photo by J. Glover.

Clematis 'Gipsy Queen' in an old chimney pot.
Photo courtesy Thorncroft Clematis Nursery.

Clematis 'Blekitny Aniol' (BLUE ANGEL™) elegantly trained
in a pot. Photo courtesy Hamlyn.

CHAPTER THREE

Cultivation and Care

The last decades of the twentieth century witnessed an explosion in the number of *Clematis* species and cultivars, particularly the large-flowered ones, made available to gardeners. *Clematis* flowers now boast an amazing range of colour, form, and size. They come in every colour except black, and they may be single, double, or semi-double, small or large. They may be beautiful nodding bells, flat open discs, or even tubular. Their growth habits vary too; some are vigorous while others are more compact. They may be climbers, scramblers, herbaceous varieties, or semi-herbaceous or woody subshrubs. Faced with all the variables, how does a gardener decide on a species or cultivar and choose a good plant? The task may not be easy but with a little thought and effort it can be done successfully.

Whatever the reason for deciding on a particular clematis—be it a species or cultivar, small- or large-flowered, evergreen or deciduous—the most important task is to purchase a good, strong-growing, healthy plant. Look for two- or three-year-old bushy plants well established in good-sized pots, preferably about 2 litres (approximately ½ gallon), with two or three strong basal stems. These are by far better than tall, single-stemmed plants on long supports, even if they are in flower, not only because the roots and shoots are much better developed but also in the event of an accidental breakage of a stem or two, there are others to continue with their growth. The more basal stems per plant, the quicker it is to establish a handsome framework of the plant.

Clematis are sold through many retail outlets, such as garden centres, specialist clematis nurseries, and supermarkets, and may also be bought by mail order. There are no set standards adhered to in the marketplace so gardeners should be careful when making selections. Before rushing to buy a clematis, whether for the garden or for a container, it would be wise to consider a few points. Make sure the plant will have adequate space to grow and mature. Likewise, consider the planting position or aspect in the garden: north, south, east, or west, exposed or sheltered. Determine the type of support; there are many natural and artificial supports from which to choose. Remember that not all clematis are natural climbers, nor are they equipped with suitable structures to coil around and make their way up. The stems of tall-growing herbaceous clematis, which have no means of twisting around such structures, will need to be trained and tied on to some form of suitable support. In addition, if the plant is meant for a container, take into account the size and shape of the container, the type of support to be placed inside the container, and the growing habit of the plant. Less vigorous, more compact clematis are more suited to container-culture, although no gardener should expect a clematis—especially those with an extensive root system—to remain in a container forever.

After deciding upon a particular species or cultivar, be it for a garden, container, glasshouse, or conservatory, consider purchasing a quality plant from a reputable specialist nursery or garden centre. Early spring and midautumn to late autumn are good times to buy plants.

Liners

Clematis liners are young plants in their first pots (10 cm or 4 in.). It is possible to buy these from some outlets, and they are relatively inexpensive. Liners, however, are not ready to be planted directly in the garden or in large containers. It is essential to pot them on and grow them with care for at least another twelve to eighteen months before planting them permanently in the garden.

Mail order

When buying plants through a mail-order specialist, select a well-known, reputable, and reliable nursery. Most specialist nurseries mail out illustrated catalogues with adequate information on each plant offered for sale. Mail-order plants usually arrive during late autumn or early spring. When the parcel arrives, do not be put off by the sight of the plant. The leaves may be dead, withered, or shrivelled, or perhaps even absent if the plant is deciduous. A close examination, however, will reveal live buds in the leaf axils and a healthy-looking root system. It is important to check that the compost is not dry. Water the plant if necessary, and leave it in a garden shed, garage, or sheltered spot in the garden until the time is right for planting. Provided it is a good-quality, healthy specimen, the plant may remain in its nursery pot for anywhere from a few days to a few weeks. If it is a tender variety, take adequate precautions—the plant will need frost-free growing conditions.

Finding the right place

To grow and flower well, evergreen and tender clematis need warm, sheltered positions in the garden. Some are only suitable for growing under glass. Pale-coloured flowers tend to be bleached in strong sunlight and are best suited for growing in shade or semi-shade. Large-flowered clematis require sheltered positions to protect their blooms from wind damage. Most members of the Alpina, Koreana, and Macropetala Groups can withstand some exposure to wind. Scented clematis perform better in sunny sites, although they demand a regular water supply. Clematis in containers cannot be expected to give a good account over many years, and regular care and maintenance are primary requisites for their successful culture, even for a short term.

Planting Clematis in the Garden

Pot-grown clematis can be planted anytime of year. The ideal time for planting is early autumn to midautumn and spring. Plant when the soil is neither frozen nor very wet, remembering that all clematis require well-drained soil. Autumn is an excellent time for planting most clematis, with the exception of some tender or evergreen plants such as *Clematis armandii*, *C. cirrhosa*, and *C. forsteri*. The upper layers of soil are usually warm and moist

A three-year-old plant with strong-growing basal stems which is ready for planting and a young plant in its first pot which is not ready for planting out in the garden.
Photo by E. Leeds.

during early autumn to midautumn and enable the roots to grow quickly and establish a good root system before the onset of winter. Autumn rains also keep the soil moist so that regular watering may not be necessary. During prolonged dry weather, however, it is important to water all newly planted clematis.

The next ideal season to plant clematis, especially the tender varieties, is early spring to midspring. As soil and air temperatures begin to rise, new plants settle down and establish quickly. If the spring is dry, newly planted clematis require a regular water supply, and clematis planted in summer require regular watering.

Soil

Fertile, loamy soil in the garden is ideal for cultivation of clematis, most of which thrive on a regular supply of balanced nutrients and moisture. In the absence of such soil, or if the soil is not in very good condition, prepare the site before planting a clematis. If the soil is heavy clay, add coarse horticultural grit or sharp sand to improve it. If the soil is sandy, add as much humus (organic matter) as possible. Well-rotted farmyard or horse manure, garden compost, leaf-mould, mushroom compost, or good-quality, proprietary, soil-based potting compost are excellent materials for improving and enriching the soil.

Although clematis are known to thrive in alkaline soils (pH value more than 7), they also grow satisfactorily on neutral to acid soil (pH value of 7 or below). For better results with extremely acidic soils, add ordinary lime (calcium carbonate), which is both easy to handle and relatively safe to use. Ideally, lime should be dug into the soil far in advance of planting. If using farmyard manure to enrich the soil, refrain from adding lime at the same time, as it reacts with the nitrogen-rich manure to release nitrogen in the form of ammonia, which may damage the plants. Annual liming is not recommended as over-liming may result in deficiencies of other soil nutrients. It is worthwhile, however, to test the soil occasionally, especially light, sandy soils, as rain tends to leach lime from it. Lime-rich mushroom compost also helps to increase soil alkalinity.

Planting hole

When planting a clematis in the garden, dig a hole at least twice as wide as the pot in which the plant is growing and at least twice as deep again. A hole 45 by 45 cm (18 by 18 in.) or larger is ideal for accommodating organic matter below and around the root ball, giving the clematis a good start for healthy growth. Loosen the base and sides of the hole with a garden fork. If the soil is heavy clay, place some coarse grit or sharp sand mixed with the soil at the bottom of the hole before placing any organic material in it. This improves drainage and prevents water logging. Place some well-rotted manure, leaf mould, or compost at the base of the planting hole to a depth of at least 10 cm (4 in.). To prevent the roots of the plant from becoming burned or damaged through direct contact with the manure or compost, cover the manure or compost with a sufficient quantity of top soil and peat or peat substitute.

Immerse the container in which the plant is growing in a bucket of water for ten to fifteen minutes to thoroughly wet the compost and enable the uptake of water by the roots. This is a very important step before planting because, once planted, the roots will need time to grow into the surrounding soil, absorb water and nutrients, and distribute adequate amounts of water to the rest of the plant. Ease the plant with its cane support out of the container and gently loosen the roots at the bottom of the root ball to encourage quick growth into the surrounding soil. Place the root ball in the prepared planting hole.

If the plant is a large-flowered cultivar, ensure that the surface of the root ball is at least 6 cm (2.25 in.) below the rim of the hole. Deep planting encourages large-flowered cultivars to develop a healthy basal root crown of buds below the soil level as a precaution against sudden wilting. *Clematis alpina*, *C. tangutica*, and *C. viticella* and their cultivars generally do not succumb to wilt and therefore deep planting is unnecessary. Similarly, evergreen and herbaceous species such as *C. armandii*, *C. cirrhosa*, *C. heracleifolia*, *C. integrifolia*, and *C. recta* should be planted with the crown of the plant level with the soil.

When the plant is in position, fill the area around the root ball with equal parts of good soil and potting compost mixed with the recommended amount of any general-purpose fertilizer. Gently firm the mixture around the root ball. Cover the base of the plant with additional organic matter used at the base of the planting hole, taking care to keep it away from the stems or vines. When mounded, it serves as a mulch to prevent excessive loss of moisture. Water the plant well, allowing at least 4 litres (about 1 gallon) of water per plant. Finally, attach a permanent label to the plant with the name of the clematis and the date of planting.

To provide a certain amount of shade for the plant's root system and to prevent excessive loss of moisture, plant a low-growing perennial or shrub close to the newly planted clematis. Avoid using slates, slabs, or tiles to shade the clematis roots as these also provide hiding places for slugs, snails, woodlice, and other insect pests.

Planting Clematis in a Container

In chapter two it was mentioned that some clematis make excellent container plants. Patios, balconies, courtyards, and other outdoor sitting areas can be brightened with clematis grown in elegant containers. Furthermore, with gardening spaces becoming more and more restricted in urban areas, growing clematis in containers can be very enjoyable, rewarding, and at times a challenging exercise. The secret of success with container-grown clematis depends on careful choice of suitable plants and routine care. Although many clematis come with labels that read, "Suitable for containers," gardeners should beware.

Oak barrels and other wooden containers, as well as those made from stone or concrete, are ideally suited for growing clematis. Unlike terracotta and plastic pots,

these other containers are better equipped to withstand fluctuating temperatures during winter and summer. Invest in good-quality containers measuring at least 45 by 45 cm (18 by 18 in.). The larger and thicker the container, the better the results. Make certain the container has adequate drainage holes; too many are better than too few. Containers are available in various shapes and sizes. An ideal container is wide-mouthed and wide-based, boasting good depth.

A mixture of soil-based and soilless compost is ideal for container-culture. Garden soil is not recommended as it becomes compact and interferes with drainage. Likewise, the level of nutrients in garden soil may not be satisfactory, and the soil may not be completely free from diseases and pests, especially vine weevil larvae, which are difficult to control.

Once the container is filled with compost, planted, and watered, it is very heavy to transport and position elsewhere, so begin by siting the empty container in its allocated place. Raise it off the ground with custom-made pot stands or half-bricks. This aids good drainage. Place a layer of small stones, pebbles, or even coarse grit over the drainage holes to prevent them from being blocked by the compost. Fill the container with a mixture of two parts loam-based compost to one part peat or peat-based

Soak the root ball in a bucket of water. Photo by J. Lindmark.

Loosen the roots and place the root ball in the prepared hole. Photo by J. Lindmark.

Place a layer of small stones, pebbles, or even coarse grit over the drainage holes to prevent blockage. Photo by R. Surman.

Insert a suitable support in the pot. Photo by R. Surman.

substitute. Scoop enough compost from the centre of the container to accommodate the plant's root ball. After immersing the plant in a bucket of water for about fifteen minutes, ease it out of its pot and place the root ball in the planting hole. Fill the area around the root ball with compost and gently firm the compost. Any remaining space should be similarly filled, but leave at least 5 cm (2 in.) space below the rim of the container to facilitate easy watering. Insert a slow-release fertilizer plug into the compost, following the recommendations given for its application, and water the plant gently but thoroughly. Plant a few annuals or a compact, low-growing perennial at the base of the clematis to provide shade and to conserve moisture. Alternatively, place a layer of horticultural grit or gravel on the surface of the compost.

Container-grown clematis need support from the time of planting. The type of support depends on where the container is sited. If the aim is to allow the plant to grow through a wall shrub or a climbing rose, insert a long bamboo cane into the compost at an angle between the container and the wall or a branch of the wall shrub. The new growths may be initially tied to the support and then allowed to scramble towards the host plant. If the container is placed on a patio, balcony, or courtyard, a suitable man-made support is required. Place the support securely in the container and train the stems onto it.

It is important to prevent or limit wind rock of container plants as it may cause stem or root damage. It also is important to spend time tying-in stems to the support and training the plant well from the bottom up to create a beautifully grown plant. Use twine, thin string, or plant ties and do not be too concerned if some new shoots accidentally break during the course of training and tying. More new shoots will break from the leaf axils, thereby promoting a handsome bushy plant.

Pinching-Out

Pinching-out involves removing the growing tips of a plant to force the development of side shoots. This method is often employed by gardeners to create a bushy plant. Leggy clematis plants benefit from this action, although care should be taken to stop pinching-out about six weeks before flowering time begins. Otherwise, the process interferes with the development of flower buds. Through trial and error, the art of pinching-out can be perfected to achieve a handsome, bushy plant with a generous display of buds and flowers.

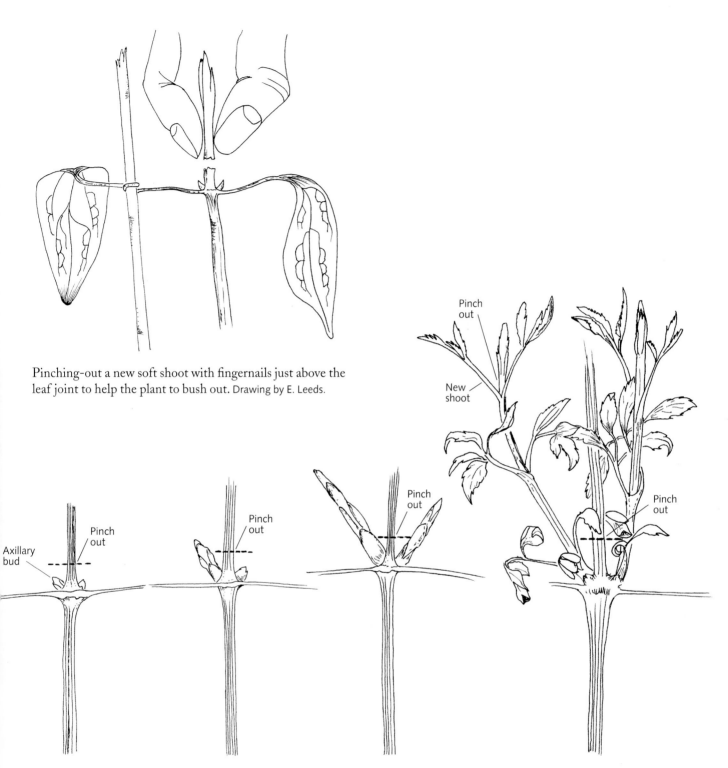

Pinching-out a new soft shoot with fingernails just above the
leaf joint to help the plant to bush out. Drawing by E. Leeds.

Stages in the development of axillary buds after pinching-out: (*from left to right*)
stage 1, stage 2, stage 3, and stage 4. Drawing by E. Leeds.

Maintaining Clematis Plants in the Garden

Routine care and maintenance enable newly planted clematis to grow into strong, healthy plants which flower well. Most clematis are voracious feeders and demand a regular supply of water throughout the growing season. When early spring arrives and the buds in the leaf axils begin to swell, it is time to commence pruning the plants, where necessary, followed by mulching and feeding. Because the time of spring's arrival varies from region to region and from country to country, it is wise to not rush pruning and tidying up clematis plants. Several newly planted clematis and all well-established plants, particularly the large- and small-flowered cultivars which require annual hard pruning, should be pruned back to at least 30–45 cm (12–18 in.) in the spring.

After pruning, mulch the plants generously with well-rotted farmyard manure, compost, or similar organic material. Take precautions when handling farmyard manure, and keep it away from stems and emerging young shoots to prevent burns or other damage. Scatter the recommended dosage of a general-purpose, inorganic granular fertilizer and a handful of bone meal or any other organic fertilizer on the mulch and fork them in. Water the plants adequately. Regular watering throughout the growing season is essential, though the amount of water needed depends on rainfall. As plant growth becomes vigorous with rising air and soil temperatures, feed the plants at least once a week with a general-purpose liquid fertilizer. Foliar feed benefits the leaves, while a high-potash tomato feed, used in place of the general-purpose liquid feed, around midspring to late spring encourages flowering. As soon as the flower buds are ready to open, stop feeding so as to prevent all the buds from opening in quick succession, thereby shortening the flowering period. Recommence feeding as soon as flowering is completed to invigorate the plants and encourage another flush of flowers, particularly in the repeat-flowering cultivars. Taper off the feeding and watering by midautumn.

Early flowering clematis

Clematis which flower on old wood in early to late spring, or even slightly later in the season, such as the Alpina, Koreana, and Macropetala Groups, as well as other atragenes; single, large-flowered cultivars such as Clematis 'Asao', C. 'Dawn', and C. 'Miss Bateman'; and all double and semi-double varieties should not be fed inorganic fertilizers until their flowering period is over. Soon after flowering, plants like these can be cleaned up by removing their dead or weak stems and by cutting back some old wood in well-established plants which may look untidy or which need to be kept within bounds. Feed the plants with a general-purpose inorganic fertilizer. Continue feeding them with a liquid fertilizer, but stop feeding those plants which may produce a second crop of flowers later in the season as soon as the buds are plump and ready to open. Recommence feeding these plants after they flower, but halt the feeding programme during late summer or early autumn.

The healthy growth and flowering capacity of early flowering clematis depend on the routine care, including feeding, given the plants during the previous, for the current, year. Little is gained by feeding plants when the soil temperature is very low. There is no harm, however, in mulching these plants and applying a handful of concentrated organic fertilizers during late winter to early spring.

Winter-flowering clematis

Certain winter-flowering evergreen clematis, such as *Clematis cirrhosa* var. *balearica* and *C. napaulensis*, may go into a state of dormancy (no active growth) for a period during summer. Such plants need not be watered regularly or fed during that time. Instead, begin the routine care of watering and feeding as the plants awake from their dormancy, usually in late summer. Refrain from overwatering clematis from regions accustomed to a certain amount of drought or dry conditions, such as the Mediterranean, parts of the United States, and New Zealand.

Maintaining Clematis Plants in Containers

Clematis growing in containers need some extra attention and routine care of watering, feeding, training, and tying-in their new growths from spring through early autumn. The amount of nutrients available in potting compost usually lasts for only four to six weeks. Compost also tends to dry out rapidly in containers, especially during hot summer months. Therefore, it is important to feed and water container-grown plants diligently.

Do not depend on a passing shower of rain. Even during heavy rainfall, only a fraction of water falls on the surface of a container and additional water should be considered. Slow-release fertilizer is a boon to container-culture. If such fertilizer has already been incorporated into the compost at the time of planting, take care not to overfeed with other general-purpose granular or liquid fertilizers.

Winter care of container plants

Clematis in containers in open gardens, with the possible exception of very mild or sheltered maritime gardens, do not enjoy the wetness, very low temperatures (−10°C or 14°F) or strong, cold winds of winter. This means that every care should be taken to shelter these plants from the elements until the arrival of warm weather. If the containers are not too heavy, move them into a glasshouse, well-lit garage, outhouse, shed, or porch. If such shelter is unavailable, position the containers at the base of a south-facing wall for protection.

Should the containers prove too heavy to move and, if the plants are hardy, prune away the top one-third of the stems and tie-in the rest to their supports to prevent wind rock and to protect the roots. A thick mulch gives added protection to the roots. If these clematis flower on ripened old wood, there will be some loss of flowers the following year.

Plants which are not very hardy but in containers too heavy to move should be wrapped in place to prevent excessive winter damage and loss. Wrap the plants with layers of horticultural fleece, and the containers with bubble wrap. Keep the compost slightly moist. During late winter or early spring, remove the horticultural fleece and prune the plants as necessary. Re-cover the clematis until all danger of frost has passed.

Spring care of container plants

Plants that overwinter in containers should be repotted in spring or, at the least, have their compost replenished. Simply remove the top 7.5–10 cm (3–4 in.) of compost, and replace it with a mixture of two parts loam-based potting compost and one part peat or suitable peat alternative. Ensure that the plant is supported securely, water it thoroughly, and commence feeding.

Repotting container plants

Not all container-grown clematis perform satisfactorily over many seasons, particularly the large-flowered culti-

vars with extensive roots. If, however, the same plant is to continue growing in a container after two or three seasons, it must be transferred to a larger container.

Successful repotting requires patience and time, especially if the containers are large and the plants are very mature. The best time for repotting clematis is early to late spring. If the plant needs pruning, do so before repotting it. Then, unless the container is too large or too heavy, ease the root ball carefully out of the container and move it to a larger pot filled with fresh potting compost. Firm the plant in, and water it. If the container is very large, lay it on its side and run a long-bladed knife between the compost and the container to loosen the root ball and ease it out. If the mouth of the container is not wide enough for the root ball to pass through, use a carving knife or similar implement to cut the outer 5–7.5 cm (2–3 in.) of the root ball before removing it. Once the root ball is out of the container, it may be necessary to reduce its size by cutting off 5–7.5 cm (2–3 in.) of roots, or even more from the outer edges. This is known as root pruning. Continue with repotting following the method outlined above for planting clematis in containers.

When repotting, refrain from forcing the plant out of its container by the stems. If canes support the plant, remove them before repotting to prevent any accidental injuries to yourself. Prune away at least one-third of the stems of clematis which flower on old wood, even if it means loss of flowers during the following season. Clematis with good, strong roots seldom die. If the clematis is too big for a container, plant it in the open garden and start over with a young plant.

A pot-bound clematis. Photo by E. Leeds.

Transplanting Established Plants

Relatively young plants can be transplanted more successfully than older, more mature plants, and transplanting is best done in late winter when the plants are dormant. When moving plants of *Clematis alpina*, *C. macropetala*, *C. montana*, or any other species, be very careful to not damage the thin, fibrous root systems. Large-flowered cultivars have "boot lace" roots, which are much thicker and better able to withstand disturbance. If the clematis is an evergreen one, the best time to transplant it is spring or late summer to early autumn. If the plant is in flower, it is best to wait until flowering is over before transplanting it.

Before transplanting, reduce the bulk of the stems or vines by pruning them down to within at least 60 cm (24 in.) of the soil level, even if it means loss of flowers in deciduous clematis which flower on the previous season's old wood. In the case of evergreen clematis, completely remove some stems and thin the plant before transplanting.

To transplant an established clematis, first insert a long bamboo cane near the plant and tie all the vines or stems to it. Using a spade, dig a circle around the plant at least 30–45 cm (12–18 in.) from its base. The aim is to lift the entire root ball. Repeat this operation a few times to cut all the roots and free the root ball from the surrounding soil. Placing the spade under the root ball, gently lift it to make sure all the roots have been cleanly cut. Place the root ball on a heavy-duty polyethylene sheet or burlap sack and keep it covered and moist until it reaches the new site. Follow the same procedure outlined above for planting a new clematis, and ensure the planting hole is wide and deep enough to receive the root ball with the shortened stems. Remember to plant it 6–7.5 cm (2.25–3 in.) deeper than the previous soil level, particularly if it is a large-flowered cultivar. Water the plant immediately after replanting. Untie the stems from the temporary cane support, and tie them to their permanent support or to the host plant through which the clematis is to grow. Spray the foliage with water at regular intervals to reduce evaporation.

CHAPTER FOUR

Pruning

Nature employs its own methods of eliminating excessive growths to ensure that flowering plants grow healthily and strongly. Within the confines of the garden, however, the main reasons for pruning clematis are to establish a neat and tidy framework, to encourage vigorous growth, and to stimulate the development of buds and flowers.

Most newly planted clematis need to be pruned back to at least 30 cm (12 in.) from the ground in the spring following the initial planting. This pruning encourages plants to produce new shoots from lower down the stems and from below the soil surface; however, certain evergreen and tender varieties, such as *Clematis armandii*, *C. forsteri*, *C. paniculata*, and their cultivars, should not be severely pruned provided the plants are strong, bushy, and healthy.

Established clematis plants fall into three major pruning categories governed by whether they flower on old wood (previous year's growths) or new wood (current year's growths) and their flowering times. Whether plants are grown in a container or in the garden, the pruning procedures are the same.

Pruning group 1

Both evergreen and deciduous clematis which flower on old ripened wood during winter or early to late spring belong to group 1 and do not usually require any major pruning. Therefore, a simple rule for these is this: If a clematis flowers before early summer, do not prune it.

This rule means that all winter- and spring-flowering *Clematis* species and their cultivars need little or no pruning, including *C. alpina*, *C. armandii*, *C. cirrhosa*, *C. forsteri*, *C. macropetala*, *C. napaulensis*, and *C. paniculata*. If, however, the plants have outgrown their allocated space or become overgrown and untidy, a certain amount of cutting back and tidying up may be undertaken after the flowering period has ended. Ideally, pruning to maintain a plant's handsome framework should be done annually. This enables the plant to produce new growths, which will be ripened by the sun during summer and early autumn and be ready to flower by the following spring or early summer.

Pruning group 2

Some clematis produce two flushes of flowers. The first display appears before early summer on old ripened growths made during the previous year(s); the second display appears during late summer on new growths made in the current year. Examples of this group include *Clematis* 'Bees Jubilee', *C.* 'Fair Rosamond', *C.* 'Miss Bateman', *C.* 'Niobe', *C.* 'Sunset', and *C.* 'The President', as well as most clematis with double or semi-double flowers, such as *C.* 'Belle of Woking', *C.* 'Daniel Deronda', *C.* 'Duchess of Edinburgh', *C.* 'Louise Rowe', *C.* 'Proteus', *C.* 'Royalty', *C.* 'Sylvia Denny', and *C.* 'Vyvyan Pennell'. Clematis in pruning group 2 do not require major pruning, but all dead and weak stems should be removed in late spring. If a certain amount of selective pruning is necessary, particularly in the case of overgrown plants, it may be undertaken immediately after the early flowering period is over, starting from the top of the plant and working downwards. It is also desirable to prune back the flowered shoots to encourage a second display of flowers. The general rule for pruning clematis in group 2 is this: Do not indulge in large-scale pruning of old wood made during the previous season(s) or there will be a loss of early flowers.

Pruning group 3

Clematis species and cultivars which flower on the current year's new growths after early summer are commonly referred to as midsummer to late summer flowering clematis. These plants need annual pruning in late winter or early spring, or even later in the season, depending on when spring arrives.

Clematis belonging to the Tangutica, Texensis-Viorna, and Viticella Groups, small-flowering species, and large-flowered cultivars, such as *Clematis gouriana*, *C. grata*, *C. hexapetala*, *C.* 'John Huxtable', *C.* 'Luther Burbank', and *C.* 'Madame Baron Veillard', belong to pruning group 3 and must be pruned very hard. A rapid and easy method of pruning these clematis is to start at the base of the stems and work upwards to the first pair of healthy, plump buds. Prune the stems just above these buds, and remove all old growths above the cuts. At times such buds may not be altogether visible. As long as the nodal points of the leaves can be established, cuts can be made just above those and all old growths removed. Such severe pruning encourages plants to produce strong new shoots and flower very well. The general rule for pruning clematis in group 3 is this: Cut back all the old stems to the lowest pair of live buds.

As the gardener becomes more experienced with pruning clematis in this group, two alternative methods can be used to control certain flowering patterns. In the first option, pruning is delayed to obtain a display of flowers later in the season. Instead of pruning during late winter or early spring, it is put off until late spring. Waiting this long means that early young growths will be pruned, which might be very disconcerting but must be done if the aim is to delay the plant's flowering time. A plant pruned in late spring does bounce back and produces flowers a month or two later than normal. An extra handful of general-purpose fertilizer gives the plant a gentle boost.

In the second option, certain well-established *Clematis* species and cultivars, including *C.* 'Helios', *C.* 'Huldine', *C.* 'Kugotia' (GOLDEN TIARA™), and *C. tangutica*, may be partially pruned to produce a continual display of flowers. To achieve this, hard prune only half the old stems or vines (from the previous years' growths), allowing the other unpruned half to come into flower early in the season. When the old growths have stopped flowering, new growths will come into flower, thus ensuring a continuous display of flowers on a single plant.

Optional pruning

Nursery catalogues and plant labels often indicate that pruning of a particular clematis may be optional or done as for pruning groups 2 or 3. Examples of such plants are *Clematis* 'Carnaby', *C.* 'Ernest Markham', *C.* 'Huldine', and *C.* 'Lady Betty Balfour', which flower on both old and new wood. If these clematis are not pruned or only lightly pruned, they will reward the gardener with early flowers produced from old wood. If, however, they are pruned very hard, the flowering period will be delayed by at least six weeks, and the plants will remain somewhat compact.

Pruning herbaceous, semi-herbaceous, and woody clematis

Herbaceous *Clematis* species and cultivars such as *C.* 'Aromatica', *C. heracleifolia*, and *C. integrifolia* can be treated just like other herbaceous perennials in the garden. With the onset of very cold winter, almost all the soft top-growth of these clematis dies back to ground level. Where winters are mild, the process of dying back may not be complete. In this case, cut the top-growth down to ground level towards the end of winter or beginning of spring. Semi-herbaceous and woody subshrubs, such as *C.* 'Durandii', *C.* 'Jouiniana', and *C. recta*, can be pruned just like herbaceous clematis by cutting the old semi-woody and woody top-growth to ground level towards the end of winter or beginning of spring.

Pruning companion clematis

Clematis grown in association with shrubs, trees, roses, conifers, heathers, and other climbers should not be hard pruned if they belong to pruning group 1 or 2. Clematis which belong to pruning group 3 can be pruned in two easy steps. Cut away all the top-growth of deciduous climbing clematis after the leaves have fallen, leaving

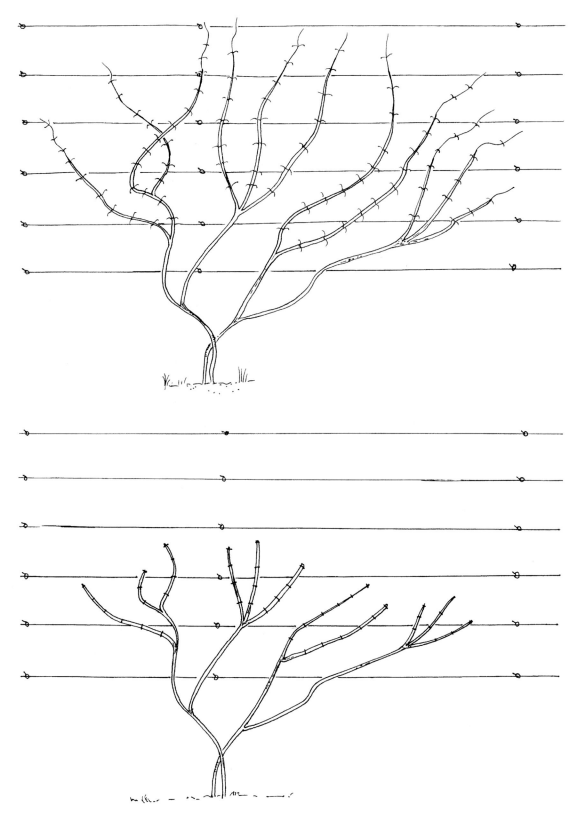

Clematis pruning group 2: (*top*) an unpruned plant after the display of early double flowers; (*bottom*) a pruned plant after weak and dead stems, as well as some old flowered shoots, have been removed to encourage a large display of flowers. Drawing by E. Leeds.

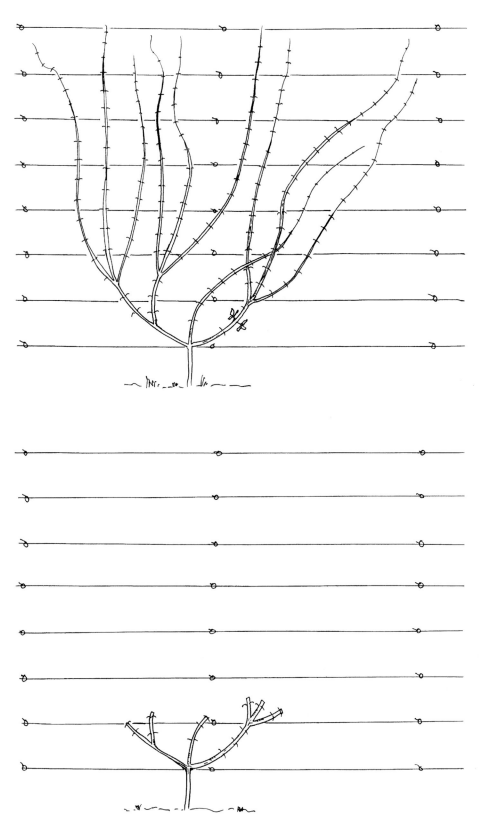

Clematis pruning group 3: (*top*) an unpruned plant; (*bottom*) a plant after all the old stems have been hard pruned. Drawing by E. Leeds.

Clematis 'Helios' before partial pruning. Photo by R. Savill.

Clematis 'Helios' after partial pruning. Note how half the old stems are retained while half are pruned back hard. Photo by R. Savill.

Regardless of the pruning group, always prune a clematis back above a live bud in the axil. Photo by J. Lindmark.

An example of a correctly pruned shoot. Note the new shoot breaking from the axil. Photo by E. Leeds.

Clematis integrifolia, a herbaceous species, before pruning.
Photo by R. Savill.

Clematis integrifolia after pruning. Photo by R. Savill.

about 2 m (6.5 ft.) of stems so that the natural supports can come into their own during winter. Complete the final pruning in early spring.

Pruning unidentified clematis

Occasionally the identity of a clematis plant is unknown, making it difficult to determine its pruning category. The label may have been lost or perhaps the plant is an established one in a recently acquired garden. Where the name of the plant is unknown, especially in an old garden, do not rush the pruning. Seek help from a clematis expert or a specialist clematis nurseryman or woman. Alternatively, assign a number to each plant and observe its flowering pattern over twelve months, recording the details of the flowering period. Using the pruning guide in this chapter, assign the plants to their respective pruning groups and maintain them accordingly.

Care after pruning

Soon after clematis are pruned, they must be fed. Use a general-purpose organic fertilizer, such as fish, blood, and bone meal, or any suitable inorganic fertilizer, following the recommended dosage given by the manufacturers. To encourage development of flower buds, add sulphate of potash. Gently fork the fertilizer into the soil surface.

Mulch the plants to conserve moisture at the roots. Use garden compost, well-rotted farmyard manure, horse manure, or any other suitable material. Handle farmyard manure and organic fertilizers with care, and wash your hands as soon as possible after using such products. When feeding and mulching are complete, remember to water the plant.

In summary, use a clean, sharp pair of secateurs for pruning and remove pruned material from the base of plants without delay. If the stems of older plants are too big for secateurs, use a narrow-bladed pruning saw or a pair of sharp loppers.

In very cold climates, do not rush the annual pruning as new growths can be damaged by severe frosts. Where winters are mild, certain clematis may burst into growth much earlier than spring and well before the time of annual pruning. If these clematis belong to pruning group 3, their new growths can be pruned away and the old stems shortened without any fear.

Establish the pruning group to which a clematis be-

Clematis 'Huldine' and 'Ernest Markham' may both be allowed to flower early in the season on old wood without severe pruning, or late in the season with hard pruning. Photo by J. Glover.

longs by reading its label or the catalogue description or by observing the months in which it flowers. Clematis which flower from late winter to early summer belong to pruning group 1. Do not prune these; any tidying up or removing of flowered stems should be done immediately after flowering. Clematis which produce two flushes of flowers—one from early spring to early summer and a second from midsummer to early autumn—belong to pruning group 2. Tidy up and remove weak and dead wood during late winter or early spring; do not indulge in large-scale, severe cutting back of old or new stems. Finally, clematis which flower from midsummer to late summer and even early autumn belong to pruning group 3. Cut back all the old stems to the lowest live buds. Vigorous plants such as *Clematis tangutica* and its cultivars can be pruned easily by gathering all the old growths in one hand and cutting them off about 30 cm (12 in.) from the ground.

Soon after pruning, mulch, feed, and water the plants. Regular watering is essential during prolonged dry spells.

CHAPTER FIVE

Propagation and Hybridization

Obtaining new, young, healthy plants from seeds, cuttings, or by the simple division of a well-established clump of herbaceous clematis is among the most gratifying aspects of gardening with clematis. Furthermore, it promotes an exchange of plants at minimal cost to the gardener. Propagating clematis is not a laborious task once the basic principles are understood.

Sexual propagation from seed produces new plants which may resemble the parent but are not identical in all respects. Though seeds may more or less breed true, there are often variations within a species due to the wide assortment of possible genetic combinations. In asexual or vegetative propagation from layers, cuttings, or division, new plants are identical to the parent, barring any sudden changes or mutations. Vegetative methods are best employed to propagate selected fine forms of species and all named cultivars.

New Plants from Seed

The flower is the reproductive unit of a flowering plant. Most clematis are bisexual or hermaphrodite, which means each flower carries both male and female parts. The male part (stamen) is composed of a filament and an anther. The female part (pistil) is composed of an ovary, style, and stigma. As each flower matures, a sequence of events takes place which leads to the development of seed. Each event is a significant part of the whole process; if one event fails, the entire process fails and no seed is produced.

Pollination is the process by which pollen is transferred from the anthers to one or more stigmas of the same flower (self-pollination) or of a flower borne on another plant but belonging to the same species (cross-pollination). External agents such as insects, birds, or wind bring about cross-pollination; at times, even the gardener may inadvertently assist in the process.

Pollination is a prerequisite for fertilization, which is the union of male and female germ cells (gametes). When the pollen grains reach the stigmas, they grow to form pollen tubes. The pollen tubes penetrate the tissues of the stigmas and travel through the styles to reach the ovary, which contains eggs (ovules). Fertilization is brought about when the male and female gametes unite. When the process is completed, each ovule commences its development into a seed.

The seed embodies the embryo, which is capable of giving rise to a new plant. As the ovules develop into seeds, the walls of the ovary enclosing the ovules undergo a series of changes to become a fruit. In clematis, successful fertilization results in a dry, single-seeded fruit (achene) which does not split to distribute its seed. A number of achenes develop from the ovary, known collectively as a head of achenes or seedhead.

Collecting seed

Seed can be collected from your own plants or those of friends, or it can be obtained through the seed exchange schemes promoted by local, national, or international clematis and horticultural societies. When gathering seed from a plant, ensure the seeds are ripe, usually brown in colour, and dry. Late summer to late autumn and early winter to midwinter are suitable times for collecting seed, depending on the time of ripening for different species and cultivars.

Collect the seedheads during dry weather. If there is a prolonged spell of wet weather, collect them and let them dry gradually in a well-ventilated, unheated room. For your own reference, attach a label to the seedheads with the name of the species or cultivar and the date of collection. It is always best to sow ripened seeds immediately, no matter what their source. Otherwise, store them carefully in labelled envelopes until the time of sowing.

Sowing seed

Most hardy clematis germinate best in cool conditions. Seed may be sown in seed trays or pots made of clay or plastic. If clay pots are used, cover the drainage holes with rocks or small stones before adding seed compost.

Assemble the following materials: clematis seed, 7.5–10 cm (3–4 in.) pots, loam-based seed compost, sharp sand or grit, a small sieve, a large basin of water containing a small quantity of general-purpose fungicide, a pane of glass, quality labels, and a pencil. Fill the container to within 1 cm (0.5 in.) of the top with the premoistened, well-drained seed compost. Using a flat piece of wood or the base of a smaller pot, gently firm the compost to prevent air pockets. Cut off the feathery styles, if present, without injuring the actual seed, and sow the seed evenly on the surface, making sure to avoid overcrowding. Allow at least 6–12 mm (0.25–0.5 in.) of space between seeds—the more space the better.

Sieve just enough compost to cover the seeds. On top of this, place a thin layer of sharp sand or grit to prevent the compost from drying out and to minimize seed disturbance. Stand the completed pot in the basin of water containing fungicide. As soon as the sand or grit shows signs of dampness, remove the pot from the water. Label the pot clearly with the name of the seed and the date of sowing.

Seedhead of *C. stans*. Photo by E. Leeds.

Seedhead of *C. viticella*. Photo by J. Lindmark.

Seedhead of *C. campaniflora*. Photo by E. Leeds.

Seedhead of *C. recta*. Photo by C. Chesshire.

Place the container in a cold greenhouse, a cold frame, or outside—always in a well-lit position, but never in direct sunlight. Place the pane of glass over the container to retain moisture and prevent disturbance by mice or birds. Check the pot regularly to ensure the compost is moist but not saturated.

Potting up seedlings

Germination may very well be erratic over several months or even years, or it may take only a couple of weeks. As long as the seeds are viable and conditions such as air, moisture, and temperature are favourable, the results will be good.

As the seedlings begin to emerge, remove the pane of glass. Let the seedlings produce two to three pairs of leaves and reach a height of 5–7.5 cm (2–3 in.) before thinking about potting up. Seedlings tend to survive and

grow extremely well in late summer to early autumn, making this an ideal time for potting up. If the seedlings are not strong enough to handle by autumn, leave them until the following spring. Reduce the watering during winter and keep the seedlings on the dry side during winter.

Remember to label the pot. Photo by E. Leeds.

Clematis seeds range in texture and size from fine and small to coarse and large. Photo by E. Leeds.

Self-sown seed of *C. tangutica*. Photo by J. Lindmark.

Sow seed evenly on the surface of the compost.
Photo by E. Leeds.

Emergence of seedlings. Photo by E. Leeds.

When the seedlings are ready, they may be pricked out individually into a 7.5-cm (3-in.) pot containing either loam-based or peat-based seedling compost. Water the container of seedlings well before pricking out and carefully turn them all out together. Holding each seedling by the leaf, gently tease out the roots and pot up the new plant. Avoid bruising or damaging the stem. If germination is erratic and some seedlings are more advanced than others, pot up only the best-developed examples. Using a dibber, ease the roots out of the container. Then, with your thumb and finger grasp the leaves of the selected seedling and pull gently. Label the pots individually with the name of the seedling and the date of potting.

Stand the pots in a sheltered spot in the open garden or in a cold greenhouse, away from direct sunlight and protected from slugs and snails. As the transplanted seedlings settle down and continue to grow, pinch-out the growing tips to encourage the plants to become bushy. Insert a short, split cane about 45 cm (18 in.) long into each pot at a short distance from the main stem and tie-in the new growths. Remember to water adequately and keep the compost moist at all times.

Once the young plants have established good root systems they can be moved into bigger, deeper pots approximately 23 cm (9 in.) in diameter. Fill the pots with a loam-based compost and label the plants. After care of the plants is essential for successful results. Allow the plants to grow in their containers until they are well established with strong stems and ready to be given permanent places in the garden.

New Plants from Layering

Layering is a simple, natural form of vegetative propagation by which a shoot is induced to root while still attached to the parent plant. Some varieties of *Clematis* self-layer, including *C.* 'Fair Rosamond' and *C.* 'Jouiniana Praecox', while others require assistance from a gardener. Although there are different methods of layering, the easiest one, and the method outlined here, is simple layering.

Late spring to early summer or late summer to early autumn are good times to attempt layering a clematis. To layer directly into the ground, dig a shallow trench about 7.5 cm (3 in.) deep along the side of the plant where the stem is to be placed. The length of the trench depends upon the number of plants being propagated. Place some organic compost or peat in the trench and mix it with the soil. Add a few handfuls of fine horticultural grit or sharp sand and gently mix this in as well. Choose a vigorous, flexible stem which can be easily bent down to soil level. Trim off its leaves. Aim to bury two or three leaf joints (nodes) in the trench. Using a sharp knife, make a small, oblique cut towards the base of the leaf joint and about 1.25 cm (0.5 in.) below it, slitting the node but not cutting through it. Dust the cut and the leaf joint with hormone rooting powder. Prepare one or two other nodes in the same way, then peg the stem securely into the soil and cover the trench.

Insert a cane into the ground to support the growing shoot tip and tie the top 45 cm (18 in.) to the cane. Water the trench and, if necessary, the parent plant. Finally, to prevent unwelcome visitors, such as cats or dogs, from digging in the trench, protect it with an elongated, dome-shaped cover made of chicken wire or stiff netting.

Water the trench regularly to keep the stem moist. If there is a prolonged dry spell, also water the parent plant. The layer should be ready after about twelve months. At that point, cut the part of the layered stem attached to the parent plant, carefully dig up the new plant, and move it to a pot filled with loam-based compost. Label and date the new plant, and keep it watered.

Clematis can also be layered into compost-filled pots. The main reason for using a pot is so that the new plant will root directly into it, making it easy to later lift the pot from the soil without damaging the root system. The new plant can be moved to a bigger pot quite easily. Start

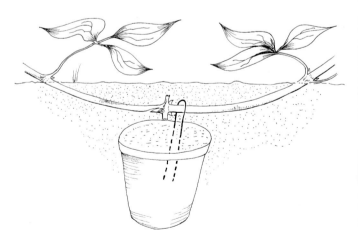

Layering into a compost-filled pot. Drawing by E. Leeds.

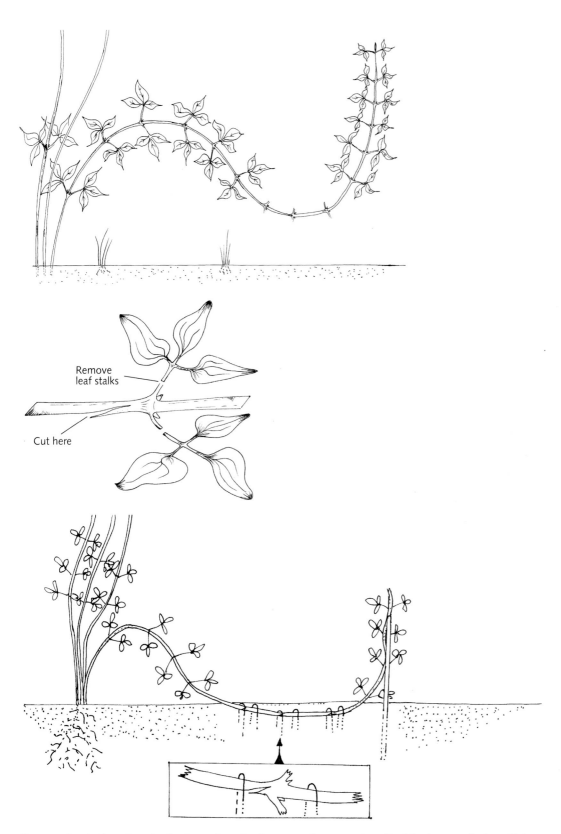

Propagation by layering: (*top*) select a length of a young, low-growing, flexible shoot and trim off the leaves; (*centre*) make a small, oblique cut towards the base of the leaf joint; (*bottom*) peg the stem securely using hairpin bends. Drawing by E. Leeds.

with a 10 cm (4 in.) pot. Fill it with compost and sink it into the ground near the parent plant. Peg the leaf joint into the pot. Check the pot regularly and keep the compost moist at all times. To obtain two or three new plants, use two or three pots and peg individual leaf joints into each pot. New plants obtained by layering in the ground or layering in a container may be potted up just like cuttings (see below) before being planted in the garden.

New Plants from Cuttings

Clematis can be propagated from softwood or semi-ripe cuttings. Softwood is the youngest, greenest part of a growing stem. The cuttings are usually taken from mid-spring to early summer and take about four to eight weeks to root. Semi-ripe cuttings use partially ripened wood. These are taken from midsummer to early autumn and take about eight to twelve weeks to root. The type of cutting normally taken to propagate clematis is known as an internodal cutting, that is, one in which the basal cut is made between two leaf joints or nodes. The materials required include a sharp pen knife or blade, seed tray or small pots, fine horticultural grit or sharp sand, cutting compost made up of equal parts peat and grit or sharp sand, general-purpose fungicide, fresh hormone rooting powder (optional for softwood cut-

tings), and propagator or clear plastic bags. Beginners may want to start with stems of the Montana Group, which are easy to propagate from cuttings, and graduate to large- and small-flowered cultivars. Hygiene is essential throughout the process.

To begin, fill the pots with a compost suitable for cuttings, firm it down, and add a layer of horticultural grit or sharp sand. Water the pots with a general-purpose fungicide and allow them to drain. Select two or three lengths of stem on the parent plant, each about 30–90 cm (12–36 in.) long, and cut them above the leaf joints. Immediately place the stems in a clear plastic bag, sealing the bag to prevent moisture loss.

Working with one stem at a time, take cuttings from the midsection of the stem because the tip is too soft and the lower part may be too woody. Cut through the stem directly above a leaf joint and make a second cut about 2.5–5 cm (1–2 in.) below the same node. To reduce moisture loss, remove one pair of leaves from the leaf joint and half the other pair. The remaining leaves on the cutting should be clean and healthy to prevent any fungal infection. Immerse the cutting in a fungicide solution and allow it to drain. If using semi-ripe wood, dip the bottom 1 cm (0.5 in.) of each cutting into rooting powder to encourage root production, and shake off any excess powder. Softwood cuttings root easily, however, and do not need to be treated with rooting powder. Insert the prepared cuttings into the compost until the

Thin, partially ripened lengths of stem make for better cutting material. Photo by R. Surman.

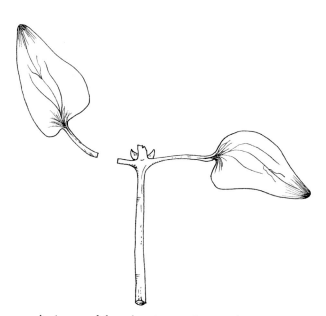

An internodal cutting. Drawing by E. Leeds.

leaf joints are at grit level and the lowest leaf is just above the surface. Label and date the cuttings.

Add some general-purpose fungicide to a small can of water and, using a fine rose spray, water the cuttings to eliminate any air pockets and allow them to settle into the compost. Place the pots of cuttings in a propagator, or cover individual pots with inverted polyethylene bags secured by elastic bands. The cover provides a humid environment. Bottom heat accelerates the rooting process but is not essential. Keep the cuttings in a well-lit area but out of direct sunlight. Check them regularly and remove any dead or infected material. Do not let the compost dry out.

Rooting normally takes about four to eight weeks. Check whether each cutting has rooted by gently pulling on a leaf. If it moves, give the cutting another week or two to develop a strong root system before potting up.

Insert cuttings into a pot of prepared compost. Drawing by E. Leeds.

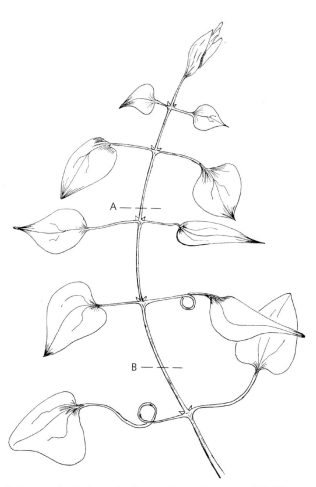

Select a suitable length of stem for cutting material. The best cutting material is between A and B. Drawing by E. Leeds.

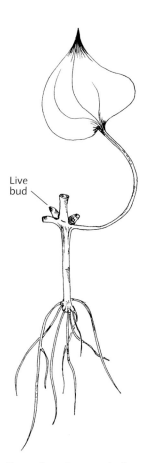

Rooted cuttings ready for potting up. Drawing by E. Leeds..

Once the cuttings are well rooted, harden them off by opening their covers gradually over a few days and exposing them to colder air.

Pot up the cuttings individually using good-quality, loam-based compost in 20 cm (8 in.) pots. Bury the original leaf joint of the cutting just below the surface of the compost. This will enable new shoots to break from the leaf joint. When the plant reaches a height of about 30 cm (12 in.), prune it back just above the first pair of leaves directly above the compost to encourage more side shoots to break from the leaf axils. Allow the plant to grow about 45 cm (18 in.) high before pruning back to the second pair of leaves. This repeated pruning ultimately results in a strong-growing, bushy plant. Water and feed the plant throughout its growing period. Continue growing the plant in its pot, and plant it out the following spring. If grown under glass, inside porches, or even in well-lit rooms or kitchen windowsills, the new plant must be hardened off gradually by introducing it to cooler air conditions before planting it outside.

New Plants from Division

Herbaceous clematis can be easily propagated by dividing large, well-established clumps into smaller sections. Late winter to early spring is the best time to do this. Cut back any old top-growth to the base and lift the plant out of the ground with a fork. Use a sharp spade or a strong carving knife to cut the clump into three or four sections, being careful to preserve the thin, fibrous roots. Replant each section to grow into a new plant.

Hybridization

New *Clematis* cultivars can be created through hybridization, a method by which one species or cultivar is cross-pollinated with another, and the new seed is sown to germinate and continue its growth. The first generation of new plants obtained by crossing two genetically inbred plants of the same species is known as first filial generation, or F_1 hybrids. These are normally full of vigour and are consistent in size, flower colour, and form. Seed from F_1 hybrids seldom breeds true.

A well-planned hybridizing or breeding programme may take detailed planning, time, and patience, but the ultimate results can be very exciting and rewarding. At the onset, list the aim of the exercise and the characteristics of the parent plants, and evaluate the possibilities of creating new hybrids with desired traits. Consider traits such as plant height; the root type (fibrous and fine or lacelike and thick); the bloom (single or double), its aspect (face up, down, or outward), colour, and overall beauty.

Selecting the parent plants for a hybridization programme can be a challenging task. Most clematis grown in gardens have a mixed pedigree, making it very difficult to predict the results of hybridization. Furthermore, very little documented genetic information is available for many species and cultivars. Although it would be useful information, heredity is only one of many factors which influence the selection of parents for hybridization purposes. Some *Clematis* cultivars make excellent pollen (male) parents, but not good seed (female) parents, and vice versa. Some may be infertile, or there may be other hidden factors preventing successful fertilization. The offspring of the first cross may not always deliver the traits a gardener is looking for, which means repeated, controlled crosses have to be made over a long period. In the final analysis, the entire process of hybridization, however scientifically approached, comes down to a matter of chance and, perhaps, luck. Therefore, choose the healthiest plants from among those you grow and have assessed for their outstanding characteristics. It may be prudent to start with the easiest crosses and graduate to more challenging ones.

To begin, assemble the following materials: a pair of fine-pointed scissors, a small camel-hair paintbrush (used by artists), muslin bags, fine twine or string, labels, and a notebook. Select two strong-growing plants, one as the seed parent and other as the pollen parent. The stigmas of the seed parent will receive the pollen grains from the anthers of the pollen parent. Because accurate record-keeping is vital, prepare a dated label with the names of both parent plants. List the seed parent first, as in *Clematis* 'Buckland Beauty' × *C.* 'Kaiu'.

Prepare the seed parent by first choosing a fully developed, plump bud which is about to open. It is advisable to choose a bud because external pollinating agents, such as bees and butterflies, will not have had the opportunity to bring about pollination. Carefully open out the tepals to expose the stamens and stigmas. Gently remove the tepals from the base of the bud and use the scissors to cut away all the stamens (filaments and anthers). Removing the stamens prevents self-pollination and is known as emasculation. Take care not to cut into the pistil in the

Propagation by division of herbaceous *C. integrifolia*. Photos by E. Leeds.

process. Carefully insert the prepared, emasculated flower bud into the muslin bag. Close and tie the bag *in situ* to prevent cross-pollination by pollinating agents.

Next, prepare the pollen parent. To make sure the stamens of the pollen parent are totally free of pollen from other cultivars of *Clematis* which may be brought in by pollinating agents, select two flowers, remove the tepals carefully, and insert each flower separately into a muslin or polyethylene bag. Close and tie the bags. The second flower serves as a reserve if additional pollen is required. Open the first bag containing the emasculated flower bud after a few days to see if the stigmas are shiny and covered with a viscous fluid, ready to receive the pollen. If so, it is time to transfer the pollen grains from the pollen parent to the receptive stigmas. If the stigmas are not ready, however, retie the bag and wait for the stigmas to become viscid and receptive.

Remove the bag from the pollen parent and, using the camel-hair paintbrush, lift and transfer the pollen from the anthers of the pollen parent to the stigmas of the seed parent. Rebag the seed parent to prevent its stigmas from receiving unwanted pollen of other clematis plants. Leave a small air space where the bag is tied to avoid condensation. Attach the prepared label to the seed parent and record the details in a notebook. To ensure that pollination is successful, repeat the procedure after two or three days using pollen from the reserve flower of the pollen parent. Cover the pollinated stigmas of the seed parent and wait two to three weeks for fertilization to take place.

If pollination is successful, fertilization takes place. The ovaries gradually begin to swell—clear proof of the development of seeds. Remove the bag to allow the sun and air to ripen the seeds. This process may take three to four months. Securely append an additional label, which should include information on the cross and the date, to the stalk of the developing seedhead.

Cover the seedhead with a muslin bag a few weeks before collecting it, even if the seeds are green. This prevents accidental damage or loss, or dispersal of seed by the wind, and protects the seedhead from rain. Wet or damp seedheads are not suitable for healthy storage. Keep an eye on the maturing seedhead. The colour of the seeds gradually changes from green to brown, and seedtails develop. (Note that members of the Viticella Group do not develop fluffy seedtails.) As the individual achenes begin to loosen, collect the seedhead, place it in a paper bag or envelope, and label it straightaway. If the seedhead was not covered or if it has become damp in some other way, leave it on a sheet of paper in a safe place so that it can dry. The seeds can be sown immediately or stored in a sealed polyethylene bag in a refrigerator for up to a year. Label the stored seeds and record all pertinent information in the notebook for future reference.

Incidentally, if the seed parent and pollen parent happen to flower at different times, it is possible to gather the pollen from the pollen parent and store it in a clearly labelled, airtight jar until the time is right for pollination of the seed parent's flower.

Selecting, naming, and registering clematis

If the hybridization is a success and all the hard work results in a worthwhile, exciting new hybrid, the next step is to assess the plant. If you have any doubts, contact an experienced clematarian, specialist nurseryman or woman, or a clematis club or society. Name the plant in accordance with the *International Code of Nomenclature for Cultivated Plants* (1995). Check with the clematis registrar of the International Clematis Registration Authority to ensure that the chosen name has not already been given to another clematis. As soon as the registrar has approved the name, the new hybrid can be recorded in the International Clematis Register.

1. Select a plump bud on the seed parent, and carefully open out the tepals to expose the stamens and stigmas.
Photo courtesy Hamlyn.

2. Remove the tepals from the base of the bud.
Photo courtesy Hamlyn.

3. Cut away all the stamens (emasculation).
Photo courtesy Hamlyn.

4. Lift pollen from the anthers of the pollen parent using a small brush. Photo courtesy Hamlyn.

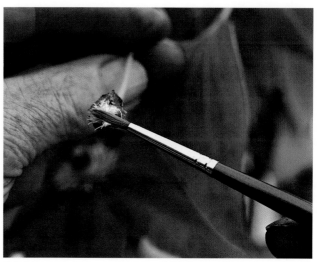

5. Place the pollen on the receptive stigmas of the seed parent.
Photo courtesy Hamlyn.

CHAPTER SIX

Clematis in North America

Maurice Horn & Linda Beutler

When J. E. Spingarn wrote "Clematis in America" for Ernest Markham's classic 1935 book, *Clematis*, interest in growing vines was declining. Selections in nursery catalogues had plummeted from a high of seventy in the 1890s to just eight varieties which were readily available at the time the book was published. This is certainly not the case today. The 1990s saw a dramatic renaissance in clematis growing throughout the United States and Canada. Gardeners in all areas of the continent are experimenting with the many forms now in commerce.

Two important hybridizers of the mid-twentieth century were Frank L. Skinner in Manitoba, who developed such cold-hardy favourites as *Clematis* 'Rosy O'Grady' and *C.* 'White Swan', and Steffen's Clematis Nursery in New York, which focused on large-flowered hybrids such as *C.* 'Sunset' and *C.* 'The First Lady'. Currently Stanley Zubrowski of Saskatchewan is carrying on Skinner's tradition. The University of British Columbia's botanic garden has introduced such worthy selections as *C.* 'Blue Ravine' and *C.* 'Lemon Bells', and the University of Nebraska has experimented with such cold-hardy species as *C. fremontii* and *C. fruticosa*.

Today North America is blessed with avid plantsmen and -women and clematis collectors who have made many plants available to gardeners through their explorations and acquisitions from hybridizers around the world. We thank them for sharing their plants and knowledge. The renaissance in clematis growing coin-cides with the booming interest in gardening in North America.

Regional Cultural Characteristics

When asked, "What clematis should I grow?" the wise plantsman must respond with another question, "Where do you garden?" Because continental North America has such an amazingly diverse array of climates and soil types, the possibilities for growing clematis need to be looked at region by region. Large-flowered hybrids grow well throughout most of the continent with only minor variations. It is with the species and their hybrids that differences in growing conditions are measured.

In the Northeast, the influence of the Atlantic Ocean mollifies the growing conditions for coastal gardeners. Such vines as the Montana Group thrive as far north as Boston. Further inland, members of the Macropetala and Viticella Groups can be trusted to survive the more changeable winters. The soil is acidic so many American species and the hybrids of *Clematis texensis* need an occasional application of lime. Wilt and mildew, which may be due in part to summer heat and humidity, are problems in sensitive, large-flowered hybrids. Some growers recommend using water polymer soil additives to keep plants from suddenly drying out. Another problem is the occasional lack of snow cover, which can put some varieties at risk; snow is often underestimated as an insulating layer. The Northeast is also beset with a vari-

Clematis 'Betty Corning', a floriferous cultivar of the Viticella Group noted for its subtle scent, was discovered in a garden in Albany, New York. Photo by J. Lindmark.

ety of pests, including blue blister beetles, Japanese beetles, deer, voles, and rabbits.

Humidity is an even greater factor in the coastal Southeast. The lack of a winter dormancy period in some areas makes it difficult to grow vines in the Alpina and Macropetala Groups. Many species and their hybrids which are native to southern climates do well, although some may become too vigorous. Try *Clematis armandii*, *C. florida*, *C. terniflora*, and *C. texensis*. High heat and continual bloom may hasten the decline of many large-flowered varieties as they literally bloom themselves to death. Heat may also diminish the ultimate size of some plants. Many areas in the South have alkaline soil. Local natives like *C. addisonii* and *C. ochroleuca* have adapted to this and demand a sweeter soil when grown elsewhere. Inland growing conditions vary depending on altitude, giving gardeners there a different range of clematis from which to choose, including many large-flowered hybrids and members of the Viticella Group.

The climate of the central continent is one of extremes, with subzero temperatures as far south as northern Texas and summer highs in the 30s (Celsius, or 90s Fahrenheit) as far north as southern Canada. In other words, clematis have to be tough to grow in the Midwest. The introduction of *Clematis alpina* and *C. macropetala* hybrids has made clematis growing less risky for gardeners here. Research and development of winter- and drought-tolerant plants have also led to the introduction of herbaceous clematis, such as *C. integrifolia* and its cultivars. Members of the Viticella Group also do very well in this climate because they can survive with-

out winter snow cover. Some large-flowered hybrids fare poorly because of wilt.

Clematis growing is justifiably popular in the Southwest because the mix of growing conditions assures something for everyone. Microclimates range from alpine to high plateau, desert, and mild coastal conditions. Although alpine and high plateau environments are difficult for any plant, gardeners have managed to grow a surprisingly broad range of clematis in these situations, including members of the Herbaceous/Integrifolia and Viticella Groups, many large-flowered hybrids, and local natives such as *Clematis hirsutissima*. The central and southern coastal areas are also able to host a wider range of clematis than had earlier been assumed. New Zealand species, members of the Viticella Group, and many large-flowered hybrids flourish here. White flies, aphids, and slugs slow down but do not discourage intrepid gardeners.

The Pacific Northwest—encompassing the region north of the San Francisco Bay area and south of southwestern British Columbia—accommodates the widest variety of clematis. Although the climate is often compared to that of southern England, the Pacific Northwest actually experiences stronger light, hotter summers, and wetter winters. Conditions west of the Cascade Mountains are characterized by mild rainy winters, warm wet springs, and hot dry summers which last into early October. As a result, mildew is a problem with the Texensis-Viorna Group. The maritime Northwest has acidic soil, so *Clematis montana* and its forms do especially well here, but *C. florida* does not. The native *C. ligusticifolia* is considered a pernicious weed by local gardeners, and earwigs, slugs, and root weevil are particular pests.

The area stretching from the east side of the Cascade Mountains to the Rockies is marked by broad plateaus and ancient mountain ranges. Summers are hot and winters severe. Many clematis suitable to the high plateau of the Southwest are at home here, and the native *Clematis occidentalis* var. *dissecta* scrambles over the forest duff.

Even areas with a direct arctic influence have amazing success with clematis. In south-central Alaska, for example, gardeners report growing members of the Alpina, Herbaceous/Integrifolia, Macropetala, Tangutica, and Viticella Groups, as well as the large-flowered hybrids with *Clematis* 'Jackmanii' influence. Although wilt and mildew are rarely problems here, moose are rampant and

Clematis texensis, a North American species referred to as "The Scarlet Lady," was widely used in modern hybrids. Photo by E. Leeds.

likely to trample clematis underfoot. Plants, therefore, must be adequately protected.

Recommendations from Gardeners

Numerous enthusiastic growers throughout the United States and Canada provided advice and specific observations about reliable clematis for their locales. Jim Fox of Anchorage, Alaska, recommends the Alpina, Macropetala, and Viticella Groups. The two best-performing large-flowered hybrids are *Clematis* 'Jackmanii' and *C.* 'Niobe'. With the renewal of interest in clematis, many Alaskan chain stores now offer untested varieties in their spring inventory. Jim is certain new large-flowered hybrids which are reliably hardy in south-central Alaska will soon be identified by the process of attrition.

In southern California, two avid gardeners share the names of their best growers. Sharon Milder, who lives in the Los Angeles area, chooses only members of the Viticella Group. Among her favourites are *Clematis* 'Polish Spirit' and *C.* 'Prince Charles'. Blanche Uyema, who lives closer inland, also recommends *C.* 'Prince Charles', as well as *C.* 'Kakio' (PINK CHAMPAGNE™), *C.* 'Niobe', *C.* 'Star of India', and *C.* 'Wyevale'.

After growing clematis in the Palo Alto area of central California for many years, Dorothy and David Rodal pulled up vines and moved to Oregon. Their Palo Alto garden, with its rare killing frosts and cool summers, successfully hosted many New Zealand species and hybrids. The Viticella Group was also dependable in their more alkaline soil. Now on Sauvie Island, near Portland, Oregon, their new favourites include *Clematis* 'Blue Boy'—a cross between *C. integrifolia* and *C. viticella*—and *C.* 'Etoile Rose'.

A core group of clematis collectors have settled in Oregon and Washington, snapping up species as soon they appear on the market at specialty nurseries. *Clematis addisonii* and *C. texensis* seem to be especially popular, as well as Japanese introductions *C.* 'Édomurasaki', *C.* 'Fujimusume', and *C.* 'Rouguchi'. New to the Northwest is the Estonian introduction *C.* 'Romantika', with its matt, nearly black-purple flowers. This cultivar stays in demand despite a tendency to mildew in hot weather. Garden designers use such locally reliable large-flowered hybrids as *C.* 'Daniel Deronda', *C.* 'Elsa Späth', *C.* 'Jadwiga Teresa', and *C.* 'Ville de Lyon'.

Southlands Nursery in Vancouver, British Columbia, reports that gardeners in the area favour clematis introduced by the University of British Columbia botanic garden. Also popular are members of the Montana Group, which easily consort with the 60-m (200-ft.) tall Douglas firs (*Pseudotsuga menziesii*) common in local gardens. The soft, gentle light of southwest Canada makes white varieties of *Clematis*, such as *C.* 'Guernsey Cream' and *C.* 'Henryi', appear luminous in the long summer evenings. A happy marriage of warming ocean and sheltering mountains also provides the area around Vancouver and Victoria with a suitable climate for clematis which are sometimes considered tender.

In a lengthy article, Richard G. Hawke (1997) summarized the results of clematis test trials completed at the Chicago Botanic Gardens. The most highly rated plants for USDA Zone 5b were *Clematis* 'Bees Jubilee', *C.* 'Comtesse de Bouchaud', *C.* 'Durandii', *C.* 'Etoile Violette', *C.* 'Grandiflora Sanguinea', *C.* 'Jouiniana Praecox', *C. macropetala*, *C.* 'Ville de Lyon', and *C.* 'Vyvyan Pennell'.

Judith Stanton gardens in the maritime Northeast. Her large garden contains 75 varieties of *Clematis*, including such favourites as *C.* 'Duchess of Albany', *C.* 'Hagley Hybrid', *C.* 'Jackmanii Superba', *C.* 'Mrs. George Jackman', and *C.* 'Rouguchi'. In Massachusetts, nursery-

Clematis texensis, a native of northeastern Texas, requires alkaline or neutral soil. Photo by K. Sugimoto.

woman and clematis specialist Sue Austin has noticed an increase in the use of small-flowered varieties because of their resistance to wilt. The Tangutica Group is increasingly sought after for this same reason. Popular large-flowered forms include *C.* 'H. F. Young', *C.* 'Marie Boisselot', *C.* 'Mrs. Cholmondeley', and *C.* 'Perle d'Azur'.

Maintaining Clematis Plants

Gardeners new to clematis are often confused by the various pruning requirements. In areas with harsh winters, especially when snow cover is absent and temperatures fluctuate unpredictably, pruning is best done in midspring. Gardeners in coastal and temperate regions can begin pruning in January or even late fall. Those living in areas of highly acidic soil can sweeten their gardens with an application of lime. Regions such as the Pacific Northwest, the Northeast, and parts of California have very heavy clay soil which must be amended to facilitate free drainage. In areas which suffer long, heavy periods of rain, gardeners need to take particular care in maintaining soil fertility because of leaching. This is especially true of containerized clematis. Several parts of North America are known for drying winter

Clematis viorna, native from southern Pennsylvania to northern Mississippi and from Ohio to southern Missouri, is commonly known as leather flower or vase vine. Photo by J. Pringle.

winds; in such areas as these, if *Clematis armandii* is hardy, it must be sheltered or the evergreen foliage will show unsightly damage and flower buds will be lost.

Gardening Style

Although basically influenced by the European gardening heritage, North American plant enthusiasts have had to adapt to widely varying growing conditions when using clematis. While still sending clematis up trellises, trees, and shrubs, as well as using them as ground cover, gardeners have additionally welcomed clematis into the mixed perennial border as a focal point rather than as a backdrop. The new crosses of *Clematis integrifolia* are especially popular in mixed plantings. With the increase of smaller gardens and condominium living, growing clematis in containers is becoming the solution to the race for space. Gardeners are beginning to seek shorter varieties to fill this need. In contrast, gardeners with larger spaces are able to integrate their clematis to reflect the scale and drama of the natural surroundings, allowing the larger varieties to achieve their full mature heights.

The quality of light varies throughout North America. In areas where midday sun is intense, subtly coloured clematis including *Clematis* 'Dawn', *C.* 'Peveril Pearl', and *C.* 'Silver Moon' fade quickly to white. Striped forms in the style of *C.* 'Nelly Moser' also lose their intensity under the sun's glare. Gardeners have learned that these flowers give a better show when grown in partial shade or in areas with only morning sun. Likewise, garden designers have led the way in creating innovative combinations, taking full advantage of clematis by using shape, scent, colour, and seedheads.

Although the classic combination of the clematis and the rose is still commonly used, gardeners are beginning to pair clematis with more surprising partners. Spring-flowering shrubs which bloom only once, such as forsythia, lilac, rhododendron, and weigela, now host clematis to add colour interest throughout the growing season. A trend has also developed towards using the smaller-flowered hybrids and species, to add detail and texture to North American gardens.

Gardening with clematis in North America is rapidly gaining popularity. The turn of the twenty-first century witnessed the birth of two new societies dedicated to spreading the word about clematis, educating not only their members but the gardening public as well. In an earlier age, North American species were appreciated overseas by collectors and hybridizers; now these same species have found popularity on their own continent. Local nurseries and mass-marketers must keep a varied selection of clematis on hand. Specialty and mail-order nurseries across the continent are unable to keep up with the demand for new varieties or for the obscure forms which find their way into the mass media. Each region is discovering what flourishes. And as clematis steadily increase in popularity, North American gardeners owe a debt of gratitude to the passionate clematis collectors willing to take chances and risks beyond the common wisdom.

CHAPTER SEVEN

Pests, Diseases, and Physiological Disorders

By adopting good gardening practices and providing proper cultivation and care of clematis, it should be possible to prevent, or at least minimize, problems caused by pests, diseases, and physiological disorders. Occasionally, however, even the most experienced clematarian may face such problems. After a proper diagnosis has been made, suitable remedies can be employed. Due to scientific research on safe and appropriate methods of dealing with garden pests and diseases, a variety of biological and organic methods, as well as chemical treatments, is available to all gardeners. It is important to take quick action when damage by pests or symptoms of diseases and disorders become visible.

Pests

The most common pests of clematis are snails, slugs, and insects such as greenflies and blackflies. These may damage a plant directly or indirectly. They may destroy parts of the plant, or even the entire plant, by feeding on it or infecting it with fungal diseases.

Snails and slugs

Symptoms of damage by snails and slugs include irregular holes in the leaves, ragged ends of young shoots emerging from below the soil surface, nibbled or chewed buds in leaf axils or shoot tips, stripped stems or vines which appear almost white, and silvery slime trails on or around the plant. To control infestations of these pests, several options are available to the gardener. One is to safeguard emerging shoots with protective covers early in the growing season. Another is to place a thick layer of horticultural grit mixed with sharp sand around the base of the plant; this makes the surface somewhat rough and prickly for snails and slugs to move with ease and destroy new shoots. Third, visit the garden nightly, especially after rain, to remove pests from plants. Fourth, cultivate the soil regularly to expose and destroy eggs. Fifth, check artificial supports such as trellises, underneath garden wall caps, and other favourite hiding places of snails during winter and remove any pests. Sixth, scatter methiocarb or metaldehyde slug pellets among the plants, or spray them with liquid metaldehyde or any other aluminum-sulphate-based product.

Mammals

Deer, rabbits, hares, mice, rats, and moles are common pests. Various symptoms of their presence in a garden, in order, include top-growth such as lower stems and leaves that has been eaten, broken shoots, gnawed roots and stems (especially during winter months), and destroyed root systems. One way to protect the garden is to erect a fence around it which is high enough to keep wild animals at bay. Another is to place 1-m (3.25-ft.) high cylindrical cages made of fine-mesh chicken wire around the base of plants; bury these at least 30 cm (12 in.) below the soil level to prevent rabbits and hares from burrowing their way in to attack the plants. Traps with poisoned baits may solve mice and rat problems. Mole scarers may help deter moles, but if these pests become a major problem, recruit the services of a professional mole trapper.

Aphids

Aphids (greenfly, blackfly) can be winged or wingless, reproduce very rapidly, and are usually found in clusters on stems, buds, and the undersides of leaves. Symptoms include stunted and distorted leaves as well as blackened or sticky stems, leaves, and buds which are covered with sooty moulds or aphid excrement (honeydew). Ladybird beetles, both adults and larvae, feed voraciously on aphids and can be very useful in controlling aphid populations. Companion plants such as French marigolds (*Tagetes patula*) attract hoverflies, which also feed on aphids. Spray heavily infested plants with a systemic insecticide containing pirimicarb, which is selective and not injurious to other harmless insects. Note, however, that pesticide resistance in some aphids is widespread. Excessive dryness at the base of plants encourages aphid infestation, so keep the area moist at all times.

Whiteflies

Whiteflies are small, about 2 mm (0.08 in.) long, active, winged insects which usually attack plants in glasshouses or conservatories. They rest on the undersides of leaves and fly off the instant plants are disturbed. Minute, flat, oval, scalelike, immature, immobile, whitish green nymphs are also found beneath young leaves. Whiteflies are not major pests of clematis. When whiteflies are a problem, however, leaves are covered with a sticky excrement (honeydew) and sooty mould. Use biological control to counter these pests. The parasitic wasp *Encarsia formosa* provides effective control in glasshouses and conservatories from midspring to midautumn. Alternatively, whiteflies in the garden or in glasshouses and conservatories may be sprayed with pirimiphos-methyl or pyrethrum.

Winter moth caterpillars

The light green caterpillars of the winter moth (*Operophtera brumata*) are 2.5 cm (1 in.) long and active during late winter and early spring. They eat plant leaves between bud burst and late spring, and may also severely damage flower buds in the axils. To control these pests, remove the caterpillars as soon as they are caught in action. After bud burst, spray plants with derris, pyrethrum, or pirimiphos-methyl.

Clematis 'Eximia' showing snail damage to tepals.
Photo by E. Leeds.

Stems of clematis stripped by the rasping tongues of snails.
Photo by E. Leeds.

Ghost swift moth caterpillars

Caterpillars of the ghost swift moth (*Hepialus* spp.) are up to 45 mm (1.8 in.) long and creamy yellow in colour with a reddish brown head. They may be a problem in some gardens. Although attacks are infrequent, these caterpillars can be very destructive pests, feeding on the roots of clematis and sometimes killing young plants. Most damage to the plants is done between late summer and midspring. Symptoms include poor plant growth or wilt during spring, and young plants suffer most. There is, unfortunately, no effective preventive measure.

Vine weevils

Vine weevils (*Otiorhynchus sulcatus*) are a very widespread and destructive garden pest. They can be a problem in containerized clematis and during propagation. Adult weevils are a dull greyish black, measuring less than 1 cm (0.5 in.) long, and have short snouts. They feed at night and hide by day. Symptoms include U-shaped notches and irregular holes in leaf margins. Control is extremely difficult, but garden hygiene and regular removal of dead leaves and other debris denies hiding places for the weevils. Spraying plants with pirimiphos-methyl around dusk may also help.

The larvae of vine weevil are about 1 cm (0.5 in.) long, plump, and creamy white, with brown heads and no legs. They are easily identified by their characteristic curled shape. The larvae emerge from the eggs laid by the adults in spring and summer and cause serious damage to the roots of the plants from autumn to spring. Plant growth is slow, plants wilt and die, and cuttings are gnawed from stems below ground level. Control of the larvae is difficult. Good garden hygiene is essential to prevent adult weevils from finding hiding places by day.

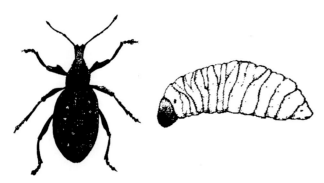

Adult vine weevil and its larva. Photo by E. Leeds. Reproduced by kind permission of the British Clematis Society.

Treatment with nematodes (*Steinernema* and *Heterorhabditis* spp.) is available, although it is effective only when the soil temperature is between 10°C (50°F) and 14°C (57°F); the treatment is more effective in heated glasshouses and conservatories than in the garden. When watered onto the potting compost in late summer, the nematodes will kill the larvae. Imidacloprid, an active chemical ingredient, is also available and may be premixed into the compost or, in the case of container-grown plants, mixed as a drench. Gardeners are advised to take such precautionary measures as examining root balls of newly bought pot-grown plants before planting.

Leaf-mining insect

The small fly (*Phytomyza vitalba*) usually attacks *Clematis vitalba*, wild clematis, and some cultivated types. It is not a serious pest and does not affect plant vigour or flowering. Symptoms include white or brown mines usually terminating in small, irregular blotches largely situated close to the leaf margins. The larvae make sinuous tunnels through the upper surfaces of the leaves, which mean the mines are hardly visible on the undersides. If the infestations are not severe, leaves may be removed and destroyed. Spraying with pirimiphos-methyl or heptenophos and permethrin will also give some control.

Red spider mite

The tiny, eight-legged red spider mite (*Tetranychus utricae*) is usually yellowish green but may appear orange red in autumn. It feeds on plant sap and is mainly a problem

Leaf showing the mines caused by the larvae of phytomyzid fly. Photo by E. Leeds.

for clematis growing in warm, sheltered areas in the garden and in glasshouses. Symptoms of red spider mite infestation include pale mottling of the upper leaf surface. Leaves gradually become dull, yellow, and dry. Close examination may reveal a fine, silky cobweb in heavily infested plants. Pesticide-resistant forms of the red spider mite are widespread and difficult to control. Biological control with a predatory mite, *Phytoseinlus persimilis*, is effective before the infestation becomes heavy. Alternatively, spraying plants thoroughly with pirimiphos-methyl or bifenthrin may control nonresistant forms. To control infestations in container-grown plants, impregnate label-sized cardboard strips with butoxycarboxim, then insert them into the compost. Attacks in glasshouses may be countered by spraying water underneath leaves and maintaining a high humidity.

Earwigs

Earwigs (*Forficula auricularia*) are yellowish brown insects about 15 mm (0.5 in.) long easily identified by a pair of curved pincers. They hide by day and surface at dusk to feed on flower tepals and young leaves. They also make holes in flower buds. Some earwigs can be collected by placing inverted pots loosely stuffed with moss, straw, or hay on the end of bamboo canes near the plants. Remove the earwigs from the pots and destroy them by dropping them into salty water. For heavy infestations of earwigs, spray plants at dusk with pirimiphos-methyl, bifenthrin, or heptenophos plus permethrin.

Diseases

Plant diseases are caused by organisms such as bacteria, fungi, and viruses. Fungal diseases are the most common in clematis.

Slime flux

When the stems of clematis are injured by mechanical means or by frost, bacteria living on the surface of the stems gain entry to the old wood within and multiply there despite low levels of oxygen. During spring, when the root pressure is high, the bacteria are forced out with the rising sap via the wounds, producing slime in the process. Hard-pruned stems of some clematis tend to suffer from slime flux after a sudden, severe frost as well. *Clematis montana* and occasionally cultivars of *C. viti-*

Earwig damage to a bud. Photo by E. Leeds.

Slime flux causes a creamy, frothy substance to ooze from the stems and collect in a small puddle on the soil surface. Photo by E. Leeds.

cella can also be affected. Slime flux causes a foul-smelling, white to pinkish, creamy slime to ooze from the stems and collect in a puddle on the soil surface around the affected plant just before the leaves break. To control it, remove the affected stems, cutting well back into healthy ones to ground level if necessary. Mulch, feed, and water the plants well. Do not uproot the plant in a hurry as new shoots may emerge from below the soil level.

Mildew

Mildew is a fungal disease to which certain *Clematis* cultivars are more susceptible than others. It spreads rapidly in dry mild weather and in conditions of shade and poor air circulation. The fungal growth, usually white and powdery, appears on leaves and stems. Leaves become yellow and fall early, the plant looks unsightly, and in very severe cases of infection buds and flowers may become distorted. To avoid mildew, mulch and water regularly, specifically around the base of the plant. Encourage air circulation by having a good air space between the trellis and the wall. If necessary, spray plants with a suitable fungicide containing buprimate and triforine early in the season and at regular intervals.

Clematis wilt

Wilt is an important fungal disease of clematis, and the causal pathogen is *Phoma clematidina*. Large-flowered cultivars vary in their susceptibility to wilt while the small-flowered species and cultivars are usually resistant to the disease. The plant can be infected via its stems, roots, or leaf joints (nodes) at or just above the soil level. When a plant is infected, the disease spreads rapidly through the stems, resulting in blackening of the vascular tissues responsible for transporting water and nutrients. Wilt caused by drought or wind damage to young stems should not be mistaken for clematis wilt brought about by this disease. Symptoms of the disease include

Buds and flowers of *C.* 'Jackmanii' affected by mildew. Photo by J. Lindmark.

sudden wilting and collapse of either a previously healthy stem(s) with or without buds and flowers, or even the whole plant. Wilted stems appear black and eventually die back. To control this disease, cut back the wilted stems below the level of infection or, if necessary, at ground level. Remove infected material as the fungus can survive in dead plant material for many months and can be dispersed by water or insects. Thoroughly disinfect any tools used to cut back wilted plants. If a plant succumbs to wilt year after year, remove and discard the whole plant and replace the soil before planting a new clematis. No effective chemical treatment is currently available.

Green flower disease
Transmitted by leafhoppers, green flower disease is an infection caused by a group of organisms known as phytoplasma, which are related to viruses. Infected flower tepals become green, misshapen, and leaflike. Unfortu-

nately, there is no cure. If the infection is severe, remove and destroy the plant to prevent spread of infection to other plants. Green flower disease should not be confused with green tepals, a disorder discussed below.

Disorders
Unlike diseases caused by other organisms, disorders are usually the result of nutritional deficiencies including vital mineral salts. Additionally, plant disorders may be caused by unsatisfactory cultural or soil conditions, irregular supplies of food or water, unsuitable growing conditions including inadequate or poor light, and inappropriate temperature range. Disorders become evident through various symptoms ranging from discoloration of leaves, greening of tepals or even the whole plant appearing unhealthy. Proper plant husbandry will help to prevent the onset of many plant disorders, although there is very little a gardener can do to combat the vagaries of weather.

Yellow leaves
Clematis fed heavily on high-potash fertilizers tend to suffer from magnesium deficiency, which causes yellowing of leaves, particularly between the veins, early in the growing season. To control this disorder, apply magnesium sulphate (Epsom salts) directly to the soil at the

Victim of clematis wilt. Photo by E. Leeds.

Yellow leaves of *C. stans*. Photo by E. Leeds.

rate of 25 grams per square meter (1 oz. per 10 sq. ft.), or dissolve 210 grams of salt in 10 litres (2.5 oz. per gallon) and spray the leaves. Add a wetting agent such as liquid soap when making up the spray.

Premature brown leaves

Many factors can cause leaves to brown, including drought, wind burn, excessive application of fertilizers (particularly when the soil is dry), water logging, pest problems, or even root diseases. Leaf tips become crispy brown and lower leaves gradually turn brown and experience premature leaf drop. To prevent premature brown leaves, mulch the plants and keep the soil moist. Check plants for pests and pest-related problems and act promptly. Follow manufacturers' recommendations when applying fertilizers and avoid overwatering or overfertilizing.

Green tepals

Some tepals of early flowering clematis fail to colour up fully due to insufficient daylight. This is a minor disorder not to be confused with green flower disease discussed earlier. Symptoms of the disorder include tepals tinged with green or entire tepals not colouring prop-erly. Control is unnecessary; as daylight becomes available, the tepals develop their right colour.

The best way to prevent pests and diseases is to maintain good garden hygiene. Where possible, rely on biological control of pests. Refrain from excessive use of chemicals in the garden, and exercise maximum care when handling pesticides and fungicides.

Early spring flower of *C.* 'Moonlight' with green tepals. Photo by M. Toomey.

PART II

Clematis 'Sunset' and *C.* 'Silver Moon' in hanging baskets. This novel method for growing clematis works for one season only. Photo by J. Glover.

CHAPTER EIGHT

Overview of Clematis Groups

The gardener's classification of *Clematis* outlined in chapter one is largely based on the flowering times of different groups. It does not take into consideration any botanical or taxonomical details, the aim being to assist gardeners select their plants according to growth habit, size and shape of flowers, and flowering times. To enhance the process of selecting and growing suitable clematis, however, salient features of each group and some cultivation tips on how to achieve good results from plants belonging to different groups are discussed in the following pages. Note that large-flowered cultivars are separated into double and semi-double, and single-flowered groups because of their different cultural requirements.

Evergreen Group

Evergreen clematis (Armandii, Cirrhosa, and Forsteri Groups) are very popular with many gardeners for the simple reason that they brighten the winter months with their foliage. A few even flower in winter, such as *Clematis cirrhosa* and its cultivars and *C. napaulensis*. Most evergreen species are natives of New Zealand, while some originate in southern Europe, India, and China. Many of them are fairly hardy in temperate gardens but require shelter from wind and frost to offer a handsome display of leaves and flowers. Most evergreen clematis make excellent conservatory and glasshouse plants. Even vigorous species, such as *C. armandii* from China, and

their cultivars can be kept in check through judicious pruning.

Evergreen clematis flower on old wood or ripened growths made during the previous year and belong to pruning group 1. Therefore, these plants do not require hard pruning. Any pruning or thinning out of superfluous old growths to keep evergreen clematis within their allocated spaces should be carried out immediately after flowering. It is important to avoid cutting back hard into the framework of the old wood, because new shoots may not necessarily break from it. It is equally important to train and tie-in the new shoots to their supports so that they mature and flower well during the following year. If plants are cut back during winter, there will be a loss of flowers during the next flowering season because the plants will not have had time to produce new flowering shoots and ripen sufficiently during summer.

On the whole, evergreen clematis require well-drained soil and resent excessive winter wetness. This is particularly true of species from New Zealand and southern Europe. Propagation by cuttings or from seed (if they are species) is recommended for this group.

Atragene Group

The atragenes (Alpina, Chiisanensis, Koreana, and Macropetala Groups) are natives of the temperate Northern Hemisphere, from Scandinavia and central Europe to Korea, Japan, and North America. The species and their cultivars are trouble-free, easy clematis to grow in any garden, as well as hardy plants admirably suited for growing specifically in cold, exposed gardens. Atragenes grow well in sun, part-shade, or shade. They can be grown on their own as specimen plants, allowed to grow through or over large shrubs or small to medium trees, planted to cascade down natural outcrops of rocks in large gardens, and are even suited for short-term container-culture. On the whole, these plants are an extremely accommodating group of clematis.

The most distinguishing feature of the atragenes is the presence of petal-like staminodes which surround the true fertile stamens. The length and arrangement of these staminodes may vary between different species. Their colour is sometimes the same as that of the tepals, or it may be different. In the Alpina and Koreana Groups, as well as many other atragenes, the staminodes are seldom longer than the stamens and almost always shorter than the tepals. On the other hand, in the Macropetala Group the outer petal-like staminodes are approximately the same length as the tepals, making the flowers look semi-double or double.

All the atragenes are deciduous, and many are strong climbers. They flower on old wood made during the previous season, mainly from leaf axils between early and late spring, but sometimes intermittently from the current season's shoot tips throughout summer and autumn. The flowers are nodding or semi-nodding and normally composed of four tepals. Many species and their cultivars flower profusely, and the seedheads are most attractive shimmering in the sunshine.

The plants establish very quickly and are not prone to many diseases, most notably clematis wilt. They are relatively pest-free too, although birds may peck out the flower buds before they are fully open. Propagation from cuttings, seed, and layering is relatively simple and easy. Plants propagated from seed, however, may not be identical to the parent plant in all respects. Propagation by vegetative method is to be recommended, although keen gardeners may wish to experiment and select seedlings grown from seed.

If these plants become overgrown or if space is limited, annually remove unwanted stems immediately after flowering and, if grown against an artificial support such as a trellis or an obelisk, train and tie-in the new growths. Refrain from large-scale cutting back of old stems dur-ing late winter months as this results in loss of flowers during the following spring.

Montana Group

The montanas are a delightful and very rewarding group of clematis and are more or less ubiquitous in many gardens in the British Isles. They are natives of northern India (Himalaya) and China, and many species and cultivars make excellent garden plants. Although they are not fully hardy in very cold climes, they are an easy group of clematis to grow elsewhere for the sheer abundance of flowers which appear from late spring onwards. Besides *Clematis montana*, other species which belong to the Montana Group and which are worth growing in the garden or under glass are *C. chrysocoma*, *C. gracilifolia*, and *C. spooneri*.

In general, the montanas are vigorous, deciduous climbers with leaves composed of three leaflets. They flower on old wood made during the previous season, and the normally four-tepalled flowers carried on thin flower stalks are borne in leaf axils in clusters or sometimes singly. Space permitting, the montanas, which belong to pruning group 1, can be allowed to grow away without any pruning; however, if pruning is necessary to keep the plants in check, it should be carried out immediately after flowering. Pruning should also be restricted to removing excessive annual growths and to retaining a framework for a spectacular display of flowers during the following season.

Like the Alpina, Koreana, and Macropetala Groups, the montanas are very accommodating plants which are excellently suited for a host of situations in the garden. They establish themselves quickly and are useful for growing either on their own or in association with large trees, for covering expansive walls or fences, or, space permitting, as ground cover plants. They may also be trained up large pillars or posts and, with judicious and conscientious annual pruning, be controlled enough to look elegant in or out of flower. If with age the lower stems become woody, train against them another low-growing or climbing variety with a different flowering period, or plant a low-growing shrub in front of them. Do not grow any member of the Montana Group close to valuable shrubs and other garden plants, as all members of the group are too vigorous.

In gardens where late, severe frosts are a problem, buds

and flowers of the Montana Group may be damaged and look unsightly. In such locations, plant the clematis against a sheltered wall or fence.

Besides the species, some excellent old and new cultivars are available to modern gardeners. These boast attractive foliage as well as single, semi-double, and even double flowers. They are robust and generally trouble-free plants. Propagation of the group is relatively easy from partially ripened cuttings or by layering.

Double and Semi-double Large-flowered Cultivars

While many *Clematis* species and cultivars distinguish themselves with small, single, dainty, and charming displays of flowers, certain old and new cultivars produce large, striking, and colourful semi-double and double flowers. These cultivars arose from planned hybridization activities, as seedlings of the much-treasured Chinese species *C. patens* or of Japanese double and semi-double cultivars introduced in the nineteenth century, or as mutations or sudden changes (sports) from other single large-flowered cultivars. Almost all of them produce semi-double or double flowers during late spring and early summer and a further display of usually single flowers in early autumn. A few cultivars, however, produce double flowers only during both flowering periods. One such example is *C.* 'Evijohill' (Josephine™). Occasionally a cultivar may bear single, semi-double, and double flowers simultaneously, as is the case with *C.* 'Louise Rowe'.

Like other early flowering clematis, semi-double and double large-flowered cultivars flower on old wood or on ripened stems of the previous season's growths. Therefore, these plants should not be pruned during late winter or early spring. If they require any tidying up, thinning out, or cutting back of old, weak, straggly stems, it should be carried out immediately after the main flowering period, that is, in early summer. No harm comes to plants if a quantity of the old, flowered stems are removed. In fact, the plants will not only look tidy but will also be invigorated, resulting in healthy new shoots emerging from below the soil level and from old, cut-back stems.

Double and semi-double large-flowered cultivars are as versatile as other groups of clematis in that they can be grown on their own as specimen plants trained on obelisks, trellises, pillars, or posts, or partnered with other suitable garden plants such as small trees, shrubs, or other climbing plants, including roses—provided their pruning requirements are similar. Some compact cultivars, as well as those needing shelter from damaging winds, can be grown in containers or in a glasshouse or conservatory.

Most double and semi-double large-flowered cultivars require some sunshine to ripen their flowering stems and, therefore, south-, east-, or west-facing aspects are ideal for cultivation and growth. Plants grown in sunny sites, particularly those facing south, require regular and adequate watering. A certain amount of light is also necessary for proper colouring of the flowers. Without adequate light, flowers of some cultivars tend to open green, although as more daylight becomes available the greenishness recedes and the right colour is restored. Furthermore, these cultivars may not perform their best, during late spring in particular, if the weather is exceptionally cold.

A majority of double and semi-double large-flowered cultivars are hardy in most regions of the British Isles and in other moderately cold areas; however, in gardens subject to severely cold winters, old flowering stems cannot survive and thus plants have no early flowers. As new flowering shoots develop with the arrival of warm weather, flower buds form which open during midsummer to late summer and early autumn. On the other hand, container-grown plants can be protected in frost-free glasshouses, or in garden sheds or garages; with the onset of warm weather they can be moved back into the garden for an early display of flowers.

In the case of certain cultivars which bear rather heavy double flowers, it pays to take extra care to train the vines against suitable supports and tie-in the flowering shoots on a regular basis. These efforts will result in a spectacular display of attractive flowers. Propagation by cuttings is recommended for all double and semi-double large-flowered cultivars.

Single Large-flowered Cultivars

A favourite group of clematis among gardeners, single large-flowered cultivars are noted for their astonishing range of colour, form, and size. The plethora of colour includes anything from delicate pinks to rich and vibrant reds, gentle blues to striking purples, and dazzling whites. Each colour is available in many different shades. Even white cultivars may appear off-white, creamy white, or brilliant, sparkling white.

With this group of clematis, a gardener must be patient and allow the plants time—at least three growing seasons—to develop a good root system and to throw up new, healthy shoots from beneath the soil surface before expecting a spectacular display of flowers. Cultivation of certain large-flowered cultivars is easier than it is with others. Start with easy cultivars, such as *Clematis* 'Comtesse de Bouchaud', *C.* 'Hagley Hybrid', or *C.* 'Ville de Lyon', and graduate to more challenging varieties. In the final analysis, the aim should be to get the newly purchased clematis to produce as many healthy, strong stems as possible through careful planting, watering, pruning, mulching, feeding, training, and tying-in of new growths.

Large-flowered cultivars can be broadly divided into two main groups based on their flowering time: early flowering (midspring to early summer) and late flowering (midsummer to midautumn to late autumn). A few may even continue flowering into early winter in mild or maritime gardens. Thus, if carefully chosen and planted, these cultivars may give a continuous display of flowers over a long period of time. Most of them are hardy in temperate gardens.

Early flowering large-flowered cultivars blossom on old wood or on the previous season's growths from late spring or early summer. Some may even flower again later in the season on the current year's shoots. These clematis belong to pruning group 1 and must not be pruned hard, which would result in loss of early flowers. Any tidying up of the plants or removal of weak stems should be carried out immediately after the main display of flowers is completed. Some cultivars develop handsome seedheads which bring added beauty to the garden; therefore, do not deadhead plants prematurely. If the old flowering stems of some cultivars succumb to severe winters, the flowering season will be delayed. The plants will have to produce new growths with the onset of warmer weather and flower later than normal. This may take anywhere from four to six weeks, sometimes longer. Some early flowering cultivars are also susceptible to clematis wilt, a fungal disease.

Late-flowering large-flowered cultivars reserve their main displays of flowers for midsummer and late summer to late autumn. They flower on new wood or on the current year's growths. Therefore, they must be pruned hard during late winter or early spring. While most late-flowering, large-flowered clematis belong to pruning group 3, exceptions are noted in the plant directory. Like some early flowering large-flowered cultivars, the late-flowering cultivars may occasionally succumb to clematis wilt.

Numerous large-flowered cultivars, both old and new introductions, are widely available to gardeners. With a few exceptions, large-flowered cultivars can be grown in association with other garden plants such as trees, shrubs, roses, and other climbers. Some varieties may be grown in medium to large containers for one or two growing seasons. They are not suitable for long-term container-culture because of their extensive root systems.

Keep pruning requirements in mind when selecting the right plant for the right position in the garden. Unlike the small-flowered species and their cultivars, large-flowered cultivars benefit from more routine care and attention, particularly during the first three years after planting. During that time they must establish themselves and continue to grow as strong, healthy, and floriferous plants. Propagation from cuttings is recommended since large-flowered cultivars do not come true from seed.

Viticella Group

Clematis viticella, also known as the purple Virgin's bower, has been cultivated since the sixteenth century and was first introduced to England in 1569 by way of southern Europe. After years of hybridization in which this species played an important role, many cultivars were made available to gardeners. Several of them are still in cultivation, and new cultivars from England, Poland, Estonia, Russia, and other countries have joined these tried and tested forms. *Clematis viticella* and its cultivars are popularly referred to as the viticellas, and their roll call is very exciting indeed.

Increasingly popular with gardeners, the viticellas are an extremely important group of clematis. They are rewarding and undemanding garden plants because of their hardiness, vigour, reliability, and floriferousness. Most viticellas are wilt-resistant, too. They flower from midsummer to early autumn or even, in mild or maritime gardens, to midautumn. Their flowers may not be the largest or the most colourful when compared to those of the large-flowered cultivars, but they are certainly graceful. The semi-nodding to nodding flowers boast various shades of blue, purple, mauve, or white. Many flowers also carry colourful stamens.

The flowers are produced from the current season's growths. Viticellas, therefore, belong to pruning group 3 and must be pruned very hard, almost to ground level, earlier in the year for a spectacular display of flowers. They can be grown on their own as specimen plants on supports such as walls, fences, free-standing trellises, pergolas, arbours, obelisks, pillars, or posts; they can also be grown in association with robust shrubs, small to medium trees, climbing roses, and other climbers. They may even be grown as ground cover. Propagation from cuttings or by layering is recommended.

Texensis-Viorna Group

In a class of its own, the exquisite scarlet-flowered *Clematis texensis* from south-central and northeastern Texas is coveted by clematis enthusiasts everywhere. It may not be readily available to many gardeners because it is difficult to propagate from cuttings and seeds are not always easy to obtain. Nevertheless, hybridizers exploited its flower colour and shape to produce several excellent, garden-worthy cultivars which are popularly referred to as texensis cultivars. These charming, old and new plants are noted for their waxy-smooth, elegantly shaped flowers, some of which are tuliplike, others bell-like and gently nodding. They flower from early summer to late autumn, certain varieties coming into flower much earlier than others. They are semi-herbaceous to herbaceous scramblers by habit and may either be cultivated on their own or in partnership with other suitable garden plants, notably small to medium-sized shrubs. Varieties with small, tuliplike flowers are especially attractive when trained on a plane where the flowers can be admired at eye level.

The Texensis-Viorna Group should be treated like other herbaceous garden perennials. During late winter or very early spring, prune back all aerial growths to ground level. With the onset of spring numerous new shoots will emerge from beneath the soil, continue growing into strong stems, and flower profusely.

Unfortunately, these cultivars are prone to mildew, which if not controlled can destroy leaves and flower buds with equal vigour. They can also be struck down by clematis wilt. Neither problem, however, should discourage gardeners from finding space for some of these plants in the garden. Propagation from cuttings is not easy. *Clematis addisonii*, *C. pitcheri*, *C. versicolor*, and *C. viorna* also belong to the Texensis-Viorna Group and rightly merit a place in any proud gardener's collection of clematis.

Tangutica Group

For the convenience of gardeners, the yellow clematis are discussed here under the extremely popular species *Clematis tangutica* from northwestern China. In fact, there are other species which have yellow flowers, including *C. graveolens*, *C. orientalis*, and *C. tibetana*.

Noted for their waxy-smooth, yellow, lantern-shaped flowers, plants sold under the name of *Clematis tangutica* are extremely variable. Therefore, it is best to seek a form which not only boasts beautiful flowers but also very attractive, relatively large seedheads. Several cultivars supposedly arisen from *C. tangutica* are widely available and make excellent, easy-to-grow garden plants. While some are quite vigorous, the new Dutch cultivars *C.* 'Helios' and *C.* 'Kugotia' (GOLDEN TIARA™) are admirably suited for small to medium-sized gardens.

Most members of this group flower continuously from early summer through autumn. Some, however, reserve their spectacular main display for late summer. The plants can withstand temperatures down to −34ºC (−30ºF) and are not too particular about sun, shade, or part shade. All of them belong to pruning group 3 and can be hard pruned during late winter or early spring. Plants may be grown on their own against strong supports or allowed to roam into large shrubs or small trees. Space permitting, they may even be grown as ground cover.

Propagation by cuttings or from seed is easy; however, there is already a certain amount of confusion about the correct identity of this group of plants raised as seedlings. Therefore, propagation by seeds, particularly of cultivars, is not recommended.

Herbaceous and Subshrubby Species and Cultivars

Although most clematis are climbers, some species and cultivars are either wholly herbaceous or subshrubby in their habit. The top-growth of truly herbaceous types dies back each winter and produces new growths from rootstocks the following spring. Similarly, in subshrubby species and cultivars the soft top-growth or nonwoody parts of the stems die back to a woody base each winter and new shoots break from them during spring. Herbaceous and subshrubby clematis (Heracleifolia and Integrifolia Groups) are very useful plants in herbaceous or mixed borders. For example, *Clematis integrifolia*, a European species introduced into cultivation as far back as 1573, and *C. heracleifolia*, a Chinese subshrubby species introduced into cultivation in 1837, are still widely grown. Likewise, there are many splendid herbaceous and subshrubby cultivars, both old and new, which are mostly trouble-free and easy to cultivate in flower borders.

Herbaceous clematis have a lax-growing habit. Depending on their height, they may be planted among other perennials in front, middle, or back of a border for support and companionship. Taller forms, such as *Clematis* 'Alionushka', *C.* 'Durandii', and *C.* 'Eriostemon', may need artificial supports; otherwise, they can be allowed to grow through small or medium-sized shrubs in mixed borders or larger perennials in herbaceous borders.

The cultural requirements of this group are similar to those for other climbing clematis. They can be treated just like other garden perennials in the borders. During late winter or early spring, cut back the old flowered stems to ground level, and mulch and feed the plants to promote new top-growth. Over time herbaceous clematis make large clumps, which should be divided every two or three years and replanted using the healthy sections.

Propagation is relatively easy by simple division, layering, or from basal cuttings. Seed-propagated plants tend to be variable.

Other Species and Cultivars

Many unusual or exotic clematis may not be widely available in nurseries or garden centres, although some may be available from specialist or unusual plants nurseries. Experienced gardeners may wish to establish their own collection of unusual clematis, mostly species, by growing plants from seed. Not all seed-propagated plants, however, are carbon copies of the parent plant. Although propagation may not be easy, the challenge of raising one's own plants can be very rewarding.

CHAPTER NINE

Directory of Clematis

Clematis 'Abundance'
VITICELLA GROUP

Synonym: *C. viticella* 'Abundance'

Origin: Rather obscure but believed to have been originally hybridized by Francisque Morel of Lyon, France, before the First World War, and subsequently given to William Robinson at Gravetye Manor. It was eventually passed on to George Jackman and Son (the head gardener, Ernest Markham died in 1937), and they named and introduced it.

Parentage and year: Hybrid of *C. viticella* × unknown pollen donor. Unknown.

Habit: Hardy, vigorous, deciduous climber.

Height: 3–4 m (10–13 ft.).

Description: A very floriferous cultivar. The single, flat, open and semi-nodding flowers, 5–7.5 cm (2–3 in.) across, are made of four, sometimes five, blunt wine-red tepals, which recurve at their edges and tips. There is a lighter shaded bar along the centre, and the veining is of a darker pink. Filaments are creamy green with yellowish anthers. The leaves are midgreen.

Pruning group: 3.

Flowering period: Midsummer to late summer.

Cultivation: Thrives in most garden soils and any aspect.

Recommended use: Ideal for a trellis, arbour, or pergola. Best grown through light-coloured foliage of host tree, conifer, or large shrub. Zones 3–9.

Clematis addisonii
TEXENSIS-VIORNA GROUP

Origin: Southeastern United States (Virginia and North Carolina).

Parentage and year: Species. 1890.

Habit: A much-branched and bushy plant with branches erect at first, later trailing or scrambling along the ground without rooting.

Height: 0.6 m (2 ft.).

Description: The single, solitary, four-tepalled flowers, borne at the ends of branches or in the axils, are small, about 1–2 cm (0.5–0.75 in.) long, and pitcher shaped. The tepals, shaped like the head of a lance, can be quite variable in colour through pale shades of reddish purple to bluish purple becoming whitish at the recurving tips. Stamens are creamy. Stems are more or less erect with simple lower leaves, whilst the upper leaves on the taller stems are compound, usually two pairs of leaflets, rarely three, with the leaf axis ending in a tendril-like structure. The lower and upper leaves are smooth and strongly blue green.

Pruning group: 3.

Flowering period: Midsummer to early autumn.

Cultivation: Tolerant of most garden soils since wild plants grow in wooded river banks (alluvial soils). Suitable for sun or semi-shade in a sheltered position in the garden, where the flowers can be viewed at close quarters. Prone to mildew. Take early precaution by spraying with a fungicide monthly from early summer. If trained on an artificial support, the stems need tying-in.

Recommended use: Place at the front of a mixed border to grow through low herbaceous plants and low shrubs. In a container it requires training and a suitable support. Zones 6–9.

Clematis aethusifolia
Origin: Northern China and Manchuria.
Parentage and year: Species. ca. 1875.
Habit: Hardy, not-so-vigorous, deciduous, semi-herbaceous climber.
Height: 1.2–2.1 m (4–7 ft.).

Description: The single, small, 1.5–2 cm (0.5–0.75 in.) long, bell-shaped, creamy yellow, scented flowers are normally composed of four tepals, which recurve, rolling back upon themselves. Anthers are beige. The leaves are distinctive with deeply dissected, fernlike leaflets.

Pruning group: 3.
Flowering period: Late summer to midautumn.
Cultivation: Tolerates most garden soils with good drainage. Prefers a sunny position to ripen flowering stems.

Recommended use: Good cover for low, artificial supports or the bare stems of other wall-trained plants. Allow it to tumble over a low wall. Zones 6–9.

Clematis afoliata
EVERGREEN GROUP
Common name: Rush-stemmed clematis
Origin: New Zealand, including North Island (Wellington) and a wide distribution in South Island to ca. 700 m (2300 ft.). Introduced into cultivation in England by Charles Willmot. Awarded RHS Award of Merit (1916).
Parentage and year: Species. 1908.
Habit: Half-hardy to hardy, semi-climbing or sprawling, evergreen shrub.

Clematis 'Abundance'. Photo by J. Lindmark.

Clematis addisonii. Photo by J. Pringle.

Height: 1.5–3 m (5–10 ft.).

Description: A unique plant which is more or less leafless in that the leaves are reduced to triangular-shaped vestiges about 6 mm (0.25 in.) across. The much-branched, congested, stiff stems are dark green to yellowish green and rushlike, becoming quite woody with age. The single, nodding, greenish yellow, scented flowers, produced solitarily or in clusters of up to five,

and measuring 1.5–2 cm (0.5–0.75 in.) across, are composed of four to six tepals and creamy stamens. Male and female flowers are borne on separate plants. Male flowers are deeper yellow in colour.

Pruning group: 1. To keep the plant from becoming an untidy mass of stems, remove some stems immediately after the main flowering period.

Flowering period: Early to late spring.

Cultivation: Tolerates most well-drained garden soils. Withstands a certain amount of drought, so overwatering should be avoided. Requires a warm, sunny position in the garden. If trained on an artificial support, the stems need tying-in.

Recommended use: An excellent plant for maritime gardens. Best grown against a sheltered warm wall, or in a conservatory or cold greenhouse in very cold areas. Zones 8–9.

Clematis 'Akaishi'

Origin: Raised in Japan by Sakata no Tane Company and named after a mountain.

Parentage and year: Unknown.

Habit: Hardy, moderately vigorous, deciduous climber.

Height: 2.4–3 m (8–10 ft.).

Description: The single, deep purple flowers, 15–20 cm (6–8 in.) across, are composed of eight boat-shaped, pointed tepals, each with wavy margins and a prominent cerise-pink central bar. Stamens are made of pinkish filaments tipped with silvery purple anthers.

Clematis aethusifolia. Photo by C. Chesshire.

Clematis afoliata. Photo by C. Chesshire.

Clematis 'Akaishi'. Photo by C. Chesshire.

Pruning group: 2.

Flowering period: Midspring to late spring and late summer.

Cultivation: Tolerates most garden soils and any aspect.

Recommended use: Suitable companion for other wall-trained shrubs, climbers, or moderately vigorous clematis which do not require annual pruning. Zones 4–9.

Clematis 'Alba'
HERBACEOUS / INTEGRIFOLIA GROUP

Synonym: *C. integrifolia* 'Alba'

Origin: Raised by Stanley J. Zubrowski of Prairie River, Saskatchewan, Canada.

Parentage and year: Selected form of *C. integrifolia*. 1985.

Habit: Hardy, deciduous, non-clinging, herbaceous perennial.

Height: 0.6 m (2 ft.).

Description: The single, nodding, bell-shaped, scented flowers are composed of four white, sometimes tinged with blue, narrow, pointed tepals, each 4–5 cm (1.5–2 in.) long, with upturned tips and ridges running from the base to the tips. Anthers are pale white. Flowers are produced on terminal shoots and upper leaf axils.

Pruning group: 3.

Flowering period: Early summer to late summer.

Cultivation: Tolerates most garden soils enriched with humus. Suitable for any aspect but produces the strongest scent in a sunny position. May need some support—pea-sticks are ideal and unobtrusive.

Recommended use: Ideal for the front of a herbaceous border. Zones 3–9.

Clematis 'Alba Luxurians'
VITICELLA GROUP

Synonym: *C. viticella* 'Alba Luxurians'

Origin: Believed to have been raised by Veitch and Son of England. Awarded RHS Award of Garden Merit.

Parentage and year: Unknown. ca. 1900.

Habit: Hardy, moderately vigorous, deciduous climber.

Height: 3–4 m (10–13 ft.).

Description: The single, 7.5-cm (3-in.) diameter, white flowers with tips shaded green are normally composed of four, sometimes up to six, blunt tepals. The green shading depends on how much sunlight the flowers enjoy. Some midsummer flowers are completely white. The delicate tepals recurve at their margins, and the beauty of the flower is enhanced by the purple-black stamens. The reverse of each tepal boasts a hint of pearly blue with a very pale green bar along the centre. The midgreen leaves are tinged with grey.

Pruning group: 3.

Flowering period: Midsummer to early autumn.

Cultivation: Tolerates most garden soils and any aspect.

Recommended use: Ideal to grow through medium-sized trees and conifers, over large open shrubs, or as a specimen on a trellis, pergola, or obelisk. Zones 3–9.

Clematis albicoma
HERBACEOUS / INTEGRIFOLIA GROUP

Origin: United States (Virginia and West Virginia).

Parentage and year: Species. Unknown.

Clematis 'Alba'. Photo by C. Chesshire.

Habit: Hardy, slender, deciduous, upright, herbaceous perennial.

Height: To 0.6 m (2 ft.).

Description: The single, solitary, nodding, urn-shaped flowers, composed of four tepals, each about 1.5–2 cm (0.5–0.75 in.) long, are borne at the tips of stems. The tepals, with a covering of silky hairs on the outside, are yellowish with a flush of bluish purple towards the base, and sharply recurve at the rounded blunt tips. The flowers are held below the topmost pair of leaves in each branch. Much-branched, ribbed stems are densely covered in short, fine, white hairs, especially at the nodes. Leaves are simple, roughly oval in shape, with entire margins occasionally interrupted by forward-pointing teeth and a few scattered hairs on the underside.

Pruning group: 3.

Flowering period: Early summer to midsummer.

Cultivation: Prefers dry, infertile soils with good drainage.

Recommended use: Ideal for container-culture or for a rockery. Zones 5–9.

Clematis 'Albiflora'
ATRAGENE GROUP

Synonym: *C. alpina* 'Albiflora'

Origin: Raised by Magnus Johnson of Södertälje, Sweden, and introduced into cultivation by Raymond Evison of Guernsey Clematis Nursery in 1991.

Parentage and year: Seedling of *C. alpina*. 1955.

Habit: Hardy, moderately vigorous, deciduous climber.

Height: 2.5–3 m (8–10 ft.).

Description: The single, creamy white flowers are made of four tepals, each 5 cm (2 in.) long. Staminodes are light yellow green. Leaves are light green and are composed of normally nine leaflets with leaf margins serrated and resembling the teeth of a saw.

Pruning group: 1. Any pruning to keep the plant tidy should be carried out immediately after the main flowering period.

Flowering period: Midspring to late spring. Few flowers in late summer.

Cultivation: Needs sharp drainage. Suitable for any aspect, but ideal for north-facing and cold aspects.

Clematis 'Alba Luxurians'. Photo courtesy Thorncroft Clematis Nursery.

Produces a better second flush of flowers in a sunny location.

Recommended use: Ideal for small gardens. Can be grown with other early flowering clematis to provide flowers low down on bare stem. Zones 3–9.

Clematis 'Albina Plena'
ATRAGENE GROUP

Synonym: *C.* 'Albino Pride'

Origin: Raised by Magnus Johnson of Södertälje, Sweden.

Parentage and year: *C. fauriei* × *C. sibirica* (F_2 hybrid). 1982.

Habit: Hardy, quite vigorous, deciduous climber.

Height: 3–4 m (10–13 ft.).

Description: The sumptuously double, bell-shaped, white flowers, 6–8 cm (2.25–3.25 in.) across, are freely produced from the old wood made during previous seasons. The flowers are composed of four outermost primary tepals, each about 4 cm (1.5 in.) long, and enclosing numerous secondary petal-like staminodes of similar length. The smooth tepals taper at both ends and are longer than broad, and wider below the middle, resembling the head of a lance. Stamens are made of greenish cream filaments and yellow anthers. Leaves are light green to midgreen and have nine leaflets.

Pruning group: 1. Tidy up after flowering.

Flowering period: Late spring to early summer.

Cultivation: Needs sharp drainage. Suitable for any aspect.

Recommended use: Ideal for a medium-sized obelisk or a trellis. May be grown through medium-sized shrubs not requiring annual pruning. Zones 4–9.

Clematis 'Alblo'
HERBACEOUS/HERACLEIFOLIA GROUP

Trade name: ALAN BLOOM

Synonym: *C.* 'Bressingham Bluebird'

Origin: Raised by Blooms of Bressingham, England. First named 'Bressingham Bluebird' by Alan Bloom,

Clematis 'Alblo' (ALAN BLOOM™). Photo by C. Chesshire.

Clematis 'Albiflora'. Photo by J. Lindmark.

Clematis 'Albina Plena'. Photo by J. Lindmark.

the founder of the nursery, and later re-named in his honour for his 90th birthday. Plant Breeders' Rights.

Parentage and year: Selected form of *C.* 'Wyevale'. Early 1990s.

Habit: Hardy, non-clinging, deciduous, woody-based subshrub.

Height: 0.6–0.9 m (2–3 ft.).

Description: The single, tubular, hyacinth-shaped flowers, 2–2.5 cm (0.75–1 in.) long and 4 cm (1.5 in.) wide, are composed of four dark blue tepals, which expand widely towards the tips and strongly recurve, revealing white filaments and yellow anthers. The flowers become more mauve with age.

Pruning group: 3.

Flowering period: Midsummer to early autumn.

Cultivation: Requires a free-draining but moist soil. Suitable for any aspect.

Recommended use: Good in the middle of a mixed or herbaceous border or as a specimen plant in a large container. Zones 5–9.

Clematis 'Alborosea'
ATRAGENE GROUP

Synonym: *C. macropetala* 'Alborosea'

Origin: Raised by Magnus Johnson of Södertälje, Sweden, from seed given to him by Hans R. Horn-Gfeller of Merligen, Switzerland.

Parentage and year: Chance seedling of *C. macropetala*. 1974.

Habit: Hardy, not-too-vigorous, compact, deciduous climber.

Height: 1.8–2.4 m (6–8 ft.).

Description: The double, nodding, mauvish pink flowers, 4–5 cm (1.5–2 in.) long, are composed of four narrow spear-shaped tepals, each boasting long veins of a darker shade running from the base to the tip. Inside the tepals is a layer of pale pink petal-like staminodes almost the same length as the tepals, but much thinner and narrower, giving the flower a spiky appearance. The pale yellow stamens are encircled by short, spoonlike staminodes.

Clematis 'Alborosea'. Photo by J. Lindmark.

Pruning group: 1.

Flowering period: Early spring to midspring, with occasional midsummer flowers.

Cultivation: Tolerates most well-drained garden soils and any aspect.

Recommended use: Ideal for container-culture or for growing on a medium-sized trellis or obelisk. Zones 3–9.

Clematis 'Alexander'
MONTANA GROUP

Synonym: *C. montana* 'Alexander'

Origin: Collected in northern India by Colonel R. D. Alexander.

Parentage and year: Selected wild form of *C. montana*. Introduced in 1961.

Habit: Vigorous, deciduous climber.

Height: To 8 m (26 ft.).

Description: The single, scented, creamy white, cup-shaped flowers, 6 cm (2.25 in.) across, are made of four broad tepals. The anthers are creamy. The leaves are much larger than those of the species *C. montana* and are light green.

Pruning group: 1. Any pruning to keep the plant in

check should be carried out immediately after the main flowering period by removing some of the old, flowered stems.

Flowering period: Midspring to late spring.

Cultivation: Tolerates most well-drained garden soils. Hardy in temperate gardens. Best in a warm, sunny position. Slow to become established and flower well.

Recommended use: Good for a large pergola. Suitable for a sheltered wall or fence. Zones 7–9.

Clematis 'Alice Fisk'

Origin: Raised by Jim Fisk of Fisk's Clematis Nursery, Suffolk, England, and named after his mother.

Parentage and year: *C.* 'Lasurstern' × *C.* 'Mrs. Cholmondeley'. 1967.

Habit: Hardy, weak-growing, deciduous climber.

Height: 1.8–2.4 m (6–8 ft.).

Description: The single, pale wisteria-blue flowers, 15–20 cm (6–8 in.) wide, are composed of usually eight pointed, textured tepals, the margins of which are toothed with shallow and somewhat rounded teeth, giving a scalloped appearance. The stamens are brown.

Pruning group: 2.

Clematis 'Alexander'. Photo by C. Chesshire.

Clematis 'Alice Fisk'. Photo by J. Lindmark.

Flowering period: Late spring to early summer and late summer.

Cultivation: Tolerates most garden soils and any aspect.

Recommended use: Ideal for small gardens. Suitable for containers or for growing on a small to medium-sized obelisk or trellis. Good companion for other not-so-vigorous, wall-trained shrubs which do not require heavy annual pruning. Zones 4–9.

Clematis 'Alionushka'
HERBACEOUS/INTEGRIFOLIA GROUP

Synonyms: *C.* 'Aljonushka', *C.* 'Alyonushka', *C. integrifolia* 'Aljonushka'

Origin: Raised by A. N. Volosenko-Valenis and M. A. Beskaravainaja of the State Nikitsky Botanic Gardens, Ukraine. Awarded British Clematis Society Certificate of Merit (1998).

Parentage and year: *C.* 'Nezhdannyi' × *C. integrifolia*. 1961.

Habit: Hardy, semi-herbaceous, moderately vigorous, non-clinging, shrubby perennial.

Height: 1.2–1.8 m (4–6 ft.).

Description: The single, nodding, delicate satiny pink, bell-shaped, 5- to 8-cm (2- to 3.25-in.) diameter flowers are composed of four, sometimes six, deeply textured and grooved tepals, each up to 6.5 cm (2.5 in.) long with a deeper pink central bar. The margins are gently scalloped and recurving. The tepals twist with

maturity. The stamens are made of yellow filaments and anthers.

Pruning group: 3.

Flowering period: Early summer to early autumn.

Cultivation: Tolerates most garden soils and any aspect. If trained on an artificial support, the stems need tying-in.

Recommended use: Grow through medium-sized shrubs where some support can be had or allow to scramble through and over prostrate shrubs and conifers. Suitable for a small to medium-sized obelisk. Zones 3–9.

Clematis 'Allanah'

Origin: Spotted first in flower in 1968 by Mrs. A. Edwards of Christchurch, New Zealand, who also named it. Raised by Alister Keay of New Zealand Clematis Nurseries, Christchurch. Introduced to the British Isles in 1984 by Jim Fisk of Fisk's Clematis Nursery, Suffolk, England.

Parentage and year: Unknown (a chance seedling). 1980.

Habit: Hardy, moderately vigorous, compact, deciduous climber.

Height: 1.8–2.4 m (6–8 ft.).

Description: The single, bright ruby-red flowers, shaded or flushed with carmine, measure 15–20 cm (6–8 in.) across and are made of six to eight widely spaced tepals, which are about 6.5 cm (2.5 in.) long

Clematis 'Alionushka'. Photo by J. Lindmark.

Clematis 'Allanah'. Photo by J. Lindmark.

and 3.5 cm (1.25 in.) wide, broad, and blunt tipped. Green filaments, flushed with maroon at first and turning to deep maroon later, and greenish anthers make up the central tuft of stamens. Leaves are divided into five leaflets, which are somewhat hairy underneath.

Pruning group: 3.

Flowering period: Early summer to late summer.

Cultivation: Tolerates most garden soils. Suitable for sun or partial shade.

Recommended use: Ideal for growing through prostrate shrubs and conifers or to cover bare lower stems of wall-trained plants. Allow to clamber in a herbaceous border or grow up a small obelisk or low support. Zones 4–9.

Clematis alpina
ATRAGENE GROUP

Origin: Native throughout the Alps from eastern France to northwestern Yugoslavia, also north to southern Germany; in the Carpathian Mountains north to southern Poland, and east to Romania; in the Balkan Mountains of Bulgaria and in the smaller areas in the Apennine Mountains of northern Italy and in west-central Yugoslavia.

Parentage and year: Species. 1768.

Habit: Hardy, moderately vigorous, deciduous climber.

Height: 2.5–3 m (8–10 ft.).

Description: The single, violet-blue flowers on short shoots are produced from the previous season's old wood. The four tepals are 2.5–5 cm (1.5–2 in.) long, nodding, and ultimately spreading widely. The four outermost staminodes are much widened with spoon-shaped tips, almost concealing the fertile stamens and pistils. White filaments carry light yellow anthers. The leaves are usually composed of nine leaflets, and the leaf margins are serrated resembling the teeth of a saw. Seedheads are attractive.

Pruning group: 1. To maintain a handsome framework of old wood on established plants, remove a few flowered stems annually, immediately after the main flowering period.

Flowering period: Midspring to late spring, with occasional flowers in midsummer.

Cultivation: Needs sharp drainage. Suitable for any aspect.

Recommended use: Ideal for a small garden, north wall, or windy, exposed sites. Suitable for container-culture. Zones 3–9.

Clematis alpina, growing in Monte Servo, Belluno, Italy. Photo by J. Lindmark.

Clematis 'Alpinist'

Origin: Raised by M. A. Beskaravainaja at the Nikitsky State Botanic Gardens, Ukraine, and named in 1977.

Parentage and year: *C.* 'Lanuginosa Candida' × pollen mixture of *C. viticella* and *C.* 'Jackmanii'. 1970.

Habit: Hardy, moderately vigorous, deciduous climber.

Height: 2.4–3 m (8–10 ft.).

Description: The single, pale lilac flowers, 12–14 cm (4.75–5.5 in.) across, are composed of six wide, oblong to rounded, gappy tepals, each tapering to a point. The stamens are made of pale filaments and greenish yellow anthers.

Pruning group: 3.

Flowering period: Midsummer to late summer.

Cultivation: Tolerates most garden soils enriched with humus. Suitable for any aspect.

Recommended use: Suitable for a pergola, obelisk, or trellis. May be grown through medium-sized to large shrubs. Zones 3–9.

Clematis 'Ametistina'

ATRAGENE GROUP

Origin: Raised by Magnus Johnson of Södertälje, Sweden.

Parentage and year: *C. fauriei* × *C. sibirica* (F_2 hybrid). 1975.

Habit: Hardy, vigorous, deciduous climber.

Clematis 'Alpinist'. Photo by M. A. Beskaravainaja.

Clematis 'Ametistina'. Photo by J. Lindmark.

Clematis alpina, growing wild in the Dolomites, Italy. Photo by B. Mathew.

Height: To 4 m (13 ft.).

Description: The mauvish pink flowers, composed of four tepals, each 4–6 cm (1.5–2.25 in.) long, boast an inner skirt of pale pink, spatula-shaped, petal-like staminodes. The midgreen to light green leaves are composed of three leaflets, which are simple or two or three lobed, with irregularly toothed margins.

Pruning group: 1. Any pruning to keep the plant tidy should be carried out immediately after the main flowering period.

Flowering period: Midspring to late spring, with occasional flowers in late summer.

Cultivation: Needs sharp drainage. Suitable for any aspect but best in sun to get summer flowers.

Recommended use: Good cover for low, bare stems of other vigorous group 1 clematis (for example, Montana Group). Suitable for a pergola or trellis, or for growing through a medium-sized tree or shrub. Zones 3–9.

Clematis 'Anders'
ATRAGENE GROUP

Synonym: *C. macropetala* 'Anders'

Origin: Raised by Magnus Johnson of Södertälje, Sweden.

Parentage and year: Selected form of *C. macropetala*. 1980.

Habit: Hardy, moderately vigorous, deciduous climber.

Height: 2–3 m (6.5–10 ft.).

Description: The nodding, lavender blue, semi-double flowers are composed of four narrow, pointed tepals, each 4–5 cm (1.5–2 in.) long, enclosing a further set of long petal-like staminodes surrounding the central fertile stamens. The edges of the tepals boast a slight silvery sheen. Flowers are borne primarily on old wood, although a few are borne on new growth.

Pruning group: 1.

Flowering period: Midspring to late spring, with some blooms in late summer.

Cultivation: Tolerates most well-drained garden soils and any aspect.

Recommended use: Suitable for container-culture. May be grown through medium-sized trees or shrubs which require no annual pruning. Allow to tumble over a low wall or fence. Zones 3–9.

Clematis 'Anders'. Photo by J. Lindmark.

Clematis 'Andrew'

Origin: Raised by Magnus Johnson of Södertälje, Sweden.

Parentage and year: Chance seedling of *C.* 'Prins Hendrik'. ca. 1952.

Habit: Hardy, moderately vigorous, compact, deciduous climber.

Height: To 2 m (6.5 ft.).

Description: The single, bluish violet flowers, 15–20 cm (6–8 in.) across, are composed of eight overlapping tepals, each with shades of purple at the base of the middle bar and wavy margins. The stamens are made of white filaments and purplish violet anthers.

Pruning group: Optional, 2, or 3. A hard pruning (group 3) results in the loss of early flowers. For late flowers, choose group 3.

Flowering period: Early summer to late summer.

Cultivation: Tolerates most garden soils and any aspect.

Recommended use: Ideal for a container or for covering bare lower stems of other not-so-vigorous wall-trained plants. Zones 4–9.

Clematis 'Andromeda'

Origin: Raised by Ken Pyne of Chingford, London, in 1987.

Parentage and year: Selected seedling of *C.* 'Jadwiga Teresa' (synonym *C.* 'Général Sikorski'). Introduced 1994.

Habit: Hardy, moderately vigorous, deciduous climber.

Height: 2.4–3 m (8–10 ft.).

Description: The early, semi-double flowers, 15–20 cm (6–8 in.) across, are produced on the previous season's old wood and carry an outer basal row of eight, and an inner row of usually six white tepals, which are broad towards the base and tapering towards the tips. A bright pink diffused stripe runs along the centre of each tepal. Single flowers are produced on new growth in late summer. The stamens are yellow and quite long.

Pruning group: 2.

Flowering period: Late spring to early summer (semi-double) and late summer (single).

Cultivation: Tolerates most garden soils. Suitable for sun or semi-shade.

Recommended use: Ideal for a pergola, arbour, large obelisk, or trellis. Zones 4–9.

Clematis 'Anita'
TANGUTICA GROUP

Origin: Raised by Rinus Zwijnenburg of Boskoop, Netherlands. Awarded RHS Certificate of Merit.

Parentage and year: Open-pollinated seed of *C. potaninii* var. *fargesii* with possibly *C. tangutica*. 1988.

Habit: Hardy, vigorous, deciduous climber.

Height: 3–4.5 m (10–14.5 ft.).

Description: The flower buds are creamy yellow. The single, pure white, semi-nodding flowers, up to 4 cm

Clematis 'Andrew'. Photo by J. Lindmark.

Clematis 'Andromeda'. Photo by M. Toomey.

(1.5 in.) across, are bowl shaped when fully opened and are made of four to six tepals. There is a prominent central boss of yellow stamens. Leaves are compound, with leaflets arranged on either side of a common leaf axis. Lower leaves are divided into three leaflets.

Pruning group: 3.

Flowering period: Early summer to late summer.

Cultivation: Tolerates most free-draining garden soils. Suitable for sun or semi-shade.

Recommended use: Ideal plant for growing through medium-sized, early flowering trees, large shrubs, or conifers. Zones 3–9.

Clematis 'Anna'

Origin: Raised by Magnus Johnson of Södertälje, Sweden, and named after a granddaughter.

Parentage and year: Seedling of *C.* 'Moonlight'. 1974.

Habit: Hardy, strong-growing but compact, deciduous climber.

Height: 2.5–3 m (8–10 ft.).

Description: A free-flowering cultivar. The single, rose-pink flowers borne on long, green, and hairy stalks, measuring 12–15 cm (4.75–6 in.) across, are composed of six or eight tepals, which are broad at the base, tapering towards the tips. Each tepal boasts a pale pink stripe. Whitish cream filaments carry reddish purple anthers. The numerous seedheads are rather large, about 7.5 cm (3 in.) across.

Pruning group: 2.

Flowering period: Late spring to early summer and late summer to early autumn.

Cultivation: Tolerates most garden soils. Best grown in a partially sunny and sheltered position to flower well and to protect and preserve flower colour.

Recommended use: Suitable for an obelisk, pergola, or arch. Zones 4–9.

Clematis 'Annemieke'
TANGUTICA GROUP

Origin: Raised by Jan Fopma of Boskoop, Netherlands. Named in 1991.

Parentage and year: Believed to be *C. serratifolia* × *C. tangutica*. Unknown.

Habit: Hardy, moderately vigorous, deciduous climber.

Height: 3–4 m (10–13 ft.).

Description: The single, small, nodding, sulphur-yellow flowers are composed of four narrow, pointed tepals, each 2.5–3 cm (1–1.25 in.) long, the tips of which gently fold backwards almost flat as the flower matures so that they look like wings. Pale purple-brown stamens contrast well with the tepal colour. Light green leaves, not too crowded, allow the delicate-looking flowers to be displayed prominently on the plant.

Pruning group: 3.

Flowering period: Midsummer to late summer.

Cultivation: Tolerates most well-drained garden soils and any aspect.

Clematis 'Anita'. Photo by C. Chesshire.

Clematis 'Anna'. Photo by J. Lindmark.

Recommended use: Suitable for a pergola or arch, or as a specimen plant supported by an obelisk or free-standing trellis. Grow naturally through medium-sized, open shrubs and trees. Zones 4–9.

Clematis 'Aoife'

EVERGREEN GROUP

Origin: Raised by Mary Toomey of Blackrock, Dublin, Ireland, and named after her daughter, Aoife (pronounced *ee-fa*). Introduced by Thorncroft Clematis Nursery.

Parentage and year: An open-pollinated seedling of possibly *C. marmoraria*. 1994.

Habit: Half-hardy, non-climbing, compact, evergreen shrub.

Height: 30–40 cm (12–16 in.) if grown vertically.

Description: The small, white, upward-facing, single flowers are 3.2–3.8 cm (1.25–1.5 in.) across and are composed of six to eight non-overlapping, spear-shaped tepals with satiny texture and veining. The centre of the flower comprises lime-green filaments and light brown anthers surrounding lime-green stigmas and styles. Very attractive finely cut, congested foliage is similar in form to parsley. When young, the foliage is light green, fading to dark green on maturity.

Pruning group: 1.

Flowering period: Early spring to midspring.

Cultivation: Prefers free-draining loam with added grit. Requires a warm aspect.

Recommended use: Best for container-culture in a cold greenhouse, alpine house, or conservatory. In warmer climates could be placed outside in an alpine bed. Zones 8–9.

Clematis 'Aotearoa'

Origin: Raised by Alister Keay of New Zealand Clematis Nurseries, Christchurch. The name in Maori means "New Zealand," which translates as "land of the long white cloud."

Parentage: Unknown. 1992.

Habit: Hardy, vigorous, deciduous climber.

Height: 3–4 m (10–13 ft.).

Description: The single, violet-purple flowers, 12.5 cm (5 in.) across, are composed of six broad, overlapping tepals with wavy margins and slightly recurved tips. The stamens comprise creamy green filaments and anthers.

Clematis 'Aoife'. Photo courtesy Thorncroft Clematis Nursery.

Clematis 'Annemieke'. Photo by C. Chesshire.

Clematis 'Aotearoa'. Photo by R. Savill.

Pruning group: 3.

Flowering period: Midsummer to late summer.

Cultivation: Tolerates most garden soils enriched with humus. Suitable for any aspect.

Recommended use: Grow with climbing roses or through a medium-sized tree or shrub. Suitable for a pergola, obelisk, or trellis. Zones 4–9.

Clematis apiifolia

Origin: China, Korea, and Japan. Introduced into cultivation in England ca. 1898.

Parentage and year: Species. 1818.

Habit: Hardy, vigorous, deciduous climber.

Height: 3.6–4.5 m (12–14.5 ft.).

Description: The single, greenish white, flat, and star-shaped flowers are borne in large clusters on terminal shoots and in leaf axils. Each flower, measuring approximately 1.5–2 cm (0.5–0.75 in.) across, is composed of four non-overlapping and spreading tepals, densely hairy on the outside, and less so inside. The prominent stamens are cream coloured. Stems are slender and somewhat hairy. Leaves are bright green, each with three rather thin, more or less triangular-shaped leaflets.

Pruning group: 3.

Flowering period: Late summer to early autumn.

Cultivation: Tolerates most well-drained garden soils but requires a sunny position to flower well.

Recommended use: Plant against a south-facing wall and fence. Allow it to grow into medium-sized, open trees or large shrubs. Zones 4–9.

Clematis 'Apple Blossom'
EVERGREEN/ARMANDII GROUP

Synonym: *C. armandii* 'Apple Blossom'

Origin: Unknown. Awarded RHS First Class Certificate and Award of Merit.

Parentage and year: Selected form of *C. armandii*. Unknown.

Habit: Half-hardy to hardy, vigorous, evergreen climber.

Height: 6 m (20 ft.) or more.

Description: The single, scented, white tinged with pink, saucer-shaped flowers, 5–6.5 cm (2–2.5 in.) across, and borne in clusters are composed of four to six non-overlapping, broad tepals. Stamens are whitish cream. Unopened buds appear more pinky, and new leaves are bronze in colour, turning to bright, dark green. Leaves are long, boat shaped with deep ribbing running their length.

Pruning group: 1.

Flowering period: Early spring to midspring.

Cultivation: Tolerates most garden soils with good drainage. Best grown against a south- or southwest-facing wall.

Recommended use: Best trained on a house or gar-

Clematis apiifolia. Photo by C. Chesshire.

Clematis 'Apple Blossom'. Photo by C. Chesshire.

den wall. Old leaves turn brown and drop in summer, so choose the planting position carefully. Too vigorous for containers. Zones 7–9.

Clematis 'Arabella'
HERBACEOUS/INTEGRIFOLIA GROUP

Origin: Raised by Barry Fretwell of Peveril Clematis Nursery, England.

Parentage and year: *C. integrifolia* × (unknown). Introduced in 1990.

Habit: Hardy, semi-herbaceous, non-clinging, compact, shrubby perennial.

Height: 1.5–1.8 m (5–6 ft.).

Description: The single, rounded, deep blue-mauve flowers are 7.5–9 cm (3–3.5 in.) wide and are composed of four to eight pear-shaped non-overlapping tepals. As the flower matures, the overall colour lightens and textured, pinky mauve central bands and veining become apparent. Finally all colours fade to a light blue as the flower reaches old age. The stamens are made of white filaments and yellow anthers.

Clematis 'Arabella'. Photo by J. Lindmark.

Pruning group: 3.

Flowering period: Continuously from late spring to early autumn.

Cultivation: Tolerates most garden soils and any aspect. If trained on an artificial support, the stems need tying-in.

Recommended use: Ideal if left to grow naturally through small to medium-sized shrubs and over prostrate conifers. Can be trained against a trellis or obelisk. Zones 4–9.

Clematis aristata

Common name: Goat's-beard

Origin: Australia (Queensland, New South Wales, Victoria, Tasmania).

Parentage and year: Species. 1817.

Habit: Half-hardy, moderately vigorous to very vigorous, evergreen climber.

Height: 3.6–4.5 m (12–14.5 ft.). May reach up to 12 m (40 ft.).

Description: This extremely variable species is not very common in cultivation. The flowers, 4–6 cm (1.5–2.25 in.) wide, can vary in colour from white through to cream, and male flowers are larger than their female counterparts. The four to seven narrow tepals recurve acutely and open to a bell shape, and the flowers are borne in clusters of five or more in the leaf axils of the upper leaves. Leaves are also variable in colour, being shiny or dull, green or purplish, occasionally with a silvery midrib depending on the form in cultivation.

Pruning group: 1.

Flowering period: Early spring to late spring.

Cultivation: Requires free-draining soil on the dry side and a sunny aspect.

Recommended use: Conservatory or cold greenhouse although may withstand very mild frost if planted against warm, sheltered, sunny parts of the garden in the mildest regions of the United Kingdom and United States. Zones 8–9.

Clematis armandii
EVERGREEN/ARMANDII GROUP

Origin: Central and southern China. Introduced by Ernest Wilson. Named in honour of French missionary Père Armand David (1826–1900).

Parentage and year: Species. 1900.

Habit: Half-hardy to hardy, vigorous, evergreen climber or scrambler.

Height: 6 m (20 ft.) or more.

Description: A universally popular evergreen clematis. Flowers are single, fragrant, and pure white. Tepals number four to six, are 5 cm (2 in.) across, and are borne in clusters of threes in the leaf axils. Stamens are cream coloured. Young leaves are pinkish bronze, becoming dark glossy green and leathery in texture with maturity. The leaves are composed of three leaflets and are up to 15 cm (6 in.) long and 5 cm (2 in.) wide.

Pruning group: 1. Any pruning to keep the plant in check should be carried out immediately after the main flowering period.

Flowering period: Early spring to midspring.

Cultivation: Best against a south- or west-facing sheltered wall. Suitable for growing into medium-sized to tall trees. Requires protection from strong, cold winds.

Recommended use: Ideal for the medium-sized to large garden. Old leaves turn brown and drop in summer, so choose the planting position carefully. Too vigorous for containers. Zones 7–9.

Clematis armandii var. *biondiana*
EVERGREEN/ARMANDII GROUP

Origin: Unknown.

Parentage and year: A variant of *C. armandii*. Unknown.

Habit: Half-hardy to hardy, moderately vigorous, evergreen climber.

Height: To 4.5 m (14.5 ft.).

Description: The single, fragrant, saucer-shaped, pure white flowers are 5 cm (2 in.) across and are borne in clusters. They are composed of four to six non-overlapping tepals and cream stamens. The leaves are narrower than those of *C. armandii*.

Pruning group: 1.

Flowering period: Early spring to midspring.

Cultivation: Requires well-drained soil. Best against a south- or southwest-facing wall.

Recommended use: Suitable for a house or garden wall, fence, or other artificial support. Old leaves turn brown and drop in summer, so choose the planting position carefully. Zones 7–9.

Clematis 'Aromatica'
HERBACEOUS GROUP

Synonym: *C.* ×*aromatica*

Origin: Raised in France prior to 1855.

Parentage and year: *C. flammula* × *C. integrifolia*. Unknown.

Habit: Hardy, semi-herbaceous, not-so-vigorous, non-clinging, somewhat upright perennial.

Height: 1.2–1.8 m (4–6 ft.).

Clematis armandii. Photo by R. Surman.

Clematis armandii var. *biondiana*. Photo by C. Chesshire.

Description: The single, small, freely borne, deep mauvish blue flowers measure 5 cm (2 in.) across and are composed of four to six narrow, ribbed, tepals which open flat. As the flower matures the margins of each tepal recurve and overlap each other, forming small tunnels on the reverse. The prominent and contrasting boss of stamens is made of cream filaments and anthers. Good forms are sweetly scented.

Pruning group: 3.

Flowering period: Late spring to early autumn.

Cultivation: Tolerates most garden soils and any aspect. Prefers gritty soil with sharp drainage. Roots resent overwatering.

Recommended use: May be grown as an individual specimen among other herbaceous perennials in a border fully supported by suitable artificial structures or nearby plants. Ideal for growing naturally through medium-sized shrubs. Zones 4–9.

Clematis 'Asagasumi'

Synonym: *C.* 'Opaline'

Origin: Raised by Yoshio Kubota of Japan. The name means "morning haze."

Parentage and year: Unknown. ca. 1957.

Habit: Hardy, moderately vigorous, deciduous climber.

Height: 2.4–3 m (8–10 ft.).

Description: The single, pearly white flowers are 10–15 cm (4–6 in.) across and are composed of six to eight oval to rounded tepals, each carrying a pale lilac central bar. The stamens are made of creamy white filaments and yellow anthers.

Pruning group: 2.

Flowering period: Late spring to early and late summer.

Cultivation: Tolerates most garden soils. Suitable for any aspect but best planted away from full sun to preserve flower colour.

Recommended use: Suitable for a medium-sized obelisk, trellis, arbour, or pergola. Grow with other wall-trained, moderately vigorous shrubs or climbers which do not require severe pruning. Zones 4–9.

Clematis 'Asao'

Origin: Raised in Japan by Kazushige Ozawa and introduced to England in the early 1980s by Raymond Evison of Guernsey Clematis Nursery.

Clematis 'Asagasumi'. Photo by C. Chesshire.

Clematis 'Aromatica'. Photo by R. Savill.

Clematis 'Asao'. Photo by M. Humphries.

Parentage and year: Unknown.

Habit: Hardy, weak-growing, compact, deciduous climber.

Height: 1.8–2.4 m (6–8 ft.).

Description: The single, large, deep pink flowers measure 15 cm (6 in.) in diameter and are composed of six to eight tepals which are much longer than broad, tapering at both ends, and slightly reflexing at the tips. The vivid colour around the edges of the tepals progressively fades to almost white towards the centre of each tepal with prominent pink veining. Anthers are yellow. The flowers open out flat with age. The leaves take on a bronze hue as they mature, although they are somewhat prone to premature yellowing.

Pruning group: 2.

Flowering period: Late spring to early summer and late summer.

Clematis 'Ascotiensis'. Photo by J. Lindmark.

Clematis 'Aureolin'. Photo by C. Chesshire.

Cultivation: Tolerates most garden soils and any aspect.

Recommended use: Suitable for container-culture or for a low garden wall, fence, or small obelisk. Zones 4–9.

Clematis 'Ascotiensis'

Origin: Raised by John Standish of Berkshire, England. Awarded RHS Award of Garden Merit.

Parentage and year: Unknown. 1874.

Habit: Hardy, vigorous, deciduous climber.

Height: 3–4 m (10–13 ft.).

Description: The single, attractive, well-formed, lavender-blue flowers are 12–13.5 cm (4.75–5.5 in.) wide and are composed of four to six wavy tepals. Filaments are greenish white with yellow-brown anthers. The leaves are broader towards the stalk and have pointed tips.

Pruning group: 3.

Flowering period: Midsummer to late summer.

Cultivation: Tolerates most garden soils and any aspect.

Recommended use: Grow naturally through medium-sized trees and shrubs. Suitable for a pergola, large obelisk, or trellis. Zones 4–9.

Clematis 'Aureolin'
TANGUTICA GROUP

Synonym: *C. tangutica* 'Aureolin'

Origin: Raised at the Boskoop Research Station, Netherlands. Awarded RHS Award of Garden Merit.

Parentage and year: Believed to be *C. tangutica* × *C. tangutica* hybrid. ca. 1979.

Habit: Hardy, moderately vigorous, deciduous climber.

Height: 3–4 m (10–13 ft.).

Description: A floriferous cultivar. The single, nodding, lanternlike, lemon-yellow flowers are composed of four broad, pointed tepals, each 4–5 cm (1.5–2 in.) long. Attractive seedheads mature whilst the plant is still flowering, and they stay on long into winter.

Pruning group: 3.

Flowering period: Midsummer to early autumn.

Cultivation: Tolerates most well-drained garden soils and any aspect.

Recommended use: Suitable for an obelisk or large trellis. Grow naturally through large, open shrubs. Zones 4–9.

Clematis australis
EVERGREEN GROUP

Origin: *New Zealand.*

Parentage and year: Species. 1899.

Habit: Half-hardy to hardy, evergreen climber or scrambler.

Height: 2 m (6.5 ft.).

Description: The single, scented, pale yellow to off-white flowers are 2 cm (0.75 in.) across and are made of five narrow, spear-shaped tepals. The flowers may be solitary or borne in clusters from the axils. Leaves are composed of three small leaflets and are normally dark green.

Pruning group: 1.

Flowering period: Early spring to midspring.

Cultivation: Needs sharp drainage and a warm, sheltered, south-facing wall.

Recommended use: Good for container-culture in the conservatory, where its scent can be enjoyed. Not suitable for very cold gardens. Zones 8–9.

Clematis 'Ballet Skirt'
ATRAGENE GROUP

Synonym: *C. macropetala* 'Ballet Skirt'

Origin: Raised by Stanley J. Zubrowski of Prairie River, Saskatchewan, Canada.

Parentage and year: Open-pollinated seedling of *C.* 'Rosy O'Grady'. 1981.

Habit: Hardy, not-too-vigorous, compact, deciduous climber.

Height: 1.6–2 m (5–6.5 ft.).

Description: The nodding, bell-shaped, compact, semi-double flowers are composed of four pale pink, pointed tepals with a full inner skirt of petal-like staminodes of a similar colour. These surround yet another set of shorter staminodes which enclose the creamy yellow stamens.

Pruning group: 1.

Flowering period: Midspring to late spring, with occasional summer flowers.

Cultivation: Tolerates most well-drained garden soils and any aspect.

Clematis australis. Photo by J. Hudson.

Recommended use: Ideal for container-culture or for growing on a small obelisk or free-standing trellis. Zones 3–9.

Clematis 'Barbara Dibley'

Origin: Raised by Rowland Jackman of George Jackman and Son, England, and named after his secretary.

Parentage and year: Unknown. 1947.

Habit: Hardy, moderately vigorous, compact, deciduous climber.

Height: 1.8–2.4 m (6–8 ft.).

Description: The single, very large, petunia-red flowers measure 15–20 cm (6–8 in.) in diameter and are composed of eight closely arranged, long, narrow, tapering tepals, each with a carmine central bar. The edges of the tepals are gently scalloped. Anthers are reddish purple.

Pruning group: 2.

Flowering period: Late spring.

Cultivation: Tolerates most garden soils. Best grown in partial shade to prevent premature fading of flower colour.

Recommended use: Suitable for container-culture and for growing on a small obelisk or trellis. May be grown as a companion for wall-trained shrubs which do not require severe pruning. Zones 4–9.

Clematis 'Barbara Dibley'. Photo by R. Surman.

Clematis 'Ballet Skirt'. Photo by J. Lindmark.

Clematis 'Barbara Jackman'

Origin: Raised by Rowland Jackman of George Jackman and Son, England, and named after his wife in 1947.

Parentage and year: Rowland Jackman's propagator, A. Voneshon, thought it might have been a seedling of *C. patens*. Introduced in 1952.

Habit: Hardy, moderately vigorous, compact, deciduous climber.

Height: 1.8–2.4 m (6–8 ft.).

Description: The single, bluish mauve flowers are 10–15 cm (4–6 in.) wide and are composed of eight broadly overlapping tepals, tapering towards the tips, each with a crimson central bar. Striking creamy stamens set off the flowers. They fade to light mauvish blue with age, but retain the colour of the central bar.

Pruning group: 2.

Flowering period: Late spring to early summer and late summer.

Cultivation: Tolerates most garden soils and any aspect. Best grown in partial shade to prevent premature fading of flower colour.

Recommended use: Suitable for an obelisk or trellis. Ideal for a patio container. Zones 4–9.

Clematis barbellata

ATRAGENE GROUP

Origin: Northwestern India, Kashmir, western Nepal, and northern Pakistan.

Parentage and year: Species. 1851.

Habit: Hardy, vigorous, deciduous climber.

Height: To 4 m (13 ft.).

Description: This species is easily identified by its flower colour. The single, reddish brown, pendulous, bell-shaped flowers, borne solitarily or in small clusters of two or three in the leaf axils of rather short shoots, are composed of four tepals, each 3.5 cm (1.25 in.) long, tapering at both ends, with sharply pointed and somewhat spreading tips, which recurve slightly. The filaments and anthers are densely hairy. Leaves composed of three leaflets are dark green, paler underneath.

Pruning group: 1.

Flowering period: Late spring to midsummer.

Cultivation: Tolerates most garden soils with good drainage. Suitable for any aspect.

Recommended use: Suitable for a large obelisk or trellis. May be trained through shrubs and small trees which do not require pruning. Zones 4–9.

Clematis 'Beauty of Richmond'

Origin: Unknown.

Parentage and year: Unknown.

Habit: Hardy, vigorous, deciduous climber.

Height: 2.5–3.6 m (8–12 ft.).

Description: The single, large, 15- to 20-cm (6- to 8-in.) wide, pale lavender-blue flowers are composed of usually six tepals with a central boss of light chocolate stamens.

Pruning group: Optional, 2, or 3. A hard pruning (group 3) results in the loss of early flowers.

Flowering period: Early summer to midsummer.

Cultivation: Tolerates most garden soils and any aspect.

Recommended use: Suitable for a large obelisk, trel-

Clematis 'Barbara Jackman'. Photo by C. Chesshire.

Clematis barbellata. Photo by C. Sanders.

lis, or arbour. If hard pruned (group 3), grow naturally up and over medium-sized trees and large open shrubs such as rhododendrons to give late-season interest. Zones 4–9.

Clematis 'Beauty of Worcester'

Origin: Raised by Richard Smith and Company, Worcester, England.

Parentage and year: *C.* 'Purpurea Elegans' × *C.* 'Countess of Lovelace'. Introduced in 1886.

Habit: Hardy, moderately vigorous, compact, deciduous climber.

Height: 1.8–2.4 m (6–8 ft.).

Description: The reddish purple, double and semi-double flowers are 12.5–15 cm (5–6 in.) across and are borne on the previous season's old wood during late

Clematis 'Beauty of Richmond'. Photo by C. Chesshire.

Clematis 'Beauty of Worcester'. Photo by C. Chesshire.

spring to early summer. They are composed of a basal row of six tepals with rounded edges and pointed tips. There are six or seven further concentric layers of tepals of a similar shape, each layer slightly smaller in diameter than the previous one, but these tepals are midblue with a hint of pink. The reverse of each tepal carries a white bar along the centre. Single flowers produced on new growths later in the current season carry six tepals. Stamens are creamy yellow with a tinge of green. Some clones are not very floriferous.

Pruning group: 2.

Flowering period: Late spring to early summer (double) and late summer to early autumn (single).

Cultivation: Tolerates most garden soils. Best grown in full or partial sun. Requires protection from strong winds.

Recommended use: Grow on a small to medium-sized obelisk or trellis. Ideal for container-culture. Zones 4–9.

Clematis 'Bees Jubilee'

Origin: Raised by Bees of Chester, England, to celebrate its 25th anniversary. Awarded RHS Award of Garden Merit.

Parentage and year: Unknown. 1958.

Habit: Hardy, weak-growing, compact, deciduous climber.

Height: 1.8–2.4 m (6–8 ft.).

Description: The single, vivid, mauvish pink flowers measure 15–20 cm (6–8 in.) across and are composed of six to eight overlapping, rounded tepals, each with a

Clematis 'Bees Jubilee' flower colour is strong when young. Photo by C. Chesshire.

carmine bar along the centre. The colour fades with maturity. A pretty central tuft has reddish cream anthers. Seedheads are striking. Leaves are divided into three leaflets.

Pruning group: 2.

Flowering period: Late spring and midsummer.

Cultivation: Tolerates most garden soils. Suitable for sun or partial shade. Slow to become established. Feed and water well.

Recommended use: Suitable for a low trellis or medium-sized obelisk. Grow naturally through open, not-too-vigorous shrubs, which require no annual pruning, such as other clematis in group 2. Zones 4–9.

Clematis 'Bella'

Origin: Raised by Uno Kivistik of Harjumaa, Estonia.

Parentage and year: Seedling of the Russian cultivar *C.* 'Serebriannyj Ruczejok' (Silver Sparkling Brook). 1982.

Habit: Hardy, moderately vigorous, compact, deciduous climber.

Height: 1.8–2.4 m (6–8 ft.).

Description: The large white, single flowers are 10–15 cm (4–6 in.) across and are composed of six, sometimes seven, broad yet pointed tepals, which overlap in the middle and taper towards the base and tip with gently scalloped and slightly incurving margins. Young flowers possess a creamy stripe which fades upon maturity. The stamens are made of white filaments and dark red anthers.

Pruning group: 3.

Flowering period: Early summer to midsummer.

Cultivation: Tolerates most garden soils. Suitable for sun or partial shade.

Recommended use: Grow through contrasting dark foliage shrubs or on a small obelisk or trellis. Ideal for container-culture. Zones 3–9.

Clematis 'Belle Nantaise'

Origin: Raised by Auguste Boisselot of Nantes, France.

Parentage and year: Unknown. 1887.

Habit: Hardy, moderately vigorous, deciduous climber.

Height: 2.5–3 m (8–10 ft.).

Description: The single, very large, 20- to 25-cm (8- to 10-in.) wide lavender-blue flowers are usually com-

Clematis 'Bella'. Photo by J. Lindmark.

Clematis 'Bees Jubilee' flower colour tends to fade with age and in strong sunlight. Photo by J. Lindmark.

Clematis 'Belle Nantaise'. Photo by Y. Aihara.

posed of six sharply pointed tepals with crinkly edges. Each tepal carries a slightly lighter blue central bar. White filaments with pale creamy yellow anthers form a fine boss of contrasting stamens.

Pruning group: 2.

Flowering period: Late spring to early summer.

Cultivation: Tolerates most garden soils and any aspect. Requires a sheltered position to prevent wind damage to the large flowers.

Recommended use: Grow naturally through large shrubs which do not require regular pruning. Zones 4–9.

Clematis 'Belle of Woking'

Origin: Raised by George Jackman and Son, England.

Parentage and year: *C.* 'Lanuginosa Candida' × *C.* 'Fortunei'. 1875.

Habit: Hardy, not very strong growing, deciduous climber.

Height: 1.8–2.4 m (6–8 ft.).

Clematis 'Belle of Woking'. Photo by C. Chesshire.

Description: The fully double flowers, which are 10 cm (4 in.) in diameter, are produced on the previous season's old wood and carry many layers of broad yet pointed, silvery mauve tepals, fading to silvery grey, soon after opening. The stamens are made of white filaments and cream anthers.

Pruning group: 2.

Flowering period: Early summer to late summer, always with double flowers.

Cultivation: Tolerates most garden soils. Best grown in full sun or partial shade. Requires protection from strong winds.

Recommended use: Ideal for container-culture. Suitable for a small to medium-sized obelisk or trellis. Grow with other wall-trained shrubs which do not require severe pruning. Zones 4–9.

Clematis 'Benedictus'

Origin: Raised by Magnus Johnson of Södertälje, Sweden, and named in honour of his son-in-law.

Parentage and year: Open-pollinated seedling of *C.* 'Nelly Moser'.

Habit: Hardy, not very vigorous, compact, deciduous climber.

Height: 2 m (6.5 ft.).

Description: The single, large flowers are borne freely from the previous season's old wood as well as the current season's new growth. Each well-formed flower, 16–20 cm (6.25–8 in.) across, is composed of six or seven tepals, slightly overlapping, broad towards the base, and tapering to points at the tips. Each tepal boasts undulating margins and central ridges running from base to tip. On opening, the flowers are light lilac, changing to almost pure white with age. Flat, white filaments with greenish and purple tinge carry reddish purple-violet anthers. Leaves are made of three leaflets, which are dark green above and lustrous light green underneath.

Pruning group: 2.

Flowering period: Early summer from old wood and midsummer to late summer from new shoots.

Cultivation: Tolerates garden soils enriched with humus. Suitable for any aspect. Best grown in a sheltered position to prevent fading of flower colour.

Recommended use: Ideal for large containers. Suitable for a small to medium-sized obelisk or trellis. Zones 4–9.

Clematis 'Beth Currie'

Trade name: VIVIENNE

Origin: Raised by Frank Meecham of Lincolnshire, England, and introduced by Raymond Evison of Guernsey Clematis Nursery. It was originally named 'Beth Currie' after the wife of the president of Loblaws, a supermarket chain, and launched in Canada.

Parentage and year. Unknown. 1980s.

Habit: Hardy, not very vigorous, compact, deciduous climber.

Height: 1.8–2.4 m (6–8 ft.).

Description: The single, plum-purple, well-formed flowers are 10–12.5 cm (4–5 in.) across and are composed of seven or eight overlapping tepals with slightly inturned margins. Each tepal boasts a crimson central bar, which fades and blends with the tepal colour nearer the tip. The flowers open wide as they mature, and the tips of the tepals recurve slightly. The off-white to creamy tuft of filaments and anthers contrasts well with the tepal colour.

Pruning group: 2.

Flowering period: Midspring to late spring and midsummer to late summer.

Cultivation: Tolerates most garden soils enriched with humus. Suitable for any aspect.

Recommended use: Ideal for container-culture. Grow on a medium-sized obelisk or trellis. Use to cover the bare lower stems of established climbers which do not need severe annual pruning. Zones 4–9.

Clematis 'Betty Corning'
VITICELLA GROUP

Synonym: *C. viticella* 'Betty Corning'

Origin: Found growing in a garden at Albany, New York, by Betty Corning, wife of Erastus Corning II (onetime mayor of Albany), and introduced into

Clematis 'Benedictus'. Photo by Jan Lindmark.

Clematis 'Beth Currie' (VIVIENNE™). Photo by C. Chesshire.

commerce by Arthur H. Steffen of Fairport, New York.

Parentage and year: Believed to be a hybrid of *C. crispa* × *C. viticella*. 1932.

Habit: Hardy, deciduous climber. Vigorous and floriferous once established.

Height: 2.5–3 m (8–10 ft.).

Description: The single, nodding, bell-shaped, slightly scented flowers measure 5–6 cm (2–2.25 in.) long and consist of four tepals, which recurve at the margins and tips. The inside of the tepals is a pale pinky mauve colour while the reverse is a pale pinky blue. The tepals are deeply veined thus adding to the texture. The stamens are yellow. Leaves are midgreen, carrying three leaflets with three lobes. A delightful cultivar.

Pruning group: 3.

Flowering period: Early summer to early autumn.

Cultivation: Tolerates most garden soils and any aspect. Produces the strongest scent in a sunny position.

Recommended use: Ideal for growing through medium-sized trees, large shrubs, or conifers. Grow with early or late-flowering climbing roses. Suitable for an obelisk, free-standing trellis, or pergola. Zones 3–9.

Clematis 'Betty Risdon'

Origin: Raised by Vince and Sylvia Denny of Denny's Clematis Nursery, Broughton, England. Named after the former treasurer of the British Clematis Society.

Parentage and year: *C.* 'Yellow Queen' (synonym

C. 'Moonlight') × *C.* 'Wada's Primrose' × *C.* 'Kathleen Wheeler'. Early 1996.

Habit: Hardy, moderately vigorous, deciduous climber.

Height: 2.5–3 m (8–10 ft.).

Description: The single, well-formed, rich plum-pink flowers measure 15–20 cm (6–8 in.) wide and are made of seven or eight gently overlapping, rounded, textured tepals with creamy pink margins and prominent ribs along the centre. Bright yellow filaments and anthers form the central tuft of stamens.

Pruning group: 2.

Flowering period: Late spring to early summer and late summer.

Cultivation: Tolerates most garden soils. Best grown in sun or partial shade. Requires a sheltered position to prevent wind damage to the large flowers.

Recommended use: Grow naturally through medium-sized trees, large, open shrubs, or as a companion for other wall-trained shrubs or fruit trees which do not require an annual severe pruning. Zones 4–9.

Clematis 'Bill MacKenzie'
TANGUTICA GROUP

Synonyms: *C. orientalis* 'Bill MacKenzie', *C. tangutica* 'Bill MacKenzie'

Origin: Open-pollinated seedling found by Bill MacKenzie, former curator of the Chelsea Physic Garden, at Waterperry Horticultural College garden, England. Awarded RHS Award of Garden Merit.

Parentage and year: Believed to be a hybrid of *C. tibetana* subsp. *vernayi* × *C. tangutica*. 1968.

Clematis 'Betty Corning'. Photo by J. Lindmark.

Clematis 'Betty Risdon'. Photo by C. Chesshire.

Habit: Hardy, vigorous, deciduous climber.

Height: To 6 m (20 ft.).

Description: An extremely floriferous cultivar. The flowers are single, bell shaped, nodding, yellow, very large, and 6–7 cm (2.25–2.75 in.) across. The four tepals are somewhat thick and fleshy, broad at the base with pointed recurving tips. Filaments are reddish brown. Anthers are brown. Attractive seedheads are silky.

Pruning group: 3.

Flowering period: Early summer to late summer.

Cultivation: Needs sharp drainage. Suitable for sun or partial shade.

Recommended use: Ideal companion for medium-sized to large trees or conifers. Suitable for a strong, large pergola, a spacious wall, or a rustic fence. Zones 4–9.

Clematis 'Blaaval'
EVERGREEN GROUP

Trade name: AVALANCHE

Origin: Raised by Robin White of Blackthorn Nursery, England. Introduced in 1999. Plant Breeders' Rights.

Parentage and year: *C. paniculata* × *C. marmoraria*. 1990.

Habit: Hardy to half-hardy, moderately vigorous, evergreen climber.

Height: 3 m (10 ft.). If left unpruned may reach a height of 4.5 m (14.5 ft.).

Description: The single, flat, waxy, greenish white flowers are 7–8 cm (2.75–3.25 in.) across, are borne in clusters, and are composed of six, sometimes as few as four or as many as seven, smooth, papery, overlapping tepals, broader than long, blunt, and with slightly undulating margins. The central boss of stamens boasts greenish filaments with creamy yellow anthers. The dark green, shiny leaves often with bronze markings and somewhat distinct veins are two to five lobed.

Pruning group: 1. To maintain a compact plant under glass, prune back after the main flowering period, leaving two or three leaf joints.

Flowering period: Midspring.

Cultivation: Requires free-draining compost, especially if planted in a container. Suitable for sun or shade. Not for excessively cold and frosty gardens.

Clematis 'Bill MacKenzie'. Photo by C. Chesshire.

Clematis 'Blaaval' (AVALANCHE™). Photo by C. Chesshire.

Recommended use: Shows up well against a dark background. Ideal for containers. Zones 7–9.

Clematis 'Black Prince'
VITICELLA GROUP

Synonym: *C. viticella* 'Black Prince'

Origin: Raised by Alister Keay of New Zealand Clematis Nurseries, Christchurch, and named by him in 1993.

Parentage and year: Unknown (a chance seedling). 1990.

Habit: Hardy, moderately vigorous, deciduous climber.

Height: 2.4–3 m (8–10 ft.).

Description: The single, very dark claret-reddish black flowers measure 9 cm (3.5 in.) across and are composed of four broad, gappy tepals with recurved tips. The stamens are made of maroon filaments and anthers. Flowers are borne on the current season's new growth.

Pruning group: 3.

Flowering period: Midsummer to late summer.

Cultivation: Tolerates most garden soils and any aspect.

Recommended use: Ideal for a pergola, obelisk, or free-standing trellis. Allow to roam into medium-sized light-coloured shrubs or conifers. Zones 4–9.

Clematis 'Blekitny Aniol'

Trade name: BLUE ANGEL™

Origin: Raised by Brother Stefan Franczak of Warsaw, Poland, and introduced in 1990.

Parentage and year: Unknown. Between 1980 and 1990.

Habit: Hardy, vigorous, deciduous climber.

Height: 3–3.6 m (10–12 ft.).

Description: The single, beautiful, pale rosy blue flowers, 7.5–10 cm (3–4 in.) wide, are composed of four to six tepals, each of which is deeply grooved along the centre. The tepals, which boast a hint of a very slight purple hue, have delicate crinkly edges and recurve gently. Stamens are creamy yellow. Leaves are midgreen.

Pruning group: 3.

Flowering period: Early summer to early autumn.

Cultivation: Tolerates most garden soils and any aspect.

Recommended use: Grow up and over medium-sized trees, large shrubs, or large, prostrate conifers. Also grow with climbing roses or in a large container with suitable supports. Zones 4–9.

Clematis 'Blue Belle'
VITICELLA GROUP

Synonym: *C. viticella* 'Blue Belle'

Origin: Raised by Ernest Markham, head gardener at Gravetye Manor. Temporarily lost to cultivation until re-introduced by Raymond Evison of Guernsey Clematis Nursery in the 1980s from a clone found in Canada.

Parentage and year: Unknown. Mid-1920s.

Clematis 'Black Prince'. Photo by R. Savill.

Clematis 'Blekitny Aniol' (BLUE ANGEL™). Photo by E. Leeds.

Habit: Hardy, vigorous, strong-growing, deciduous climber.

Height: 3–4 m (10–13 ft.).

Description: The single, partially nodding, fully rounded, deep violet-blue flowers measure 9 cm (3.5 in.) across, are composed of six tepals, and are borne very freely. Yellow anthers contrast well with the colour of the tepals. Leaves are midgreen with five leaflets which may or may not be divided into further parts.

Pruning group: 3.

Flowering period: Midsummer to early autumn.

Cultivation: Tolerates most garden soils and any aspect.

Recommended use: Shows up well against a light background, whether over a tree or large shrub, or on its own up a trellis or any other suitable support. Grow with other climbers against a wall. Zones 3–9.

Clematis 'Blue Bird'
ATRAGENE GROUP

Synonym: *C. macropetala* 'Blue Bird'

Origin: Raised by Frank L. Skinner of Dropmore, Manitoba, Canada.

Parentage and year: *C. macropetala* × *C. alpina*. 1962.

Habit: Hardy, moderately vigorous, deciduous climber.

Height: 2.4–3 m (8–10 ft.).

Description: The semi-double, bell-shaped, mauvish blue flowers are composed of four narrow, twisted tepals, each 5–6 cm (2–2.25 in.) long, giving the flower a gappy appearance. The inner skirt of petal-like sta-

minodes is a paler blue on the outside and surrounds a creamy white centre of stamens. The main flush of flowers is on old wood. Leaves are composed of three leaflets, and the serrated leaf margins resemble the teeth of a saw.

Pruning group: 1. Any pruning to keep the plant tidy should be carried out immediately after the main flowering period.

Flowering period: Midspring to late spring, with some late summer blooms.

Cultivation: Tolerates most well-drained garden soils and any aspect.

Recommended use: Suitable for a medium-sized obelisk or trellis, or as a companion for shrubs which require no annual pruning. Grow in large containers. Zones 3–9.

Clematis 'Blue Boy'
HERBACEOUS/INTEGRIFOLIA GROUP

Origin: Raised by Frank L. Skinner of Dropmore, Manitoba, Canada.

Parentage and year: *C. integrifolia* × *C. viticella*. 1947.

Habit: Hardy, deciduous, moderately vigorous, non-clinging, herbaceous perennial.

Height: 1.5–1.8 m (5–6 ft.).

Description: The bell-shaped, nodding, hyacinth-blue to midblue flowers are 5–7.5 cm (2–3 in.) wide and are composed of four tepals, each with a slight silvery sheen, a delicately textured surface, and gently notched edges. The stamens are made of white filaments and yellow anthers. Thick and dense leaves are

Clematis 'Blue Belle'. Photo by C. Chesshire.

Clematis 'Blue Bird'. Photo by J. Lindmark.

produced from numerous shoots emerging from the base.

Pruning group: 3.

Flowering period: Early summer to late summer.

Cultivation: Tolerates most garden soils and any aspect.

Recommended use: Plant in open ground and allow to scramble or train up an obelisk or trellis taking care to tie-in the strong-growing shoots. Not recommended as a companion for other trees, shrubs, or conifers because mature plants throw numerous basal shoots with thick, dense foliage, which may damage the supportive plants and their leaves in particular. Zones 4–9.

Clematis 'Blue Dancer'
ATRAGENE GROUP

Synonym: *C. alpina* 'Blue Dancer'

Origin: Raised by Raymond Evison of Guernsey Clematis Nursery.

Parentage and year: Unknown. Late 1980s.

Habit: Hardy, moderately vigorous, deciduous climber.

Height: 2.4–3 m (8–10 ft).

Description: The single, nodding, pale blue flowers are composed of four narrow, twisting, pointed tepals, each 5–7.5 cm (2–3 in.) long, with silvery veins running along the length. Short, pale creamy green, spoon-shaped, petal-like staminodes enliven the flowers. Leaves are bright green and divided into leaflets.

Pruning group: 1. Any pruning to keep the plant tidy should be carried out immediately after the main flowering period.

Flowering period: Midspring to late spring.

Cultivation: Tolerates most well-drained garden soils and any aspect.

Clematis 'Blue Boy' growing through *Rosa rugosa*. Photo by C. Chesshire.

Recommended use: Grow through wall-trained shrubs or supported by a medium-sized obelisk or a trellis. Suitable for container-culture. Zones 3–9.

Clematis 'Blue Gem'

Origin: Raised by George Jackman and Son, England.

Parentage and year: *C. lanuginosa* × *C.* 'Standishii'. 1875.

Habit: Hardy, moderately vigorous, deciduous climber.

Height: 2.5–3.5 m (8–12 ft.).

Description: The single, light blue flowers measure 12.5–15 cm (5–6 in.) across, are borne from the upper axils, and are composed of six to eight overlapping tepals terminating in sharp, flexible tips. White filaments tipped with purple-red anthers constitute the stamens.

Pruning group: 3.

Flowering period: Midsummer to late summer.

Cultivation: Tolerates most garden soils and any aspect.

Recommended use: Suitable for a pergola, large obelisk, or trellis. Grow with medium-sized shrubs or climbing roses. Zones 4–9.

Clematis 'Blue Ravine'

Origin: Raised by Conrad Eriandson of Abbottsford, British Columbia, Canada.

Parentage and year: Open-pollinated hybrid believed to be *C.* 'Nelly Moser' × *C.* 'Ramona'. ca. 1978.

Habit: Hardy, moderately vigorous, deciduous climber.

Height: 2–3 m (6.5–10 ft.).

Description: The single, soft violet flowers are 15–20 cm (6–8 in.) in diameter and open flat with seven or

Clematis 'Blue Gem'. Photo by C. Chesshire.

Clematis 'Blue Ravine'. Photo by C. Chesshire.

Clematis 'Blue Dancer'. Photo by C. Chesshire.

Clematis 'Bonstedtii'. Photo by C. Chesshire.

Clematis 'Boskoop Beauty'. Photo by J. Lindmark.

eight wavy-edged tepals, each carrying a slightly deep violet central bar with veins radiating from it. Dark purple-red stamens have white styles in the centre.

Pruning group: 2.

Flowering period: Late spring to early summer and late summer.

Cultivation: Tolerates most garden soils with adequate drainage. Prefers a sheltered position in sun or partial shade.

Recommended use: Grow on a fence, trellis, or arbour. Allow to climb up a small tree or scramble over shrubs which do not require pruning. Zones 4–9.

Clematis 'Bonstedtii'
HERBACEOUS/HERACLEIFOLIA GROUP

Synonym: *C.* ×*bonstedtii*

Origin: Unknown.

Parentage and year: Believed to be *C. heracleifolia* × *C. stans*. Unknown.

Habit: Hardy, herbaceous, non-clinging semi-woody shrub.

Height: 1–1.2 m (3.25–4 ft.).

Description: The single, small, tubular, hyacinth-like, pale bluish white flowers measure 2–2.5 cm (0.75–1 in.) long and are composed of four tepals, the tips of which roll back upon themselves with age. The stamens are made of white filaments and yellow anthers.

Pruning group: 3.

Flowering period: Early summer to late summer.

Cultivation: Requires free-draining garden soil. Suitable for any aspect.

Recommended use: Plant in herbaceous borders. Use as ground cover in front of climbing clematis. Suitable for large containers. Zones 4–9.

Clematis 'Boskoop Beauty'

Origin: Raised by J. de Vink of Boskoop, Netherlands.

Parentage and year: Open-pollinated seedling of *C.* 'Nelly Moser'. ca. 1960.

Habit: Hardy, moderately vigorous, compact, deciduous climber.

Height: 2.8–3 m (8–10 ft.).

Description: Not very floriferous. The single, large, pale lilac flowers are 21.5 cm (8.5 in.) across and composed of six or seven tepals which are gappy at the base. The margins are wavy, and an attractive, prominent, lilac-purple stripe runs along the centre, from the base to the tip of each tepal. Creamy filaments with dark red anthers and prominent white styles distinguish the flowers.

Pruning group: Optional, 2, or 3. A hard pruning (group 3) results in the loss of early flowers. For early flowers, choose group 2; for late flowers, group 3.

Flowering period: Early summer to late summer.

Cultivation: Tolerates most garden soils. Best grown in partial shade to preserve flower colour. Requires a sheltered position to prevent wind damage to the large flowers.

Recommended use: Grow as a companion for other wall-trained shrubs where its sparse flowering will not be too evident. Zones 4–9.

Clematis 'Bowl of Beauty'
EVERGREEN/ARMANDII GROUP

Synonym: *C. armandii* 'Bowl of Beauty'

Origin: Raised by Jan Fopma of Boskoop, Netherlands.

Parentage and year: Selected form of *C. armandii*. 1992.

Habit: Half-hardy to hardy, vigorous, evergreen climber.

Height: To 6 m (20 ft.) or more.

Description: The single, pure white flowers, 5 cm (2 in.) across, are bowl shaped when young, becoming flatter as the four to six tepals mature. Stamens are creamy white. Foliage is bright, dark green and glossy.

Pruning group: 1.

Flowering period: Early spring to midspring.

Cultivation: Tolerates most well-drained garden soils. Best against a south- or southwest-facing wall or fence.

Recommended use: Grow against a warm wall or fence. Old leaves turn brown and drop in summer, so choose the planting position carefully. Zones 7–9.

Clematis brachiata

Origin: Central and southern Africa. Awarded RHS Award of Merit (1975).

Parentage and year: Species. 1800.

Habit: Tender, rather vigorous, semi-evergreen climber.

Height: 3–3.6 m (10–12 ft.).

Description: The single, semi-nodding flowers measure 2–4 cm (0.75–1.5 in.) wide and normally consist of four or five white tepals with a greenish tinge. These are borne laterally from leaf axils or in terminal panicles and are sometimes scented. The greenish yellow anthers are prominent. Leaves are midgreen and may be simple or sometimes in threes; leaflets are somewhat papery with finely toothed margins.

Pruning group: 3.

Flowering period: Early to late autumn.

Cultivation: Requires well-drained compost and a

Clematis 'Bowl of Beauty'. Photo by C. Chesshire.

Clematis brachiata. Photo by C. Chesshire.

very warm, sheltered position. Tends to be less vigorous in containers.

Recommended use: Not for cold, exposed gardens. Grow in a conservatory or frost-free greenhouse. Zones 8–9.

Clematis brachyura

Origin: South Korea.

Parentage and year: Species. 1877.

Habit: Hardy, deciduous, semi-herbaceous, non-clinging shrub.

Height: 0.9–1.5 m (3–5 ft.).

Description: The single, starlike, pure white, and faintly scented flowers, which are green in bud, are produced in threes in leaf axils and terminally. Each flower is 2.5–5 cm (1–2 in.) wide and composed of four non-overlapping, narrow tepals. The creamy yellow stamens are prominent. Flowers are not produced in abundance. Stems are erect and ribbed. Leaves are dull, may be simple, trifoliate, or even pinnate with many leaflets.

Pruning group: 3.

Flowering period: Early summer to late summer.

Cultivation: Tolerates most garden soils with good drainage. Produces the strongest scent in a sunny position. If trained on an artificial support, the stems need tying-in.

Recommended use: Place midway or at the back of a herbaceous border among other plants. Zones 7–9.

Clematis 'Bravo'

TANGUTICA GROUP

Origin: Raised by Willem Brandenburg and Dr. van Vooren at Wageningen, Netherlands.

Parentage and year: Probably *C. tangutica*. 1990s.

Habit: Hardy, not-so-vigorous, compact, deciduous climber.

Height: 2.4–3 m (8–10 ft.).

Description: The single, yellow, nodding flowers are made of four broad tepals that open flat when fully mature with reflexed tips. The prominent anthers are reddish brown.

Pruning group: 3.

Flowering period: Midsummer to late summer.

Cultivation: Tolerates most well-drained garden soils and any aspect.

Recommended use: Grow through open, large

shrubs. Suitable for a medium-sized obelisk or trellis. Zones 4–9.

Clematis brevicaudata

Origin: Northern, northeastern, and western China, North Korea, western Mongolia, and parts of Russia.

Parentage and year: Species. 1818.

Habit: Hardy, vigorous, deciduous climber.

Height: 4–5 m (13–16 ft.).

Description: The single, scented, small flowers, measuring 2 cm (0.75 in.) across, are produced in lateral and terminal clusters. Each flower is composed of four or five narrow, non-overlapping tepals, which are

Clematis 'Bravo'. Photo by C. Chesshire.

Clematis brevicaudata. Photo by C. Chesshire.

creamy white, flushed with green or yellow, and covered with fine hairs on the inner and outer surfaces. The tepals open flat and slightly recurve at the tips. The stamens consist of cream filaments and yellow anthers. Young stems are ribbed, covered in fine hairs, and boast a purple colouring. Leaves are usually arranged in threes, but sometimes are pinnate with five to seven leaflets.

Pruning group: 3.

Flowering period: Late summer to midautumn.

Cultivation: Tolerates most garden soils with good drainage. Best scent in a sunny aspect.

Recommended use: Very effective growing up and over large shrubs or trees. Suitable for growing over a spacious wall or fence. Zones 5–9.

Clematis 'Broughton Bride'
ATRAGENE GROUP

Origin: Raised by Vince and Sylvia Denny of Denny's Clematis Nursery, Broughton, England. Named in 1998.

Parentage and year: A second- or third-generation seedling selection of open-pollinated *C. koreana* seed obtained from Dortmund, Germany, in 1987.

Habit: Hardy, moderately vigorous, deciduous climber.

Height: 2.4–3.6 m (8–12 ft.).

Description: Flowers in the first flush are borne on short axillary shoots and are normally single, semi-nodding, and composed of four white tepals, each of which is 7.5–9 cm (3–3.5 in.) long, wide at the base, and tapering smartly to a point at the tip. Noticeable lilac speckles on the outside of the tepals are an added feature. The tight tuft of staminodes is cream in colour. Flowers in the second flush produced later in the season, though not in abundance, are shorter, 5–6.4 cm (2–2.5 in.) long, very full, and resemble a ballet skirt. Stems are very dark purplish brown in colour and slightly hairy. Leaves are roughly oval in shape but widest towards the stalk, light to midgreen. The nine leaflets taper to a point, and the leaf margins have forward-pointing teeth.

Pruning group: 1. Any pruning to keep the plant tidy should be carried out immediately after the main flowering period.

Flowering period: Late spring and early summer to midsummer.

Cultivation: Requires well-drained soil. Suitable for any aspect.

Recommended use: Suitable for a free-standing trellis, obelisk, arbour, or similar artificial supports. May be grown through large shrubs or wall-trained plants which do not require annual pruning. Zones 6–9.

Clematis 'Broughton Star'
MONTANA GROUP

Synonym: *C. montana* 'Broughton Star'

Origin: Raised by Vince and Sylvia Denny of Denny's Clematis Nursery, Broughton, England. Awarded British Clematis Society Certificate of Merit (1998).

Parentage and year: *C.* 'Marjorie' × *C.* 'Picton's Variety'. 1988.

Habit: Moderately vigorous, deciduous climber.

Height: To 6 m (20 ft).

Description: The double and semi-double, deep pink flowers up to 6 cm (2.25 in.) across are composed of four large outer tepals with many smaller inner ones. Veins of tepals are prominent and deeper pink in colour. Leaves are attractive with a bronze tinge when young, turning dark green when mature. Leaf margins are notched with forward-pointing teeth.

Clematis 'Broughton Bride'. Photo by R. Kirkman.

Pruning group: 1. Any pruning to keep the plant in check should be carried out immediately after the main flowering period by removing some of the old, flowered stems.

Flowering period: Late spring to early summer.

Cultivation: Needs sharp drainage. Not universally hardy. Suitable for any aspect in temperate gardens but produces best flower colour in a sunny position.

Recommended use: One of the less vigorous montana varieties which might suit the smaller garden. Grow through medium-sized or large trees and conifers. Zones 7–9.

Clematis 'Brunette'
ATRAGENE GROUP

Synonym: *C.* 'Catullus'

Origin: Raised by Magnus Johnson of Södertälje, Sweden.

Parentage and year: *C. koreana* var. *lutea* × *C. fauriei*. 1979.

Habit: Hardy, deciduous climber.

Height: 2–3 m (6.5–10 ft.).

Description: The small, nodding, bell-shaped, plum-purple flowers are composed of four spear-shaped textured tepals, each 3.5–4.5 cm (1.25–1.75 in.) long, with heavy ridging running from the base to the tip. Bright green leaflets have serrated margins.

Pruning group: 1.

Flowering period: Early spring to midspring.

Cultivation: Tolerates most well-drained garden soils enriched with humus. Suitable for any aspect.

Recommended use: Suitable for a small to medium-sized pergola, obelisk, or trellis. Use for container-culture, gradually potting on into larger containers at least every two years. Zones 3–9.

Clematis 'Broughton Star'. Photo by C. Chesshire.

Clematis 'Brunette'. Photo by J. Lindmark.

Clematis buchananiana

Origin: Himalayan region from Kashmir to northern Myanmar, northern India, southwestern China, Tibet, and North Vietnam.

Parentage and year: Species. 1818.

Habit: Hardy, strong-growing, deciduous climber.

Height: 4–5 m (13–16 ft.).

Description: The single, nodding, bell-shaped, tubular, greenish yellow to creamy yellow, scented flowers are borne in a clusterlike fashion and measure 2–2.5 cm (0.75–1 in.) wide. Each one consists of four tepals, which are ribbed, densely hairy on the outside, separate, and recurve strongly at the tips. Filaments and anthers are hairy, threadlike, and creamy. Young stems are grooved and are covered in yellowish to brownish hairs. Leaves are densely hairy beneath, with five or seven leaflets arranged in pairs on either side of a common leaf axis, or may be trifoliate with three leaflets. Leaf margins are coarsely toothed like a saw.

Pruning group: 3.

Flowering period: Late summer to early autumn.

Cultivation: Tolerates most free-draining garden soils. Requires a sunny aspect because the plant comes into flower somewhat late in the season.

Recommended use: A good garden plant and worth the effort to find a good form with creamy yellow flowers. Grow through medium-sized to large trees or on a large pergola, obelisk, or trellis. Suitable for a conservatory, where this vigorous clematis will give an impressive display of furry flowers. Zones 7–9.

Clematis 'Buckland Beauty'

TEXENSIS-VIORNA GROUP

Origin: Raised by Everett Leeds of Buckland, Surrey, England, from seed donated by Wim Snoeijer of the Netherlands to the British Clematis Society seed exchange. Named in 1999.

Parentage and year: Chance seedling of *C. texensis* (possibly × *C. pitcheri*). 1991.

Habit: Hardy, moderately vigorous, herbaceous, deciduous climber.

Height: 1.6–2.4 m (5–8 ft.).

Description: The single, semi-nodding, pitcher-shaped, pink-mauve flowers, 3–3.5 cm (1.25–1.5 in.) long, are composed of four fleshy, deeply ribbed, fused tepals that open about three-quarters along their length nearer the recurving tips with mauve shading, revealing their pale yellow, thick sides and pale greenish undersides. Cream filaments and yellow anthers make up the stamens. The flowers are solitary and are borne from the leaf axils and terminal shoots. Young leaves are light green, and with age the mature leaves become dark green. The leaflets arranged on either side of a central axis are oval in outline with entire leaf margins. The leaf axis occasionally terminates in a slender, tendril-like structure.

Pruning group: 3.

Flowering period: Late spring to late summer.

Cultivation: Tolerates most well-drained garden soils enriched with humus. Suitable for any aspect.

Recommended use: Ideal for short-term container-

Clematis buchananiana. Photo by S. Kuriyama.

Clematis 'Buckland Beauty'. Photo by E. Leeds.

culture. May be grown through medium-sized shrubs. Suitable for an obelisk or trellis. Zones 4–9.

Clematis 'Burford Bell'
TEXENSIS-VIORNA GROUP

Synonym: *C. pitcheri* 'Burford Bell'

Origin: Raised by John Treasure, Treasures of Tenbury, England. Named in 1991.

Parentage and year: Open-pollinated chance seedling of *C. pitcheri*.

Habit: Hardy, slender, deciduous climber. Vigorous for its type but not aggressively so.

Height: 3–4 m (10–13 ft.).

Description: The single, small, nodding, greenish purple-blue bell-shaped flowers, up to 3 cm (1.25 in.) long, are composed of four thick tepals, which recurve but not completely. The insides of the tepals are purple. The large, compound leaves have entire margins but sometimes with one large, blunt lobe.

Pruning group: 3.

Flowering period: Midsummer to early autumn.

Cultivation: Tolerates most garden soils. Suitable for sun or partial shade.

Recommended use: Grow through large shrubs, medium-sized trees, and conifers. Best sited where it is

possible to look up and into the small flowers. Zones 4–9.

Clematis 'Burford Variety'
TANGUTICA GROUP

Synonym: *C. tangutica* 'Burford Variety'

Origin: Found in John Treasure's garden at Burford House, Worcestershire, England, and introduced by Treasures of Tenbury.

Parentage and year: Believed to be *C. tangutica* × *C. tibetana* subsp. *vernayi*. 1970s.

Habit: Hardy, moderately vigorous, deciduous climber.

Height: 3–4 m (10–13 ft.).

Description: The single, nodding, yellow flowers are composed of four broad, pointed tepals, each 4 cm (1.5 in.) long, which remain almost closed, giving the flower a very rounded effect. Chocolate-brown stamens contrast with the tepal colour. The flowers are followed by long-lasting, fluffy seedheads.

Pruning group: 3.

Flowering period: Midsummer to midautumn.

Cultivation: Tolerates most well-drained garden soils and any aspect.

Recommended use: Suitable for a pergola, large obe-

Clematis 'Burford Bell'. Photo by C. Chesshire.

Clematis 'Burford Variety'. Photo by C. Chesshire.

lisk, or trellis or let it roam into trees and large, open shrubs. Zones 4–9.

Clematis 'Burford White'
ATRAGENE GROUP

Synonym: *C. alpina* 'Burford White'

Origin: Grown in northern Wales and introduced by Raymond Evison, while at Treasures of Tenbury, England.

Parentage and year: Chance seedling of *C. alpina*. 1985.

Habit: Hardy, moderately vigorous, deciduous climber.

Height: 2–3 m (6.5–10 ft.).

Description: The flowers are creamy white, fuller and more bell shaped compared to other members of the Alpina Group. The four tepals are 5 cm (2 in.) long. Staminodes are light green with rounded tips and hairy. Leaves are light green and finely cut.

Pruning group: 1. Any pruning to keep the plant tidy should be carried out immediately after the main flowering period.

Clematis 'Burford White'. Photo by C. Chesshire.

Flowering period: Midspring to late spring, with some flowers in late summer.

Cultivation: Needs sharp drainage. Produces a second flush of flowers when grown in a sunny position.

Recommended use: Ideal for small gardens with cold or north-facing aspects. Small enough for container-culture. Zones 3–9.

Clematis 'Burma Star'

Origin: Raised by Barry Fretwell of Peveril Clematis Nursery, England.

Parentage and year: Unknown. ca. 1990.

Habit: Hardy, moderately vigorous, compact, deciduous climber.

Height: 1.8–2.4 m (6–8 ft.).

Description: The single, rich velvety purple flowers, measuring 11.5–12.5 cm (4.5–5 in.) in diameter, are composed of six to eight tepals boasting reddish hues along the centre. Anthers are deep red.

Pruning group: 2.

Flowering period: Late spring and late summer.

Cultivation: Tolerates most garden soils and any aspect.

Recommended use: Ideal for container-culture or for growing on a small obelisk or trellis. May also be a companion for small to medium-sized shrubs which do not require pruning. Zones 4–9.

Clematis 'Burma Star'. Photo by M. Bracher.

Clematis 'C. W. Dowman'. Photo courtesy Pennells Nurseries.

Clematis campaniflora. Photo by C. Chesshire.

Clematis 'C. W. Dowman'

Origin: Raised by Walter Pennell of Pennell and Sons nursery and named in 1961 after an employee.

Parentage and year: Mixed seed sown in 1953.

Habit: Hardy, moderately vigorous, compact, deciduous climber.

Height: 1.8–2.4 m (6–8 ft.).

Description: The single, small, pale pink flowers are 10–15 cm (4–6 in.) wide and made of six to eight tepals, each with a deep pink central bar consisting of two or three pink streaks, which gradually fade towards the tip. Golden yellow filaments are tipped with reddish brown anthers.

Pruning group: Optional, 2, or 3. A hard pruning (group 3) results in the loss of early flowers.

Flowering period: Late spring to midsummer.

Cultivation: Tolerates most garden soils and any aspect.

Recommended use: Ideal for container-culture or for growing on a small obelisk or trellis. Useful for covering bare lower stems of wall-trained shrubs. Zones 4–9.

Clematis campaniflora
VITICELLA GROUP

Origin: Portugal and southwestern Spain.

Parentage and year: Species. Introduced into England in 1810.

Habit: Hardy, vigorous, deciduous climber.

Height: 3–6 m (10–20 ft.).

Description: The single flowers are borne either solitarily or in small clusters of two or three on long, slender stalks. They are nodding, bell shaped, white tinged with violet, and 2 cm (0.75 in.) long. The four tepals per flower are longer than broad and pointed, and they recurve gently and somewhat twist at their tips. Stamens are greenish cream. Young stems are slightly hairy. Leaves and leaflets are slightly bluish.

Pruning group: 3.

Flowering period: Early summer to late summer.

Cultivation: Tolerates most garden soils and any aspect.

Recommended use: Grow through large shrubs and medium-sized trees. Allow it to ramble along a wall or fence. Suitable for a large trellis or pergola. Zones 3–9.

Clematis 'Campanile'
HERBACEOUS/HERACLEIFOLIA GROUP

Synonym: *C. heracleifolia* 'Campanile'

Origin: Raised by Victor Lemoine of Nancy, France.

Parentage and year: *C. heracleifolia* × *C. stans*. ca. 1900.

Habit: Hardy, deciduous, non-clinging, woody sub-shrub.

Height: 0.9–1.2 m (3–4 ft.).

Description: Pale blue, tubular, single flowers are 2.5–3 cm (1–1.25 in.) long, with a pale whitish bar down the centre of each of the four tepals. The tips of the tepals curl backwards in a loop on mature flowers. Flowers are borne from leaf axils on the top half of stems and have no apparent scent.

Pruning group: 3.

Flowering period: Midsummer to early autumn.

Cultivation: Tolerates well-drained garden soils and any aspect.

Recommended use: Ideal for the herbaceous border. Zones 5–9.

Clematis 'Capitaine Thuilleaux'

Synonym: *C.* 'Souvenir du Capitaine Thuilleaux'

Origin: Raised by J. Thuilleaux of France and named after a son killed in the First World War.

Parentage and year: Unknown. 1918.

Habit: Hardy, moderately vigorous, compact, deciduous climber.

Height: 1.8–2.4 m (6–8 ft.).

Description: The single, large, pointed, pale pink-grey flowers are 15–20 cm (6–8 in.) in diameter and composed of six to eight overlapping tepals, each with a broad strawberry-pink central bar. Stamens are golden brown.

Pruning group: 2.

Flowering period: Late spring to early summer and late summer to early autumn.

Cultivation: Tolerates most garden soils. Best grown in partial shade as flower colour fades in full sun.

Recommended use: Grow up and over moderately vigorous shrubs which do not require annual pruning. May also be allowed to clamber through other wall-trained shrubs or small fruit trees. Ideal for container-culture. Zones 4–9.

Clematis 'Carmen Rose'
ATRAGENE GROUP

Synonym: *C. ochotensis* 'Carmen Rose'

Origin: Kamchatka. Raised by Magnus Johnson of Södertälje, Sweden.

Parentage and year: Seedling selected from first sowing of *C. ochotensis* seed from Eric Hultén. 1950.

Habit: Hardy, moderately vigorous, deciduous climber.

Height: 2.4–3 m (8–10 ft.).

Description: The single, nodding, bell-shaped, pur-

Clematis 'Campanile'. Photo by C. Chesshire.

Clematis 'Capitaine Thuilleaux'. Photo courtesy British Clematis Society Slide Library.

plish pink flowers are composed of four narrow, twisted tepals, each 5–6 cm (2–2.25 in.) long, with attractive crimped edges and a central boss of pale pink staminodes completely hiding the fertile stamens. Leaf margins are coarsely serrated, resembling the teeth of a saw.

Pruning group: 1.

Flowering period: Late spring to early summer.

Cultivation: Tolerates most well-drained garden soils and any aspect. Pinch out the tips of young growth to promote a good, bushy vine structure.

Recommended use: Train through medium-sized trees or open shrubs which do not require annual pruning. Grow as a companion to other wall-trained plants. Zones 3–9.

Clematis 'Carmencita'
VITICELLA GROUP

Synonym: *C. viticella* 'Carmencita'

Origin: Raised by Magnus Johnson of Södertälje, Sweden.

Parentage and year: Seedling of *C.* 'Södertälje'. 1952.

Habit: Hardy, vigorous, deciduous climber.

Height: 3–4 m (10–13 ft.).

Description: A very floriferous cultivar. The single, nodding, carmine-pink flowers are 6 cm (2.25 in.) across and are composed of four to six broad tepals, each of which is deeply veined especially along the centre. The tepals have slightly frilly, recurved margins, and the stamens are formed of green filaments carrying dark purplish mauvish black anthers. The leaves are midgreen with five to seven leaflets arranged on both sides of the leaf axis in pairs. Leaflets may be in threes or three lobed.

Pruning group: 3.

Flowering period: Midsummer to late summer.

Cultivation: Tolerates most garden soils and any aspect but produces most vibrant flower colour in sun or semi-shade.

Recommended use: Ideal as a specimen planting supported by an obelisk or similar free-standing structures. Suitable for growing through medium-sized trees and conifers or over large shrubs. Best over an arbour or pergola where the nodding flowers can be viewed from below. Zones 3–9.

Clematis 'Carmen Rose'. Photo by E. Leeds.

Clematis 'Carmencita'. Photo by J. Lindmark.

Clematis 'Carnaby'

Origin: Raised in the United States by an unknown person.

Parentage and year: Unknown. Introduced in 1983 by Treasures of Tenbury, England.

Habit: Hardy, moderately vigorous, compact, deciduous climber.

Height: 1.8–2.4 m (6–8 ft.).

Description: The single, raspberry pink flowers measure 15–20 cm (6–8 in.) wide and are composed of six to eight slightly reflexing tepals, each carrying an intensely pink central bar. The tepal margins are crimped, and the central tuft of stamens is made of white filaments and dark red anthers.

Pruning group: Optional, 2, or 3. A hard pruning (group 3) results in the loss of early flowers.

Flowering period: Late spring to late summer.

Cultivation: Tolerates most garden soils. Best grown out of strong sun to preserve flower colour.

Recommended use: Ideal for container-culture. Grow through small to medium-sized shrubs or with other moderately vigorous, wall-trained shrubs or fruit trees. Zones 4–9.

Clematis 'Caroline'

Origin: Raised by Barry Fretwell of Peveril Clematis Nursery, England.

Parentage and year: Unknown. ca. 1992.

Habit: Hardy, moderately vigorous, compact, deciduous climber.

Height: 1.8–2.4 m (6–8 ft.).

Description: The single, small, well-formed, firm, pinkish white flowers measure 10–12.5 cm (4–5 in.) wide and are normally composed of six pointed, non-overlapping tepals, each with a deeper pink bar towards the base. White filaments and pale yellow anthers form the central mass of stamens.

Pruning group: 3.

Clematis 'Caroline'. Photo by C. Chesshire.

Clematis 'Carnaby'. Photo by R. Savill.

Flowering period: Early summer to early autumn.

Cultivation: Tolerates most garden soils. Produces best and long-lasting flower colour when planted out of full sun.

Recommended use: Grow over dark, prostrate conifers and groundcover plants such as heathers, or up and over grey- or silver-leaved small shrubs. Looks well on a small arch or an obelisk as a specimen planting. Suitable for containers. Zones 4–9.

Clematis 'Chalcedony'

Origin: Raised by Ellis Strachen of Plymouth, England.

Parentage and year: *C.* 'Vyvyan Pennell' × *C.* 'Marie Boisselot'. 1976.

Habit: Hardy, strong-growing, deciduous climber.

Height: 2.4–3 m (8–10 ft.).

Description: The double, ice-blue flowers are 12.5–15 cm (5–6 in.) wide and have many layers of broad, pointed tepals, approximately 50 to 60 in number, of which a large majority have gently scalloped edges. Stamens are inconspicuous and are made of cream filaments and anthers. The late summer flowers of the second flush are also double, but they are smaller with less tepals. Leaves may be simple or with three leaflets and somewhat leathery in texture.

Pruning group: 2.

Flowering period: Late spring to early summer (double), and late summer (double).

Cultivation: Tolerates most garden soils. Best grown out of full sun. Requires protection from strong winds.

Recommended use: Grow on a medium-sized obelisk or trellis. May also be grown as a companion for other not-too-vigorous, wall-trained shrubs which do not require pruning. Zones 4–9.

Clematis 'Charissima'

Origin: Raised by Walter Pennell of Pennell and Sons nursery and named in 1974 by Sheila Gilbert, an employee at the nursery.

Parentage and year: *C.* 'Nelly Moser' × *C.* 'Kathleen Wheeler'. 1961.

Habit: Hardy, moderately vigorous, deciduous climber.

Height: 2.5–3 m (8–10 ft.).

Clematis 'Chalcedony'. Photo by C. Chesshire.

Clematis 'Charissima'. Photo by R. Surman.

Description: The single, cerise-pink flowers are 15–20 cm (6–8 in.) in diameter and are composed of six to eight broad, overlapping tepals with gently undulating margins, tapering towards the apex. Each tepal is distinguished by a deeper coloured central bar and delicate veining. Whitish pink filaments carry dark maroon anthers. Leaves have prominent veining.

Pruning group: 2.

Flowering period: Late spring to early summer and late summer.

Cultivation: Tolerates most garden soils. Requires a sheltered position. Best grown in partial shade to prevent premature fading of flower colour.

Recommended use: Suitable for a medium-sized obelisk, trellis, or pergola. Grow with wall-trained shrubs or fruit trees which do not require annual pruning. Ideal for a small garden. Zones 4–9.

Clematis chiisanensis
ATRAGENE GROUP

Origin: South Korea.

Parentage and year: Species. 1913.

Habit: Hardy, moderately vigorous, deciduous climber or scrambler.

Height: 2–3 m (6.5–10 ft.).

Description: The single, pendulous flowers are borne solitarily or in groups of threes on the old wood from the previous season and on the current season's new growth. The four nodding tepals are 5 cm (2 in.) long and vary in colour from pale yellow to a brownish orange-yellow. The tepals are heavily ribbed and have spurs (similar to those found in the flowers of *Aqui-*

legia) near the base, where they are a darker shade of colour.

Pruning group: 1. Any pruning to keep the plant tidy should be carried out immediately after the main flowering period.

Flowering period: Late spring to summer.

Cultivation: Needs sharp drainage, especially in a container. Suitable for sun or semi-shade in a sheltered position.

Recommended use: Grow at the back of a sunny border. Zones 5–9.

Clematis 'Chili'
ATRAGENE GROUP

Synonyms: *C. macropetala* 'Chili', *C. macropetala* 'Harry Smith'

Origin: Raised by Harry Smith of Sweden from wild seed collected in the Chili region of China.

Parentage and year: Selected form of *C. macropetala*. 1922.

Habit: Hardy, moderately vigorous, compact, deciduous climber.

Height: 2–2.5 m (6.5–8 ft.).

Description: The nodding, pale grey-blue semi-double flowers are composed of four broad tepals, each 4 cm (1.5 in.) long, with pointed tips, enclosing at least another four narrower and slightly shorter petal-like staminodes of a similar colour. Right in the heart of

Clematis chiisanensis. Photo by J. Lindmark.

Clematis 'Chili'. Photo by J. Lindmark.

the flower is an inner cluster of pale lilac staminodes surrounding the fertile stamens.

Pruning group: 1.

Flowering period: Midspring to late spring and late summer.

Cultivation: Tolerates most well-drained garden soils and any aspect.

Recommended use: Ideal for container-culture. Allow it to tumble over a low wall or fence. Grow on a small to medium-sized obelisk or trellis. Zones 3–9.

Clematis chinensis

Origin: Central, southern, and eastern China and North Vietnam.

Parentage and year: Species. 1757.

Habit: Hardy, moderately vigorous, semi-evergreen to deciduous climber.

Height: 3–4 m (10–13 ft.).

Description: The clusters of numerous white, scented flowers are borne from the leaf axils. Each flower is 3–4 cm (1.25–1.5 in.) wide and is composed of four narrow, non-overlapping tepals, which are 6–10 mm (0.25–0.5 in.) long, open flat, and bend backwards exposing prominent, creamy yellow stamens. The ribbed stems are somewhat hairy at the nodes. Leaves usually carry five leaflets arranged in pairs with the lower pair composed of three leaflets.

Pruning group: 3.

Flowering period: Late summer to early autumn.

Cultivation: Tolerates most garden soils but prefers good drainage. Produces the strongest scent in a sunny position. Root crown needs some protection in hard winters.

Recommended use: Suitable for growing up and over medium-sized shrubs and trees. Train on a pergola, trellis, or obelisk. Zones 6–9.

Clematis 'Christian Steven'

Origin: Raised by M. A. Beskaravainaja of the State Nikitsky Botanic Gardens, Ukraine, and named after the Gardens' founder, in honour of the 200th anniversary of his birth.

Parentage and year: *C.* 'Gipsy Queen' × *C.* 'Lawsoniana'. 1975.

Habit: Hardy, moderately vigorous, deciduous climber.

Height: 2.4–3 m (8–10 ft.).

Description: The single, open flowers, 12–16 cm (4.75–6.25 in.) across, are composed of six or seven overlapping, broad yet pointed, bluish purple tepals with wavy edges. Mature tepals fade to an even shade of dark blue. The contrasting prominent stamens are made of white filaments and brownish wine anthers.

Pruning group: 3.

Flowering period: Midsummer to late summer.

Cultivation: Tolerates most garden soils enriched with humus. Suitable for any aspect.

Recommended use: Grow on a medium-sized obelisk or trellis, or up and over large shrubs. Zones 3–9.

Clematis chinensis. Photo by C. Chesshire.

Clematis 'Christian Steven'. Photo by C. Chesshire.

Clematis chrysocoma

MONTANA GROUP

Origin: China.

Parentage and year: Species. 1886.

Habit: Semi-hardy, deciduous climber or scrambler. A second form is not as compact as the one described here and is a strong climber to 6 m (20 ft.).

Height: To 2 m (6.5 ft.).

Description: Single, solitary flowers are white tinged with pink. The four to six tepals, each 1.8–2.5 cm (0.75–1 in.) long, open to a cup shape and then open fully flat with a central boss of short yellow stamens. The stems, leaflets, leaf, and flower stalks are covered with brownish yellow hairs.

Pruning group: 1.

Flowering period: Early summer to late summer.

Cultivation: Needs sharp drainage and a sunny, sheltered position. Hardy only in maritime or mild temperate gardens.

Recommended use: Suitable for container-culture or a cold greenhouse. The more rampant form is ideal for a sheltered garden wall and for growing through large trees. Zones 8–9.

Clematis chrysocoma 'Hybrid'

MONTANA GROUP

Origin: Unknown.

Parentage and year: Unknown.

Habit: Vigorous, deciduous climber.

Height: 4.5–6 m (14.5–20 ft.).

Description: The single, shallow cup-shaped flowers are composed of four broad, pale pink tepals, each 7.5

Clematis chrysocoma. Photo by J. Lindmark.

Clematis chrysocoma 'Hybrid'.
Photo courtesy British Clematis Society Slide Library.

cm (3 in.) wide. The stamens are made of white filaments and yellow anthers. Leaves are attractive, downy, and bronzy green when young, gradually turning greener with age.

Pruning group: 1. Any pruning to keep the plant in check should be carried out immediately after the main flowering period by removing some of the old, flowered stems.

Flowering period: Late spring.

Cultivation: Tolerates most well-drained garden soils. Half-hardy to hardy in temperate gardens. Requires a sheltered, sunny position to flower well.

Recommended use: Grow on a wall or fence. Zones 7–9.

Clematis 'Cicciolina'
VITICELLA GROUP

Synonym: *C. viticella* 'Cicciolina'

Origin: Raised and introduced by Hans Vermeulen of the Netherlands. Named after an Italian actress known as La Cicciolina.

Parentage and year: Seedling of *C. viticella* 'Minuet'. 1996.

Habit: Hardy, moderately vigorous, deciduous climber.

Height: 3–3.7 m (10–12 ft.).

Description: The single, striking, semi-nodding, deep pinkish red flowers, up to 6 cm (2.5 in.) in diameter are composed of generally four tepals, each with a creamy white stripe along the centre. The tepals are neatly veined, and the edges are deeper red in colour. The stamens are cream coloured.

Pruning group: 3.

Flowering period: Midsummer to early autumn.

Cultivation: Tolerates most garden soils and any aspect.

Recommended use: Allow it to roam into a small tree or large shrub. Suitable for a large obelisk, trellis, or pergola. Zones 3–9.

Clematis cirrhosa
EVERGREEN/CIRRHOSA GROUP

Origin: Southern Europe, Mediterranean borders from Spain to Israel, and also North Africa.

Parentage and year: Species. 1596.

Habit: Half-hardy to hardy, vigorous, evergreen climber.

Height: Up to 4.5 m (14.5 ft.).

Description: Single, small, nodding, cream-green flowers (can be slightly variable) are 4 cm (1.5 in.) long and have four tepals. The inside of the tepals is covered with brown-purple blotches. Leaves may be simple, or

Clematis 'Cicciolina'. Photo by R. Savill.

Clematis cirrhosa. Photo by J. Lindmark.

made of three lobes or three leaflets which may be further divided. Leaf margins are usually toothed, and the leaves are generally dark green and glossy.

Pruning group: 1. Any pruning to keep the plant in check should be carried out immediately after the main flowering period by cutting back to 1 m (3.25 ft.) from the ground once the plant is well established.

Flowering period: Midwinter to early spring, earlier under glass or in a warm, sheltered position.

Cultivation: Prefers sharp drainage and a warm, sunny position to ripen the flowering wood.

Recommended use: Suitable for a pergola, trellis, or wall. Zones 7–9.

Clematis cirrhosa var. *balearica*
EVERGREEN/CIRRHOSA GROUP

Common name: Fern-leafed clematis

Origin: Balearic Islands, Spain. Awarded RHS Award of Garden Merit.

Parentage and year: A variant of *C. cirrhosa*. 1783.

Habit: Half-hardy to hardy, quite vigorous, evergreen climber.

Height: 4.75–7 m (15.25–23 ft.).

Description: Not very floriferous. The single, small, nodding, bell-shaped, lemon-scented, creamy white flowers are composed of four narrow, slightly recurving tepals, each 4 cm (1.5 in.) long, with maroon-brown speckles on the inside. The stamens are made of green filaments and yellow anthers. The flowers tend to turn pink with age and form attractive fluffy balls. Very finely cut leaves turn bronzy purple in winter.

Pruning group: 1. Any pruning to keep the plant in check should be carried out immediately after the main flowering period by cutting back to 1 m (3.25 ft.) from the ground once the plant is well established.

Flowering period: Midwinter to early spring.

Cultivation: Tolerates most well-drained and somewhat gritty garden soils. Requires a warm position to flower well.

Recommended use: Grow on a warm, south- or southwest-facing wall or fence. Not suitable for a very small garden. Zones 7–9.

Clematis cirrhosa var. *balearica*. Photo by B. Mathew.

Clematis 'Claudius'

ATRAGENE GROUP

Synonym: *C.* 'Citra'

Origin: Raised by Magnus Johnson of Södertälje, Sweden.

Parentage and year: *C. koreana* var. *fragrans* × *C.* 'Alborosea'. 1979.

Habit: Hardy, moderately vigorous, deciduous climber.

Height: 2–2.5 m (6.5–8 ft.).

Description: Flowers are nodding with four greenish

Clematis 'Claudius'. Photo by J. Lindmark.

Clematis coactilis. Photo by J. Pringle.

yellow, pointed tepals, which have a pink tinge at the base and are each 4.5–5 cm (1.75–2 in.) long. Staminodes are light green with purplish tinge. Leaves are made of nine leaflets, and the leaf margins are deeply serrated with forward-pointing teeth.

Pruning group: 1.

Flowering period: Late spring to early summer.

Cultivation: Needs sharp drainage. Suitable for sun or shade.

Recommended use: Best in a sheltered position at the back of a border on trellis or wall. Ideal for small gardens. Zones 5–9.

Clematis coactilis

HERBACEOUS/INTEGRIFOLIA GROUP

Origin: United States (southern Virginia).

Parentage and year: Species. 1942.

Habit: Hardy, upright, semi-woody, herbaceous perennial.

Height: 20–40 cm (8–16 in.).

Description: The solitary, nodding flowers, 2–3 cm (0.75–1.25 in.) long, are composed of four tepals which recurve at the somewhat rounded, blunt tips. The colour varies from pale white to white slightly tinged with green or pale purple. The anthers are creamy white. The flower is distinguished by its dense covering of silky hairs on the tepals and flower stalks. Much-branched stems are densely covered in short, fine, white hairs, and the simple, pale green leaves are velvety-hairy on the underside.

Pruning group: 3.

Flowering period: Late spring to early summer.

Cultivation: Prefers dry, somewhat infertile soils with extremely good drainage. Suitable for any aspect.

Recommended use: Best as a specimen plant in a container where growing conditions can be regulated in a cool greenhouse or conservatory. Suitable for a rockery or scree garden. Zones 8–9.

Clematis 'Colette Deville'

Origin: Raised by André Leroy of France.

Parentage and year: Unknown. ca. 1885.

Habit: Hardy, moderately vigorous, deciduous climber.

Height: 2.5–3.6 m (8–12 ft.).

Description: The single, gappy, deep mauve flowers, measuring 15 cm (6 in.) in diameter, are composed of six to eight non-overlapping tepals, which are deeply veined. The body colour of the tepals gradually pales towards the centre. The central mass of stamens is made of reddish filaments and creamy red anthers.

Pruning group: 2.

Flowering period: Late spring to early summer and late summer to early autumn.

Cultivation: Tolerates most garden soils. Best grown in partial shade to prevent premature fading of flower colour. Requires protection from strong winds.

Recommended use: Grow on a medium-sized obelisk, trellis, or arbour. Allow to roam naturally through medium-sized shrubs which do not require annual pruning. Zones 4–9.

Clematis columbiana
ATRAGENE GROUP

Origin: North America (British Columbia south to Colorado and Oregon).

Parentage and year: Species. 1838.

Habit: Semi-woody, moderately vigorous, deciduous scrambler or climber.

Height: 1–1.5 m (3.25–5 ft.) or more.

Description: Flowers are solitary, nodding, and bell shaped with four purple-blue to pale lavender-purple or rosy purple, semi-spreading tepals, each 2.5–6 cm (1–2.25 in.) long. Staminodes are creamy and about one-third the length of the tepals. Leaves are compound, and the nine leaflets have a few teeth or are distinctly three lobed.

Clematis 'Colette Deville'. Photo by C. Chesshire.

Pruning group: 1.

Flowering period: Late spring.

Cultivation: Needs sharp drainage. Prefers partial shade.

Recommended use: Ideal for container-culture, a scree garden or alpine bed, or growing through low shrubs. Zones 3–9.

Clematis columbiana var. *tenuiloba*
ATRAGENE GROUP

Synonym: *C. tenuiloba*

Origin: Western United States.

Parentage and year: A variant of *C. columbiana*. 1880.

Habit: Low mound-forming, deciduous alpine.

Height: 10–15 cm (4–6 in.).

Description: Single, semi-nodding, purple-blue to reddish purple flowers made of four tepals, each 2–3 cm (0.75–1.25 in.) long, are held above the low mat of foliage. The four outer staminodes are purplish violet whilst the inner ones are white and somewhat hairy. Greenish filaments tipped with creamy yellow anthers constitute the innermost stamens. Leaves divided into three to nine leaflets are further dissected into many narrow lobes. The plant multiplies vegetatively by underground shoots from swollen stems (rhizomes).

Pruning group: 1.

Flowering period: Late spring.

Cultivation: Needs sharp drainage. Suitable for any aspect.

Recommended use: Good for container-culture or an alpine house or bed. Zones 3–9.

Clematis 'Columbine'
ATRAGENE GROUP

Synonym: *C. alpina* 'Columbine'

Origin: Raised by Ernest Markham, head gardener at Gravetye Manor.

Parentage and year: Seedling of *C. alpina* (possibly *C. sibirica* × *C. alpina*). 1937.

Habit: Hardy, deciduous climber or scrambler.

Height: 2–3 m (6.5–10 ft.).

Description: The single, nodding, pale blue flowers are composed of four tepals, each 5 cm (2 in.) long. The staminodes are greenish creamy white, and the leaves are pale green.

Pruning group: 1. Any pruning to keep the plant tidy

should be carried out immediately after the main flowering period.

Flowering period: Midspring to late spring.

Cultivation: Needs sharp drainage. Suitable for any aspect, especially north- and east-facing aspects.

Recommended use: Good for containers or small gardens. Zones 3–9.

Clematis 'Columella'
ATRAGENE GROUP

Origin: Raised by Magnus Johnson of Södertälje, Sweden.

Parentage and year: *C. koreana* var. *fragrans* × *C.* 'Rosy O'Grady'. 1979.

Habit: Hardy, moderately vigorous, deciduous climber.

Height: 2–3 m (6.5–10 ft.).

Description: The single, nodding, bell-shaped, rosy pink flowers, measuring 5–6.5 cm (2–2.5 in.) long, are composed of four or five long, narrow, pointed tepals, which boast prominent darker pink continuous veins running from the base to the tip, and pale creamy white edges to the tepal margins. There is an inner skirt of pale whitish lemon staminodes encircling the cream filaments and yellow anthers.

Pruning group: 1.

Flowering period: Late spring.

Cultivation: Needs sharp drainage and a sunny position.

Recommended use: Useful for container-culture, at the back of a border, or for growing through medium-sized shrubs or small trees. Zones 5–9.

Clematis 'Comtesse de Bouchaud'

Synonym: *C.* 'Comtesse de Bouchard'

Origin: Raised by Francisque Morel of Lyon, France, ca. 1900. Named after the wife of Comte de Bouchaud, who gardened at Chasselay (Rhône). Awarded RHS Award of Garden Merit.

Parentage and year: Unknown. 1903.

Clematis columbiana var. *tenuiloba*. Photo by J. Lindmark.

Clematis 'Columbine'. Photo by R. Surman.

Habit: Hardy, moderately vigorous, compact, deciduous climber.

Height: 1.8–2.4 m (6–8 ft.).

Description: A very floriferous cultivar. The single, mauvish pink flowers are 10–15 cm (4–6 in.) in diameter and usually formed of six wide, well-rounded, slightly overlapping and recurving, textured tepals, each deeply veined and distinctively grooved along the centre. The central boss of stamens is composed of white filaments and pale yellow anthers. The leaves are divided into three or five leaflets.

Pruning group: 3.

Flowering period: Early summer to late summer.

Cultivation: Tolerates most garden soils and any aspect.

Recommended use: Ideal for growing over prostrate conifers and other groundcover or low-growing plants including roses. Suitable for container-culture. Zones 4–9.

Clematis connata

Origin: Himalaya, India, Kashmir, and southwestern China.

Parentage and year: Species. 1824.

Habit: Hardy, vigorous, deciduous climber.

Height: 5–7 m (16–23 ft.).

Description: The bell-shaped, pendent, slightly fragrant flowers are borne in axillary clusters from new wood. Each flower, 3–4 cm (1.25–1.5 in.) long, consists of four yellowish green tepals, each tapering to a point and recurving. Both sides of the tepals are covered with very fine hairs. The anthers are creamy green. The stems are slightly grooved, and the base of each pair of common stalks of leaves forms a thick disclike collar around the stem at each node. Leaves are glossy green, sometimes bluish beneath, and carry three or five leaflets.

Pruning group: 3.

Flowering period: Early autumn to midautumn.

Clematis 'Columella'. Photo by J. Lindmark.

Cultivation: Tolerates most garden soils but prefers good drainage. Best grown in full sun to ripen the stems and obtain the maximum number of flowers.

Recommended use: Grow through medium-sized trees, conifers, or large shrubs. Plant against a warm wall or fence. Suitable for a pergola. Zones 6–9.

Clematis 'Constance'
ATRAGENE GROUP

Synonym: *C. alpina* 'Constance'

Origin: Raised in Hull, England, by Kathleen Goodman, and introduced by Raymond Evison of Guernsey Clematis Nursery.

Parentage and year: Seedling of *C.* 'Ruby'. 1992.

Habit: Hardy, moderately vigorous, deciduous climber.

Height: 2.5–3 m (8–10 ft.).

Description: Semi-double, semi-nodding, deep pink flowers are 5 cm (2 in.) long. The outer layer of petal-like staminodes is as colourful and as long as the tepals, hence the semi-double appearance of the flowers. Leaves are composed of three leaflets, and leaf margins are serrated, resembling the teeth of a saw.

Pruning group: 1. Any pruning to keep the plant tidy should be carried out immediately after the main flowering period.

Flowering period: Midspring to late spring.

Clematis connata. Photo courtesy British Clematis Society Slide Library.

Clematis 'Comtesse de Bouchaud'. Photo by J. Lindmark.

Clematis 'Constance'. Photo by R. Kirkman.

Cultivation: Needs sharp drainage. Suitable for any aspect.

Recommended use: Ideal for small gardens. May be grown in containers. Zones 3–9.

Clematis 'Continuity'
MONTANA GROUP

Synonym: *C. chrysocoma* 'Continuity'

Origin: Raised by Albert Voneshan of George Jackman and Son, England.

Parentage and year: Selected form of *C. chrysocoma*. 1958.

Habit: Strong-growing, deciduous subshrub or scrambler.

Height: To 2 m (6.5 ft.).

Description: The single, pale pink flowers, measuring 5 cm (2 in.) across, are composed of four, sometimes up to six, broad, satiny textured, spreading and slightly wavy tepals held on long stalks, up to 20 cm (8 in.). White filaments with creamy white anthers constitute the stamens. The leaf stalks are also remarkably long, up to 15 cm (6 in.), and are less hairy than those of the species *C. chrysocoma*.

Pruning group: 1.

Flowering period: Early summer to late summer.

Cultivation: Tolerates most well-drained garden soils. Half-hardy to hardy in temperate gardens only. Requires a sheltered, warm position in the garden preferably near a south-facing wall.

Recommended use: Best in a conservatory or cold greenhouse. Zones 8–9.

Clematis 'Continuity'. Photo by M. Humphries.

Clematis 'Corona'

Origin: Raised by Tage Lundell of Helsingborg, Sweden. Introduced to the British Isles in 1972 by Treasures of Tenbury, England.

Parentage and year: Chance seedling of *C.* 'Nelly Moser'. 1955.

Habit: Hardy, moderately vigorous, low-growing, compact, deciduous climber.

Height: 1.2–1.8 m (4–6 ft.).

Description: The single, rich velvety crimson flowers, borne in abundance during spring, are 10–15 cm (4–6 in.) wide and are composed of six to eight tepals, rather blunt at the tips. White filaments are tipped with red anthers. The late summer flowers are smaller and paler in colour.

Pruning group: 2.

Clematis 'Corona'. Photo by J. Lindmark.

Flowering period: Late spring to early summer and late summer.

Cultivation: Tolerates most garden soils. Best grown in partial shade to prevent premature fading of flower colour.

Recommended use: Ideal for container-culture. Suitable for a small obelisk, or grow through low shrubs and prostrate conifers. Zones 4–9.

Clematis 'Corry'
TANGUTICA GROUP

Origin: Raised by Pieter G. Zwijnenburg of Boskoop, Netherlands.

Parentage and year: *C. tangutica* × *C. tibetana* subsp. *vernayi* 'Orange Peel'. 1975.

Habit: Hardy, quite vigorous, deciduous climber.

Clematis 'Corry'. Photo by C. Chesshire.

Height: 3–4 m (10–13 ft.).

Description: The single, nodding, deep yellow flowers are made of four tepals, each 3–3.5 cm (ca. 1.25 in.) long, with a central boss of dark brownish purple stamens.

Pruning group: 3.

Flowering period: Midsummer to early autumn.

Cultivation: Tolerates most well-drained garden soils.

Recommended use: Grow through large, open shrubs or medium-sized trees. Suitable for a pergola, obelisk, or free-standing trellis. Zones 4–9.

Clematis 'Côte d'Azur'
HERBACEOUS/HERACLEIFOLIA GROUP

Synonym: *C. heracleifolia* 'Côte d'Azur'

Origin: Raised by Victor Lemoine of Nancy, France.

Parentage and year: *C. heracleifolia* × *C.* 'Jouiniana'. ca. 1900.

Habit: Hardy, deciduous, non-clinging, woody subshrub.

Height: 0.9–1.2 m (3–4 ft.).

Description: Light blue, tubular, single flowers are composed of four narrow tepals, each 2–2.5 cm (0.75–1 in.) long, with a paler shade down the centre, and tepal tips fully turning back upon themselves as the flower matures. Flowers are borne in clusters from long stalks in the leaf axils beginning about halfway up the stems to the tip. There is no detectable scent.

Pruning group: 3.

Flowering period: Midsummer to midautumn.

Clematis 'Côte d'Azur'. Photo by C. Chesshire.

Cultivation: Tolerates most well-drained garden soils and any aspect.

Recommended use: Ideal for the herbaceous border, giving colour at the end of the growing year. Zones 5–9.

Clematis 'Countess of Lovelace'

Origin: Raised by George Jackman and Son, England.

Parentage and year: *C.* 'Sophia Plena' × *C.* 'Jackmanii' hybrid. 1871.

Habit: Hardy, moderately vigorous, deciduous climber.

Height: 1.8–2.4 m (6–8 ft.).

Description: The double flowers, measuring 15–18 cm (6–7 in.) in diameter and produced on the previous season's old wood, are composed of an outermost layer of pale mauve tepals followed by successive smaller layers of narrower, and more pointed, blue-mauve tepals. Each of the numerous tepals carries a white bar on the reverse. The central tuft of stamens is whitish. Single flowers are the rule later, on the current season's new shoots. Greenish cream filaments carry light yellow anthers.

Clematis 'Countess of Lovelace'. Photo by J. Lindmark.

Pruning group: 2.

Flowering period: Late spring to early summer (double) and early autumn (single).

Cultivation: Tolerates most garden soils. Requires generous feeding to flower well. Best grown in full sun or partial shade.

Recommended use: Suitable for container-culture. May also be grown on a small obelisk or trellis. Zones 4–9.

Clematis 'Crépuscule'

HERBACEOUS/HERACLEIFOLIA GROUP

Origin: Raised by Victor Lemoine of Nancy, France.

Parentage and year: *C. tubulosa* × *C. stans*. ca. 1900.

Habit: Hardy, semi-herbaceous, non-clinging, woody-based perennial.

Height: 1–1.2 m (3.25–4 ft.).

Description: The tubular, hyacinth-like, pale purple-blue flowers, measuring 2–4 cm (0.75–1.5 in.) long, are borne in clusters from the upper leaf axils of erect and semi-erect woody stems. As each flower matures, the four tepals, which are textured and have edges of small rounded teeth, open and recurve fully back on themselves. White filaments and yellow anthers make up the stamens.

Pruning group: 3.

Flowering period: Early summer to late summer.

Cultivation: Requires free-draining garden soils. Suitable for any aspect.

Recommended use: Grow in herbaceous or mixed borders. May be grown in large containers. Zones 4–9.

Clematis 'Crépuscule'. Photo by C. Chesshire.

Clematis 'Crimson King'

Synonym: *C.* 'Crimson Star' (in the United States)

Origin: Raised by George Jackman and Son, England. Awarded RHS Award of Merit.

Parentage and year: Unknown.

Habit: Hardy, moderately vigorous, deciduous climber.

Height: 2.5–3 m (8–10 ft.).

Description: The single, gappy, crimson-coloured flowers are 15–20 cm (6–8 in.) in diameter and composed of five to seven broad, overlapping, pointed tepals, which tend to recurve along the margins with age. White filaments carry distinctly purplish brown anthers. Occasionally semi-double flowers may appear.

Pruning group: 2.

Flowering period: Early summer to late summer.

Cultivation: Tolerates most garden soils. Best grown in partial shade to prevent premature fading of flower colour. Requires protection from strong winds.

Recommended use: Grow through large, open shrubs which do not require annual pruning. May be used to furnish a medium-sized obelisk or trellis. Allow to scramble through wall-trained shrubs which do not require annual pruning. Zones 4–9.

Clematis 'Crimson King'. Photo by J. Lindmark.

Clematis crispa

TEXENSIS-VIORNA GROUP

Common names: Blue jasmine, marsh clematis, curly clematis

Origin: Southeastern United States.

Parentage and year: Species. Before 1726.

Habit: Slender, semi-woody, deciduous climber.

Height: 2 m (6.5 ft.).

Description: The single, nodding and semi-nodding, solitary, bell-shaped flowers are 3–4 cm (1.25–1.5 in.) long and vary in colour from light blue to blue purple. The four tepals are joined at the base, have crisped or undulate margins, and recurve at the tips forming a complete loop. The stamens are pale green. Flower stalks are long, measuring 7.5 cm (3 in.). Prominent seedheads appear after flowering. Leaves are divided into five or seven small, smooth, roughly oval leaflets with entire margins and three apparent veins from the base.

Pruning group: 3.

Flowering period: Midsummer to midautumn.

Cultivation: Found in marsh land (mainly acid) in the wild, but tolerates neutral soil conditions in the garden. Plants best grown from seed, although there will be some variation in colour and perhaps size.

Recommended use: Ideal for container-culture or growing through small to medium-sized shrubs and over heathers or prostrate conifers. Zones 5–9.

Clematis cunninghamii

Common name: Cunningham's clematis

Origin: New Zealand (North Island).

Parentage and year: Species. 1837.

Habit: Half-hardy, evergreen scrambler or climber.

Clematis crispa. Photo by J. Pringle.

Height: 3–3.6 m (10–12 ft.).

Description: The semi-nodding, mildly lemon scented flowers are 2–3 cm (0.75–1.25 in.) across and are produced in clusters. Each flower is composed of four to eight greenish yellow, pointed tepals, which open outwards and slightly backwards, exposing yellow anthers. Male and female flowers are borne on separate plants. Male flowers are slightly larger than their female counterparts. The vine growth is congested, and leaves are very narrow, dark green, each carrying three leaflets, which are somewhat thin with tawny-coloured hairs beneath.

Pruning group: 1.

Flowering period: Early spring to late spring.

Cultivation: Requires a sharp-draining compost and a sunny, sheltered aspect.

Recommended use: Ideal for container-culture in a cool greenhouse or conservatory. Zones 8–9.

Clematis 'Cyanea'
ATRAGENE GROUP

Synonym: *C. alpina* 'Cyanea'

Origin: Raised by Magnus Johnson of Södertälje, Sweden.

Parentage and year: Believed to be *C. alpina* × *C. macropetala*. 1950.

Habit: Hardy, moderately vigorous, deciduous climber.

Height: 2–3 m (6.5–10 ft.).

Description: The semi-double, nodding, darkish blue flowers are composed of four pointed tepals, each 4–5 cm (1.5–2 in.) long, with faint silvery lines running along its length. There is an inner layer of another four lighter, shorter, silvery blue spoon-shaped, petal-like staminodes surrounding greenish yellow filaments and yellow anthers. Leaves are midgreen and divided into nine leaflets, and the leaf margins are irregularly serrated.

Clematis 'Cyanea'. Photo by J. Lindmark.

Pruning group: 1. Any pruning to keep the plant tidy should be carried out immediately after the main flowering period.

Flowering period: Midspring to late spring.

Cultivation: Tolerates most well-drained garden soils and any aspect.

Recommended use: Grow with other wall-trained shrubs, or on a medium-sized obelisk or trellis, or through small trees. Allow to tumble over a low wall. Suitable for container-culture. Zones 3–9.

Clematis 'Cylindrica'

HERBACEOUS/INTEGRIFOLIA GROUP

Synonym: *C. cylindrica*

Origin: Found possibly in Gordon and Thompson's old nursery at Mile End in London.

Parentage and year: Believed to be *C. integrifolia* × *C. crispa*. First recorded under its synonym in 1799.

Habit: Hardy, deciduous, non-clinging, sprawling, herbaceous perennial.

Height: 0.9–1.2 m (3–4 ft.).

Description: The single, deep purple-blue, nodding, bell-shaped flowers are composed of four narrow, twisted tepals, each 3–4.5 cm (1.25–1.75 in.) long. Greenish white filaments and golden yellow anthers make up the contrasting stamens.

Pruning group: 3.

Flowering period: Early summer to early autumn.

Cultivation: Tolerates most garden soils and any aspect. If trained on an artificial support, the stems need tying-in.

Recommended use: Plant in mixed borders amongst other herbaceous plants where it will find its own natural support from neighbouring plants. Zones 4–9.

Clematis 'Daniel Deronda'

Origin: Raised by Charles Noble of Sunningdale, England. Named after the main character in George Eliot's 1876 novel of the same title. Awarded RHS Award of Garden Merit.

Parentage and Year: Unknown. 1882.

Habit: Hardy, strong-growing, deciduous climber.

Height: 2.4–3 m (8–10 ft.).

Description: Large, star-shaped, flattish flowers, measuring 18–20 cm (7–8 in.) wide, normally are formed of eight pointed, dark blue-purple tepals, each with faint off-white lines along the centre, recurving margins, and a central mass of cream filaments and anthers. The first flush of flowers produced from late spring to early summer may be semi-double or single while those appearing in late summer are usually single. Attractive and novel spherical seedheads with a gentle twist of the seedtails at the top are an added feature.

Pruning group: 2.

Flowering period: Late spring to late summer (semi-double or single).

Cultivation: Tolerates most garden soils. Best grown in sun or partial shade. Requires protection from strong winds.

Clematis 'Cylindrica'. Photo by C. Chesshire.

Clematis 'Daniel Deronda'. Photo by C. Chesshire.

Recommended use: Suitable for a medium-sized obelisk, trellis, arbour, or pergola. Grow naturally through other wall-trained shrubs which do not require severe pruning. Zones 4–9.

Clematis 'Dawn'

Origin: Raised by Tage Lundell of Helsingborg, Sweden, and introduced to the British Isles in 1969 by Treasures of Tenbury, England.

Parentage and year: Seedling of *C.* 'Moonlight' × *C.* 'Nelly Moser'. 1960.

Habit: Hardy, moderately vigorous, compact, deciduous climber.

Height: 2.5–3 m (8–10 ft.).

Description: The single, pearly pink flowers are 15–20 cm (6–8 in.) wide and are composed of usually eight, but sometimes six or seven, broad and overlapping tepals, each tapering to a blunt tip. The colour deepens towards the margins. White filaments carry carmine anthers. Leaves may be simple or divided into three leaflets. The young leaves are quite bronzy, becoming green as they age.

Pruning group: 2.

Flowering period: Late spring to early summer and occasionally late summer.

Cultivation: Tolerates most garden soils. Best grown out of strong sunlight to prevent premature fading of flower colour.

Recommended use: Grow with other wall-trained shrubs or small trees. Suitable for a sheltered pergola, trellis, or arch. Zones 4–9.

Clematis 'Denny's Double'

Origin: Raised by Vince and Sylvia Denny of Denny's Clematis Nursery, Broughton, England.

Parentage and year: *C.* 'Silver Moon' × *C.* 'Duchess of Edinburgh'. Introduced in 1985.

Habit: Hardy, moderately vigorous, deciduous climber.

Height: 1.8–2.4 m (6–8 ft.).

Description: The double, pale lavender-blue flowers measure 10–15 cm (4–6 in.) wide and carry many layers of long tepals, which get progressively shorter towards the centre, giving a mophead effect. Stamens are composed of white filaments and creamy yellow anthers.

Pruning group: 2.

Flowering period: Late spring to early summer (double), and late summer (double).

Cultivation: Tolerates most garden soils. Best grown in full sun or semi-shade. Requires protection from strong winds.

Recommended use: Grow on a small to medium-sized obelisk or trellis. May also be grown naturally through other wall-trained, not-so-vigorous shrubs which do not require severe pruning. Suitable for short-term container-culture. Zones 4–9.

Clematis 'Dawn'. Photo by C. Chesshire.

Clematis 'Denny's Double'. Photo by C. Chesshire.

Clematis denticulata

Origin: South America (Argentina predominantly, Bolivia, Brazil, Chile, Paraguay, Peru, and Uruguay).

Parentage and year: Species. 1825.

Habit: Tender to half-hardy, vigorous climber.

Height: 3–4 m (10–13 ft.).

Description: The single, greenish white, scented flowers borne in lateral and terminal clusters are made of four, sometimes five or six, broad and elliptical tepals 0.7–1.3 cm (0.25–0.5 in.) long. The flowers can be unisexual or bisexual. The leaves are divided into five leaflets, which may be arranged in pairs on either side of a central axis sometimes further divided or two or three lobed.

Pruning group: 2 or 3. A hard pruning (group 3) results in the loss of early flowers.

Flowering period: Midsummer to late summer.

Cultivation: Tolerates most garden soils but not too fertile. Requires a warm, sunny aspect.

Recommended use: Grow on a wall or fence, or through medium-sized trees or large shrubs. Best as a conservatory plant in very cold gardens. Zones 8–9.

Clematis 'Docteur Le Bêle'

Origin: Unknown. Named after a French clematarian, Jules Le Bêle.

Parentage and year: Unknown.

Habit: Hardy, moderately vigorous, deciduous climber.

Height: 2.4–3 m (8–10 ft.).

Description: The single, gappy, mauvish pink flowers measure 10–13 cm (4–5 in.) across and are composed of four to six non-overlapping, pear-shaped, textured tepals, each with three central grooves of a slightly darker shade running from the base to the tip. The stamens comprise cream filaments and yellow anthers.

Pruning group: 3.

Flowering period: Midsummer to late summer.

Cultivation: Tolerates most garden soils and any aspect.

Recommended use: Suitable for a pergola, medium-sized obelisk, or trellis. Grow with moderately vigorous conifers and medium-sized shrubs. Zones 4–9.

Clematis 'Doctor Ruppel'

Origin: Raised by Dr. Ruppel of Argentina and introduced to the British Isles by Jim Fisk of Fisk's Clematis Nursery, Suffolk, England. Awarded RHS Award of Garden Merit.

Parentage and year: Unknown. 1973.

Habit: Hardy, moderately vigorous, compact, deciduous climber.

Height: 2.5–3 m (8–10 ft.).

Description: The single, large, rosy pink flowers are

Clematis denticulata.
Photo courtesy British Clematis Society Slide Library.

Clematis 'Docteur Le Bêle'. Photo by E. Leeds.

15–20 cm (6–8 in.) wide and are composed of six to eight overlapping tepals, each with a carmine central bar, gently notched to slightly wavy margins and tapering to a point. The large stamens are golden.

Pruning group: 2.

Flowering period: Late spring to early summer and late summer.

Cultivation: Tolerates most garden soils and any aspect. Withstands strong sunlight.

Recommended use: Grow through medium-sized shrubs or in containers. Ideal to cover the bare stems of wall-trained shrubs which do not require annual pruning. Zones 4–9.

Clematis 'Dorothy Tolver'

Origin: Raised by Jonathan Gooch and named after his mother-in-law. Introduced by Thorncroft Clematis Nursery.

Parentage and year: *C.* 'Vyvyan Pennell' × *C.* 'Niobe'. 1993.

Clematis 'Doctor Ruppel'. Photo by E. Leeds.

Habit: Hardy, vigorous, deciduous climber.

Height: 2.5–3.6 m (8–12 ft.).

Description: The single, medium-sized to large, deep mauvish pink flowers, measuring 10–15 cm (4–6 in.) in diameter, are composed of six overlapping tepals with a satin sheen, being mauve at the base, heavily overlaid with deep mauve pink. Each tepal boasts slightly crimped edges and tapers to a point. The anthers are buttercup yellow.

Pruning group: 2.

Flowering period: Late spring to early summer and early autumn to midautumn.

Cultivation: Tolerates most garden soils and any aspect.

Recommended use: Suitable for a medium-sized obelisk or trellis. Grow with other wall-trained shrubs which do not require severe annual pruning. Zones 4–9.

Clematis 'Dorothy Walton'

Synonym: *C.* 'Bagatelle'

Origin: Raised by a customer of and introduced by Jim Fisk of Fisk's Clematis Nursery, Suffolk, England. Named after the customer's wife.

Parentage and year: Unknown. Before 1978.

Habit: Hardy, vigorous, deciduous climber.

Height: 3–3.6 m (10–12 ft.).

Description: The single, mauvish pink flowers, measuring 10 cm (4 in.) wide, are usually composed of six to eight long, pointed tepals and reddish brown stamens.

Clematis 'Dorothy Tolver'. Photo by C. Chesshire.

Pruning group: 3.

Flowering period: Early summer to late summer.

Cultivation: Tolerates most garden soils and any aspect.

Recommended use: Grow naturally through medium-sized trees and large shrubs. Also grow with climbing roses or other wall-trained shrubs. Zones 4–9.

Clematis 'Dovedale'
MONTANA GROUP

Synonym: *C.* ×*vedariensis* 'Dovedale'

Origin: Raised by Barry Fretwell of Peveril Clematis Nursery, England.

Parentage and year: *C. chrysocoma* × *C.* 'Picton's Variety'. ca. 1996.

Habit: Hardy, moderately vigorous, deciduous climber.

Height: 4.6–6 m (14.5–20 ft.).

Description: The single, rounded, slightly cup-shaped, pale pink flowers measure 7–7.5 cm (2.75–3 in.) across and are composed of four to seven broad tepals, which overlap only near the base, with rounded, blunt yet gently pointed tips and with central bars of a deeper shade. The whole surface has prominent veining of yet a deeper pink, and the central boss of prominent stamens comprises greenish cream filaments and creamy yellow anthers. The dark green foliage has undersides tinged with reddish brown.

Pruning group: 1.

Flowering period: Midspring to late spring.

Cultivation: Tolerates most well-drained garden soils and any aspect.

Recommended use: Ideal to grow into open, medium-sized to large trees or along a sheltered boundary fence and wall. Zones 5–9.

Clematis 'Duchess of Albany'
TEXENSIS-VIORNA GROUP

Synonym: *C. texensis* 'Duchess of Albany'

Origin: Raised by George Jackman and Son, England. Awarded RHS Award of Garden Merit.

Clematis 'Dovedale'. Photo by E. Leeds.

Clematis 'Duchess of Albany'. Photo by C. Chesshire.

Clematis 'Dorothy Walton'. Photo by C. Chesshire.

Parentage and year: *C. texensis* × *C.* 'Star of India'. 1890.

Habit: Hardy, vigorous, deciduous, herbaceous climber.

Height: 2.5–3 m (8–10 ft.).

Description: The single, 5- to 6-cm (2- to 2.25-in.) long, tuliplike flowers are composed of four to six clear pink tepals, each with recurving tip and a darker pink bar along the centre. The leaves are midgreen.

Pruning group: 3.

Flowering period: Midsummer to late summer.

Cultivation: Tolerates most garden soils. Suitable for full sun or partial shade. Prone to mildew. Take early precaution by spraying with a fungicide monthly from

Clematis 'Duchess of Edinburgh'. Photo by C. Chesshire.

Clematis 'Duchess of Sutherland'. Photo by D. Harding.

late spring. New shoots at soil level need protection from slugs and snails.

Recommended use: Grow through medium-sized trees or large shrubs. It holds many of its flowers erect if it is grown over other prostrate, robust garden plants, showing off the tuliplike flowers to the best advantage. Zones 4–9.

Clematis 'Duchess of Edinburgh'

Origin: Raised by George Jackman and Son, England.

Parentage and year: Unknown. 1874.

Habit: Hardy, moderately vigorous, deciduous climber.

Height: 1.8–2.4 m (6–8 ft.).

Description: The fully double flowers, borne on the previous season's old wood and the current season's new growth, are 10–12.5 cm (4–5 in.) wide and are composed of several layers of narrow, white tepals, which tend to recurve at the tips. White filaments and cream anthers constitute the central mass of stamens. Early flowers may be tinged with green.

Pruning group: 2.

Flowering period: Early summer to late summer (always double).

Cultivation: Tolerates most garden soils. Best grown in full sun or partial shade. Requires protection from cold winds.

Recommended use: Grow through other moderately vigorous, wall-trained shrubs which do not require pruning. Train on a small to medium-sized obelisk or trellis. Zones 4–9.

Clematis 'Duchess of Sutherland'

Origin: Raised by George Jackman and Son, England.

Parentage and year: Unknown. 1934.

Habit: Hardy, deciduous climber. Vigorous once established.

Height: 2.4–3 m (8–10 ft.).

Description: The single, rather flattish, rosy carmine-pink flowers measure 15–17 cm (6–7 in.) across and are composed of six tepals, which are broad in the middle and tapering to sharp points, with a slightly deeper colour along the margins. Bright cream stamens contrast well with the tepal colour.

Pruning group: 2 or 3. If the old vines are not pruned

or lightly pruned, there may be a short display of some double flowers, although the main crop of single flowers is produced from the new, current season's wood.

Flowering period: Late spring and midsummer to late summer.

Cultivation: Tolerates most garden soils and any aspect. May take some time to establish itself.

Recommended use: Grow naturally through medium-sized trees and shrubs or on a trellis or pergola. Zones 4–9.

Clematis 'Durandii'
HERBACEOUS / INTEGRIFOLIA GROUP

Synonym: *C. ×durandii*

Origin: Raised by Durand Frères of France.

Parentage and year: *C. integrifolia* × *C.* 'Jackmanii'. 1874.

Habit: Hardy, strong-growing, non-clinging, herbaceous perennial.

Clematis 'Durandii'. Photo by J. Lindmark.

Height: 0.9–1.8 m (3–6 ft.).

Description: The single, semi-nodding, indigo-blue flowers open flat and measure 9–11 cm (3.5–4.5 in.) wide. They are composed of four to six firm, blunt but pointed tepals, each prominently ribbed along the centre and recurving along the edges with maturity. The reverse of each tepal boasts a deep midblue colouring. The striking central tuft of stamens, made of white filaments shaded with blue at the base, carries golden yellow anthers. Leaves are simple, dark green, and broad at the base, tapering towards the apex like the head of a lance head. A floriferous cultivar.

Pruning group: 3.

Flowering period: Early summer to early autumn.

Cultivation: Tolerates most garden soils and any aspect. If trained on an artificial support, the stems need tying-in. Remove some old woody stems when the plant is well established and forms a large clump.

Recommended use: Allow to scramble naturally through mixed borders or low and prostrate conifers or shrubs. Train on a trellis or other suitable supports. Zones 4–9.

Clematis 'Early Sensation'
EVERGREEN GROUP

Origin: Raised by Graham Hutchins of County Park Nursery, Essex, England. Named and introduced by A. N. M. Rijnbeek of Boskoop, Netherlands.

Parentage and year: Unclear. Believed to be *C.* 'Fairy' × *C. paniculata*. 1990s.

Clematis 'Early Sensation'. Photo by C. Chesshire.

Habit: Half-hardy, compact, evergreen shrub.

Height: To 2 m (6.5 ft.).

Description: The single, pure white, bowl-shaped flowers are normally composed of seven, sometimes six or eight, rounded yet pointed, overlapping tepals and an attractive centre of greenish cream stamens. The leaves are dark green and deeply dissected.

Pruning group: 1.

Flowering period: Early spring to midspring.

Cultivation: Requires a free-draining compost if grown in a container.

Recommended use: Best grown under glass in a cool greenhouse or conservatory. Zones 7–9.

Clematis 'Edith'

Origin: Raised by Raymond Evison, while at Treasures of Tenbury, England, and named after his mother. Awarded RHS Award of Garden Merit.

Parentage and year: Open-pollinated seedling of *C.* 'Mrs. Cholmondeley'. 1974.

Habit: Hardy, moderately vigorous, compact, deciduous climber.

Height: 2–2.5 m (6.5–8 ft.).

Description: The single, white flowers, measuring 12 cm (4.75 in.) in diameter, are composed of six to eight tepals, each with a distinct greenish yellow central bar during late spring. Flowers, which appear later in the season, do not feature the prominent green along the central bars. Tepal margins bend down, and tepal tips reflex gently as the flowers mature. White filaments and dark red anthers set off the flowers.

Pruning group: 2.

Flowering period: Late spring to early summer and late summer.

Cultivation: Tolerates most garden soils and any aspect.

Recommended use: Ideal for container-culture or growing through low-growing, small to medium-sized shrubs which do not require annual pruning, or conifers. May also be grown on a small obelisk or short trellis. Zones 4–9.

Clematis 'Édomurasaki'

Origin: Raised by Seijūrō Arai of Japan. The name means "Tokyo purple."

Parentage and year: *C.* 'Asagasumi' × *C.* 'The President'. 1952.

Habit: Hardy, moderately vigorous, deciduous climber.

Height: 2.4–3 m (8–10 ft.).

Description: The single, deep purplish blue flowers are 15–18 cm (6–7 in.) across and are composed of six to eight broad yet pointed, overlapping tepals with a velvety sheen. The stamens are made of greenish cream filaments and rich red anthers.

Pruning group: 2.

Flowering period: Late spring to early summer and late summer.

Clematis 'Edith'. Photo by E. Leeds.

Clematis 'Édomurasaki'. Photo by J. Lindmark.

Cultivation: Tolerates most garden soils. Best grown in sun or partial shade. Occasionally, early foliage is plentiful and pale green. Young plants can be slow to establish themselves.

Recommended use: Grow with other wall-trained plants which do not require annual pruning. Suitable for a medium-sized obelisk or trellis. Zones 4–9.

Clematis 'Édouard Desfossé'

Origin: Raised by Desfossé of Orléans, France. Awarded RHS Award of Merit (1936).

Parentage and year: *C. patens* × *C. lanuginosa*. 1880.

Habit: Hardy, not very vigorous, compact, deciduous climber.

Height: 1.2–1.8 (4–6 ft.).

Description: The single, rather large, somewhat gappy, violet-mauve flowers measure 17–22 cm (7–9 in.) in diameter and are composed of six to eight pointed tepals, each with a deep reddish purple central bar, slightly undulating margins, and gently reflexed tips. There is a central mass of prominent reddish purple stamens. The flowers, as they open, boast a velvety silky sheen, which is lost as they mature.

Pruning group: 2.

Flowering period: Late spring, early summer, and midsummer.

Cultivation: Tolerates most garden soils and any aspect. Requires a sheltered position to prevent wind damage to the large flowers.

Recommended use: Ideal for container-culture or for covering the bare stems of wall-trained roses and shrubs. Zones 4–9.

Clematis 'Edward Prichard'
HERBACEOUS GROUP

Synonym: *C.* 'Edward Pritchard'

Origin: Raised by Russell V. Pritchard of Australia.

Parentage and year: *C. recta* × *C. heracleifolia* var. *davidiana*. Before 1950.

Habit: Hardy, deciduous, non-clinging and somewhat lax, herbaceous perennial.

Height: 0.9–1.2 m (3–4 ft.).

Description: The masses of fragrant, pale mauvish pink flowers, which are 4 cm (1.5 in.) across, have a crosslike arrangement of four wedge-shaped, narrow, delicate tepals, displaying the deepest colouring towards the tips. The stamens are made of white fila-

ments and yellow anthers. The leaves are divided into five leaflets and are irregularly lobed, with margins coarsely toothed like a saw. Seed of this cultivar is not viable.

Pruning group: 3.

Flowering period: Midsummer to late summer.

Cultivation: Tolerates most garden soils and any aspect. Needs support to prevent the plant from flopping, unless grown as ground cover. Not a long-lived plant.

Recommended use: Plant in mixed or herbaceous borders and allow to scramble through plants nearby or provide an artificial support to show off the slender, arching stems which carry an abundance of flowers. Zones 4–9.

Clematis 'Édouard Desfossé'. Photo by J. Lindmark.

Clematis 'Edward Prichard' flower detail. Photo by E. Leeds.

Clematis 'Edward Prichard' in the garden. Photo by E. Leeds.

Clematis 'Ekstra'. Photo courtesy Thorncroft Clematis Nursery.

Clematis 'Eleanor of Guildford'. Photo courtesy Notcutts Nurseries.

Clematis 'Ekstra'

Origin: Raised by Uno Kivistik of Harjumaa, Estonia.

Parentage and year: Seedling of *C.* 'Serebriannyj Ruczejok'. 1982.

Habit: Hardy, compact, deciduous climber.

Height: 1–2 m (3.25–6.5 ft.).

Description: The single, fairly large, light blue-violet flowers, borne in great profusion and measuring 10–14 cm (4–5.5 in.) across, are composed of six or seven tepals, the centres of which gradually fade to light blue contrasting with deep blue veining. White filaments with dark purple-violet anthers constitute the prominent central mass of stamens.

Pruning group: 3.

Flowering period: Midsummer to late summer.

Cultivation: Tolerates most garden soils enriched with humus. Suitable for any aspect. Requires a position sheltered from strong winds.

Recommended use: Ideal for large containers. Suitable for a small to medium-sized obelisk or trellis. Grows with small to medium-sized shrubs or prostrate conifers with silver or golden foliage. Zones 4–9.

Clematis 'Eleanor of Guildford'

Origin: Raised by Ken Pyne of Chingford, London. First flowered in 1989. The cultivar was selected by the Borough of Guildford in Surrey, England, as its plant for the new millennium and was named in commemoration of three queens bearing that name, who resided in the town during the last millennium. Introduced by Notcutts Nurseries of Woodbridge, Suffolk, England, in April 2000.

Parentage and year: Chance seedling of *C.* 'Richard Pennell'. 1987.

Habit: Hardy, moderately vigorous, deciduous climber.

Height: 2–3 m (6.5–10 ft.).

Description: The rather large, pearly pink flowers measure 15–20 cm (6–8 in.) across and are composed of eight fairly rounded, slightly overlapping tepals, which taper to points and boast a pronounced deeper pink shading along the margins. Each tepal carries well-defined ribs. The flowers frequently appear semi-double when petal-like sterile stamens take on the function of small secondary tepals. The stamens are well spread and distinct with cream filaments carrying yellow anthers. The leaves are deep glossy-green with nine leaflets.

Pruning group: 2.

Flowering period: Late spring to early summer, with sporadic flowering in late summer and autumn.

Cultivation: Tolerates most garden soils. Best grown away from direct sun to preserve flower colour.

Recommended use: Suitable for a medium-sized obelisk, trellis, or arch. Grows with medium-sized shrubs which do not require annual pruning. Zones 4–9.

Clematis 'Elegija'

Synonyms: *C.* 'Elegia', *C.* 'Elegiia'

Origin: Raised by A. N. Volosenko-Valenis and named by M. A. Beskaravainaja, both of the State Nikitsky Botanic Gardens, Ukraine. The translation of the name is "elegy."

Parentage and year: *C.* 'Jackmanii' × *C.* 'Lanuginosa Candida'.

Habit: Hardy, moderately vigorous, deciduous climber.

Height: 2.5–3.5 m (8–12 ft.).

Description: The single, somewhat gappy, bluish purple flowers are 12–15 cm (4.75–6 in.) across and are composed of five or six tepals, each egg shaped in outline with a purple-violet central bar and hairy on the underside with margins bent outwards and terminating in a blunt recurved tip. Greyish filaments carry purplish red anthers. Leaves have three or five leaflets and are hairy beneath. Flowers are produced profusely on the current season's growth.

Pruning group: 3.

Flowering period: Midsummer to late summer.

Clematis 'Elegija'. Photo by C. Chesshire.

Cultivation: Tolerates most garden soils. Prefers an open, sunny aspect.

Recommended use: Suitable for an obelisk, trellis, or pergola. Grow with other wall-trained shrubs or climbers. Zones 4–9.

Clematis 'Elgar'. Photo by J. Lindmark.

Clematis 'Elgar'

Origin: Unknown.

Parentage and year: Unknown. 1990s.

Habit: Hardy, moderately vigorous, deciduous climber.

Height: 2–3 m (6.5–10 ft.).

Description: The single to almost semi-double, bluish mauve flowers measure 15–20 cm (6–8 in.) across and are composed of six to eight (when single) to eleven to twelve (when semi-double) tepals with pointed tips, which recurve as the flower matures, giving the appearance of a floppy habit. Young flowers display a more reddish colour on the tepals. There is a whitish central bar on the reverse of the tepals with purple ribbing and mauvish blue margins. Pale mauve filaments and yellow anthers make up the stamens.

Pruning group: 2.

Flowering period: Late spring to early summer and late summer.

Cultivation: Tolerates most garden soils. Best grown in full sun or partial shade.

Clematis 'Elizabeth'. Photo by M. Bracher.

Recommended use: Suitable for a medium-sized obelisk or a trellis. Would make a useful container plant for a few years before being planted out. Zones 4–9.

Clematis 'Elizabeth'
MONTANA GROUP

Synonym: *C. montana* 'Elizabeth'

Origin: Raised by Rowland Jackman of George Jackman and Son, England. Awarded RHS Award of Garden Merit.

Parentage and year: Selected form of *C. montana*. 1958.

Habit: Vigorous, deciduous climber.

Height: 7–10 m (23–30 ft.).

Description: The single, vanilla-scented, pale pink flowers with a satiny sheen measure 6 cm (2.25 in.) across and are composed of four slightly gappy tepals. The central boss has pale yellow stamens. Leaves bronze when young, turning to midgreen with age.

Pruning group: 1. Any pruning to keep the plant in check should be carried out immediately after the main flowering period by removing some of the old, flowered stems.

Flowering period: Late spring to early summer, with occasional flowers in late summer.

Cultivation: Suitable for sun or partial shade, although flowers may be paler, bordering on white, when in shade. Produces the strongest scent and colour in a sunny position.

Recommended use: Grow through medium-sized to large trees and conifers. Zones 7–9.

Clematis 'Elsa Späth'

Trade name: BLUE BOY (in Australia)

Synonym: *C.* 'Xerxes'

Origin: Raised by L. Späth of Berlin, Germany. Awarded RHS Award of Garden Merit.

Parentage and year: Unknown. 1891.

Habit: Hardy, moderately vigorous, compact, deciduous climber.

Height: 1.8–2.1 m (6–7 ft.).

Description: The single, early, rounded, rich dark blue flowers fade with time to paler mauvish blue with a hint of pink and measure 15–17 cm (6–7 in.) in diameter. They are composed of usually six, sometimes seven or eight, broad, overlapping tepals. A mass of white filaments and dark red anthers constitutes the stamens. Flowers produced later in the season are smaller.

Pruning group: 2.

Flowering period: Early summer to midsummer and early autumn.

Cultivation: Tolerates most garden soils and any aspect.

Recommended use: Ideal for containers. May be grown to cover bare lower stems of moderately vigorous wall-trained shrubs and roses which do not require severe annual pruning. Suitable for a small obelisk or short trellis. Zones 4–9.

Clematis 'Elvan'
VITICELLA GROUP

Synonym: *C. viticella* 'Elvan'

Origin: Raised by Barry Fretwell of Peveril Clematis Nursery, England.

Parentage and year: Unknown, but possibly a selected form of *C. viticella*. 1979.

Habit: Hardy, vigorous, deciduous climber.

Clematis 'Elsa Späth'. Photo by C. Chesshire.

Height: 3–4 m (10–13 ft.).

Description: A very floriferous cultivar. The single, small 5-cm (2-in.) purple, nodding flowers carry four tepals with a diffused pale white bar along the midrib. Tepals may recurve gently at the tips. Yellowish green anthers are carried on greenish filaments. Leaves are light green and are composed of five to seven leaflets.

Pruning group: 3.

Clematis 'Elvan'. Photo by E. Leeds.

Flowering period: Midsummer to late summer.

Cultivation: Tolerates most garden soils and any aspect.

Recommended use: Ideal specimen plant on an obelisk. Shows up well against a light background. Suitable for training through medium-sized trees, conifers, or large shrubs or on a trellis against a white wall. Zones 3–9.

Clematis 'Emilia Plater'

Origin: Raised by Brother Stefan Franczak of Warsaw, Poland, and named after a Polish heroine.

Parentage and year: Unknown. 1989.

Habit: Hardy, quite vigorous, deciduous climber.

Height: 2.5–3 m (8–10 ft.).

Description: The single, small, violet-blue flowers, measuring 10 cm (4 in.) in diameter, are produced freely over a long period and are composed of four broad, rather rounded tepals, which are semi-nodding at first but open and slightly recurve as they mature. Each tepal boasts a darker violet-veined central bar,

Clematis 'Emilia Plater'. Photo by C. Chesshire.

textured upper surface, and crimped margins. The leaves are midgreen with five to seven leaflets.

Pruning group: 3.

Flowering period: Midsummer to late summer.

Cultivation: Tolerates most garden soils and any aspect.

Recommended use: Ideal companion for medium-sized shrubs and climbing roses. May be grown to great advantage on a pergola, medium-sized obelisk, or trellis. Zones 4–9.

Clematis 'Empress of India'

Origin: Raised by Thomas Cripps and Son of Tunbridge Wells, England.

Parentage and year: *C.* 'Fairy Queen' × *C.* 'Ville de Lyon'. Before 1912.

Habit: Hardy, moderately vigorous, deciduous climber.

Height: 2.5–3 m (8–10 ft.).

Description: The single, well-shaped, mauvish red flowers measure 15–18 cm (6–7 in.) in diameter and are composed of six tepals, each with a deeper reddish purple central bar. Anthers are pale brown.

Pruning group: 2.

Flowering period: Early summer to late summer.

Cultivation: Tolerates most garden soils and any aspect. Requires a sheltered position to prevent wind damage to the flowers.

Recommended use: Grow as a companion for climbing roses and other wall-trained shrubs which do not require annual pruning. Suitable for a medium-sized pergola, trellis, or obelisk. Zones 4–9.

Clematis 'Entel'

Origin: Raised by Uno Kivistik of Harjumaa, Estonia. The name is the first word in a nursery rhyme.

Parentage and year: *C.* 'Hagley Hybrid' × *C.* 'Alba Luxurians'. 1984.

Habit: Hardy, not-so-vigorous, deciduous climber.

Height: 2–2.5 m (6.5–8 ft.).

Description: The single, small, well-formed, pale pinkish mauve flowers produced in great profusion measure 8–10 cm (3.25–4 in.) in diameter and are composed of six to eight tepals with gently notched edges and sharp flexible tips. Anthers are pale greenish yellow. Leaves have five leaflets arranged in pairs on both sides of the leaf axis.

Pruning group: 3.

Flowering period: Midsummer to late summer.

Cultivation: Tolerates most garden soils and any aspect.

Recommended use: Grow up and over medium-sized prostrate conifers or shrubs. Suitable for an obelisk or short trellis. Attractive when allowed to tumble over a low wall or fence. Zones 4–9.

Clematis 'Eriostemon'
HERBACEOUS/INTEGRIFOLIA GROUP

Synonym: *C.* ×*eriostemon*

Origin: Unclear, believed to be raised in the Netherlands.

Parentage and year: *C. integrifolia* × *C. viticella*. ca. 1830.

Habit: Hardy, deciduous, non-clinging, sprawling, semi-woody shrub.

Clematis 'Empress of India'. Photo by J. Lindmark.

Clematis 'Entel'. Photo by C. Chesshire.

Height: 1.8–2.4 m (6–8 ft.).

Description: The single, nodding, bell-shaped, dark purple-blue flowers are 6.5–9 cm (2.5–3.5 in.) across and are composed of four tepals, which open wide and recurve with age. Greenish white filaments and pale yellow anthers make up the stamens.

Pruning group: 3.

Flowering period: Early summer to late summer.

Cultivation: Tolerates most garden soils and any aspect. If trained on an artificial support, the stems need tying-in.

Recommended use: Grow naturally through other mixed border plants, prostrate shrubs, and conifers. Zones 4–9.

Clematis 'Ernest Markham'

Origin: Raised by Ernest Markham, head gardener at Gravetye Manor, and named by Rowland Jackman of George Jackman and Son, England, in December 1937, after Markham's death.

Parentage and year: Unknown. Before 1937.

Habit: Hardy, vigorous, deciduous climber. Though a strong grower, somewhat shy to flower in abundance.

Height: 3–3.6 m (10–12 ft.).

Description: The single, rounded, rich petunia-red flowers measure 10–15 cm (4–6 in.) in diameter and are composed of six broad, overlapping tepals which taper to a point, with crimped margins. The stamens are beige in colour and not prominent.

Pruning group: Optional, 2, or 3. Plants that are not pruned or lightly pruned produce early flowers from old wood.

Flowering period: Early summer to late summer or early autumn.

Cultivation: Tolerates most garden soils. Suitable for

Clematis 'Eriostemon'. Photo by J. Lindmark.

Clematis 'Ernest Markham'. Photo by C. Chesshire.

any aspect but flowers better when grown in a sunny position. Flowering period can be extended by using a combination of both pruning groups.

Recommended use: Grow up and over medium-sized trees or large shrubs. Suitable for a trellis, arbour, pergola, or pillar. Zones 4–9.

Clematis 'Etoile de Malicorne'

Origin: Raised by A. Girault of Orléans, France.

Parentage and year: Unknown. Before 1968.

Habit: Hardy, moderately vigorous, deciduous climber.

Height: 2.5–3 m (8–10 ft.).

Description: The single, rich purple-blue flowers are 15–17 cm (6–7 in.) wide and composed of eight broad, slightly overlapping, pointed tepals, which remain cupped for some time, soon after opening. Each tepal carries a narrow, reddish purple central bar, and the base colour tends to fade as the flower matures. The reverse of each tepal is midblue with a whitish bar. The stamens are made of white filaments and dark red anthers.

Pruning group: 2.

Flowering period: Late spring to early summer and early autumn.

Cultivation: Tolerates most garden soils and any aspect.

Recommended use: Grow where the young cupped flowers can be enjoyed. Shows up well against a light background, such as a silver-leaved shrub which does not require pruning. Zones 4–9.

Clematis 'Etoile de Paris'

Origin: Raised by Christen of Versailles, France.

Parentage and year: Unknown. ca. 1885.

Habit: Hardy, fairly vigorous but compact, deciduous climber.

Height: 1.8–2.4 m (6–8 ft.).

Description: The single, rather large, well-formed, deep mauvish blue flowers measure 15–17 cm (6–7 in.) across and are composed of eight short, fine-pointed tepals, each with a reddish central bar. The tepals are slightly gappy at the base. White filaments and dark red anthers make up the central boss of stamens. Leaves in threes are small and leathery.

Pruning group: 2.

Flowering period: Late spring to early summer and late summer.

Cultivation: Tolerates most garden soils and any aspect. Requires a sheltered position to prevent wind damage to the flowers.

Recommended use: Ideal against a white wall or other light background. Grow with wall-trained shrubs or roses which do not require pruning. Suitable as a specimen plant on an obelisk or trellis, or in a large container. Zones 4–9.

Clematis 'Etoile Rose'
TEXENSIS-VIORNA GROUP

Synonym: *C. texensis* 'Etoile Rose'

Origin: Raised by Victor Lemoine of Nancy, France. Awarded RHS Award of Garden Merit.

Parentage and year: *C.* ×*globulosa* (*C. hirsutissima* var.

Clematis 'Etoile de Malicorne'. Photo by J. Lindmark.

Clematis 'Etoile de Paris'. Photo by C. Chesshire.

Clematis 'Etoile Rose' growing up *Picea pungens* f. *glauca*. Photo courtesy Thorncroft Clematis Nursery.

scottii × *C. texensis*) × unknown variety of *C. viticella*. 1903.

Habit: Hardy, vigorous, deciduous climber. Normally herbaceous in habit with new shoots emerging from below ground level.

Height: 3–4 m (10–13 ft.).

Description: A strong-growing, floriferous cultivar. The single, nodding and semi-nodding flowers are open bell shaped, 5–7.5 cm (2–3 in.) across, with the four tepals recurving at the tips. Inside the tepals, the base colour is light pink with a deep cherry-pink bar along the centre, whilst on the outside the same bar is apparent along the centre of each tepal, but with a more pronounced light pink margin.

Pruning group: 3.

Flowering period: Midsummer to early autumn.

Cultivation: Tolerates most garden soils. Suitable for sun or partial shade. Can be prone to mildew. Take early precaution by spraying with a fungicide monthly from late spring to the end of flowering period. New shoots at soil level need protection from slugs and snails.

Recommended use: Grow through medium-sized trees or over a pergola, arbour, or arch, where it is possible to view the inside of the flowers. Ideal companion for climbing roses. Zones 4–9.

Clematis 'Etoile Violette'
VITICELLA GROUP

Synonym: *C. viticella* 'Etoile Violette'

Origin: Raised by Francisque Morel of Lyon, France. Awarded RHS Award of Garden Merit.

Parentage and year: Unknown. 1885.

Habit: Hardy, deciduous climber. Quite vigorous once established.

Height: 3–4 m (10–13 ft.).

Description: The single, semi-nodding, somewhat gappy, dark purple flowers, measuring 6–9 cm (2.25–3.5 in.) across, are produced in great profusion over a long flowering period on the new season's stems. There are four to six velvety textured tepals with a central boss of contrasting creamy yellow stamens. Leaves are midgreen with usually five leaflets.

Pruning group: 3.

Flowering period: Midsummer to late summer.

Cultivation: Tolerates most garden soils and any aspect.

Recommended use: Can be used as a specimen plant on an obelisk, pergola, or trellis. Shows up well against a light background. Grow naturally through medium-sized trees, conifers, or large shrubs. Makes a splendid companion for climbing roses with yellow or salmon-coloured flowers. Zones 3–9.

Clematis 'Etoile Rose'. Photo by J. Lindmark.

Clematis 'Etoile Violette'. Photo by J. Lindmark.

Clematis 'Evifive'

Trade name: LIBERATION

Origin: Raised by Raymond Evison of Guernsey Clematis Nursery. Named in 1995 to commemorate the 50th anniversary of the liberation of the Channel Islands from German occupation. Plant Breeders' Rights.

Parentage and year: Unknown (open-pollinated chance seedling). Before 1990.

Habit: Hardy, strong-growing, deciduous climber.

Height: 2.4–3 m (8–10 ft.).

Description: The single, striking cerise-pink flowers, 10–20 cm (4–8 in.) wide, are formed of six to eight broad, blunt-tipped, slightly overlapping tepals, each with gently notched or scalloped edges and carrying a deep cerise central band. Pinkish grey filaments and golden yellow anthers make up the contrasting stamens.

Pruning group: 2.

Flowering period: Late spring to early summer and late summer. Early flowers during late spring are much larger than those borne during late summer.

Cultivation: Tolerates most garden soils and any aspect. Requires protection from strong winds.

Recommended use: Ideal for growing naturally through small trees or medium-sized to large shrubs which do not require annual pruning. Suitable for a pergola, trellis, or arch. Zones 4–9.

Clematis 'Evifour'

Trade name: ROYAL VELVET

Origin: Raised by Raymond Evison of Guernsey Clematis Nursery. Plant Breeders' Rights.

Parentage and year: Unknown (a chance seedling). 1993.

Habit: Hardy, moderately vigorous, compact, deciduous climber.

Height: 2 m (6.5 ft.).

Description: The single flowers, 10–15 cm (4–6 in.) wide, are composed of six to eight overlapping, velvet-purple tepals, each with a reddish purple central bar. Pinkish white filaments carry dark red anthers. Flowers are borne in abundance.

Pruning group: 2.

Flowering period: Late spring to early summer and early autumn.

Cultivation: Tolerates most garden soils and any aspect.

Recommended use: Suitable for the small garden. Ideal for a small obelisk or trellis. May also be grown and trained in a large container or planted in the ground to hide the bare lower stems of other wall-

Clematis 'Evifive' (LIBERATION™). Photo by J. Lindmark.

Clematis 'Evifour' (ROYAL VELVET™). Photo by J. Lindmark.

trained plants which do not require severe pruning. Zones 4–9.

Clematis 'Evijohill'

Trade name: JOSEPHINE

Origin: An unnamed clematis originally bought by Josephine Hill in 1980 for her English garden and introduced by Guernsey Clematis Nursery in 1998. Plant Breeders' Rights.

Parentage and year: Unknown (a chance seedling). Mid-1990s.

Habit: A compact, hardy, deciduous climber.

Height: 1.8–2.4 m (6–8 ft.).

Description: The sumptuous double flowers, 10–12.5 cm (4–5 in.) in diameter, are composed of a basal row of six to eight lilac-pink, broad but pointed tepals, each with a tinge of green and a deeper pink central bar. Each successive layer is slightly shorter than the previous one, and the tepals are similar in colour but are narrower. As the flowers mature the green tinge fades away. Only double flowers are produced throughout the flowering season. There are no stamens.

Pruning group: 2.

Flowering period: Early summer to early autumn.

Cultivation: Tolerates most garden soils. Best grown in full sun. Requires protection from strong winds. If green-tinged flowers are desired, plant in partial shade. Spent flowers tend to look unsightly and can be removed.

Recommended use: Grow on a small obelisk or trellis. Ideal for container-culture. Zones 4–9.

Clematis 'Evione'

Trade name: SUGAR CANDY

Origin: Raised by Raymond Evison of Guernsey Clematis Nursery. Plant Breeders' Rights.

Parentage and year: Unknown (a chance seedling). Introduced in 1994.

Habit: Hardy, moderately vigorous, deciduous climber.

Height: 2.4–3 m (8–10 ft.).

Description: The single, pale pinkish mauve flowers, 15–18 cm (6–7 in.) across, are composed of six to eight tapering and pointed tepals, each with a deeper pink veined central bar. The stamens carry greyish pink filaments and yellow anthers.

Pruning group: 2.

Flowering period: Late spring to early summer and early autumn.

Cultivation: Tolerates most garden soils. Best grown out of full sun to preserve flower colour.

Recommended use: Suitable for a medium-sized pergola, arbour, or trellis. Grow through large shrubs which require little or no pruning. Zones 4–9.

Clematis 'Evirida'

Trade name: PISTACHIO

Synonym: *C. florida* 'Evirida'

Origin: Raised by Raymond Evison of Guernsey Clematis Nursery. Plant Breeders' Rights.

Parentage and year: Sport of *C.* 'Evison'. Introduced in 1999.

Habit: Half-hardy, moderately vigorous, deciduous climber.

Clematis 'Evijohill' (JOSEPHINE™). Photo by J. Lindmark.

Clematis 'Evione' (SUGAR CANDY™). Photo by C. Chesshire.

Height: 2.4–3 m (8–10 ft.).

Description: The single, creamy white flowers, 8 cm (3.25 in.) across, are composed of six broad yet pointed, overlapping tepals surrounding a centre of pinkish grey anthers, in the middle of which is a green tuft of aborted stigmas. Late flowers in autumn carry a greenish tinge to the tepals.

Pruning group: Optional, 2, or 3. A hard pruning (group 3) results in the loss of early flowers.

Flowering period: In the garden, early summer to early autumn. Under glass, to late autumn.

Cultivation: Tolerates well-drained garden soils enriched with humus. Requires a warm, sheltered position.

Recommended use: In temperate regions, grow in a container in a conservatory or cold greenhouse. Zones 6–9.

Clematis 'Evisix'

HERBACEOUS GROUP

Trade name: PETIT FAUCON

Origin: Raised by Raymond Evison of Guernsey Clematis Nursery. Plant Breeders' Rights.

Parentage and year: Chance seedling of *C.* 'Daniel Deronda' (seed parent) and either *C. integrifolia* or *C.* 'Eriostemon' (pollen parent). 1989.

Habit: Hardy, non-clinging, herbaceous perennial.

Height: 0.75–1 m (2.5–3.25 ft.).

Description: Exquisite single, deep blue, nodding flowers, 7–9 cm (2.75–3.5 in.) wide, are made of four to six tepals. As the flower bud opens, the tepals twist slightly to expose a central boss of vivid orange-yellow stamens. When the flower opens fully, the tepals become intensely blue, almost steel blue, and the stamens become creamy white. Seedheads are almost silvery white. Light green simple leaves have bronze colouring when young, becoming dark green with age.

Pruning group: 3.

Flowering period: Midsummer to early autumn.

Cultivation: Tolerates most garden soils and any aspect. If trained on an artificial support, the stems need tying-in.

Recommended use: Grow through low or prostrate shrubs and conifers. Plant among other herbaceous plants which will support the stems in a border. Can be trained on a trellis or obelisk. Zones 3–9.

Clematis 'Evista'

Trade name: EVENING STAR

Origin: Raised by Raymond Evison of Guernsey Clematis Nursery. Plant Breeders' Rights.

Parentage and year: Unknown. Introduced in 1997.

Habit: Hardy, moderately vigorous, deciduous climber.

Height: 2.4–3 m (8–10 ft.).

Description: The single, plum-mauve flowers, measuring 15–20 cm (6–8 in.) across, are composed of six to eight broad yet pointed tepals, which overlap when young, but as the flower matures the tepals tend to twist and the margins crinkle. Each tepal carries a cerise bar running lengthways and matched on the reverse by three purple-red veins. The prominent boss has golden yellow stamens. Late season flowers are not quite so large or numerous.

Pruning group: 2.

Clematis 'Evirida' (PISTACHIO™). Photo by J. Lindmark.

Clematis 'Evisix' (PETIT FAUCON™). Photo by J. Lindmark.

Flowering period: Late spring to late summer.

Cultivation: Tolerates most garden soils. Best grown in sun or partial shade. Requires a sheltered position to prevent wind damage to the large flowers.

Recommended use: Suitable for a medium-sized obelisk or trellis or may be grown as a companion for other wall-trained plants which do not require severe annual pruning. Ideal for container-culture. Zones 4–9.

Clematis 'Evithree'

Trade name: ANNA LOUISE

Origin: Raised by Raymond Evison of Guernsey Clematis Nursery. Introduced in 1993. Plant Breeders' Rights.

Parentage and year: Unknown (a chance seedling). Before 1990.

Habit: Hardy, moderately vigorous, compact, deciduous climber.

Height: 1.8–2.4 m (6–8 ft.).

Description: A free-flowering cultivar. The single, striking, violet flowers, measuring 10–15 cm (4–6 in.) across, are composed of six to eight tepals, each with a red-purple bar along the centre. Anthers are light reddish brown.

Pruning group: 2.

Flowering period: Late spring to early summer and early autumn.

Cultivation: Tolerates most garden soils and any aspect.

Recommended use: Ideal for small gardens and large containers. Grow on a short obelisk or trellis. Zones 4–9.

Clematis 'Evitwo'

Trade name: ARCTIC QUEEN

Origin: Raised by Raymond Evison of Guernsey Clematis Nursery. Introduced in 1994. Plant Breeders' Rights.

Parentage and year: Unknown (a chance seedling). 1989.

Habit: Hardy, moderately vigorous, deciduous climber.

Height: 1.8–2.4 m (6–8 ft.).

Description: This extremely floriferous cultivar produces fully double flowers on both old wood from the previous season and new growth in the current one.

Clematis 'Evista' (EVENING STAR™). Photo by J. Lindmark.

Clematis 'Evithree' (ANNA LOUISE™). Photo by J. Lindmark.

Clematis 'Evitwo' (ARCTIC QUEEN™). Photo by J. Lindmark.

The creamy white flowers, 10–18 cm (4–7 in.) wide, carry a dozen or more pointed and overlapping tepals. Stamens are made of white filaments and yellow anthers.

Pruning group: 2.

Flowering period: Early summer to early autumn (double).

Cultivation: Tolerates most garden soils. Best grown in sun or partial shade. Requires protection from strong winds.

Recommended use: Grow with other wall-trained plants which do not require severe pruning. Ideal for container-culture. Zones 4–9.

Clematis 'Fair Rosamond'

Synonym: *C.* 'Fair Rosamund'

Origin: Raised by George Jackman and Son, England.

Parentage and year: Unknown. 1871.

Habit: Hardy, fairly vigorous but compact, deciduous climber.

Height: 2.5–3 m (8–10 ft.).

Description: The single, blush white flowers, 10–15 cm (4–6 in.) in diameter, are composed of six to eight overlapping, pointed tepals, which have a diffused pink central bar becoming pale and almost indistinct with age. A conspicuous central boss of dark purple-red anthers contrasts well with the tepal colour. Flower buds are very plump, slightly hairy, and globose. The well-formed, rounded, golden seedheads are long lasting. Some clones may emit a scent of violets.

Pruning group: 2.

Flowering period: Late spring to midsummer.

Cultivation: Tolerates most garden soils. Best grown out of full sun as flower colour fades, but the plant does require some sun to enhance the scent. Prefers a west-facing aspect.

Recommended use: Grow through dark foliage plants or with wall-trained shrubs which do not require pruning. Ideal for container-culture. Zones 4–9.

Clematis 'Fairy Queen'

Origin: Raised by Thomas Cripps and Son of Tunbridge Wells, England.

Parentage and year: Unknown. First displayed in 1875.

Habit: Hardy, vigorous, deciduous climber.

Height: 3–3.6 m (10–12 ft.).

Description: The single, large, pale pink flowers, 15–20 cm (6–8 in.) in diameter, are composed of eight broad, slightly gappy tepals, each with a mauvish pink central bar and intense veining. Yellow filaments carry dark reddish purple anthers.

Pruning group: Optional, 2, or 3. For early flowers, choose group 2; for late flowers, group 3.

Flowering period: Late spring or midsummer to late summer.

Cultivation: Tolerates most garden soils. Best grown in partial shade to preserve flower colour.

Recommended use: Shows up well against a dark background or with dark-leaved plants. Ideal for a trellis, pergola, or arch. Zones 4–9.

Clematis 'Fair Rosamond'. Photo by M. Toomey.

Clematis 'Fairy Queen'. Photo by C. Chesshire.

Clematis fasciculiflora

EVERGREEN GROUP

Synonym: *C. montana* var. *fasciculiflora*

Origin: Southwestern China (Yunnan).

Parentage and year: Species. 1889.

Habit: Half-hardy to hardy, vigorous, evergreen climber and scrambler.

Height: Up to 6 m (20 ft.).

Description: The single flowers are white to cream, 2 cm (0.75 in.) across and 3–4 cm (1.25–1.5 in.) long, nodding, and bell shaped. They are borne in axillary clusters of one to a few together. There are four tepals per flower. Each leaf is composed of three leaflets up to 10 cm (4 in.) long and no more than 5 cm (2 in.) wide. The leaves are roughly oval in outline, entire, and dark green with a silvery vein down the middle.

Pruning group: 1.

Flowering period: Early spring to midspring.

Cultivation: Requires a warm, sunny aspect and a wall or medium-sized tree on which to climb.

Recommended use: Best as a large conservatory plant. Zones 7–9.

Clematis fauriei

ATRAGENE GROUP

Origin: Japan.

Parentage and year: Species. 1899.

Habit: Hardy, compact, deciduous climber.

Height: To 2 m (6.5 ft.).

Description: The single, semi-nodding, bell-shaped, plum-purple to violet-purple flowers measure 5.5–7 cm (2.25–2.75 in.) across and are composed of four broad yet pointed tepals, each with recurving tip and prominent veining running from base to tip. There is an inner ring of paddle-shaped, pale purplish white staminodes completely hiding the fertile stamens from view. The leaves are pale green and finely cut.

Pruning group: 1.

Flowering period: Midspring to late spring and late summer.

Cultivation: Tolerates most well-drained garden soils and any aspect.

Recommended use: Suitable for a small obelisk or trellis. Allow to tumble over a low wall or grow through medium-sized shrubs which do not require annual pruning. Ideal for container-culture. Zones 3–9.

Clematis fasciculiflora. Photo by E. Leeds.

Clematis fauriei. Photo by C. Chesshire.

Clematis finetiana
EVERGREEN/ARMANDII GROUP

Origin: Central, eastern, and southern China.

Parentage and year: Species. 1904.

Habit: Half-hardy to hardy, moderately vigorous, semi-evergreen climber.

Height: To 4 m (13 ft.).

Description: The single, star-shaped, scented, greenish white flowers, 2–4 cm (0.75–1.5 in.) across, borne in axillary clusters of three to seven, are composed of four to six spear-shaped, pointed and spreading tepals that overlap at the base. The stamens are made of greenish white filaments, much shorter than the tepals, and creamy yellow anthers. Leaves made of three leaflets are somewhat leathery or tough, narrow, and roughly oval in shape but widest towards the leaf stalk, tapering to acute tips, bright green, smooth, and three veined.

Pruning group: 1.

Flowering period: Late spring to early summer.

Cultivation: Tolerates most garden soils with good drainage. Requires a warm, frost-free situation.

Recommended use: Grow on a warm, south-facing wall or in a cool greenhouse or conservatory. Zones 7–9.

Clematis 'Fireworks'

Origin: Raised by John Treasure, Treasures of Tenbury, England. Awarded RHS Award of Garden Merit.

Parentage and year: *C.* 'Maureen' × *C.* 'Nelly Moser'. Early 1980s.

Habit: Hardy, vigorous, deciduous climber.

Height: 2.5–3 m (8–10 ft.).

Description: The single, large, bluish purple flowers, 18–20 cm (7–8 in.) wide, are composed of six to eight tepals, each with a conspicuous twist, gently notched margins, and a bright cerise central bar. The reverse of each tepal boasts a greenish bar and mauve margins. The tepal tips tend to recurve slightly. The filaments are pale cream, and the anthers are dark red.

Pruning group: 2.

Clematis finetiana in the wild; Shizong-Xingyi, China. Photo by Phillip Cribb.

Clematis 'Fireworks'. Photo by R. Surman.

Flowering period: Late spring to early summer and early autumn.

Cultivation: Tolerates most garden soils and any aspect. Requires a sheltered position to prevent wind damage to the large flowers.

Recommended use: Grow as a specimen plant on an obelisk or with other plants on an arbour, trellis, or pergola. Zones 4–9.

Clematis flammula

Synonym: *C. recta* subsp. *flammula*

Origin: Southern Europe, northern Africa, and northern Iran.

Parentage and year: Species. Introduced into cultivation in 1590.

Habit: Hardy, vigorous, deciduous climber.

Height: 3–4.5 m (10–14.5 ft.) or more.

Description: A very floriferous species. Single, pure white, strongly scented flowers are borne laterally and terminally in large clusters. Each flower measures 2–3 cm (0.75–1.25 in.) across and is composed of four narrow, blunt-tipped tepals with a covering of very fine hairs beneath. The anthers are creamy white. Stems are green and grooved. Leaves are glossy deep green with a number of leaflets.

Pruning group: 3.

Flowering period: Late summer to midautumn.

Cultivation: Tolerates most garden soils but thrives in well-drained conditions. Produces the strongest scent in a sunny position. Moderately drought-resistant.

Recommended use: Plant against a wall or fence where the scent can be enjoyed. Grow with other vigorous small- and large-flowered cultivars which bloom at the same time and require similar pruning. Suitable for a pergola. Zones 4–9.

Clematis flammula. Photo by C. Chesshire.

Clematis 'Floralia'
ATRAGENE GROUP

Origin: Raised by Magnus Johnson of Södertälje, Sweden.

Parentage and year: *C. macropetala* × *C. ochotensis*. Introduced to the United Kingdom in 1980s.

Habit: Hardy, compact, deciduous climber.

Height: 1.8–2.4 m (6–8 ft.).

Description: The nodding, semi-double, powder-blue flowers are composed of four broad tepals, each 4 cm (1.5 in.) long and tapering to a point. The tepals of early flowers are sometimes tinged with green as they open. Flowers are borne on old wood from the previous season on purple-red stalks, and there is often a small flush of flowers later in the summer.

Pruning group: 1.

Flowering period: Midspring to late spring and late summer.

Cultivation: Tolerates most well-drained garden soils and any aspect.

Recommended use: Ideal for container-culture. Grow through small to medium-sized shrubs or on an obelisk or trellis. Zones 3–9.

Clematis 'Flore Pleno'
VITICELLA GROUP

Synonyms: *C. viticella* 'Mary Rose', *C.* 'Purpurea Plena'

Origin: This cultivar has an interesting history. A similar flower was mentioned in John Parkinson's *Par-adisi* (1629) and first illustrated in Robert Thurber's *Twelve Months of Flowers* (1730) as *Clematis viticella* 'Purpurea Plena'. Names given prior to Linneaus (ca. 1753), however, have no value, and a herbarium specimen at Leiden Herbarium, believed to have been secured by Adriaan van Royen (1704–1779) or by his son David (1727–1799), is labelled *C. viticella* 'Flore Pleno'. This clematis was then lost from cultivation until Barry Fretwell of Peveril Clematis Nursery, England, brought it back into commerce in 1981, coinciding with the raising of Henry VIII's flagship *Mary Rose* off Portsmouth in the English Channel.

Parentage and year: Unknown. Before 1623.

Habit: Hardy, deciduous climber. Vigorous once established.

Height: 3–4 m (10–13 ft.).

Description: The small, smoky amethyst, sterile flowers, measuring 4–5 cm (1.5–2 in.) wide and produced in profusion, are fully double rosettes with a spiky appearance. Leaves are similar to those of *C. viticella*, being light to midgreen and made of five to seven leaflets.

Pruning group: 3.

Flowering period: Midsummer to early autumn.

Cultivation: Tolerates most garden soils. Suitable for sun or partial shade.

Recommended use: Shows up well against a white or light background, such as a wall or through a medium-sized to large conifer or a tree with light-coloured foliage. Zones 3–9.

Clematis 'Floralia'. Photo by J. Lindmark.

Clematis 'Flore Pleno'. Photo by J. Lindmark.

Clematis florida

Origin: Southern and southeastern China. Naturalized in Japan.

Parentage and year: Species. First introduced from cultivated specimens in Japan in 1776.

Habit: Half-hardy, moderately vigorous, semi-evergreen to mostly deciduous, slender climber.

Height: 1.8–2.4 m (6–8 ft.), occasionally to 3 m (10 ft.).

Description: The single, solitary, pearly white flowers, are carried on slender, hairy stalks with a pair of leaflike structures (bracts) at the halfway point. Each flower, measuring 7.5–10 cm (3–4 in.) wide, is composed of four to six tepals, pointed, sometimes overlapping at their base and with grooves along the centre from base to tip. On the reverse of the tepal is a pale green bar running along the centre. The prominent stamens are a stunning feature, made of white filaments shading to dark purple and finally into purple-black anthers. Late season flowers are tinged with green. Stems are wiry and grooved. Leaves are deep green and glossy, divided into five to nine leaflets.

Pruning group: 2.

Flowering period: In the garden, late spring, with sporadic flowering to early autumn; under glass, late spring, with sporadic flowering to late autumn.

Cultivation: Requires well-drained but moist soil in a warm, sunny, and sheltered location if planted in the garden.

Recommended use: Best as a conservatory or glasshouse plant. Grow in containers with a suitable support. Train and tie-in the stems to achieve a spectacular display of flowers. Zones 6–9.

Clematis foetida
EVERGREEN GROUP

Origin: New Zealand.

Parentage and year: Species. 1846.

Habit: Half-hardy to hardy, vigorous, evergreen climber or scrambler.

Height: 5–6 m (16–20 ft.).

Description: The single, small, scented, yellowish flowers, 2.5 cm (1 in.) across, are borne in great profusion. Tepals number five to eight. Sometimes female plants are not scented. Leaves are deep green, smooth or slightly hairy, and divided into three leaflets.

Pruning group: 1.

Flowering period: Early spring.

Cultivation: Requires a warm, sunny aspect.

Recommended use: Grow in a cold greenhouse or conservatory. Zones 7–9.

Clematis forsteri
EVERGREEN GROUP

Origin: New Zealand.

Parentage and year: Species. 1791.

Habit: Half-hardy to hardy, moderately vigorous, evergreen climber or scrambler.

Height: 2 m (6.5 ft.).

Description: Male and female flowers are borne on separate plants. An abundance of single, lemon-scented, semi-nodding, open, star-shaped, creamy lime-green flowers, 2–3 cm (0.75–1.25 in.) wide, are produced on the previous season's old wood. Tepals number five to eight. Leaves are dark green and composed of three leaflets. Leaf shape and size vary considerably, and botanists are still trying to sort this particular group of the genus.

Pruning group: 1.

Flowering period: Early spring to midspring.

Cultivation: Requires a sunny, sheltered position.

Recommended use: Male plants recommended because the flowers and leaves are much larger than those of female. Grow in a container under glass in a conservatory or cold greenhouse to enjoy the scent. Move outdoors during the summer. Zones 8–9.

Clematis florida. Photo by C. Chesshire.

Clematis forsteri. Photo by M. Toomey.

Clematis 'Foxtrot'
VITICELLA GROUP

Synonym: *C. viticella* 'Foxtrot'

Origin: Raised by Barry Fretwell of Peveril Clematis Nursery, England.

Parentage and year: Unknown. 1990s

Habit: Hardy, moderately vigorous, deciduous climber.

Height: 2.4–3 m (8–10 ft.).

Description: The single, small, bluish purple flowers, 7.5–9 cm (3–3.5 in.) across, are composed of four or five broad, spear-shaped tepals, each with white centres most prominently at the base and fading towards the tip by way of deep veining. On mature flowers the tepal margins tend to be gently undulating and in the tips recurving, giving a blunt appearance. The tepal colour is complemented by light green filaments and dark brown anthers.

Pruning group: 3.

Flowering period: Midsummer to late summer.

Cultivation: Tolerates most garden soils and any aspect.

Recommended use: Ideal for a pergola, large trellis, or obelisk. Grow up and over large shrubs and on tall conifers. Zones 4–9.

Clematis 'Foxy'
ATRAGENE GROUP

Synonym: *C. alpina* 'Foxy'

Origin: Raised by Raymond Evison of Guernsey Clematis Nursery.

Parentage and year: Sport of *C.* 'Frankie'. 1980s.

Habit: Hardy, moderately vigorous, deciduous climber.

Height: 2.4–3 m (8–10 ft.).

Description: The single, small, pale pink, bell-shaped, nodding flowers are composed of four narrow, sharp-pointed, spear-shaped tepals 5 cm (2 in.) long, with a darker shading near the base and on the thin ridges and lines running from the base towards the tips. There is an inner skirt of staminodes shaded pale pink, and the foliage is light green with serrated margins resembling the teeth of a saw.

Pruning group: 1.

Flowering period: Midspring to late spring.

Cultivation: Tolerates most well-drained garden soils and any aspect.

Recommended use: Ideal for small gardens and for north-facing aspects. Suitable for a medium-sized pergola or trellis or with other wall-trained plants which do not require annual pruning. Suitable for container-culture. Zones 3–9.

Clematis 'Fragrant Spring'
MONTANA GROUP

Synonym: *C. montana* 'Fragrant Spring'

Origin: Unknown.

Parentage and year: Unknown.

Habit: Vigorous, deciduous climber.

Height: 6–9 m (20–29 ft.).

Description: The single, saucer-shaped, scented, light pink-mauve flowers are made of four broad, rounded tepals and yellow stamens. The attractive leaves are bronze coloured.

Clematis 'Foxtrot'. Photo by E. Leeds.

Clematis 'Foxy'. Photo by C. Chesshire.

Pruning group: 1. Any pruning to keep the plant in check should be carried out immediately after the main flowering period by removing some of the old, flowered stems.

Flowering period: Midspring to late spring.

Cultivation: Tolerates most well-drained garden soils. Hardy in temperate gardens. Suitable for any aspect but produces the strongest scent in a sunny position.

Recommended use: Suitable for a large pergola or arch. Grow over a boundary wall or fence or through large, open trees. Zones 7–9.

Clematis 'Frances Rivis' (Dutch form)
ATRAGENE GROUP

Synonyms: *C. alpina* 'Francis Rivis, *C. alpina* 'Frances Rives'

Origin: Unclear but probably around Boskoop, Netherlands.

Parentage and year: Selected seedling, possibly *C. ochotensis* × *C. alpina*. Unknown.

Habit: Hardy, moderately vigorous, deciduous climber.

Height: 2.4–3 m (8–10 ft.).

Description: The single, nodding, bright deep blue flowers, measuring 4.5–5 cm (1.75–2 in.) long, are composed of four broad tepals, which are pointed yet shorter and wider in the middle than the English form. Unlike the tepals of the English form, the margins do not twist and turn. There is an inner skirt of short, whitish cream staminodes, which surrounds the yellow stamens.

Pruning group: 1.

Flowering period: Early to late spring, with occasional flowers in late summer.

Cultivation: Dislikes wet, badly drained soils. Suitable for any aspect.

Recommended use: Grow on a medium-sized obe-

Clematis 'Frances Rivis' (Dutch form). Photo by E. Leeds.

Clematis 'Frances Rivis' (English form). Photo by C. Chesshire.

Clematis 'Fragrant Spring'. Photo by R. Surman.

lisk or trellis or through shrubs which do not require severe annual pruning. Zones 3–9.

Clematis 'Frances Rivis' (English form)
ATRAGENE GROUP

Synonyms: *C. alpina* 'Blue Giant', *C. alpina* 'Francis Rivis', *C. alpina* 'Frances Rives'

Origin: Raised by Sir Cedric Morris of England. Awarded RHS Award of Garden Merit.

Parentage and year: Selected seedling, possibly *C. ochotensis* × *C. alpina*. 1965.

Habit: Hardy, moderately vigorous, deciduous climber.

Height: 2.5–3 m (8–10 ft.).

Description: Single, deep sky blue flowers have four tepals, each 6 cm (2.25 in.) long. White petal-like stamens form a central cluster. Leaves are composed of three leaflets, and leaf margins are serrated, resembling the teeth of a saw.

Pruning group: 1. Any pruning to keep the plant tidy should be carried out immediately after the main flowering period.

Flowering period: Midspring to late spring, with a few flowers in late summer.

Cultivation: Needs sharp drainage. Suitable for any aspect.

Recommended use: Good for small gardens and patios. Ideal for north- and east-facing aspects. Zones 3–9.

Clematis 'Frankie'
ATRAGENE GROUP

Synonym: *C. alpina* 'Frankie'

Origin: Raised by Frank Meecham of Lincolnshire, England, and introduced by Raymond Evison of Guernsey Clematis Nursery.

Parentage and year: Seedling of *C. alpina*. 1990.

Habit: Hardy, moderately vigorous, deciduous climber or scrambler.

Height: 2.5–3 m (8–10 ft.).

Clematis 'Frankie'. Photo by R. Savill.

Description: The single, midblue flowers have four broad tepals, each 5 cm (2 in.) long, and creamy white staminodes. The outer ring of tepals is tinged with pale blue at the tips. Leaves are composed of three leaflets, and the leaf margins are serrated, resembling the teeth of a saw.

Pruning group: 1. Any pruning to keep the plant tidy should be carried out immediately after the main flowering period.

Flowering period: Midspring to late spring.

Cultivation: Needs sharp drainage. Suitable for any aspect.

Recommended use: Good for small gardens and patios. Ideal for north- or east-facing aspects. Zones 3–9.

Clematis 'Freckles'
EVERGREEN/CIRRHOSA GROUP

Synonym: *C. cirrhosa* 'Freckles'

Origin: Raised by Raymond Evison of Guernsey Clematis Nursery from wild seed collected in the Balearic Islands, Spain, and named after one of his daughters. Awarded RHS Award of Garden Merit.

Parentage and year: Open-pollinated wild species seed. Introduced in 1989.

Habit: Half-hardy to hardy, quite vigorous, evergreen climber.

Height: 3–4 m (10–13 ft.).

Description: The single, nodding, creamy pink flowers are held on long stalks, and the four tepals are 4–5 cm (1.5–2 in.) long, with reddish maroon speckling on the insides. The leaves are larger than those of *C. cirrhosa*.

Clematis 'Freckles'. Photo by D. Harding.

Pruning group: 1. Any pruning to keep the plant in check should be carried out immediately after the main flowering period by cutting back to 1 m (3.25 ft.) from the ground once the plant is well established.

Flowering period: Midautumn to late autumn.

Cultivation: Thrives in well-drained and somewhat gritty soils in a sunny, warm position. Occasionally plants go into a summer dormancy before putting on new growth prior to the flowering season. Refrain from overwatering particularly during dormancy.

Recommended use: Best at the back of a border on a wall or fence. Zones 7–9.

Clematis 'Freda'
MONTANA GROUP

Synonym: *C. montana* 'Freda'

Origin: Raised by Freda Deacon of Woodbridge, Suffolk, England, and introduced by Jim Fisk of Fisk's Clematis Nursery, Suffolk, England.

Parentage and year: Seedling of *C.* 'Pink Perfection'. 1985.

Habit: Moderately vigorous, deciduous climber.

Height: To 6 m (20 ft.).

Description: The single, deep cherry pinkish red flowers are 5 cm (2 in.) across and have four tepals with paler pink bars down their centres. The attractive bronze leaves turn midgreen with maturity.

Clematis 'Freda'. Photo by E. Leeds.

Pruning group: 1. Any pruning to keep the plant in check should be carried out immediately after the main flowering period by removing some of the old, flowered stems.

Flowering period: Late spring to early summer.

Cultivation: Needs sharp drainage. Suitable for sun or partial shade but gives deepest colour when planted in full sun.

Recommended use: Good for the small garden. Ideal with medium-sized trees and conifers. Suitable for a pergola or free-standing, large, and sturdy trellis. Zones 7–9.

Clematis fremontii
HERBACEOUS/INTEGRIFOLIA GROUP

Origin: United States (central-northern Kansas, south-central Nebraska, and in parts of southern and eastern Missouri).

Parentage and year: Species. 1875.

Habit: Erect, compact, herbaceous perennial.

Height: Up to 40 cm (16 in.), occasionally taller.

Description: The nodding to semi-nodding, pitcher-shaped, solitary and terminal flowers, measuring 2–4 cm (0.75–1.5 in.) long, are produced from the current season's growth. Each flower is composed of four thick, purple or pale blue-lavender, slightly hairy tepals, creamy yellow within, with margins which slightly spread towards the strongly recurved, pale greenish tips. The stamens are creamy white. The stems are rather stout and hairy, and carry several pairs of simple, broadly oval to rounded leaves with smooth to coarsely toothed margins and conspicuous netlike veining.

Clematis fremontii. Photo by R. Kirkman.

Pruning group: 3.

Flowering period: Midsummer onwards.

Cultivation: Difficult to grow. Requires extremely good drainage since plants in the wild are found on rocky hillsides with limestone soils. Quite drought-resistant in its natural habitat and therefore should not be overwatered. Prefers to be kept virtually dry and resents winter wet. Requires a warm, sheltered location in the garden to grow and flower successfully.

Recommended use: Best grown as a container plant in a cold greenhouse where growing conditions can be monitored and regulated. Zone 4.

Clematis fruticosa

Origin: Mongolia and northern China.

Parentage and year: Species. Unknown.

Habit: Hardy, non-climbing, twiggy, deciduous sub-shrub.

Height: 0.5–1.2 m (1.8–4 ft.).

Description: The single, semi-nodding, bell-shaped, yellow flowers are 2–4.5 cm (0.75–1.75 in.) across and composed of four thick, broad yet pointed tepals borne singly or in groups of two or three on terminal shoots. The tips of the tepals curve slightly backwards revealing red anthers. Leaves are deep green, thick, and leathery.

Pruning group: 3.

Flowering period: Midsummer to early autumn.

Cultivation: In the wild grows on dry rocky banks, scrubby hillsides, cliffs, and river gravels. Needs sharp drainage. Poor soils appear to be the norm. Suitable for any aspect.

Recommended use: Ideal for container-culture or an alpine scree bed. Zones 5–9.

Clematis 'Fryderyk Chopin'

Origin: Raised by Brother Stefan Franczak of Warsaw, Poland, and named after the famous Polish-born composer.

Parentage and year: Chance seedling. 1995.

Habit: Hardy, moderately vigorous, compact, deciduous climber.

Height: 1.2–2.4 m (4–8 ft.).

Description: The single, neat, purple-red flowers, measuring 10–15 cm (4–6 in.) across, are composed of six oval tepals, which overlap at the base and have irregularly notched and slightly wavy margins terminating in gently recurving tips. Creamy white, short filaments with deep purple-red anthers contrast and harmonize with the tepal colour. Flowers are produced profusely over a long period of time.

Pruning group: 2.

Flowering period: Early summer to late summer.

Cultivation: Tolerates most garden soils and any aspect.

Recommended use: Suitable for a medium-sized obelisk, free-standing trellis, pole, or post. Grow with other not-too-vigorous wall-trained shrubs which do not require annual pruning. Zones 4–9.

Clematis 'Fryderyk Chopin'. Photo by M. Humphries.

Clematis 'Fujimusume'. Photo by J. Lindmark.

Clematis 'Fujimusume'

Origin: Raised by Seijūrō Arai of Japan.

Parentage and year: *C.* 'Asagasumi' × *C.* 'The President'. 1952.

Habit: Hardy, strong-growing, compact, deciduous climber.

Height: 2–2.5 m (6–8 ft.).

Description: Flower buds are very large and plump with a dense covering of short, whitish hairs. The single, rather large, flattish, light blue flowers, measuring 16–18 cm (6.25–7 in.) in diameter, are composed of six to eight tepals, with a smooth, velvety texture, slightly overlapping and tapering towards the tips. There is a prominent central boss of golden yellow stamens. Flowers borne later in the season are smaller. Seedheads are well-shaped, attractive, and golden. Large, glossy, dark green leaves with entire margins enliven the plant.

Pruning group: Optional, 2, or 3. A hard pruning (group 3) results in the loss of early flowers.

Flowering period: Early summer to midsummer and late summer.

Cultivation: Tolerates most garden soils. Best grown away from direct sunshine in a sheltered place.

Recommended use: Suitable for a small obelisk, pillar, or small arch. Excellent for container-culture. Zones 4–9.

Clematis fusca

Origin: Northern China and islands north of the Japanese mainland.

Parentage and year: Species. First mentioned in 1840.

Habit: Hardy, moderately vigorous, deciduous climber. Some shorter forms are self-supporting.

Height: 1–3 m (3.25–10 ft.).

Description: The single, nodding or semi-nodding, urn-shaped, dark purple flowers, 2–3 cm (0.75–1.25 in.) long, are composed of four tepals, which are covered in short, woolly brown hairs. Each tepal is deeply ribbed with its tip slightly recurving, exposing the pale green undersides and creamy yellow stamens. The leaves are divided into five to nine leaflets, which are roughly oval in outline but widest toward the stalk. Some leaflets are broadly lobed, and the leaf margins are smooth edged or entire. Prominent seedheads are produced after flowering.

Pruning group: 3.

Flowering period: Early summer to early autumn.

Cultivation: Needs sharp drainage. Tolerates most garden soils and any aspect.

Recommended use: Ideal for container-culture or to grow through another wall-trained shrub. Shows up well against a light or white background. Zones 3–9.

Clematis fusca var. *violacea*

Synonym: *C. ianthina* var. *ianthina*

Origin: China and Korea.

Parentage and year: A variant of *C. fusca*. First mentioned in 1859.

Habit: Hardy, not-so-vigorous, deciduous climber.

Height: 1.8–2.4 m (6–8 ft).

Description: The single, small, nodding to semi-nodding, urn-shaped brownish purple flowers, 2–3 cm (0.75–1.25 in.) long, are composed of four ribbed tepals, which recurve at their tips exposing purple-blue

insides and creamy green anthers. The flowers are followed by large seedheads.

Pruning group: 3.

Flowering period: Early to late summer.

Cultivation: Prefers sharp drainage. Tolerates most garden soils and any aspect.

Recommended use: Ideal for container-culture. Shows up well against a light or white background. Zones 3–9.

Clematis 'G. Steffner'
ATRAGENE GROUP

Origin: Raised by Gustaf Steffner of Åmål, Sweden.

Parentage and year: *C. macropetala* × *C. sibirica*. ca. 1945.

Habit: Hardy, moderately vigorous, deciduous climber.

Height: 3–4 m (10–13 ft.).

Description: The nodding, single flowers, 8–12 cm (3.25–4.75 in.) across, are composed of four narrow, pointed, light bluish purple tepals which spread and open flat, with the tips turned upwards. The spatula-shaped, creamy white to white staminodes vary in length and form and are not petal-like. The stamens are greyish white.

Pruning group: 1. Any pruning to keep the plant tidy should be carried out immediately after the main flowering period.

Flowering period: Early to late spring.

Cultivation: Tolerates most well-drained garden soils and any aspect.

Recommended use: Grow through open shrubs

Clematis fusca. Photo by C. Chesshire.

Clematis fusca var. *violacea*. Photo by C. Chesshire.

Clematis 'G. Steffner'. Photo by J. Lindmark.

which do not require annual pruning, or with other wall-trained plants. Suitable for a pergola or obelisk. Ideal for north-facing locations. Zones 3–9.

Clematis 'Gabriëlle'

Origin: Unknown.

Parentage and year: Unknown.

Habit: Hardy, moderately vigorous, deciduous climber.

Height: 2.5–3 m (8–10 ft.).

Description: The single, mauvish blue flowers, 13–15 cm (5–6 in.) across, comprise six non-overlapping, boat-shaped tepals having slight tapering towards the tip, each grooved but not prominently so from the base to the tip. At the base there is a green shading which fades into the main tepal colour. The stamens are made of cream filaments and maroon anthers.

Pruning group: 2.

Flowering period: Late spring and late summer.

Cultivation: Tolerates most garden soils. Requires protection from strong winds.

Recommended use: Plant with wall-trained roses and shrubs or on a sheltered arbour or pergola. Zones 4–9.

Clematis gentianoides
EVERGREEN GROUP

Common name: Bushy clematis

Origin: Australia (Tasmania).

Parentage and year: Species. 1818.

Habit: Half-hardy, low, sprawling, bushy, evergreen herbaceous perennial or subshrub.

Height: 45–60 cm (18–24 in.).

Description: The single, scented, white flowers, 3–6 cm (1.25–2.25 in.) across, consist of four to eight narrow, spreading, upward-facing tepals. Flowers are borne on erect, terminal shoots and sometimes from leaf axils. The simple, undivided leaves are green to purplish green and rather fleshy and thick. Male and female flowers are borne on separate plants. Male flowers boast prominent greenish cream stamens whereas female ones have bunched styles, which if pollinated, make showy seedheads.

Pruning group: 1.

Flowering period: Early to late spring.

Cultivation: Prefers gritty, open, and fast-draining soil in sun or partial shade.

Recommended use: Best for container-culture in an alpine house, conservatory, or cold greenhouse. Zones 8–9.

Clematis gentianoides. Photo by S. Kuriyama.

Clematis 'Gabriëlle'. Photo by M. Humphries.

Clematis 'Georg'
ATRAGENE GROUP

Origin: Raised by Magnus Johnson of Södertälje, Sweden, and named after a gardening colleague, Georg Wettergren.

Parentage and year: *C. macropetala* × *C. fauriei*. 1985.

Habit: Hardy, moderately vigorous, compact, deciduous climber.

Height: 1.8–2.4 m (6–8 ft.).

Description: The open, bell-shaped, semi-double, purple-indigo flowers are composed of four broad yet pointed, silvery edged tepals, each 4 cm (1.5 in.) long and surrounding an inner skirt of similar coloured staminodes with paler tips. Leaves are bright green.

Pruning group: 1.

Flowering period: Midspring to late spring, with sporadic flowering in summer.

Cultivation: Tolerates most well-drained garden soils and any aspect.

Recommended use: Ideal for container-culture, or on a small to medium-sized obelisk or free-standing trellis. Can also be grown with open shrubs which require no annual pruning. Zones 3–9.

Clematis 'Georg Ots'

Origin: Raised by Maria F. Sharonova of Moscow and named after an Estonian singer.

Parentage and year: *C.* 'Luther Burbank' × pollen mixture. 1972.

Habit: Hardy, compact, deciduous climber.

Height: 1.8–2.4 m (6–8 ft.).

Description: The single, flat, violet-blue flowers, 13–15 cm (5–6 in.) across, are composed of six broad, spear-shaped and heavily textured tepals, which overlap at the base. Each tepal carries distinct veining on either side of three grooves; this veining is a slightly lighter shade and runs from the base to the tip. The centre of the flower is completed by the stamens made of white filaments and dark purple anthers.

Pruning group: 3.

Clematis 'Georg'. Photo by J. Lindmark.

Clematis 'Georg Ots'. Photo by J. Lindmark.

Flowering period: Midsummer to late summer.

Cultivation: Tolerates most garden soils enriched with humus. Suitable for any aspect.

Recommended use: Grow in a container or over a medium-sized shrub or prostrate conifer. Zones 3–9.

Clematis 'Gillian Blades'

Origin: Raised by Jim Fisk of Fisk's Clematis Nursery, Suffolk, England, and named after one of his secretaries. Awarded RHS Award of Garden Merit.

Parentage and year: Seedling of *C.* 'Lasurstern'. Introduced in 1975.

Habit: Hardy, not-so-vigorous, compact, deciduous climber.

Height: 1.8–2.4 m (6–8 ft.).

Description: The single, pure white flowers, 15–20 cm (6–8 in.) wide and opening flat, are composed of six to eight pointed tepals with gently notched and slightly undulating margins. The stamens are golden. Early flowers may be tinged with blue.

Pruning group: 2.

Flowering period: Late spring and late autumn.

Cultivation: Tolerates most garden soils and any aspect.

Recommended use: Ideal for container-culture. May be grown through low, prostrate conifers or shrubs which do not require annual pruning. Good against a red brick pillar or wooden post. Zones 4–9.

Clematis 'Gipsy Queen'

Origin: Raised by Thomas Cripps and Son of Tunbridge Wells, England.

Parentage and year: *C. patens* × *C.* 'Jackmanii'. 1877.

Habit: Hardy, vigorous, deciduous climber.

Height: 3–3.6 m (10–12 ft.).

Description: The single, velvety, violet-purple flowers, 12–14 cm (4.75–5.5 in.) wide, are composed of four to six broad and smooth tepals. They are blunt tipped but narrow at the base, giving the flower an open appearance. Dull white filaments and dark red anthers constitute the central mass of stamens. This cultivar is often confused with *C.* 'Jackmanii' and *C.* 'Jackmanii Superba'.

Pruning group: 3.

Flowering period: Midsummer to early autumn.

Cultivation: Tolerates most garden soils and any aspect.

Recommended use: Grow through medium-sized trees and large shrubs, or with other wall-trained shrubs or roses. Suitable for a medium-sized to large obelisk, pergola, or arbour. Shows up well against a light background. Zones 4–9.

Clematis 'Gladys Picard'

Origin: Raised by Jim Fisk of Fisk's Clematis Nursery, Suffolk, England, and named after one of his secretaries.

Clematis 'Gillian Blades'. Photo by C. Chesshire.

Clematis 'Gipsy Queen'. Photo by C. Chesshire.

Parentage and year: Unknown. 1975.

Habit: Hardy, moderately vigorous, deciduous climber.

Height: 2.5–3 m (8–10 ft.).

Description: The single, rather large, delicate mauvish pink flowers, 15–20 cm (6–8 in.) wide, are composed of eight broad, overlapping, and veined tepals. When young, the tepal margins slightly curve inwards, but the flower opens flat with age and, if in full sun, will fade to white. White filaments carrying golden anthers make up the central boss of stamens.

Pruning group: 2.

Flowering period: Late spring to early summer and late summer.

Cultivation: Tolerates most garden soils and any aspect. Best grown out of full sun to preserve delicate flower colour. Requires a sheltered position to prevent wind damage to the large flowers. Shows up well against a dark background.

Recommended use: Suitable for a pergola, freestanding trellis, or arch. Plant with other dark-leaved, wall-trained shrubs which do not require annual pruning. Zones 4–9.

Clematis 'Gladys Picard' flower colour fades to white with age. Photo by C. Chesshire.

Clematis glycinoides
EVERGREEN GROUP

Common name: Forest clematis

Origin: Australia.

Parentage and year: Species. 1818.

Habit: Half-hardy, very vigorous, evergreen climber.

Height: 3–4.6 m (10–14.5 ft.). Up to 20 m (66 ft.) in its natural habitat.

Description: The starry, white or greenish white flowers, 2–2.5 cm (0.75–1 in.) across, each with four narrow tepals, are borne from the upper leaf axils and stem tips. The anthers carry a small appendage (additional structure). Leaves are textured and shiny and have three leaflets, which are roughly oval in outline, with entire or sparsely toothed margins.

Pruning group: 1.

Flowering period: Early spring to midspring.

Cultivation: Requires cool, moist conditions, sharp drainage, and a sunny position.

Recommended use: Grow in a greenhouse or conservatory. Zone 9.

Clematis 'Glynderek'

Origin: Raised by Derek Mills of Dulwich, England, and introduced by Fisk's Clematis Nursery, Suffolk, England.

Parentage and year: Unknown. 1985.

Habit: Hardy, moderately vigorous, deciduous climber.

Height: 2.4–3 m (8–10 ft.).

Description: The early, deep blue, double flowers,

Clematis 'Glynderek'. Photo by C. Chesshire.

10–15 cm (4–6 in.) in diameter, are borne on the previous season's old wood and formed of an outer base layer of six tepals, followed by several inner layers of shorter tepals of a similar colour. In the centre are dark purple filaments and anthers. Late summer flowers are single and are produced from the current season's new wood.

Pruning group: 2.

Flowering period: Late spring to early summer (double) and late summer (single).

Cultivation: Tolerates most garden soils. Best grown in full sun. Requires protection from strong winds.

Recommended use: Grow with other not-so-vigorous, wall-trained shrubs which do not require severe pruning. Suitable for an arbour, pergola, or medium-sized obelisk or trellis. Zones 4–9.

Clematis 'Golden Harvest'
TANGUTICA GROUP

Origin: Found growing on the trials ground of the old experimental station, Boskoop, Netherlands, by Chris Sanders of Bridgemere Nurseries, England, and named by him.

Parentage and year: Believed to be *C. serratifolia* × *C. tangutica*. 1991.

Habit: Hardy, moderately vigorous, deciduous climber.

Height: 3–4 m (10–13 ft.).

Description: The single, small, deep yellow flowers are made of four narrow, pointed tepals which spread and open outward until they are almost flat, resembling small wings. The very prominent, contrasting stamens are dark purple brown.

Pruning group: 3.

Flowering period: Midsummer to late summer.

Cultivation: Tolerates most well-drained garden soils and any aspect.

Recommended use: Grow naturally through medium-sized shrubs or trees, or against a wall or fence. Suitable for a pergola or arch. Zones 4–9.

Clematis 'Golden Harvest'. Photo by C. Sanders.

Clematis 'Gothenburg'

MONTANA GROUP

Synonym: *C. montana* 'Gothenburg'

Origin: Raised at the Gothenburg Botanical Gardens, Sweden.

Parentage and year: Selected form of *C. montana*. Early 1980s.

Habit: Moderately vigorous, deciduous climber.

Height: To 6 m (20 ft.).

Description: The single, rounded, creamy pink flowers, 4–6 cm (1.5–2.25 in.) across, are held on long flower stalks. Leaves are deep bronzy green with a silver stripe down the centre of each leaflet.

Pruning group: 1. Any pruning to keep the plant in check should be carried out immediately after the main flowering period by removing some of the old, flowered stems.

Flowering period: Late spring to early summer.

Cultivation: Needs sharp drainage. Suitable for sun or partial shade.

Recommended use: Grow through medium-sized to large trees and conifers in full sun to gain the best variegation and colour from the leaves. Zones 7–9.

Clematis gouriana

Origin: Northern India, Himalaya, Nepal, and western and southern China.

Parentage and year: Species. 1814.

Habit: Hardy, vigorous, variable, deciduous climber.

Height: 4.6–6 m (14.5–20 ft.).

Description: The numerous, distinctively scented, creamy white flowers, each 2.5–3 cm (1–1.25 in.)

Clematis 'Gothenburg'. Photo by C. Chesshire.

across, are borne in lateral and terminal panicles. Each flower consists of four or five narrow tepals, which, as the flower matures, spread widely, droop backwards, and the tips recurve. Both surfaces of the tepals are covered with very fine, minute, soft hairs with more beneath. Young flowers exhibit a greenish tinge. The prominent cream stamens give the flower a spiky appearance. The filaments are threadlike, gradually thickening towards the top. The leaves are large, coarse, and light green. Stems are grooved along their length and when mature are tinged with mauve brown and become woody.

Pruning group: 3.

Flowering period: Midsummer to midautumn.

Cultivation: Tolerates most garden soils. Suitable for any aspect but produces the strongest scent in a sunny position.

Recommended use: Train through large trees or conifers. Suitable for a strong pergola or trellis. Zones 3–9.

Clematis 'Grace'

TANGUTICA GROUP

Origin: Raised by Frank L. Skinner of Dropmore, Manitoba, Canada.

Parentage and year: *C. serratifolia* × *C. ligusticifolia*. 1925.

Habit: Hardy, moderately vigorous, deciduous climber.

Height: 3–3.6 m (10–12 ft.).

Description: The single, small, creamy white flowers, 4–5 cm (1.5–2 in.) across, are composed of four spear-shaped tepals, which open flat, exposing the prominent central boss of pale wine-red stamens.

Pruning group: 3.

Flowering period: Midsummer to late summer.

Cultivation: Tolerates most well-drained garden soils. Best in full sun or partial shade.

Recommended use: Grow through medium-sized shrubs or trees or over a pergola. Suitable for an obelisk or free-standing trellis. Zones 4–9.

Clematis gracilifolia

MONTANA GROUP

Origin: Discovered by Ernest Wilson in western China.

Parentage and year: Species. 1908.

Clematis gouriana. Photo by J. Lindmark.

Clematis 'Grace'. Photo by C. Chesshire.

Habit: Not very hardy in cold gardens. Vigorous, deciduous climber.

Height: 2–4 m (6.5–13 ft.).

Description: The single, white flowers are carried on slender stalks in groups of two to four from the leaf axils of wood made the previous year. The four tepals are 15 mm (0.5 in.) long. The interesting, pretty leaves have three leaflets, or five to seven leaflets arranged in pairs on both sides of the leaf axis and terminating in a single leaflet. The leaflets tend to be somewhat hairy with coarsely serrated edges.

Pruning group: 1.

Flowering period: Late spring.

Cultivation: Needs sharp drainage and a frost-free, sunny position.

Recommended use: Grow in a sheltered aspect against a south- or west-facing wall. Zones 6–9.

Clematis grandiflora

Origin: Sierra Leone, French Guinea, Congo (Brazzaville), Angola, Uganda, southern Ethiopia, and Congo (Zaire).

Parentage and year: Species. 1829.

Habit: Not very hardy in cold gardens. Very vigorous, evergreen climber.

Height: To 12 m (40 ft.).

Description: The few, nodding, bell-shaped flowers,

each 3–4.5 cm (1.25–1.75 in.) long, are composed of four thick tepals, yellowish green on the outside and pale yellowish brown on the inside. Each tepal carries five to seven longitudinal veins and slightly recurved tips. Greenish stamens are shorter than the tepals. Young leaves and flowers are hairy; young stems are green but on maturity become brown, ribbed, and smooth. The seed is the largest in the genus, being up to 12 cm (4.75 in.) long including the tail.

Pruning group: 2.

Flowering period: In warm gardens, early autumn to early spring. Under glass, autumn.

Cultivation: In the wild grows in heavy soil. Requires a very warm location in cultivation.

Recommended use: An attractive plant for a very large conservatory or frost-free, warm greenhouse. Zones 8–9.

Clematis 'Grandiflora'
MONTANA GROUP

Synonym: *C. montana* 'Grandiflora'

Origin: Collected in northern India and introduced into cultivation by Veitch and Son of England. Awarded RHS Award of Garden Merit.

Parentage and year: Selected form of *C. montana*. ca. 1844.

Habit: Vigorous, deciduous climber.

Height: To 12 m (40 ft.) or more.

Description: The single, saucer-shaped, pure white flowers are 10 cm (4 in.) across and made of four broad, round-edged tepals. White filaments and dis-

Clematis gracilifolia. Photo by C. Chesshire.

Clematis grandiflora. Photo by Y. Aihara.

tinct yellow anthers make up the prominent stamens. Leaves are dark green.

Pruning group: 1. Any pruning to keep the plant in check should be carried out immediately after the main flowering period by removing some of the old, flowered stems.

Flowering period: Midspring to late spring.

Cultivation: Tolerates well-drained garden soils and any aspect. Hardy in temperate gardens.

Recommended use: A perfect plant for the large garden. Grow through large trees and conifers. Suitable for a large pergola, wall, and boundary fence. Zones 6–9.

Clematis grata

Origin: Eastern Afghanistan to Nepal, southern Tibet, and southern China.

Parentage and year: Species. 1830.

Habit: Hardy, vigorous, deciduous climber.

Height: 3.6–4.75 m (12–15.25 ft.).

Description: The numerous, greenish cream, scented flowers, each 1.5–2 cm (0.5–0.75 in.) wide, are borne in panicles. Each flower consists of four or five narrow, spreading tepals, which as they mature, droop backwards and the tips bend under, showing off prominent cream filaments and anthers. The shallowly grooved stems on reaching maturity are a mauve brown. The leaves are midgreen.

Pruning group: 3.

Flowering period: Late summer to midautumn.

Cultivation: Tolerates most garden soils but prefers good drainage. Suitable for any aspect but produces the strongest scent in a sunny position.

Recommended use: Allow to scramble up medium-sized trees or strong artificial supports such as a pergola or trellis. If space permits, allow it to grow as a groundcover plant. Zones 4–9.

Clematis 'Gravetye Beauty'
TEXENSIS-VIORNA GROUP

Synonym: *C. texensis* 'Gravetye Beauty'

Origin: Raised by Francisque Morel of Lyon, France, and given to William Robinson of Gravetye Manor, who named it after his home.

Parentage and year: *C. texensis* × unknown. ca. 1900.

Habit: Hardy, moderately vigorous, deciduous climber. Normally herbaceous in habit with new shoots emerging from below ground level.

Height: 1.8–2.4 m (6–8 ft.).

Clematis grata. Photo by E. Leeds.

Clematis 'Grandiflora'. Photo by J. Lindmark.

Description: The single, rich red, satin-textured flowers are 6–8 cm (2.25–3.25 in.) across and normally face upwards towards the sky. The four to six tepals are narrow, pointed, with some incurving margins and slightly recurving tips, and the exterior colour is a paler pink. When young, the flowers resemble small tulips, but as they mature, the tepals open out more so than do the tepals of other, similar cultivars, fully exposing the reddish brown stamens.

Pruning group: 3.

Flowering period: Midsummer to midautumn.

Cultivation: Tolerates most garden soils. Produces best flower colour in sun or partial shade. Slightly prone to mildew but not to such a degree as are some of the other cultivars of *C. texensis*. Take early precaution by spraying with a fungicide monthly from early summer. New shoots at soil level need protection from slugs and snails.

Recommended use: Grow and train the vines horizontally to enjoy the flowers by looking down into them. Ideal for growing over prostrate conifers, heathers, and a low wall. Zones 4–9.

Clematis 'Green Velvet'
EVERGREEN GROUP

Origin: Raised by Graham Hutchins of County Park Nursery, Essex, England.

Parentage and year: *C. petriei* 'Princess' × *C. australis*. 1987.

Habit: Half-hardy to hardy, not-too-vigorous, compact, evergreen climber.

Height: 2 m (6.5 ft.).

Description: The single, fragrant, all-male, pale greenish white flowers are 3–4 cm (1.25–1.5 in.) wide and composed of five or six spear-shaped, non-overlapping tepals, which are covered with dense, short hairs on both surfaces. The stamens made of pale green filaments and white anthers harmonize with the tepal colour. The deep green leaves consist of nine, almost rounded leaflets, each 10–15 mm (ca. 0.5 in.) across. The leaf margins are scalloped with rounded teeth.

Clematis 'Gravetye Beauty'. Photo by J. Lindmark.

Clematis 'Green Velvet'.
Photo courtesy Thorncroft Clematis Nursery.

Pruning group: 1.

Flowering period: Late spring.

Cultivation: Needs sharp drainage and a warm position.

Recommended use: Best for container-culture in a cool greenhouse or conservatory. Zones 7–9.

Clematis grewiiflora

Synonym: *C. grewiaeflora*

Origin: Himalaya, northern India, Nepal, southwestern China, and southern Tibet.

Parentage and year: Species. 1818.

Habit: Tender, vigorous, deciduous climber.

Height: 3.6–4.75 m (12–15.25 ft.).

Description: The urn-shaped, nodding, yellowish brown flowers, measuring 3 cm (1.25 in.) long, are borne singly or in small clusters of three. Each flower consists of four tepals which are broader towards the base and flare outwards slightly at their tips. The tepals have shallow ridges running along their length. The whole plant is covered in yellowish brown fine hairs, especially the young flower buds and leaves, which give the plant a velvety appearance. The greenish yellow stamens often protrude beyond the tips of the tepals.

Pruning group: 2.

Flowering period: In the garden, late winter to early spring. Under glass, midwinter.

Cultivation: Tolerates well-drained garden soils. Requires a mild, warm, sheltered position.

Recommended use: Grow in a large conservatory or frost-free greenhouse. Zones 8–9.

Clematis 'Guernsey Cream'

Origin: Raised by Raymond Evison of Guernsey Clematis Nursery.

Parentage and year: Unknown. Introduced in 1989.

Habit: Hardy, not-so-vigorous, compact, deciduous climber.

Height: 1.8–2.4 m (6–8 ft.).

Description: An extremely floriferous cultivar. The single, creamy yellow flowers, 12–15 cm (5–6 in.) wide, are composed of eight overlapping, pointed tepals. Each tepal carries a slightly deeper creamy central stripe, which is tinged with green in young flowers. As flowers mature, the tepals fade to light cream and can look unsightly. The stamens are somewhat short and not very colourful.

Pruning group: 2.

Flowering period: Late spring to early summer and late summer.

Cultivation: Tolerates most garden soils. Best grown out of full sun to preserve flower colour.

Recommended use: Ideal against a dark background of prostrate conifers or medium-sized shrubs which do not require annual pruning. Suitable for a small to

Clematis grewiiflora. Photo by R. Kirkman.

Clematis 'Guernsey Cream'. Photo by R. Surman.

medium-sized obelisk or trellis. May be grown in a large container. Zones 4–9.

Clematis 'Guiding Star'

Origin: Raised by Thomas Cripps and Son of Tunbridge Wells, England.

Parentage and year: Unknown but probably a hybrid of *C. lanuginosa*. Before 1866.

Habit: Hardy, moderately vigorous, deciduous climber.

Height: 2.5–3 m (8–10 ft.).

Description: The single, large, glossy lavender-blue flowers measure 11 cm (4.5 in.) across and are composed of six to eight sharp-pointed tepals with deep lavender veining. White filaments and brown anthers form the central tuft of stamens.

Pruning group: 3.

Flowering period: Midsummer to late summer.

Cultivation: Tolerates most garden soils and any aspect.

Recommended use: Grow on a pergola, trellis, or obelisk. Suitable with wall-trained shrubs, other climbers, and roses. Ideal against a light background. Zones 4–9.

Clematis 'H. F. Young'

Origin: Raised by Walter Pennell of Pennell and Sons nursery and named after the director responsible for the company's Grimsby shop and nursery. Awarded RHS Award of Garden Merit.

Parentage and year: Unknown. Probably sown in 1954, but named in 1962.

Clematis 'Guiding Star'. Photo by C. Chesshire.

Habit: Hardy, moderately vigorous, deciduous climber.

Height: 2.4–3 m (8–10 ft.).

Description: The single, well-shaped, midblue flowers are 15–20 cm (6–8 in.) across and composed of six to eight overlapping tepals with rounded edges and pointed tips. On the reverse, the tepals carry a greenish white bar fading into the mauvish blue background.

Pruning group: 2.

Flowering period: Late spring to early summer and early autumn.

Cultivation: Tolerates most garden soils. Prefers sun or partial shade.

Recommended use: Suitable for a pergola, arbour, large trellis, or obelisk. Zones 4–9.

Clematis 'Hagley Hybrid'

Synonym: *C.* 'Pink Chiffon' (in the United States)

Origin: Raised by Percy Picton of Old Court Nurseries, Colwall, England. Introduced in 1956 by Jim Fisk of Fisk's Clematis Nursery, Suffolk, England.

Parentage and year: Unknown. ca. 1945.

Habit: Hardy, not-so-vigorous, compact, deciduous climber.

Height: 1.8–2.4 m (6–8 ft.).

Clematis 'H. F. Young'. Photo by R. Surman.

Description: A very floriferous and popular cultivar. The single, saucer-shaped, shell-pink flowers measure 10–15 cm (4–6 in.) wide and are composed of five or six boat-shaped, pointed tepals, with crimped edges. White filaments and wine-red anthers make up the contrasting stamens.

Pruning group: 3.

Flowering period: Early summer to early autumn.

Cultivation: Tolerates most garden soils. Best grown out of direct sunlight to preserve flower colour.

Recommended use: Best grown with other low shrubs or prostrate conifers. Suitable for a low wall or fence. May be grown in a large container on a terrace, patio, or balcony where it is sheltered from strong winds. Zones 4–9.

Clematis 'Hainton Ruby'

Origin: Raised by Keith and Carol Fair of Valley Clematis, England.

Parentage and year: *C.* 'Niobe' × *C.* 'W. E. Gladstone'. Introduced in 1993.

Habit: Hardy, moderately vigorous, deciduous climber.

Height: 2.5–3 m (8–10 ft.).

Description: The single, rich plum-red flowers measure 15 cm (6 in.) in diameter and are composed of six to eight overlapping, broad yet pointed tepals.

Clematis 'Hainton Ruby'. Photo by K. Fair.

Clematis 'Hagley Hybrid'. Photo by M. Toomey.

On mature flowers the colour pales slightly along the centre, and the margins curve upwards so that the tepals take on a slight boat shape. The stamens are dark wine red.

Pruning group: 2.

Flowering period: Late spring to early summer and late summer.

Cultivation: Tolerates most garden soils. Best grown in sun or partial shade.

Recommended use: Shows up well against a light background. Grow with other wall-trained shrubs and roses which do not require pruning. Suitable for a trellis, arbour, or pergola. Zones 4–9.

Clematis 'Hakuōkan'

Synonym: *C.* 'Haku Ookan'

Origin: Raised by Esio Kubota of Japan. The name means "white royal crown."

Parentage and year: Unknown. ca. 1957.

Habit: Hardy, moderately vigorous, compact, deciduous climber.

Height: 1.8–2.4 m (6–8 ft.).

Description: The mostly single, rich, royal purple flowers are 15–17 cm (6–7 in.) wide and are composed of seven or eight overlapping, pointed tepals, which tend to incurve slightly along their lengths. The conspicuous central boss consists of creamy white stamens. Semi-double flowers may appear occasionally.

Pruning group: 2.

Flowering period: Late spring to early summer and late summer.

Cultivation: Tolerates most garden soils. Requires protection from strong winds.

Recommended use: Grow against a light-coloured wall. Ideal for a small to medium-sized obelisk or trellis. May be grown up and over shrubs with silver or gold leaves. Zones 4–9.

Clematis 'Hanaguruma'

Origin: Raised by Gorō Jōsha of Japan. The name means "wheel of blossom."

Parentage and year: Unknown. 1985.

Habit: Hardy, moderately vigorous, compact, deciduous climber.

Height: 1.8–2.4 m (6–8 ft.).

Description: The single, deep pink, rounded flowers, 10–15 cm (4–6 in.), are composed of six to eight broad, overlapping, gently pointed tepals, each with textured grooves running along the centre from base to tip. The stamens are yellow.

Pruning group: 2.

Flowering period: Late spring to early summer and late summer.

Cultivation: Tolerates most garden soils and any aspect.

Recommended use: Grow with wall-trained shrubs or roses which do not require annual pruning. Suitable for a small obelisk, trellis, or arch. Zones 4–9.

Clematis 'Hakuōkan'. Photo by Y. Aihara.

Clematis 'Hanaguruma'. Photo by C. Chesshire.

Clematis 'Heather Herschell'
HERBACEOUS GROUP

Origin: Raised by Barry Fretwell of Peveril Clematis Nursery, England. Introduced early 1990s.

Parentage and year: Selected form of *C.* 'Eriostemon'. Unknown.

Habit: Hardy, moderately vigorous, non-clinging, deciduous, herbaceous perennial.

Height: 1.8–2.4 m (6–8 ft.).

Description: The single, bell-shaped, nodding, bright warm-pink flowers are 7.5 cm (3 in.) across and are composed of four tepals, which are deeply grooved along the centre and gently notched at the edges. The tips of the tepals recurve with maturity. The stamens are made of white filaments and pale green-yellow anthers.

Pruning group: 3.

Flowering period: Early summer to late summer.

Cultivation: Tolerates most garden soils and any aspect. If trained on an artificial support, the stems need tying-in.

Recommended use: Plant in mixed borders and allow to grow through other herbaceous plants, low shrubs, or small trees. Zones 4–9.

Clematis 'Helen Cropper'

Origin: Raised by Vince and Sylvia Denny of Denny's Clematis Nursery, Broughton, England, and named after a granddaughter.

Parentage and year: Unknown. Introduced in 1985.

Habit: Hardy, moderately vigorous, deciduous climber.

Height: 1.8–2.4 m (6–8 ft.).

Description: The first flush of semi-double flowers, measuring 15–18 cm (6–7 in.) in diameter, is borne on the previous season's old wood and is formed of an outer row of six to eight large, pink, overlapping, blunt-tipped, curled-edged, and textured tepals, spread over with deep dusky mauvish pink, reminiscent of raspberry ripple ice-cream. There is another row of about 15 much smaller tepals having the same colouring and texture. A second crop of single flowers appears in late summer from the current season's new growth. The filaments are white shading to pink with deep red anthers.

Pruning group: 2.

Flowering period: Late spring to early summer (semi-double) and late summer (single).

Cultivation: Tolerates most garden soils and any aspect. Requires a sheltered position to prevent wind damage to the large flowers.

Recommended use: Ideal for container-culture. Grow on a low obelisk or trellis, through medium-sized shrubs, or with wall-trained, not-so-vigorous climbers and roses which do not require severe pruning. Zones 4–9.

Clematis 'Helios'
TANGUTICA GROUP

Synonym: *C. tangutica* 'Helios'

Origin: Raised at the Boskoop Research Station, Netherlands.

Parentage and year: Unknown. Possibly a hybrid of *C. tangutica* × *C.* 'Golden Harvest'. 1988.

Clematis 'Heather Herschell'. Photo by C. Chesshire.

Clematis 'Helen Cropper'. Photo by V. Denny.

Clematis 'Helios'. Photo by M. Toomey.

Habit: Hardy, moderately vigorous, compact, deciduous climber.

Height: To 2 m (6.5 ft.) or slightly more.

Description: Flowers are single, slightly nodding, bright yellow and 6.5–9 cm (2.5–3.5 in.) across. The tepals number four, each 3.5–4.5 cm (1.25–1.75 in.) long, opening quite flat, with the pointed tips reflexing like a Turk's cap. Stamens are dark purple. The flowers are held proud of the bright green leaves on long stalks. This cultivar makes a final show of attractive seedheads.

Pruning group: 3.

Flowering period: Late spring to early autumn, the earliest cultivar of *C. tangutica* if left unpruned or partially pruned.

Cultivation: Needs sharp drainage. Suitable for sun or partial shade.

Recommended use: Ideal for the small, modern garden. Suitable for short-term container-culture, growing on a free-standing trellis in a mixed border, or cov-

Clematis 'Helsingborg'. Photo by J. Lindmark.

ering bare stems of climbing roses or wisteria. Grow through medium-sized shrubs or small to medium-sized trees. Zones 4–9.

Clematis 'Helsingborg'
ATRAGENE GROUP

Synonym: *C. alpina* 'Helsingborg'

Origin: Raised by Tage Lundell of Helsingborg, Sweden. Introduced by Raymond Evison of Guernsey Clematis Nursery. Awarded RHS Award of Garden Merit.

Parentage and year: *C. ochotensis* × *C. alpina*. 1970.

Habit: Hardy, moderately vigorous, deciduous climber.

Height: 2.5–3 m (8–10 ft.).

Description: The flowers with four slightly twisted, blue-purple tepals measure 5 cm (2 in.) long and are slightly paler at the margins. Each flower has an inner skirt of pale purple petal-like staminodes, similar in colour to the reverse side of the tepals. Leaves are light green.

Pruning group: 1.

Flowering period: Midspring to late spring.

Cultivation: Needs sharp drainage. Suitable for any aspect, even cold ones.

Recommended use: Ideal for small gardens, container-culture, and covering bare lower stems of *C. montana* varieties and other climbers such as wisteria. Zones 3–9.

Clematis 'Hendersoni'
HERBACEOUS/INTEGRIFOLIA GROUP

Synonyms: *C. integrifolia* 'Hendersonii', *C. integrifolia* 'Henderson'

Origin: Possibly raised by Henderson of Pineapple Nursery, England. A selected form received the RHS Award of Merit in 1965 when it was exhibited at the Chelsea Flower Show.

Parentage and year: *C. viticella* × *C. integrifolia*. 1835.

Habit: Hardy, deciduous, non-climbing, herbaceous perennial.

Height: 0.6–0.9 m (2–3 ft.).

Description: The bell-shaped, slightly scented single flowers are composed of four deep midblue, pointed tepals, each 5.5–6.5 cm (2.25–2.5 in.) long. As they mature the tepals twist in different directions, exposing the yellow anthers in the centre. The edges of the tepals are curved in an irregular fashion, adding to the beauty of the flower. The outside of the tepals has prominent darker coloured ridges starting at the base and receding towards the tip.

Pruning group: 3.

Flowering period: Midsummer to late summer.

Cultivation: Tolerates most garden soils. Suitable for any aspect but produces the strongest scent in a sunny position.

Recommended use: Ideal for a herbaceous border. Zones 3–9.

Clematis 'Henryi'

Synonym: *C.* 'Bangholm Belle'

Origin: Raised by Isaac Anderson-Henry of Edinburgh, Scotland. Awarded RHS Award of Garden Merit (1873).

Parentage and year: *C. lanuginosa* × *C.* 'Fortunei'. 1870.

Habit: Hardy, vigorous, deciduous climber.

Height: 3–3.6 m (10–12 ft.).

Description: The single, white flowers, 15–20 cm (6–8 in.) wide, are composed of eight smooth, overlapping, and pointed tepals. A large central boss of white filaments and coffee-coloured anthers enhances the flowers. Leaves are in threes, large, and slightly tough.

Clematis 'Hendersoni' finding its way into a hosta. Photo by J. Lindmark.

Pruning group: 2.

Flowering period: Late spring to late summer.

Cultivation: Tolerates most garden soils and any aspect. Best grown in a sheltered spot.

Recommended use: Shows up well against a dark background. Suitable for an obelisk, trellis, or pergola. Grows with other shrubs which do not require pruning. Zones 4–9.

Clematis heracleifolia
HERBACEOUS / HERACLEIFOLIA GROUP

Origin: Central and eastern China.

Parentage and year: Species. Introduced into cultivation in Britain in 1837.

Habit: Hardy, woody-based, deciduous, semi-herbaceous subshrub.

Height: 0.6–0.9 m (2–3 ft.).

Description: The dense, short clusters of small, hyacinth-shaped, nodding or partly nodding, deep blue or purple-blue, tubular flowers, 1.5–2 cm (0.5–0.75 in.) across, and somewhat hairy on the outside, are composed of four tepals, each 1.5–3 cm (0.5–1.25 in.) long, which recurve at their expanded, blunt, frilled tips as they mature. Pale yellow filaments and anthers make up the stamens, which almost reach the mouth of the tubular portion of the flower. Male and female flowers are separate but borne on the same plant. Leaves are dark green, divided into three leaflets, and held on long stalks.

Clematis 'Henryi'. Photo courtesy Thorncroft Clematis Nursery.

Pruning group: 3.

Flowering period: Early summer to early autumn.

Cultivation: Requires free-draining but moist garden soils. Suitable for any aspect.

Recommended use: Plant in a herbaceous or mixed border or grow as a specimen plant in a large container. Zones 5–9.

Clematis heracleifolia var. *davidiana*
HERBACEOUS / HERACLEIFOLIA GROUP

Origin: Found by French missionary Père Armand David (1826–1900) near Beijing, China.

Parentage and year: A variant of *C. heracleifolia*. 1863.

Habit: Hardy, non-clinging, deciduous, wholly herbaceous perennial.

Height: 1 m (3.25 ft.).

Description: The single, tubular, hyacinth-like, light mauve to grey-blue flowers are borne in dense clusters at the upper nodes or leaf joints. Each flower is 2–2.5 cm (0.75–1 in.) long and 4 cm (1.5 in.) wide and is composed of four tepals, narrow in the tubelike part of the flower, expanding widely towards the tips, and

Clematis heracleifolia. Photo by C. Chesshire.

recurving with maturity. The stamens are made of white filaments and pale yellow anthers. The flowers are very sweetly scented, and the large, thick, leathery leaves also emit scent when they dry in the autumn. Male and female flowers are borne on separate plants.

Pruning group: 3.

Flowering period: Early summer to early autumn.

Cultivation: Requires free-draining but moist garden soils. Suitable for any aspect but produces the strongest scent in a sunny position. Easy to propagate from the underground rhizomes by which the plant spreads.

Recommended use: Plant in a mixed or herbaceous border or grow as a specimen plant in a large container. Zones 5–9.

Clematis 'Herbert Johnson'

Origin: Raised by Walter Pennell of Pennell and Sons nursery and named in 1973 after the company's managing director.

Parentage and year: *C.* 'Vyvyan Pennell' × *C.* 'Percy Picton'. 1962.

Habit: Hardy, moderately vigorous, deciduous climber.

Height: 2.5–3 m (8–10 ft.).

Description: The single, large, reddish mauve flowers measure 15–20 cm (6–8 in.) wide and are composed of eight broad and overlapping tepals. Maroon stamens are somewhat lost in the flower colour. Leaves are large and simple or with three leaflets.

Pruning group: 2.

Flowering period: Late spring to late summer.

Cultivation: Tolerates most garden soils when planted in sun or partial shade.

Recommended use: Ideal companion for roses and other wall-trained shrubs. Suitable for a pergola, obelisk, or trellis. Zones 4–9.

Clematis hexapetala
HERBACEOUS GROUP

Synonym: *C. angustifolia*

Origin: Northern China, Manchuria, Mongolia, Siberia, Korea, and Japan.

Parentage and year: Species. 1762.

Habit: Hardy, erect, deciduous, herbaceous perennial.

Height: To 1 m (3.25 ft.).

Clematis heracleifolia var. *davidiana*. Photo by D. Harding.

Clematis 'Herbert Johnson'. Photo courtesy Pennells Nurseries.

Description: The single, white flowers, 2.5–4 cm (1–1.5 in.) across, are composed of normally four, sometimes seven or eight, narrow, blunt-tipped tepals, velvety hairy on the inside and smooth outside. The tepals tend to spread and droop slightly as the flowers mature. The stamens are made of greenish white filaments and yellow anthers. Leaves are somewhat leathery.

Pruning group: 3.

Flowering period: Early summer to late summer.

Cultivation: Prefers well-drained soil. Plant in sun or partial shade. If trained on an artificial support, the stems need tying-in.

Recommended use: Suitable for a herbaceous or mixed border. Zones 3–9.

Clematis 'Highdown'
MONTANA GROUP

Synonym: *C.* ×*vedrariensis* 'Highdown'

Origin: Unknown.

Parentage and year: *C. chrysocoma* × *C. montana* var. *rubens*. Unknown.

Habit: Vigorous, deciduous climber.

Height: To 6 m (20 ft.).

Description: The single, saucer-shaped, rose-pink flowers, 5 cm (2 in.) across, are composed of four to six rounded tepals on slender, hairy stalks. The undersides of the tepals are a darker shade of pink. The leaves retain a downy appearance.

Pruning group: 1. Any pruning to keep the plant in check should be carried out immediately after the main flowering period by removing some of the old, flowered stems.

Flowering period: Late spring to early summer.

Cultivation: Tolerates most well-drained garden soils. Hardy in temperate gardens. Suitable for any aspect.

Recommended use: Suitable for a pergola or large trellis. Ideal for a boundary fence or wall. Zones 7–9.

Clematis hirsutissima
HERBACEOUS/TEXENSIS-VIORNA GROUP

Common name: Sugar-bowls (in the United States)

Origin: Mountainous regions of western and parts of southwestern United States.

Clematis 'Highdown'. Photo by J. Treasure.

Clematis hirsutissima growing wild at Grand Mesa, Colorado, United States. Photo by R. Ratko.

Clematis hexapetala. Photo by J. Lindmark.

Parentage and year: Species. 1814.

Habit: Hardy, herbaceous, non-climbing shrub.

Height: 20–50 cm (8–20 in.).

Description: The small, solitary and terminal flowers, held on erect stems, are nodding and tubular shaped. Each flower, 2–3 cm (0.75–1.25 in.) long, is composed of four thick, leathery, pointed tepals, which open outwards slightly from about three-quarters of the way to the tips. The colour is quite variable from clear purple, brownish purple to dark bluish purple, and the flowers, stems, and leaves are covered in soft long hairs. The stamens are yellow.

Pruning group: 3.

Flowering period: Midspring to midsummer.

Cultivation: Requires very fast draining soils and dislikes being too wet during the winter. Suitable for any aspect.

Recommended use: Best grown in an alpine bed or as a specimen plant in a container where it can be given winter protection from excessive rain. Zones 6–9.

Clematis hirsutissima var. *scottii*
HERBACEOUS/TEXENSIS-VIORNA GROUP

Synonym: *C. douglasii* var. *scottii*

Origin: Northwestern United States (Rocky Mountains area).

Parentage and year: A variant of *C. hirsutissima*. 1885.

Habit: Hardy, herbaceous perennial.

Height: 30–46 cm (12–18 in.).

Description: The single, solitary, terminal, urn- to pitcher-shaped flowers, 2.5–4 cm (1–1.5 in.) long, are composed of four, rarely five, purple-blue, broad yet pointed thick, hairy tepals, which gently recurve at the tip and are borne on short perpendicular hairy stems. Almost hidden from view are yellow stamens. The leaflets are arranged in pairs on either side of a central axis and are undivided. They are usually five lobed, mainly shaped like the head of a lance, tapering at both ends, much longer than broad, and wider below the middle. Leaf stalks, stems, and flowers are all covered in tiny hairs.

Clematis hirsutissima var. *scottii* growing in Burford House Gardens. Photo by N. Hall.

Pruning group: 3.

Flowering period: Midspring to midsummer.

Cultivation: Requires fast-draining soils. Suitable for full sun. Very slow to establish itself and flower.

Recommended use: Ideal for the front of a herbaceous border or for container-culture. Zones 6–9.

Clematis 'Honora'

Origin: Discovered and named by Mrs. A. Edwards of Christchurch, New Zealand. The name is Maori.

Parentage and year: Possibly a sport from *C.* 'Gipsy Queen'. ca. 1995.

Habit: Hardy, moderately vigorous, deciduous climber.

Height: 3–4 m (10–13 ft.).

Description: The single, solitary, rich violet-purple flowers, 18 cm (7 in.) across, are composed of six tepals, long pointed, and shaded with burgundy, with small gaps between them at the base and a deeper purple central bar running from the base to the tip. The margins of tepals are wavy. As the flower matures, the tepals twist and bend backwards. Creamy filaments and anthers make up the attractive stamens. Leaves are made of five leaflets. Stems are somewhat hairy.

Pruning group: Optional, 2, or 3. A hard pruning (group 3) results in the loss of early flowers. For late flowers, choose group 3.

Flowering period: Early summer to early autumn.

Cultivation: Tolerates most garden soils and any aspect.

Recommended use: Grow with other wall-trained plants. Suitable for a medium-sized obelisk or a trellis.

If group 3 pruning is utilized, grow naturally through shrubs or conifers. Zones 4–9.

Clematis 'Horn of Plenty'

Origin: Raised by K. Maarse Dzn. Jr. of the Netherlands. Awarded RHS Award of Garden Merit.

Parentage and year: Unknown. ca. 1962.

Habit: Hardy, moderately vigorous, deciduous climber.

Height: 2–3 m (6.5–10 ft.).

Description: The single, rosy mauve flowers, 15–20 cm (6–8 in.) in diameter, are composed of six to eight overlapping, blunt-tipped tepals, each with a deeper coloured central bar with veining and slightly notched margins. Prominent stamens have reddish anthers.

Pruning group: Optional, 2, or 3. A hard pruning (group 3) delays flowering time.

Flowering period: Late spring to early summer and late summer.

Cultivation: Tolerates most garden soils and any aspect.

Recommended use: Best on an obelisk, trellis, or pergola if no pruning or light pruning (group 2) is undertaken. Grow through other suitable shrubs if hard pruning (group 3) is used. Zones 4–9.

Clematis 'Horn of Plenty'. Photo by C. Chesshire.

Clematis 'Honora'. Photo by C. Chesshire.

Clematis 'Huldine'

Origin: Raised by Francisque Morel of Lyon, France, and given to William Robinson of Gravetye Manor. Exhibited by Robinson's head gardener, Ernest Markham. Awarded RHS Award of Merit (1934).

Parentage and year: Unknown. Before 1914.

Habit: Hardy, vigorous, deciduous climber. A strong growing and floriferous cultivar.

Height: 3–4.6 m (10–14.5 ft.).

Description: The single, well-held, small, and numerous pearly white flowers, 7.5–10 cm (3–4 in.) wide, are usually composed of six non-overlapping translucent tepals, each boasting three pinkish mauve central bars on their under surface. The margins of the tepals are slightly incurved, but the tips are recurved. White filaments and bright yellow anthers make up the stamens.

Pruning group: 3. For early flowers, retain a few old stems.

Flowering period: Midsummer to late summer.

Cultivation: Tolerates most garden soils. Best in full sun or partial shade.

Recommended use: Ideal for a large trellis, arch, or pergola. Grow through medium-sized trees and large shrubs. Best where the undersurface of the flowers can be viewed with ease. Zones 4–9.

Clematis 'Huvi'

Origin: Raised by Uno Kivistik of Harjumaa, Estonia.

Parentage and year: *C.* 'Pöhjanael' × *C.* 'Niobe'. 1986.

Habit: Hardy, moderately vigorous, compact, deciduous climber.

Height: 1.8–2.4 m (6–8 ft.).

Description: The single, non-overlapping, deep carmine red flowers, 12–14 cm (4.75–5.5 in.) across, are composed of six boat-shaped tepals, each with incurving wavy margins at the base, becoming reflexed towards the tip. The central rib of the tepal has a reddish mauve colour between the grooving which runs from base to tip. The anthers are pinky white.

Clematis 'Huldine'. Photo by J. Lindmark.

Pruning group: 2.

Flowering period: Early summer to late summer.

Cultivation: Tolerates most garden soils enriched with humus. Suitable for any aspect.

Recommended use: Ideal for container-culture. Suitable for an obelisk or trellis. Zones 3–9.

Clematis 'Hybrida Sieboldii'

Synonyms: *C.* 'Hybrida Sieboldiana', *C.* 'Ramona'

Origin: Raised by B. Droog of Boskoop, Netherlands.

Parentage and year: Seedling of *C. lanuginosa*. 1874.

Habit: Hardy, moderately vigorous, deciduous climber.

Height: 2.5–3 m (8–10 ft.).

Description: The single, rather large, lavender blue flowers, 15–20 cm (6–8 in.) wide, are composed of six to eight tepals and contrasting red anthers. The leaves with entire margins are quite large.

Clematis 'Huvi'. Photo by R. Savill.

Clematis 'Hybrida Sieboldii'. Photo by C. Chesshire.

Pruning group: 2 or 3. A hard pruning (group 3) results in the loss of early flowers.

Flowering period: Early summer to late summer.

Cultivation: Tolerates most garden soils. Prefers sun or partial shade.

Recommended use: Good for a pergola, trellis, or obelisk. May also be trained through medium-sized trees and large shrubs. Method of pruning will dictate its use in the garden. Zones 4–9.

Clematis 'Imperial'

Origin: Raised by Magnus Johnson of Södertälje, Sweden.

Parentage and year: Chance seedling of *C.* 'Lasurstern'. 1955.

Habit: Hardy, moderately vigorous, deciduous climber.

Height: 2.4–3 m (8–10 ft.).

Description: The single and semi-double, pale purplish pink flowers, 15–20 cm (6–8 in.) across, are composed of eight, sometimes six or seven, overlapping, rounded but pointed tepals shaded darker along the centre. Mature tepals fade to white at the margins. The stamens are made of white filaments and purplish violet anthers, which on maturity turn yellowish. When semi-double flowers are produced, there is an inner row of narrower and shorter tepals overlaid. Large leaves carry three smooth, rounded leaflets.

Pruning group: 2.

Flowering period: Late spring to early summer and late summer.

Clematis 'Imperial'. Photo by C. Chesshire.

Cultivation: Tolerates most garden soils and any aspect.

Recommended use: Grow with other wall-trained plants which do not require annual pruning. Suitable for a medium-sized obelisk or trellis. Zones 4–9.

Clematis integrifolia
HERBACEOUS/INTEGRIFOLIA GROUP

Origin: Central and eastern Europe.

Parentage and year: Species. Introduced into cultivation in Britain in 1573.

Habit: Hardy, deciduous, non-clinging, woody-based, herbaceous perennial or subshrub.

Height: 0.6–0.9 m (2–3 ft.).

Description: The solitary, nodding, bell-shaped flowers on long stalks, borne terminally or laterally at the uppermost leaf joints, each 3–5 cm (1.25–2 in.) long, are composed of four pointed, half-spreading, and recurving tepals, which are invariably twisted. The colour of the flowers can be variable depending on the clone, from mauvish blue to deep blue. Pale cream filaments, which are somewhat hairy towards the upper part, carry yellow anthers. Attractive seedheads have shiny, silvery, and feathery seedtails. Slender, ribbed stems rise from the ground annually. Leaves without stalks are simple and undivided with prominent veins. Upper leaves are usually smaller than the lower.

Pruning group: 3.

Flowering period: Early summer to early autumn.

Cultivation: Tolerates most garden soils and any aspect. Forms a clump as the plant gets established and can be divided in the autumn.

Recommended use: A splendid garden plant for the front half of a herbaceous or mixed border. Provide suitable supports to prevent the slender stems from flopping around too much. Zones 4–9.

Clematis integrifolia. Photo by J. Lindmark.

Clematis integrifolia var. *latifolia*
HERBACEOUS/INTEGRIFOLIA GROUP

Origin: Reportedly the Altai Mountains of northern Asia.

Parentage and year: A variant of *C. integrifolia*. 1885.

Habit: Hardy, deciduous, non-clinging, herbaceous perennial.

Clematis integrifolia var. *latifolia*. Photo by J. Lindmark.

Height: 0.9–1.2 m (3–4 ft.).

Description: The bell-shaped, slightly scented, single flowers, 5 cm (2 in.) across, are composed of four midblue tepals, which open out fully with recurving tips and incurving margins. The outside of the tepals is paler in colour with prominent ribbing from base to tip. Thick pale cream filaments and yellow anthers make up the prominent stamens.

Pruning group: 3.

Flowering period: Early summer to late summer.

Cultivation: Tolerates most garden soils enriched with humus. Suitable for any aspect but produces the strongest scent in a sunny position.

Recommended use: Grow in the middle of a herbaceous border. Zones 3–9.

Clematis intricata

Synonym: *C. intricata* 'Harry Smith'

Origin: China and North Korea. Raised from seed collected in the wild by Harry Smith of Sweden.

Clematis intricata. Photo by J. Lindmark.

Parentage and year: Selected clone of the species. 1831.

Habit: Hardy, moderately vigorous, deciduous climber.

Height: To 3 m (10 ft.).

Description: The single, small, nodding, yellow to greenish yellow flowers, borne singly or in a group of two or three from the leaf axils or terminally, are composed of four elliptical, spreading tepals, each 1–2.5 cm (0.5–1 in.) long, often streaked with purple brown to purple on the outside. As the flowers mature, the tips, which may be pointed or rounded and blunt, recurve gently. The stamens are reddish brown. The leaves are bluish green, and somewhat leathery with usually five to seven leaflets arranged in pairs on both sides of a central axis.

Pruning group: 3.

Flowering period: Late spring to late summer.

Cultivation: Tolerates most well-drained garden soils. Best grown in sun or partial shade.

Recommended use: Grow through medium-sized to large shrubs. Suitable for an obelisk, trellis, or pergola. Zones 5–9.

Clematis 'Iola Fair'

Origin: Raised by Keith Fair of Valley Clematis Nursery.

Parentage and year: *C.* 'Niobe' × *C.* 'W. E. Gladstone'. Introduced in 1995.

Habit: Hardy, moderately vigorous, compact, deciduous climber.

Height: 1.8–2.4 m (6–8 ft.).

Description: The single, luminous, pale lavender flowers, 13–15 cm (5–6 in.) wide, are composed of six tepals, which are tinged with pink at their base and have incurving margins and pointed tips. The stamens are wine red.

Pruning group: 2.

Flowering period: Late spring to early summer and late summer.

Cultivation: Tolerates most garden soils. Best grown in partial shade to preserve flower colour.

Recommended use: Grow on a small to medium-sized obelisk or low trellis. Train through other wall-trained shrubs and roses which do not require annual pruning. Zones 4–9.

Clematis 'Ishobel'

Origin: Raised by Alec Medlycott of Watford, Hertfordshire, England.

Parentage and year: Unknown.

Habit: Hardy, vigorous, deciduous climber.

Height: 2.4–3.6 m (8–12 ft.).

Description: The single, rather large, white flowers, 15–20 cm (6–8 in.) wide, are composed of eight overlapping tepals, boasting a centre of prominent brown stamens. The tepals have attractive, gently notched edges.

Pruning group: 2.

Flowering period: Late spring to early summer and late summer.

Cultivation: Tolerates most garden soils and any aspect.

Recommended use: Ideal against a dark background.

Clematis 'Iola Fair'. Photo by K. Fair.

Clematis 'Ishobel'. Photo by C. Chesshire.

Grow with other wall-trained shrubs which do not require annual pruning, or on a pergola, obelisk, or trellis. Zones 4–9.

Clematis ispahanica

Origin: Western and northern Iran and Turkmenistan.

Parentage and year: Species. 1845.

Habit: Hardy, deciduous, non-clinging, subshrub.

Height: 1.5–1.8 m (5–6 ft.).

Description: The rather small, white flowers, 2–2.5 cm (0.75–1 in.) across, are borne on terminal shoots and in leaf axils. Each flower is composed of four narrow, pointed, widely spreading tepals. The stamens are made of white filaments and deep purplish anthers. Lower parts of the stems become woody as the plant matures. Leaves with five or seven leaflets are somewhat leathery.

Clematis ispahanica. Photo by E. Leeds.

Clematis 'Ivan Olsson'. Photo by C. Chesshire.

Pruning group: 3.

Flowering period: Midsummer to late summer.

Cultivation: Tolerates most garden soils but prefers sharp drainage and some sun. If trained on an artificial support, the stems need tying-in.

Recommended use: Grow over low artificial supports or with other not-so-vigorous wall-trained plants. Zones 6–9.

Clematis 'Ivan Olsson'

Origin: Raised by Magnus Johnson of Södertälje, Sweden, from seed given to him by his late friend, Mr. Olsson of Gothenburg.

Parentage and year: Open-pollinated seedling of *C.* 'The President'. 1955.

Habit: Hardy, not-so-vigorous, compact, deciduous climber.

Height: 1.8–2.4 m (6–8 ft.).

Description: The single, ice-blue flowers, 8–14 cm (3.25–5.5 in.) wide, carry eight or more tepals, with deeper blue margins. The filaments are white to greenish white, and the anthers are purple.

Pruning group: 2.

Flowering period: Late spring to early summer and late summer.

Cultivation: Tolerates most garden soils and any aspect.

Recommended use: Ideal for container-culture. Suitable on a short trellis or small obelisk, or growing through low shrubs which do not require annual pruning. Zones 4–9.

Clematis 'Jackmanii'

Origin: Raised by George Jackman and Son, England. Awarded RHS First Class Certificate (1863).

Parentage and year: *C. lanuginosa* × *C.* 'Hendersoni' × *C.* 'Atrorubens'. 1858.

Habit: Hardy, vigorous, deciduous climber.

Height: 3–3.6 m (10–12 ft.).

Description: A widely grown, universally popular and free-flowering cultivar. The single, gently semi-nodding, dark velvet-purple flowers, 10 cm (4 in.) wide, are composed of four to six broad, slightly twisted, gappy, blunt, and rough-textured tepals, each with reddish purple grooves along its centre. Anthers are greenish cream.

Pruning group: 3.

Flowering period: Early to late summer.

Cultivation: Tolerates most garden soils and any aspect.

Recommended use: Ideal specimen plant on a trellis, obelisk, or pergola. Grow up and over large shrubs and small trees. Zones 3–9.

Clematis 'Jackmanii Alba'

Origin: Raised by Charles Noble of Sunningdale, England.

Parentage and year: *C.* 'Jackmanii' × *C.* 'Fortunei'. Before 1877.

Habit: Hardy, vigorous, deciduous climber.

Height: 3–3.4 m (10–12 ft.).

Description: The light bluish mauve double flowers, borne on the previous year's old wood early in the season, are 12.5 cm (5 in.) wide. Each flower is composed of many layers of textured, pointed tepals of uneven length. The colour of these tepals fades to white as the flower matures. Some tepals may be tinged with green, and on the reverse of each one there is a greenish bar. White filaments and light brown anthers form the central mass of stamens. Single flowers, consisting of six white tepals, are produced on the current year's growth during midsummer to late summer.

Pruning group: Optional, 2, or 3. For early flowers, do not prune back to the previous year's wood.

Flowering period: Early summer to midsummer (double) and late summer (single).

Cultivation: Tolerates most garden soils and any aspect. Best grown in full or partial sun.

Recommended use: Suitable for a large trellis, obelisk, arbour, or pergola. Grow up and over or through small trees and large shrubs which do not require regular pruning. Zones 4–9.

Clematis 'Jackmanii Rubra'

Origin: Obscure. Variously attributed to Houry of France, Charles Noble of Sunningdale, England, and George Jackman and Son, England.

Parentage and year: Unknown. Possibly late 1800s to early 1900.

Habit: Hardy, strong-growing, deciduous climber.

Clematis 'Jackmanii Alba'. Photo by E. Leeds.

Clematis 'Jackmanii Rubra' early flowers are usually semidouble. Photo by J. Lindmark.

Clematis 'Jackmanii'. Photo by J. Lindmark.

Height: 3–3.6 m (10–12 ft.).

Description: The early, semi-double flowers, 12.5 cm (5 in.) in diameter, are produced on the previous season's old wood, and carry six tapering, crimson tepals tinged with purple, upon which are arranged more layers of shorter, similar coloured tepals. The filaments and anthers are creamy yellow. Single flowers are produced later in the season on the current year's new growth.

Pruning group: 2.

Flowering period: Early summer (double) to late summer (single).

Cultivation: Tolerates most garden soils and any aspect.

Recommended use: Suitable for a pergola, arbour, medium-sized to large obelisk, or trellis. Grow with other wall-trained plants or through large shrubs which do not require major pruning. Zones 4–9.

Clematis 'Jackmanii Superba'

Origin: Raised by Thomas Cripps and Son of Tunbridge Wells, England.

Parentage and year: Unknown. 1878 or 1880.

Habit: Hardy, vigorous, deciduous climber.

Height: 3–3.6 m (10–12 ft.).

Description: The single, dark velvety mauve flowers, 13–14 cm (5–5.5 in.) wide, are composed of four tepals, similar in shape to and broader than those of *C.* 'Jackmanii'. The deeper reddish purple flush along the middle of the tepals, however, fades as the flower matures. Greenish cream filaments carry beige anthers.

Pruning group: 3.

Flowering period: Early to late summer.

Cultivation: Tolerates most garden soils and any aspect.

Recommended use: Ideal for a trellis, pergola, or obelisk. Grow through medium-sized trees, especially fruit trees, to give late summer interest. Peg out in island beds and use as ground cover. Zones 3–9.

Clematis 'Jacqueline du Pré'
ATRAGENE GROUP

Synonym: *C. alpina* 'Jacqueline du Pré'

Origin: Raised by Barry Fretwell of Peveril Clematis Nursery, England. Named after the famous cellist.

Parentage and year: Unknown. 1985.

Habit: Hardy, moderately vigorous, deciduous climber.

Height: 2.4–3 m (8–10 ft.).

Description: The small, bell-shaped, nodding, rosy mauvish pink flowers are composed of four broad yet tapering tepals, each 6.3 cm (2.5 in.) long, with darker shaded veins running from base to tip and wavy, silver-pink margins. The inside of the tepals are paler, and there is an inner skirt of spoon-shaped, pale pink staminodes surrounding the pale cream, fertile stamens. The leaf margins are serrated, resembling the teeth of a saw.

Pruning group: 1. Any pruning should be carried out immediately after the main flowering period.

Flowering period: Early May to mid-May.

Cultivation: Tolerates well-drained garden soils enriched with organic material. Suitable for any aspect.

Recommended use: Ideal for colder parts of the gar-

Clematis 'Jackmanii Superba'. Photo by C. Chesshire.

Clematis 'Jacqueline du Pré'. Photo by C. Chesshire.

den. Grow on an obelisk, pergola, or trellis. Looks good on a boundary wall. Zones 3–9.

Clematis 'Jacqui'
MONTANA GROUP

Synonym: *C. montana* 'Jacqui'

Origin: Found in the garden of Jacqui Williams of Hertfordshire, England, and introduced to commerce by Priorswood Clematis Nursery, Ware, England.

Parentage and year: Chance seedling. Mid-1990s.

Habit: Vigorous, deciduous climber.

Height: To 6 m (20 ft.).

Description: Slightly scented, single and semi-double, white flowers up to 7.5 cm (3 in.) in diameter are borne at the same time on the previous season's old wood. The undersides of the tepals are slightly tinged with pink, and the leaves are light to midgreen.

Pruning group: 1. Any pruning to keep the plant in check should be carried out immediately after the main flowering period by removing some of the old, flowered stems.

Flowering period: Midspring to late spring.

Cultivation: Tolerates most well-drained garden soils. Hardy in temperate gardens. Produces the strongest scent in a warm position.

Recommended use: Suitable for a large pergola. Allow to roam into large trees and conifers. Zones 7–9.

Clematis 'Jadwiga Teresa'

Synonym: *C.* 'Général Sikorski'

Origin: Raised by Brother Stefan Franczak of Warsaw, Poland, and sent to Vladyslaw Noll as *C.* 'Jadwiga Teresa'. Noll renamed it *C.* 'Général Sikorski' and introduced it commercially in 1975. Introduced to the British Isles in 1980 by Fisk's Clematis Nursery, Suffolk, England. Awarded RHS Award of Garden Merit.

Parentage and year: Unknown. 1965.

Habit: Hardy, compact, deciduous climber.

Height: 1.8–2.4 m (6–8 ft.).

Description: A floriferous cultivar. The single, freely produced, well-rounded flowers, 12–15 cm (4.75–6 in.) wide, are composed of six broadly overlapping mauvish blue tepals, each with a hint of pinkish red emerging from the base and extending halfway along its length, and with gently notched margins. Central boss of stamens is made of creamy white filaments and bright yellow anthers.

Pruning group: 2.

Flowering period: Early summer to early autumn.

Cultivation: Tolerates most garden soils. Best grown in full or partial sun.

Recommended use: Ideal for a pergola, obelisk, or arch, or for growing with wall-trained shrubs which do not require pruning. Good container specimen. Zones 4–9.

Clematis 'James Mason'

Origin: Raised by Barry Fretwell of Peveril Clematis Nursery, England. Named after the renowned actor.

Clematis 'Jacqui'. Photo by E. Leeds.

Clematis 'Jadwiga Teresa'. Photo by D. Harding.

Parentage and year: *C.* 'Marie Boisselot' × *C.* 'Lincoln Star'. 1984.

Habit: Hardy, moderately vigorous, deciduous climber.

Height: 1.8–2.4 m (6–8 ft.).

Description: The single, large, white flowers, 15–20

cm (6–8 in.) wide, are composed of eight overlapping tepals, tapering to fine points, and each with three deep grooves along the centre and undulating margins. The flower boasts a prominent central boss of stamens made of white filaments and dark maroon anthers.

Pruning group: 2.

Flowering period: Late spring to early summer and late summer.

Cultivation: Tolerates most garden soils and any aspect.

Recommended use: Shows up well against a dark background. Ideal for container-culture. Grow through conifers and other medium-sized shrubs or with other wall-trained plants which do not require annual pruning. Suitable for a medium-sized obelisk in a sheltered place to prevent wind damage. Zones 4–9.

Clematis 'Jan Lindmark'
ATRAGENE GROUP

Synonym: *C. macropetala* 'Jan Lindmark'

Origin: Raised in Sweden by Jan Lindmark. Named by Magnus Johnson of Södertälje, Sweden. Introduced

Clematis 'James Mason'. Photo by C. Chesshire.

Clematis 'Jan Lindmark'. Photo by J. Lindmark.

commercially by Raymond Evison of Guernsey Clematis Nursery.

Parentage and year: Seedling of *C.* 'Blue Bird'.

Habit: Hardy, moderately vigorous, compact, deciduous climber.

Height: 2–2.5 m (6.5–8 ft.).

Description: The purple-mauve flowers, composed of four tepals, each with darker streaks, 3.5 cm (1.25 in.) long, open out revealing an inner skirt of petal-like staminodes, which are paler in colour and are twisted and kinked in form, giving a spidery appearance to the whole flower.

Pruning group: 1.

Flowering period: Spring. One of the first cultivars of *C. macropetala* to flower.

Cultivation: Requires sharp-draining garden soils enriched with humus. Suitable for any aspect, even a cold one.

Recommended use: Ideal for the small garden or container-culture. Shows up well against a white or light background. Zones 3–9.

Clematis 'Jan Pawel II'

Synonym: *C.* 'John Paul II'

Origin: Raised by Brother Stefan Franczak of Warsaw, Poland, and introduced into commerce in 1982 by Fisk's Clematis Nursery, Suffolk, England. Named after Pope John Paul II.

Parentage and year: Unknown. Before 1981.

Habit: Hardy, vigorous, deciduous climber.

Height: 2.5–3 m (8–10 ft.).

Description: The single, creamy white flowers with pink trails, which become more prominent in late summer, occasionally as a pink bar, measure 13–14 cm (5–5.5 in.) across and are composed of six firm, broad, creased, overlapping, and pointed tepals. The stamens are made of creamy white filaments with dark wine-red anthers.

Pruning group: 2 or 3. A hard pruning (group 3) delays flowering.

Flowering period: Midsummer to late summer.

Cultivation: Tolerates most garden soils and any aspect. Best grown in partial shade to preserve flower colour.

Recommended use: Suitable for an obelisk, trellis, or pergola. If using pruning group 3, grow naturally through dark-leaved shrubs or conifers. Zones 4–9.

Clematis japonica

Origin: Japan.

Parentage and year: Species. 1784.

Habit: Moderately vigorous, deciduous climber.

Height: 2.5–3 m (8–10 ft.).

Description: The single, brownish red, nodding, bell-shaped flowers, 3 cm (1.25 in.) long, are borne singly or in clusters. The four tepals are somewhat fleshy, recurve at the tips, and are on the whole smooth and shiny except for the hairy margin. Flower colour is variable and also a lighter shade where the flower stalk meets the top of the flower. The flower stalks carry a small pair of leaflike growths (bracts) about 4 cm (1.5 in.) from the flower. Leaves are covered with short,

Clematis 'Jan Pawel II'.
Photo courtesy Thorncroft Clematis Nursery.

Clematis japonica. Photo by C. Chesshire.

stiff hairs and carry three leaflets, which are coarsely toothed. The foliage tends to smother the flowers.

Pruning group: 1.

Flowering period: Late spring to summer.

Cultivation: Needs a sheltered position in sun or partial shade.

Recommended use: A novel garden plant. Not for containers or very cold gardens. Zones 6–9.

Clematis 'Jasper'

Origin: Raised by Rinus Zwijnenburg of Boskoop, Netherlands.

Parentage and year: Open-pollinated seedling of *C. potaninii* var. *fargesii*. Pollen parent believed to be *C. rehderiana*. 1989.

Habit: Hardy, moderately vigorous, deciduous climber.

Height: 2.5–3 m (8–10 ft.).

Description: The single, small, fragrant, semi-nodding, creamy white flowers, 2–3 cm (0.75–1.25 in.) wide, are composed of four or five broad, blunt-tipped tepals with recurving tips. The anthers are greenish yellow. The flowers are borne in clusters.

Pruning group: 3.

Flowering period: Midsummer to late summer.

Cultivation: Tolerates most garden soils. Suitable for any aspect but produces the strongest scent in a sunny position.

Recommended use: Grow through other shrubs, trees, and conifers, or on an arbour, trellis, or pergola. Zones 4–9.

Clematis 'Jeffries'
EVERGREEN/ARMANDII GROUP

Synonym: *C. armandii* 'Jeffries'

Origin: Found by Raymond Evison of Guernsey Clematis Nursery, growing over a shed at the former old nursery of Jeffries of Cirencester, England.

Parentage and year: Selected form of *C. armandii*. Unknown.

Habit: Half-hardy to hardy, vigorous, evergreen climber.

Height: 5–6 m (16–20 ft.).

Description: The single, scented, saucer-shaped, white flowers are composed of four to six non-overlapping and gappy tepals. The leaves are long and narrow with pointed tips.

Pruning group: 1.

Flowering period: Early spring to midspring, with occasional summer flowers.

Clematis 'Jasper'. Photo by C. Chesshire.

Clematis 'Jeffries'. Photo by S. Kuriyama.

Cultivation: Tolerates most well-drained garden soils. Requires a warm, sunny position with protection from cold winds.

Recommended use: Grow on a south-facing wall or fence. Zones 7–9.

Clematis 'Jingle Bells'
EVERGREEN/CIRRHOSA GROUP

Synonym: *C. cirrhosa* 'Jingle Bells'

Origin: Raised by nurseryman Robin Savill of Pleshey, England.

Parentage and year: Chance seedling of *C.* 'Freckles'. 1992.

Habit: Half-hardy to hardy, vigorous, evergreen climber.

Height: 4.5–6 m (14.5–20 ft.).

Description: Cream-coloured buds develop into single, small, nodding, bell-shaped flowers composed of four broad, white tepals 5–6 cm (2–2.25 in.) long, and the stamens are made of greenish filaments and pale yellow anthers. The dark green leaves show off the flowers to the best effect.

Pruning group: 1. Any pruning necessary to keep the plant in check should be carried out immediately after

the main flowering period by cutting back to 1 m (3.25 ft.) from the ground once the plant is well established.

Flowering period: Late autumn to early spring.

Cultivation: Tolerates most garden soils with good drainage. Requires a sunny, warm, frost-free position facing south or southwest to flower well.

Recommended use: Ideal to cover a wall, fence, or unsightly garden building. May be grown through open, medium-sized to large trees. Not recommended for the small garden. Zones 7–9.

Clematis 'Joan Baker'
VITICELLA GROUP

Origin: Raised by Bill Baker of Tidmarsh, Herne, England.

Parentage and year: *C.* 'Etoile Rose' × (*C. campaniflora* × *C. viticella* hybrid). Early 1980s.

Habit: Hardy, moderately vigorous, deciduous climber.

Height: 2.4–3 m (8–10 ft.).

Description: The single, nodding and semi-nodding flowers, 6–6.5 cm (2.25–2.5 in.) across, are composed of four pinkish mauve tepals. These are narrow at the base, not overlapping, and halfway along their length they widen into a slight arrowhead shape with heavily textured margins which turn inwards. Three central grooves, which are shaded a deeper colour, run the length of each tepal. Nearer to the base, the tepal colour shades into a very pale mauve, and the stamens are greenish yellow.

Pruning group: 3.

Flowering period: Early summer to late summer.

Clematis 'Jingle Bells'. Photo by C. Chesshire.

Clematis 'Joan Baker'. Photo by C. Chesshire.

Cultivation: Tolerates most garden soils and any aspect. Best grown in an open situation to prevent any occurrence of mildew.

Recommended use: Ideal for a medium-sized obelisk or trellis. Grow through medium-sized to large shrubs and conifers. Zones 4–9.

Clematis 'Joan Picton'

Origin: Raised by Percy Picton of Old Court Nurseries, Colwall, England. Introduced by Fisk's Clematis Nursery, Suffolk, England.

Parentage and year: Unknown. 1974.

Habit: Hardy, not-so-vigorous, compact, deciduous climber.

Height: 1.8–2.4 m (6–8 ft.).

Description: A very free-flowering cultivar. The single, pale lilac flowers, measuring 15–20 cm (6–8 in.) across, are composed of seven or eight tepals, which are somewhat narrower towards the base and wider towards the top end. Each tepal boasts a slightly prominent darker central bar, which elegantly contrasts with the tepal colour. Greenish white filaments are tipped with dark purple-red anthers.

Pruning group: 2.

Flowering period: Late spring to early summer and late summer.

Cultivation: Tolerates most garden soils and any aspect. Requires protection from strong winds.

Recommended use: Ideal for container-culture. Grow on a medium-sized trellis or obelisk. Allow to scramble over low-growing, open shrubs which do not require severe annual pruning. Zones 4–9.

Clematis 'Joe'
EVERGREEN GROUP

Synonym: *C. cartmanii* 'Joe'

Origin: Seed sent to Margaret and Henry Taylor of Invergowrie, Scotland, by Joe Cartman, Christchurch, New Zealand. Sown 30 June 1983.

Parentage and year: Believed to be *C. marmoraria* × *C. paniculata*. 1983–1984.

Clematis 'Joan Picton'. Photo by C. Chesshire.

Clematis 'Joe'. Photo by I. Holmåsen.

Habit: Half-hardy to hardy, non-clinging evergreen climber or scrambler.

Height: 2 m (6.5 ft.) if trained and tied-in; otherwise makes a compact mound.

Description: A very floriferous cultivar. Clusters of greenish buds open to single, snowy white, showy, male flowers 2.5 cm (1 in.) wide on short stalks. The tepals usually number six, but may be few as five or as many as eight. The leaves are finely dissected, long lasting, and glossy.

Pruning group: 1.

Flowering period: In the garden, early spring to midspring; under glass, even earlier.

Cultivation: Prefers well-drained, gritty soil.

Recommended use: Best grown in a sheltered alpine bed where it can scramble, or in a container in a cold greenhouse or conservatory. Zones 7–9.

Clematis 'John Gould Veitch'

Origin: Japan. Found by John Gould Veitch and sent to John Standish of Berkshire, England, along with Robert Fortune's plants. The plant was then transferred to the Veitch nursery.

Parentage and year: Semi-double form of *C. patens*. 1862.

Habit: Hardy, not-so-vigorous, deciduous climber.

Height: 2–2.5 m (6.5–8 ft.).

Description: The semi-double flowers, 10–15 cm (4–6 in.) across, are made of six to eight rows of staminodes, which are initially lavender-blue fading to almost white with a blue tinge. The petal-like staminodes are wider at the base, tapering towards a slightly

hairy tip, which ends in sharp, flexible points. White filaments carrying yellow anthers make up the stamens. The flowers are always semi-double and are produced from ripened, previous season's wood. A very fine plant.

Pruning group: 2.

Flowering period: Early summer and late summer.

Cultivation: Tolerates most garden soils but prefers a semi-shaded, sheltered position.

Recommended use: Plant with medium-sized shrubs or moderately vigorous climbing roses. Suitable for an obelisk or trellis. Zones 4–9.

Clematis 'John Gudmundsson'

Origin: Raised by John Gudmundsson, an amateur gardener of Helsingborg, Sweden. Named in 1986 by Krister Cedargren and Company, Helsingborg.

Parentage and year: Unknown. 1950.

Habit: Hardy, not-so-vigorous, compact, deciduous climber.

Height: 1.8–2.4 m (6–8 ft.).

Description: The single, violet-blue flowers, 12–15 cm (4.75–6 in.) across, are composed of six to eight tepals, each with a deeper reddish purple central bar, and margins with very small rounded teeth. The stamens are deep reddish purple.

Pruning group: 2.

Flowering period: Late spring to early summer and late summer.

Cultivation: Tolerates most garden soils and any aspect.

Recommended use: A good subject for container-

Clematis 'John Gould Veitch'. Photo by J. Lindmark.

Clematis 'John Gudmundsson'. Photo by M. Brown.

culture. Ideal for a small obelisk or short trellis. Useful for covering the bare lower stems of wall-trained shrubs and roses. Zones 4–9.

Clematis 'John Huxtable'

Origin: Raised by John Huxtable of Devon and introduced by Rowland Jackman of George Jackman and Son, England.

Parentage and year: Chance seedling of *C.* 'Comtesse de Bouchaud'. 1967.

Habit: Hardy, moderately vigorous, compact, deciduous climber.

Clematis 'John Huxtable'. Photo by C. Chesshire.

Clematis 'John Warren'. Photo by R. Surman.

Height: 2.5–3 m (8–10 ft.).

Description: The single, translucent, creamy white flowers, 11–12 cm (4.5–4.75 in.) across, are composed of six tapering, textured tepals with slightly recurving tips. The stamens are made of white filaments and yellow anthers.

Pruning group: 3.

Flowering period: Midsummer to late summer.

Cultivation: Tolerates most garden soils and any aspect.

Recommended use: Ideal to grow over shrubs with dark foliage or with climbing roses and other wall-trained shrubs. Suitable for a trellis, obelisk, or small arch. Zones 4–9.

Clematis 'John Warren'

Origin: Raised by Walter Pennell of Pennell and Sons nursery. Named in 1968 after the then principal of Lincoln College of Agriculture, England.

Parentage and year: Unknown. Probably raised between 1950 and 1956.

Habit: Hardy, moderately vigorous, compact, deciduous climber.

Height: 2.5–3 m (8–10 ft.).

Description: The single, rather large flowers, 20–23 cm (8–9 in.) across, are composed of 6–8 overlapping, pointed tepals with a base colour of pinky grey overlaid with a deeper pink stripe along the middle. The tepal margins are also richly coloured, but the colour fades with age. The stamens are reddish, and the leaves may be simple or divided into three parts or a combination of both kinds.

Pruning group: 2.

Flowering period: Late spring to early summer and late summer.

Cultivation: Tolerates most garden soils. Requires a sheltered position to prevent wind damage to the large flowers.

Recommended use: Ideal for a semi-shaded area of the garden on a trellis, obelisk, or pergola. Would also suit being grown through a medium-sized shrub which does not require severe annual pruning. Zones 4–9.

Clematis 'Jouiniana'
HERBACEOUS/HERACLEIFOLIA GROUP

Synonym: *C.* ×*jouiniana*

Origin: Raised at the nursery of Simon-Louis Frères

in France and named after Emile Jouin, the nursery manager.

Parentage and year: *C. heracleifolia* var. *davidiana* × *C. vitalba*. ca. 1900.

Habit: Hardy, deciduous, vigorous, non-clinging, herbaceous, woody shrub.

Height: 1.8–2.4 m (5–8 ft.) if grown supported; 0.9–1.2 m (3–4 ft.) if allowed to scramble.

Description: The large clusters of small flowers, 2–3 cm (0.75–1.25 in.) wide, are borne from terminal stems and upper leaf axils. Each flower is composed of four yellowish white, narrow, spreading tepals, which open fully and slightly recurve, becoming suffused with lilac as they mature. The prominent stamens have white filaments and yellow anthers. The leaves are large, coarse, uninteresting, and dull green.

Pruning group: 3.

Flowering period: Late summer to early autumn.

Cultivation: Tolerates most garden soils and any aspect but flourishes in a free-draining site with annual feed and mulch. If trained on an artificial support, the stems need tying-in.

Recommended use: Ideal for ground cover or as a centrepiece on an island bed if grown over a low, sturdy tripod. Not suitable for small gardens. Zones 3–9.

Clematis 'Jouiniana Praecox'
HERBACEOUS / HERACLEIFOLIA GROUP

Origin: Unknown. Awarded RHS Award of Garden Merit.

Parentage and year: Believed to be *C. heracleifolia* × *C.* 'Jouiniana'. Unknown.

Habit: Hardy, deciduous, vigorous, herbaceous, non-clinging, woody subshrub.

Height: 1.8–2.4 m (6–8 ft.) if grown supported. 0.9–1.2 m (3–4 ft.) if allowed to scramble. If used as ground cover will encompass up to 2.4 m (8 ft.) in diameter.

Description: The single flowers comprise four, rarely five or six, pale mauve, narrow tepals up to 4 cm (1.5 in.) in diameter, the deepest colour being near the tips. Each tepal has a ridge along the margins and the tips curve back upon themselves. The central boss of prominent stamens consists of white filaments and yellow anthers. Large, coarse leaves have serrated edges.

Pruning group: 3.

Flowering period: Midsummer to early autumn.

Cultivation: Tolerates most garden soils and any aspect.

Recommended use: Ideal for ground cover or as a centrepiece on an island bed if grown over a low tripod. Zones 3–9.

Clematis 'Jubileijnyj-70'

Synonym: *C.* 'Jubileinyi 70'

Origin: Raised by M. A. Beskaravainaja and A. N. Volosenko-Valenis of the State Nikitsky Botanic Gardens, Ukraine. Named to commemorate the 100th anniversary of the birth of Lenin (1870–1924). The name means "jubilee."

Parentage and year: *C.* 'Jackmanii' × *C.* 'Gipsy Queen'. 1965.

Habit: Hardy, fairly vigorous, deciduous climber.

Clematis 'Jouiniana'. Photo by J. Lindmark.

Clematis 'Jouiniana Praecox'. Photo by R. Surman.

Height: 3–3.6 m (10–12 ft.).

Description: A free-flowering cultivar. The single, deep lilac-purple, velvety flowers, 9–12 cm (3.5–4.75 in.) in diameter, are composed of normally six, sometimes four or five, tepals with wavy edges. The anthers are yellow. The rich colour of the flower fades with age. The compound leaves consist of five leaflets.

Pruning group: 3.

Flowering period: Midsummer to late summer.

Cultivation: Tolerates most garden soils and any aspect.

Recommended use: Grow naturally through other shrubs and small trees. Suitable for a pergola, post, or trellis. Zones 4–9.

Clematis 'Jubileijnyj-70'. Photo by J. Lindmark.

Clematis 'Juuli'. Photo by J. Lindmark.

Clematis 'Juuli'

HERBACEOUS/INTEGRIFOLIA GROUP

Origin: Raised by Uno Kivistik of Harjumaa, Estonia.

Parentage and year: *C. integrifolia* × *C. viticella*. 1984.

Habit: Hardy, herbaceous, non-clinging shrub.

Height: 1.2–1.5 m (4–5 ft.).

Description: A very floriferous cultivar. The small, single, outward-facing flowers, 7.5–9 cm (3–3.5 in.) across, are borne in great profusion on the current season's wood and comprise five or six spoon-shaped, non-overlapping purplish blue tepals with prominent central grooves tinged with pinkish purple. As the flowers mature the margins fade to pale blue, leaving a more prominent central rib marking. A striking central boss of prominent stamens is composed of cream filaments and golden yellow anthers.

Pruning group: 3.

Flowering period: Midsummer to late summer.

Cultivation: Tolerates most garden soils enriched with humus. Suitable for any aspect. If vertical growth is required, the stems need tying-in.

Recommended use: Ideal underplanted in a rose bed where it can be left to scramble at will. Grow in a container where it can overflow or allow it to tumble over a low wall, shrubs, and prostrate conifers. Zones 3–9.

Clematis 'Kacper'

Trade name: CASPAR

Origin: Raised by Brother Stefan Franczak of Warsaw, Poland, and named after one of the three biblical Wise Men.

Parentage and year: Unknown. ca. 1970.

Habit: Hardy, moderately vigorous, deciduous climber.

Clematis 'Kacper' (CASPAR™). Photo by C. Chesshire.

C. 'Maria Louise Jensen'
C. 'Marie Boisselot'
C. 'Masquerade'
C. 'Matka Teresa'
C. 'Maureen'
C. 'Midnight'
C. 'Mikelite'
C. 'Miniseelik'
C. 'Minister'
C. 'Miss Bateman'
C. 'Monte Cassino'
C. 'Moonlight'
C. 'Mrs. Bush'
C. 'Mrs. Cholmondeley'
C. 'Mrs. Hope'
C. 'Mrs. N. Thompson'
C. 'Mrs. P. B. Truax'
C. 'Mrs. P. T. James'
C. 'Myōjō'
C. 'Natacha'
C. 'Natascha'
C. 'Negritjanka'
C. 'Negus'
C. 'Nelly Moser'
C. 'Nikolaj Rubtzov'
C. 'Niobe'
C. 'Olimpiada-80'
C. 'Paddington'
C. 'Pat Coleman'
C. patens
C. 'Perle d'Azur'
C. 'Perrin's Pride'
C. 'Peveril Pearl'
C. 'Pink Fantasy'
C. 'Pink Pearl'
C. 'Pöhjanael'
C. 'Polish Spirit'
C. 'Poulala' (ALABAST™)
C. 'Poulvo' (VINO™)
C. 'Prince Charles'
C. 'Prince Philip'
C. 'Princess of Wales'
C. 'Prins Hendrik' (PRINCE
    HENDRIK™)
C. 'Rahvarinne'
C. 'Red Cooler'
C. 'Rhapsody'
C. 'Richard Pennell'
C. 'Romantika'
C. 'Rouge Cardinal'
C. 'Rüütel'
C. 'Satsukibare'

C. 'Saturn'
C. 'Scartho Gem'
C. 'Sealand Gem'
C. 'Seranata'
C. 'Sheila Thacker'
C. 'Sho-un'
C. 'Signe'
C. 'Silver Moon'
C. 'Sir Garnet Wolseley'
C. 'Snow Queen'
C. 'Special Occasion'
C. 'Sputnik'
C. 'Star of India'
C. 'Strawberry Roan'
C. 'Sunset'
C. 'Susan Allsop'
C. 'Sympatia'
C. 'Tartu'
C. 'Teksa'
C. 'Tentel'
C. 'The Bride'
C. 'The First Lady'
C. 'The President'
C. 'The Vagabond'
C. 'Titania'
C. 'Torleif'
C. 'Twilight'
C. 'Ulrique'
C. 'Valge Daam'
C. 'Vanessa'
C. 'Victoria'
C. 'Ville de Lyon'
C. 'Viola'
C. 'Violet Charm'
C. 'Vivienne Lawson'
C. 'Voluceau'
C. 'Vostok'
C. 'W. E. Gladstone'
C. 'W. S. Callick'
C. 'Wada's Primrose'
C. 'Warszawska Nike'
C. 'Westerplatte'
C. 'Wilhelmina Tull'
C. 'Will Goodwin'
C. 'William Kennett'
C. 'Yukikomachi'
C. 'Yvette Houry'

Viticella Group
C. 'Abundance'
C. 'Alba Luxurians'
C. 'Betty Corning'

C. 'Black Prince'
C. 'Blue Belle'
C. campaniflora
C. 'Carmencita'
C. 'Cicciolina'
C. 'Elvan'
C. 'Etoile Violette'
C. 'Flore Pleno'
C. 'Foxtrot'
C. 'Joan Baker'
C. 'Kasmu'
C. 'Kermesina'
C. 'Lisboa'
C. 'Little Nell'
C. 'Madame Julia Correvon'
C. 'Margot Koster'
C. 'Minuet'
C. 'Mrs. T. Lundell'
C. 'Pagoda'
C. 'Purpurea Plena Elegans'
C. 'Royal Velours'
C. 'Södertälje'
C. 'Tango'
C. 'Triternata Rubromarginata'
C. 'Venosa Violacea'
C. viticella
C. 'Walenburg'

Texensis-Viorna Group
C. addisonii
C. 'Buckland Beauty'
C. 'Burford Bell'
C. crispa
C. 'Duchess of Albany'
C. 'Etoile Rose'
C. 'Gravetye Beauty'
C. hirsutissima
C. hirsutissima var. *scottii*
C. 'Kaiu'
C. 'Lady Bird Johnson'
C. 'Phil Mason'
C. pitcheri
C. 'Princess Diana'
C. 'Sir Trevor Lawrence'
C. texensis
C. versicolor
C. viorna

Tangutica Group
C. 'Anita'
C. 'Annemieke'
C. 'Aureolin'

C. 'Bill MacKenzie'
C. 'Bravo'
C. 'Burford Variety'
C. 'Corry'
C. 'Golden Harvest'
C. 'Grace'
C. 'Gravetye Variety'
C. 'Helios'
C. 'Kugotia' (GOLDEN TIARA™)
C. ladakhiana
C. 'Lambton Park'
C. orientalis
C. serratifolia
C. tangutica
C. tangutica subsp. *obtusiuscula*
C. tibetana subsp. *vernayi*
C. tibetana subsp. *vernayi*
    Ludlow, Sherriff & Elliot

Herbaceous Group
C. 'Alba'
C. albicoma
C. 'Alblo' (ALAN BLOOM™)
C. 'Alionushka'
C. 'Arabella'
C. 'Aromatica'
C. 'Blue Boy'
C. 'Bonstedtii'
C. 'Campanile'
C. coactilis
C. 'Côte d'Azur'
C. 'Crépuscule'
C. 'Cylindrica'
C. 'Durandii'
C. 'Edward Prichard'
C. 'Eriostemon'
C. 'Evisix' (PETIT FAUCON™)
C. fremontii
C. 'Heather Herschell'
C. 'Hendersoni'
C. heracleifolia
C. heracleifolia var. *davidiana*
C. hexapetala
C. integrifolia
C. integrifolia var. *latifolia*
C. 'Jouiniana'
C. 'Jouiniana Praecox'
C. 'Juuli'
C. 'Lauren'
C. 'Lord Herschell'
C. mandschurica
C. 'Mrs. Robert Brydon'

C. 'New Love'
C. ochroleuca
C. 'Olgae'
C. 'Pamela'
C. 'Pamiat Serdtsa'
C. 'Pangbourne Pink'
C. 'Pastel Blue'
C. 'Pastel Pink'
C. 'Purpurea'
C. recta
C. 'Rosea'
C. 'Sander'
C. 'Sinij Dozhdj' (BLUE RAIN™)
C. socialis
C. songarica

C. stans
C. 'Tapestry'
C. 'Wyevale'

Other Species and Cultivars

C. aethusifolia
C. apiifolia
C. aristata
C. brachiata
C. brachyura
C. brevicaudata
C. buchananiana
C. chinensis
C. connata
C. cunninghamii
C. denticulata

C. flammula
C. florida
C. fruticosa
C. fusca
C. fusca var. *violacea*
C. gouriana
C. grandiflora
C. grata
C. grewiiflora
C. intricata
C. ispahanica
C. japonica
C. lanuginosa
C. lasiandra
C. lasiantha

C. ligusticifolia
C. obvallata
C. 'Paul Farges' (SUMMER SNOW™)
C. peterae
C. phlebantha
C. pierotii
C. potanini
C. ranunculoides
C. rehderiana
C. veitchiana
C. virginiana
C. vitalba
C. 'Western Virgin'
C. williamsii

APPENDIX 2

Clematis by Flower Colour

RED

C. 'Abundance'
C. 'Allanah'
C. 'Barbara Dibley'
C. 'Black Prince'
C. 'Buckland Beauty'
C. 'Carmencita'
C. 'Carnaby'
C. 'Charissima'
C. 'Cicciolina'
C. 'Corona'
C. 'Crimson King'
C. 'Docteur Le Bêle'
C. 'Empress of India'
C. 'Ernest Markham'
C. 'Evifive' (LIBERATION™)
C. 'Gravetye Beauty'
C. 'Hainton Ruby'
C. 'Huvi'
C. 'Jackmanii Rubra'
C. 'Kardynal Wyszynski' (CARDINAL WYSZYNSKI™)
C. 'Keith Richardson'
C. 'Kermesina'
C. 'Lady Bird Johnson'
C. 'Lansdowne Gem'
C. 'Madame Édouard André'
C. 'Madame Julia Correvon'
C. 'Niobe'
C. 'Olimpiada-80'
C. 'Poulvo' (VINO™)
C. 'Purpurea Plena Elegans'
C. 'Red Cooler'

C. 'Rouge Cardinal'
C. 'Rüütel'
C. 'Sir Trevor Lawrence'
C. 'Södertälje'
C. texensis
C. versicolor
C. 'Ville de Lyon'
C. 'Voluceau'
C. 'W. S. Callick'
C. 'Westerplatte'

BLUE

C. 'Alblo' (ALAN BLOOM™)
C. 'Alice Fisk'
C. alpina
C. 'Alpinist'
C. 'Anders'
C. 'Andrew'
C. 'Aromatica'
C. 'Ascotiensis'
C. 'Beauty of Richmond'
C. 'Beauty of Worcester'
C. 'Belle Nantaise'
C. 'Blekitny Aniol' (BLUE ANGEL™)
C. 'Blue Belle'
C. 'Blue Bird'
C. 'Blue Boy'
C. 'Blue Dancer'
C. 'Blue Gem'
C. 'Blue Ravine'
C. 'Boskoop Beauty'
C. 'Campanile'

C. 'Chalcedony'
C. 'Chili'
C. 'Columbine'
C. 'Countess of Lovelace'
C. 'Crépuscule'
C. 'Cyanea'
C. 'Cylindrica'
C. 'Denny's Double'
C. 'Durandii'
C. 'Édouard Desfossé'
C. 'Ekstra'
C. 'Elsa Späth' (BLUE BOY™ in Australia)
C. 'Elvan'
C. 'Emilia Plater'
C. 'Eriostemon'
C. 'Etoile de Malicorne'
C. 'Etoile de Paris'
C. 'Evisix' (PETIT FAUCON™)
C. 'Evithree' (ANNA LOUISE™)
C. 'Floralia'
C. 'Frances Rivis' (Dutch form)
C. 'Frances Rivis' (English form)
C. 'Frankie'
C. fremontii
C. 'Fujimusume'
C. 'Gabriëlle'
C. 'Georg Ots'
C. 'Glynderek'
C. 'Guiding Star'
C. 'H. F. Young'

C. 'Helsingborg'
C. 'Hendersoni'
C. heracleifolia
C. heracleifolia var. davidiana
C. 'Hybrida Sieboldii'
C. integrifolia
C. integrifolia var. latifolia
C. 'Ivan Olsson'
C. 'Jadwiga Teresa'
C. 'John Gould Veitch'
C. 'John Gudmundsson'
C. 'Juuli'
C. 'Kasugayama'
C. 'Ken Donson'
C. 'Kiri Te Kanawa'
C. 'Königskind'
C. 'Lady Betty Balfour'
C. 'Lady Northcliffe'
C. 'Lagoon'
C. 'Lasurstern'
C. 'Laura'
C. 'Lawsoniana'
C. 'Lilactime'
C. 'Lisboa'
C. 'Lord Nevill'
C. macropetala
C. 'Maidwell Hall'
C. 'Maria Louise Jensen'
C. 'Masquerade'
C. 'Midnight'
C. 'Minister'
C. 'Mrs. Bush'
C. 'Mrs. Cholmondeley'

C. 'Mrs. Hope'
C. 'Mrs. James Mason'
C. 'Mrs. P. B. Truax'
C. 'Mrs. P. T. James'
C. 'Mrs. Robert Brydon'
C. 'Multi Blue'
C. 'Natacha'
C. 'Negus'
C. 'New Love'
C. ochotensis
C. 'Odorata' (Atragene Group)
C. 'Olgae'
C. 'Pamela Jackman'
C. 'Pastel Blue'
C. 'Pauline'
C. 'Perle d'Azur'
C. 'Prairie River'
C. 'Prince Charles'
C. 'Prins Hendrik' (PRINCE HENDRIK™)
C. 'Rhapsody'
C. 'Sandra Denny'
C. 'Saturn'
C. 'Sealand Gem'
C. 'Sheila Thacker'
C. 'Sho-un'
C. 'Signe'
C. 'Sinij Dozhdj' (BLUE RAIN™)
C. 'Sir Garnet Wolseley'
C. socialis
C. 'Sputnik'
C. 'Teshio'
C. 'The First Lady'
C. 'The President'
C. 'Ulrique'
C. 'Vanessa'
C. 'Violet Charm'
C. 'W. E. Gladstone'
C. 'Wesselton'
C. 'Will Goodwin'
C. 'William Kennett'
C. 'Wyevale'
C. 'Yukikomachi'
C. 'Yvette Houry'

PINK
C. 'Alborosea'
C. 'Alionushka'
C. 'Ametistina'
C. 'Anna'
C. 'Asao'
C. 'Ballet Skirt'

C. 'Bees Jubilee'
C. 'Broughton Star'
C. 'Capitaine Thuilleaux'
C. 'Carmen Rose'
C. 'Caroline'
C. chrysocoma 'Hybrid'
C. 'Columella'
C. 'Comtesse de Bouchaud'
C. 'Constance'
C. 'Dawn'
C. 'Doctor Ruppel'
C. 'Dorothy Tolver'
C. 'Dorothy Walton'
C. 'Dovedale'
C. 'Duchess of Sutherland'
C. 'Edward Prichard'
C. 'Eleanor of Guildford'
C. 'Elizabeth'
C. 'Etoile Rose'
C. 'Evijohill' (JOSEPHINE™)
C. 'Fairy Queen'
C. 'Foxy'
C. 'Freda'
C. 'Gothenburg'
C. 'Hagley Hybrid'
C. 'Hanaguruma'
C. 'Heather Herschell'
C. 'Helen Cropper'
C. 'Highdown'
C. 'Imperial'
C. 'Jacqueline du Pré'
C. 'Jan Lindmark'
C. 'John Warren'
C. 'Kakio' (PINK CHAMPAGNE™)
C. 'King George V'
C. 'Kirimäe'
C. 'Lilacina'
C. 'Lincoln Star'
C. 'Lucey'
C. 'Margaret Hunt'
C. 'Margot Koster'
C. 'Markham's Pink'
C. 'Mayleen'
C. 'Miss Crawshay'
C. montana var. rubens
C. 'Natascha'
C. 'Nelly Moser'
C. 'New Dawn'
C. 'Odorata' (Montana Group)
C. 'Pafar' (PATRICIA ANN FRETWELL™)
C. 'Pangbourne Pink'

C. 'Pastel Pink'
C. 'Peveril Pearl'
C. 'Picton's Variety'
C. 'Piilu'
C. 'Pink Fantasy'
C. 'Pink Flamingo'
C. 'Pink Pearl'
C. 'Pink Perfection'
C. 'Princess Diana'
C. 'Propertius'
C. 'Proteus'
C. 'Rosea'
C. 'Rosy O'Grady'
C. 'Rosy Pagoda'
C. 'Ruby'
C. 'Scartho Gem'
C. 'Strawberry Roan'
C. 'Sunset'
C. 'Tango'
C. 'Tapestry'
C. 'Triternata Rubromarginata'
C. 'Twilight'
C. 'Vera'
C. 'Violet Elizabeth'
C. 'Walter Pennell'
C. 'Warwickshire Rose'
C. 'Willy'

PURPLE
C. 'Akaishi'
C. 'Alborosea'
C. 'Aotearoa'
C. 'Beth Currie' (VIVIENNE™)
C. 'Brunette'
C. 'Burford Bell'
C. 'Burma Star'
C. 'Christian Steven'
C. columbiana var. tenuiloba
C. 'Daniel Deronda'
C. 'Édomurasaki'
C. 'Elegija'
C. 'Etoile Violette'
C. 'Evifour' (ROYAL VELVET™)
C. fauriei
C. 'Fireworks'
C. 'Foxtrot'
C. 'G. Steffner'
C. 'Georg'
C. 'Gipsy Queen'
C. 'Hakuōkan'
C. 'Helsingborg'
C. 'Jackmanii'
C. 'Jackmanii Superba'

C. 'Jenny Caddick'
C. 'Jubilenyj-70'
C. 'Karin'
C. 'Kasmu'
C. 'Kathleen Dunford'
C. 'Kuba'
C. 'Lauren'
C. 'Luther Burbank'
C. 'Madame Grangé'
C. 'Maureen'
C. 'Mikelite'
C. 'Miniseelik'
C. 'Monte Cassino'
C. 'Mrs. N. Thompson'
C. 'Myōjō'
C. 'Paddington'
C. 'Perrin's Pride'
C. 'Pöhjanael'
C. 'Polish Spirit'
C. 'Pruinina'
C. 'Purple Spider'
C. 'Rahvarinne'
C. 'Red Beetroot Beauty'
C. 'Richard Pennell'
C. 'Romantika'
C. 'Serenata'
C. 'Star of India'
C. 'Susan Allsop'
C. 'Tage Lundell'
C. 'Tartu'
C. 'Tentel'
C. 'The Vagabond'
C. 'Venosa Violacea'
C. 'Viola'
C. 'Vivienne Lawson'
C. 'Vostok'
C. 'Warszawska Nike'
C. 'Wilhelmina Tull'

MAUVE
C. 'Arabella'
C. 'Barbara Jackman'
C. 'Belle of Woking'
C. 'Betty Corning'
C. 'Colette Deville'
C. 'Édouard Desfossé'
C. 'Elgar'
C. 'Entel'
C. 'Evione' (SUGAR CANDY™)
C. 'Evista' (EVENING STAR™)
C. 'Fragrant Spring'
C. 'Herbert Johnson'
C. 'Horn of Plenty'

C. 'Iola Fair'
C. 'Joan Baker'
C. 'Joan Picton'
C. 'Jouiniana'
C. 'Jouiniana Praecox'
C. 'Kathleen Wheeler'
C. 'Lady Caroline Nevill'
C. 'Lady Londesborough'
C. 'Laura'
C. 'Louise Rowe'
C. 'Madame Baron Veillard'
C. 'Miriam Markham'
C. 'Mrs. Spencer Castle'
C. 'Nikolaj Rubtzov'
C. 'Pamiat Serdtsa'
C. 'Prince Philip'
C. 'Royal Velours'
C. 'Royalty'
C. 'Satsukibare'
C. 'Silver Moon'
C. 'Sympatia'
C. 'Teksa'
C. 'Thyrislund'
C. 'Torleif'
C. 'Veronica's Choice'
C. 'Victoria'
C. viticella
C. 'Vyvyan Pennell'
C. 'Walenburg'

WHITE
C. 'Alba'
C. 'Alba Luxurians'
C. 'Albiflora'
C. 'Albina Plena'
C. 'Alexander'
C. 'Andromeda'
C. 'Anita'
C. 'Aoife'

C. apiifolia
C. 'Apple Blossom'
C. armandii
C. armandii var. biondiana
C. 'Asagasumi'
C. 'Bella'
C. 'Blaaval' (AVALANCHE™)
C. 'Bowl of Beauty'
C. brachiata
C. brevicaudata
C. 'Broughton Bride'
C. 'Burford White'
C. campaniflora
C. chrysocoma
C. denticulata
C. 'Duchess of Edinburgh'
C. 'Edith'
C. 'Evirida' (PISTACHIO™)
C. 'Evitwo' (ARCTIC QUEEN™)
C. 'Fair Rosamond'
C. fasciculiflora
C. flammula
C. 'Flore Pleno'
C. florida
C. gentianoides
C. 'Gillian Blades'
C. gouriana
C. 'Grace'
C. gracilifolia
C. grata
C. 'Henryi'
C. hexapetala
C. 'Huldine'
C. 'Ishobel'
C. ispahanica
C. 'Jackmanii Alba'
C. 'Jacqui'
C. 'James Mason'
C. 'Jan Pawel II'

C. 'Jasper'
C. 'Jeffries'
C. 'Jingle Bells'
C. 'Joe'
C. 'John Huxtable'
C. 'Kaiu'
C. ligusticifolia
C. 'Little Nell'
C. 'Madame van Houtte'
C. mandschurica
C. 'Margaret Jones'
C. 'Marie Boisselot'
C. marmoraria
C. 'Matka Teresa'
C. meyeniana
C. 'Miss Bateman'
C. montana
C. montana var. wilsonii
C. 'Mrs. George Jackman'
C. 'Nunn's Gift'
C. 'Pamela'
C. paniculata
C. 'Pat Coleman'
C. 'Paul Farges' (SUMMER SNOW™)
C. 'Peveril'
C. 'Plena'
C. potaninii
C. 'Poulala' (ALABAST™)
C. 'Purpurea'
C. recta
C. 'Riga'
C. 'Robusta'
C. sibirica
C. 'Sieboldii'
C. 'Snow Queen'
C. 'Snowbird'
C. 'Snowdrift'

C. songarica
C. spooneri
C. 'Sylvia Denny'
C. terniflora
C. 'The Bride'
C. 'Titania'
C. 'Valge Daam'
C. virginiana
C. vitalba
C. 'Western Virgin'
C. 'White Columbine'
C. 'White Moth'
C. 'White Swan'
C. 'White Wings'

YELLOW
C. 'Annemieke'
C. 'Aureolin'
C. australis
C. 'Bill MacKenzie'
C. 'Bravo'
C. chiisanensis
C. coactilis
C. 'Corry'
C. 'Golden Harvest'
C. 'Helios'
C. 'Kugotia' (GOLDEN TIARA™)
C. 'Lambton Park'
C. 'Lemon Bells'
C. 'Lemon Chiffon'
C. 'Moonlight'
C. rehderiana
C. serratifolia
C. tangutica
C. tangutica subsp. obtusiuscula
C. tibetana subsp. vernayi
C. 'Wada's Primrose'

APPENDIX 3

Trade and Cultivar Names

C. ALABAST™, see *C.* 'Poulala'
C. ALAN BLOOM™, see *C.* 'Alblo'
C. ANNA LOUISE™, see *C.* 'Evithree'
C. ARCTIC QUEEN™, see *C.* 'Evitwo'
C. AVALANCHE™, see *C.* 'Blaaval'
C. BLUE ANGEL™, see *C.* 'Blekitny Aniol'
C. BLUE BOY™ (in Australia only), see *C.* 'Elsa Späth'
C. BLUE RAIN™, see *C.* 'Sinij Dozhdj'
C. CARDINAL WYSZYNSKI™, see *C.* 'Kardynal Wyszynski'
C. CASPAR™, see *C.* 'Kacper'
C. EVENING STAR™, see *C.* 'Evista'
C. GOLDEN TIARA™, see *C.* 'Kugotia'

C. JOSEPHINE™, see *C.* 'Evijohill'
C. LIBERATION™, see *C.* 'Evifive'
C. PATRICIA ANN FRETWELL™, see *C.* 'Pafar'
C. PETIT FAUCON™, see *C.* 'Evisix'
C. PINK CHAMPAGNE™, see *C.* 'Kakio'
C. PISTACHIO™, see *C.* 'Evirida'
C. PRINCE HENDRIK™, see *C.* 'Prins Hendrik'
C. ROYAL VELVET™, see *C.* 'Evifour'
C. SUGAR CANDY™, see *C.* 'Evione'
C. SUMMER SNOW™, see *C.* 'Paul Farges'
C. VINO™, see *C.* 'Poulvo'
C. VIVIENNE™, see *C.* 'Beth Currie'

Hybridizers and Nurseries Mentioned in the Directory of Clematis

Anderson-Henry, Isaac, Hay Lodge, Edinburgh, Scotland.*

Baron Veillard of Orléans, France.*

Bees of Chester, England.*

Blooms of Bressingham, Diss, Norfolk, IP22 2AB, England.

Boisselot, Auguste, Nantes, France.*

Caddick's Clematis Nursery, Lymm Road, Thelwall, Warrington, Cheshire, WA4 2TG, England.

Cripps, Thomas, and Son, Tunbridge Wells, England.*

Denny's Clematis Nursery, Broughton, Lancashire, England.*

Desfossé, Orléans, France.*

Evison, Raymond J., The Guernsey Clematis Nursery, Domarie Vineries, Les Sauvagées, St. Sampson, Guernsey, GY2 4FD, Channel Islands.

Fisk, Jim, Fisk's Clematis Nursery, Suffolk, England.*

Fopma, Jan, Boskoop, Netherlands.*

Frères, Simon-Louis, France.*

Fretwell, Barry, Peveril Clematis Nursery, Christow, Nr. Exeter, Devon, EX6 7NG, England.

Goos and Koenemann of Germany.*

Hutchins, Graham, County Park Nursery, Essex Gardens, Hornchurch, Essex, RM11 3BU, England.

J. Bouter and Zoon, Boskoop, Netherlands.

Jackman, George, and Son, Woking, Surrey, England.*

Jerard, M. L., Potters Lane, Lansdowne Valley, R.D. 2, Christchurch, New Zealand 8021.

Johnson, Magnus, Södertälje, Sweden.*

Keay, Alister, New Zealand Clematis Nurseries, 67 Ngaio Street, St. Martins, Christchurch 2, New Zealand.

Kivistik, Uno, Roogoja Talu, Karlaküla, Kose 75101, Harjumaa, Estonia. (Now trading as Family Kivistik.)

Lemoine, Victor, Nancy, France.*

Morel, Francisque, Lyon, France.*

Noble, Charles, Sunningdale, Berkshire, England.*

Noll, Vladyslaw, Warsaw, Poland.*

Olesen, Mogens, Poulsen Roser International, Denmark.

Pennell, Walter, Pennell and Sons, Newark Road, South Hykeham, Lincoln, Lincolnshire, LN6 9NT, England.

Picton, Percy, The Old Court Nurseries, Colwall, Worcestershire, England.*

Pineapple Nursery, St. John's Wood, London, England.*

Savill, Robin, Clematis Specialist, 2 Bury Cottages, Bury Road, Pleshey, Chelmsford, Essex, CM3 1HB, England.

Scott's Clematis Nursery, Earlswood, Solihull, Birmingham, England.

Späth, L., Berlin, Germany.*

Standish, John, Ascot, Berkshire, England.*

Steffen, Arthur H., Fairport, New York, United States.*

Swadwick, George, Worth Park Nurseries, Horley, Surrey, England.*

Treasures of Tenbury, Burford House Gardens, Tenbury Wells, Worcestershire, WR15 8HQ, England.

Veitch and Son, Coombe Wood Nursery, Langley, Slough, England.*

Vilmorin, Vèrriere le Buisson, France.*

Watkinson, Frank, Doncaster, England.*

Westphal, Friedrich Manfred, Peiner Hof 7, 25497 Prisdorf, Germany.

White, Robin, Blackthorn Nursery, Kilmeston, Alresford, SO24 0NL, England.

Wyevale Nurseries, Hereford, England.

Zwijnenburg Jr., Pieter G., Halve Raak 18, 2771 AD Boskoop, Netherlands.

Zwijnenburg, Rinus, Boskoop, Netherlands.

No longer trading

APPENDIX 5

Nursery List

AUSTRALIA
Alameda Homestead Nursery
112-116, Homestead Road,
  Berwick
Victoria 3806
David and Judith Button
Wholesale

Clematis Cottage Nursery
41, Main Street
Sheffield 7306, Tasmania
Todd Miles
Retail; wholesale

AUSTRIA
Jungpflanzenbaumschule
  Alexander Mittermayr
Griesbach, A-4770 Andorf
Retail; wholesale

CANADA
Adera Nurseries
1971 Wain Road RR#4
Sidney, British Columbia V8L
  4R4
Retail; wholesale

Barrons Flowers
Box 250
2800 Hurricane Road
Fonthill, Ontario L0S 1E0
Wholesale

Clearview Horticultural Prod-
  ucts
5343-264th Street, RR#1
Aldergrove, British Columbia
  V4W 1K4
Wholesale

Connon Nurseries
1724 Concession IV
Rockton, Ontario L0R 1X0
Wholesale

Gardenimport
P.O. Box 760
Thornhill, Ontario L3T 4A5
Mail order; retail

Humber Nurseries
8386 Highway 50, RR#8
Brampton, Ontario L6T 3Y7
Retail

Linwell Gardens
344 Read Road, RR#36
St. Catherines, Ontario L2R
  7K6
Wholesale

Mason Hogue Gardens
2340 Durham Road #1, RR#4
Uxbridge, Ontario L9P 1R4
Mail order (in Canada); retail

Skinner Nurseries
Box 220
Roblin, Manitoba R0L 1P0
Retail

Zubrowski, Stanley
P.O. Box 26
Prairie River, Saskatchewan
  S0E 1J0
Mail order; retail; wholesale

DENMARK
Hansen, Flemming
Solbakken 22
Ugelbølle DK 8410 Rønde
Retail; wholesale

ENGLAND
Adams Plants of Cambridge
Rosewood, Taylors Lane,
  Buckden
Cambridge PE18 9TD
Carole and John Adams
Retail

Baines Paddock Nursery
Haverthwaite, Ulverston
Cumbria LA12 8PF
T. H. Barker and Son
Mail order; retail

Beamish Clematis Nursery
Burntwood Cottage, Stoney
  Lane, Beamish
Durham DH9 0SJ
Retail

Blooms of Bressingham
Diss, Norfolk IP22 2AB
Retail; wholesale

Bridgemere Nurseries
Bridgemere, Nantwich
Cheshire CW5 7QB
Retail; wholesale

Busheyfields Nursery
Herne, Herne Bay
Kent CT6 7LJ
J. Bradshaw and Son
Retail; wholesale

Caddick's Clematis Nursery
Lymm Road, Thelwall, War-
  rington
Cheshire WA4 2TG
Mail order; retail; export

Clematis Specialist
2 Bury Cottages, Bury Road,
Pleshey, Chelmsford
Essex CM3 1HB
Robin Savill
Mail order; retail; wholesale

Country Clematis
31, Sefton Lane, Maghull
Merseyside L31 8AE
Steve Gilsenan
Retail; wholesale

County Park Nursery
Essex Gardens, Hornchurch
Essex RM11 3BU
Graham Hutchins
Retail

Darby Nursery Stock
Old Feltwell Road, Meth-
   wold, Thetford
Norfolk IP26 4PW
Wholesale

Floyds Climbers and Clematis
77 Whittle Avenue, Compton
   Bassett, Calne
Wiltshire SN11 8QS
Wholesale

Glyndley Nurseries
Hailsham Road, Pevensey
East Sussex BN24 5BS
Wholesale

Goscote Nurseries
Systen Road, Cossington,
   Leicester
Leicestershire LE7 4UZ
Retail; wholesale; exports to
European Community countries

Great Dixter Nurseries
Northiam, Rye
East Sussex TN31 6PH
Retail; exports to European
Community countries

The Guernsey Clematis
   Nursery
Domarie Vineries, Les
   Sauvagées, St. Sampson
Guernsey GY2 4FD
Raymond J. Evison
Wholesale

The Hawthornes
Marsh Road, Hesketh Bank,
   Nr. Preston
Lancashire PR4 6XT
Retail

Haybridge Nurseries
Springacres, Dudnill,
   Cleobury Mortimer, Kid-
   derminster
Worcestershire DY14 0DH
Joe Link
Wholesale

Hollybrook Nursery
Exmouth Road, West Hill,
   Ottery St. Mary
Devon EX11 1JZ
Retail

John Richards Nurseries
Camp Hill, Malvern
Worcestershire WR14 4BZ
Wholesale

Liss Forest
Petersfield Road, Greatham
Hampshire GU33 6EX
Wholesale

Longstock Park Gardens
Longstock, Stockbridge
Hampshire SO20 6EH
Retail

M. Oviatt-Ham
Ely House, Green Street,
   Willingham
Cambridge CB4 5JA
Wholesale; exports

Notcutts Nursery
Woodbridge
Suffolk IP12 4AF
Retail; wholesale

Orchard Nurseries
Tow Lane, Foston, Nr.
   Grantham
Lincolnshire NG32 2IE
Retail

Oxney Clematis at Hanging
   Gardens Nurseries
Ongar Road West, (A414)
   Writtle-by-Pass, Writtle
Essex CM1 3NT
Retail

Paddocks Nursery
Sutton, Tenbury Wells
Worcestershire WR25 8RJ
Retail; wholesale

Pennell and Sons
Newark Road, South Hyke-
   ham, Lincoln
Lincolnshire LN6 9NT
Retail; wholesale

Peveril Clematis Nursery
Christow, Nr. Exeter
Devon EX6 7NG
Retail

Priorswood Clematis
Widbury Hill, Ware
Hertfordshire SG12 7QH
Retail; wholesale; exports

Quantock Climbing Plants
Bagborough, Taunton
Somerset TA4 3EP
Mike Cheadle
Retail; wholesale

Roseland House Nursery
Chacewater, Truro
Cornwall TR4 8QB
Charles Pridham
Retail

S. F. Hoddinott and Son
New Leaf Plants
Amberley Farm, Cheltenham
   Road
Evesham WR11 6LW
Wholesale

Scottclem
1 Huish Lodge, Instow
Devon EX39 4LT
Retail; exports

Sheila Chapman Clematis at
   Crowther Nurseries
Ongar Road, Abridge
Essex RM4 1AA
Retail

Sherston Parva Nursery
Malmesbury Road, Sherston
Wiltshire SN16 0NX
Retail; exports

Taylors Nurseries
Sutton Road, Sutton Askern,
   Doncaster
South Yorkshire DN6 9JZ
Retail

Thorncroft Clematis Nursery
The Lings, Reymerston, Nor-
   wich
Norfolk NR9 4QG
Ruth and Jonathon Gooch
Mail order; retail; exports

Top Plants
Broad Lane, North Curry,
   Taunton
Somerset TA3 6EE
Wholesale

Treasures of Tenbury
Burford House Gardens, Ten-
   bury Wells
Worcestershire WR15 8HQ
Mail order; retail; wholesale

Two Ways Nursery
Cleeve Road, Middle Little-
   ton, Evesham
Worcestershire WR11 5JT
Retail; wholesale

Woodcote Park Nursery
Ripley Road, Send, Woking
Surrey GU23 7LT
Retail; wholesale

Woodland Barn Nurseries
Lichfield Road, Abbots
   Bromley, Rugeley
Staffordshire WS15 3DN
Tony Slater
Wholesale

ESTONIA
Family Kivistik
Roogoja Talu, Karlaküla
Kose 75101, Harjumaa
Retail; wholesale

FINLAND
Puutarhakeskus Sofianletho
Sofianlehdonkatu 12
00610 Helsinki

FRANCE
ELLEBORE
La Chamotière
61360 St. Jouin de Blavou
Retail

La Vallée Blonde
L'Hôtellerie, RN 13
14100 Lisieux
Retail

Le Jardin des Clématites
5 bis allée du Fond du Val, BP
172
76135 Mont St. Aignan
Retail

Pépinière Botanique
Jean Thoby
Château de Gaujacq
40330 Amou
Retail

Pépinière Rhône Alpes
3549 route de Paris
01440 Viriat
Retail

SNC N. Albouy Geoffroy
Jardin d'Acclimatation
Bois de Boulogne
75116 Paris
Retail

Travers
Cour Charette
45650 St. Jean Le Blanc
Retail

GERMANY
Baumschul-Center
    Schmidtlein
Oberer Bühl 18
91090 Effeltrich
Retail; wholesale

Kruse, Wilhelm Clematis-
    gärtnerei
Wallenbrückerstrasse 14
49328 Melle 7
Mail order; retail

Mayer, Robert
Gartenbau, An der Schleuse
96129 Strullendorf bei Bam-
berg
Wholesale

Münster, Klaus
Baumschulen
Bullendorf 19-20
25335 Altenmoor
Retail; wholesale

Sachs, Lothar
Clematisgärtnerei
Großstückweg 10
01445 Radebeul
Retail

Straver, Adrian
Gartenbau, Zum Waldkreuz
    97
46446 Emmerich Elte
Retail; wholesale

Westphal, Friedrich Manfred
Peiner Hof 7
D-25497 Prisdorf
Mail order; retail

IRELAND
Woodtown Nurseries
Stocking Lane
Woodtown, Rathfarnham
Dublin 16
Wholesale

JAPAN
Chikuma Engei
1-19-27 Sugo Miyamae Ku
Kawasaki City 216-0015
Wholesale

Clema Corporation
270-17 Hachibudaira, Higa-
shino
Nagaizumi Machi, Suntoo
Gun
Shizuoka Ken 441-0931
Wholesale

Hayakawa Engei
65, Nakahongo Izumi Cho
Anjo City, Aicha Prefecture
    444-1221
Wholesale

Kasugai Engei
1709-120 Kakino Tsurusato
    Machi
Toki City, Gifu Prefecture
    509-5312
Kozo Sugimoto
Mail order (in Japan only);
wholesale

Ozawa Engei
951 Shimo-Asao Asao Ku
Kawasaki City, Kanagawa
    Prefecture 215-0022
Kazushige Ozawa
Wholesale

Shonan Clematis Nursery
3-7-24 Tsuzido-Motomachi
Fujisawa City, Kanagawa Prefecture 247-0043
Mail order (in Japan only);
wholesale

NETHERLANDS
Bulk, Rein en Mark
Rijneveld 115
2771 XV, Boskoop
Wholesale; exports

Bulkyard Plants
P.O. Box 56
2779 AB, Boskoop
Retail; wholesale

Kuijf, Henk J.M.
Mennonietenbuurt 116A
1427BC Uithoorn

Werf, Ruud van der
Goudserijweg 60
2771 AK Boskoop
Retail; wholesale; exports

Westerhoud, Ed
Boomwekerijen
Reijerskoop 305a
2771 BL Boskoop
Wholesale; exports

Zoest, Jan van
Azalealaan 29
2771 ZX Boskoop
Wholesale

Zoest, Peter van
Randenburgseweg 21
2811 PS Reeuwijk
Wholesale

Zwijnenburg Jr., Pieter G.
Halve Raak 18
2771 AD Boskoop
Retail; wholesale

NEW ZEALAND
Cadsonbury Plant Breeders
28 Vardon Crescent
Christchurch 8006
Robin and Lorna Mitchell
Retail

M. L. Jerard and Company
Potters Lane, Lansdowne Val-
ley, R.D.2
Christchurch 8021
Michael Jerard
Wholesale

New Zealand Clematis Nurseries
67 Ngaio Street, St. Martins
Christchurch 2
Wholesale

POLAND
Szczepan Marczyñski
Szkolka Pojemnikowa
ul. Duchnicka 25
05-800 Pruszków
Retail; wholesale; trade exports

SWEDEN
Cedergren and Company
    Plantskola
Box 16016
250 16 Rââ
Krister Cedergren
Mail order; retail; wholesale

SWITZERLAND
Forster, Alfred
CH-3207 Golaten
Retail

Lehmann Baumschulen AG
CH-3294 Büren an der Aare
Retail

Meier, Ernst AG
Garten-Center
CH-8630 Tann-Rüti
Retail

UNITED STATES
Chalk Hill Clematis Farm
P.O. Box 1847
11720 Chalk Hill Road
Healdsburg, California 95448
Mail order; retail

Collector's Nursery
16804 NE 102nd Avenue
Battle Ground, Washington
    98604
Mail order

Completely Clematis Specialty Nursery
217 Argilla Road
Ipswich, Massachusetts 01938
Mail order; retail

D. S. George Nurseries
2491 Penfield Road
Fairport, New York 14450
Mail order

Donahue's Clematis Specialists
P.O. Box 366
420 SW 10th Street
Faribault, Minnesota 55021
Mail order; retail; wholesale

Forestfarm
990 Tetherow Road
Williams, Oregon 97544
Mail order

Greer Gardens
1280 Goodpasture Island Road
Eugene, Oregon 97401
Mail order

Gutmann Nurseries
19131 NW Dairy Creek Road
Cornelius, Oregon 97113
Wholesale

Heronswood Nursery
7530 NE 288th Street
Kingston, Washington 98346
Mail order; retail

Joy Creek Nursery
20300 NW Watson Road
Scappoose, Oregon 97056
Mail order

New Life Nurseries
192 Starry Road
Sequim, Washington 98382
Frank Snow
Retail

Siskiyou Rare Plant Nursery
2825 Cummings Road
Medford, Oregon 97501
Mail order

Wayside Gardens
1, Garden Lane
Hodges, South Carolina
    29695
Mail order; retail

National Clematis Collections and Display Gardens

NATIONAL CLEMATIS COLLECTIONS

The National Council for the Conservation of Plants and Gardens (NCCPG) in the United Kingdom administers a National Plant Collections scheme. Although all national collections are open to the public, some, due to location or size, may have restricted access; details of this kind are not listed. To view restricted-access collections, please write to the collection holder and make the appropriate arrangements. The following nurseries and individuals are holders of clematis collections.

Clematis—all groups
Raymond J. Evison
The Guernsey Clematis Nursery
Domarie Vineries, Les Sauvagées, St. Sampson
Guernsey GY2 4FD, Channel Islands

Atragene group
M. Oviatt-Ham
Ely House, Green Street, Willingham
Cambridgeshire CB4 5JA, England

Alpina group
Mrs. J. Floyd
39, Arundel Gardens, Winchmore Hill
London N21 3AG, England

Herbaceous group
M. Brown
Clematis Corner, 15, Plough Close
Shillingford, Wallingford
Oxfordshire OX10 7EX, England

C. texensis, C. viticella, and herbaceous group
Treasures of Tenbury
Burford House Gardens, Tenbury Wells
Worcestershire WR15 8HQ, England

C. texensis and cultivars
Mr. and Mrs. J. Hudson
The Mill, 21 Mill Lane
Cannington, Bridgewater
Somerset TA5 2HB, England

Orientalis group
Chris Sanders
Bridgemere Nurseries
Bridgemere, Nantwich
Cheshire CW5 7QB, England

Viticella group
Robin Savill
Clematis Specialist
2 Bury Cottages, Bury Road, Pleshey, Chelmsford
Essex CM3 1HB, England

D. Stuart
Longstock Park Gardens
Longstock, Stockbridge
Hampshire SO20 6EH, England

CLEMATIS DISPLAY GARDENS
Two gardens are operated in association with the British Clematis Society.

Bourne Hall Display Garden
Bourne Hall Park, Spring Street, Ewell
Surrey KT17 1UF, England

Helmsley Walled Garden
Cleveland Way, Helmsley
York YO6 5AH, England

Height: 1.8–2.4 m (6–8 ft).

Description: The single, large, intense violet-blue flowers, 20–23 cm (8–9 in.) in diameter, are composed of six to eight broad, overlapping tepals with deeper colouring along the middle and finely scalloped margins. White filaments and red anthers constitute the stamens. The leaves are large, dark green, and pointed.

Pruning group: 2.

Flowering period: Late spring to early summer and late summer.

Cultivation: Tolerates most garden soils. Best grown out of full sun. Requires a sheltered position to prevent wind damage to the large flowers.

Recommended use: Shows up well against a light background. Grow with other wall-trained shrubs. Suitable for a pergola, obelisk, or trellis with other clematis from pruning group 2. Zones 4–9.

Clematis 'Kaiu'
TEXENSIS-VIORNA GROUP

Origin: Raised by Erich Pranno of Kaiu, Estonia, and named after his village.

Parentage and year: *C. viorna* × possibly *C. viticella*. 1982.

Habit: Hardy, compact, herbaceous climber.

Height: 1.5–1.8 m (5–6 ft.).

Description: The single, pitcher-shaped, nodding flowers 3–4 cm (1.25–1.5 in.) long, are composed of four greyish white tepals, which in young flowers are tinged with pale purple. As the flower matures the colour becomes whiter and the pointed tips of the tepals gently curve outwards and upwards. The stamens are pale cream.

Pruning group: 3.

Flowering period: Midsummer to late summer.

Cultivation: Tolerates most garden soils and any aspect.

Recommended use: Ideal for large containers or for growing on a small trellis. Suitable for growing over prostrate conifers and medium-sized shrubs with dark foliage. Zones 3–9.

Clematis 'Kakio'
Trade name : PINK CHAMPAGNE
Origin: Raised by Kazushig Ozawa of Japan.
Parentage and year: *C.* 'Star of India' × *C.* 'Crimson

Clematis 'Kaiu'. Photo by C. Chesshire.

Clematis 'Kakio' (PINK CHAMPAGNE™).
Photo courtesy Thorncroft Clematis Nursery.

King'. ca. 1971. The cultivar 'Star of India' in Japan is believed to be different from the 'Star of India' that is grown and sold elsewhere.

Habit: Hardy, moderately vigorous, compact, deciduous climber.

Height: 1.8–2.4 m (6–8 ft.).

Description: The single flowers, 14–16.5 cm (5.5–6.5 in.) wide, are composed of six to eight overlapping, pointed tepals. The base colour of the tepals is pink and is deepest at the margins, fading to a central mauvish bar covered with pink veins. The anthers are bright yellow.

Pruning group: 2.

Flowering period: Late spring to early and late summer.

Cultivation: Tolerates most garden soils and any aspect.

Recommended use: Ideal for container-culture. Grow on a small to medium-sized obelisk or trellis. Plant with other not-so-vigorous, wall-trained climbers which do not require severe pruning. Zones 4–9.

Clematis 'Kardynal Wyszynski'

Trade name: CARDINAL WYSZYNSKI

Origin: Raised by Brother Stefan Franczak of Warsaw, Poland, and named after a former archbishop of Warsaw who became a cardinal in 1952. Introduced into the British Isles by Fisk's Clematis Nursery, Suffolk, England.

Parentage and year: Unknown. 1986.

Habit: Hardy, quite vigorous, deciduous climber.

Height: 2.5–3.6 m (8–12 ft.).

Description: The single, glowing crimson flowers, 15–20 cm (6–8 in.) in diameter, are composed of six to eight overlapping and pointed tepals. The stamens are brown.

Pruning group: 3.

Flowering period: Early summer to late summer.

Cultivation: Tolerates most garden soils and all aspects except north.

Recommended use: Grow naturally through other trees and shrubs or with other wall-trained plants. Ideal for a pergola, obelisk, or trellis. Zones 4–9.

Clematis 'Karin'

Origin: Raised by Magnus Johnson of Södertälje, Sweden, and named after his daughter.

Parentage and year: Chance seedling of *C.* 'Lasurstern'. 1955.

Habit: Hardy, moderately vigorous, deciduous climber.

Height: 2.1–3 m (7–10 ft.).

Description: The single, occasionally semi-double, pinkish purple flowers, 14–16 cm (5.5–6.25 in.) across, are composed of six to eight tepals, which overlap from the base to halfway along their length from where they gently taper to points. The margins are wavy, the surfaces are textured and veined, and grooves run from the tip to the base where the colour is a deeper shade. The stamens are made of white filaments shaded pink and dark purple anthers.

Pruning group: 2.

Flowering period: Early summer to late summer

Cultivation: Tolerates most garden soils enriched with humus. Suitable for any aspect.

Recommended use: Ideal for a pergola, medium-sized obelisk, or trellis. Zones 4–9.

Clematis 'Kasmu'
VITICELLA GROUP

Synonym: *C. viticella* 'Signe'

Origin: Raised by Uno Kivistik of Harjumaa, Estonia. Named after a peninsula in the Gulf of Finland.

Parentage and year: Unknown.

Habit: Hardy, moderately vigorous, deciduous climber.

Height: 2.5–3 m (8–10 ft.).

Description: The single, dark purple flowers with

Clematis 'Karin'. Photo by J. Lindmark.

Clematis 'Kardynal Wyszynski' (Cardinal Wyszynski™). Photo by R. Surman.

velvet sheen, 10–15 cm (4–6 in.) across, are normally composed of six tepals with light purple veining. On the reverse of each tepal is a pronounced white stripe. Yellow stamens contrast well with the flower colour.

Pruning group: 3.

Flowering period: Midsummer to late summer.

Cultivation: Tolerates most garden soils. Prefers a bright, sunny position.

Recommended use: Shows up well against a light background. Use in natural planting with other shrubs and prostrate conifers. Suitable for a pergola, trellis, or obelisk. Zones 4–9.

Clematis 'Kasugayama'

Origin: Japan. Raised by Gen Sakurai of Japan. Named after Mount Kasuga.

Parentage and year: Unknown. ca. 1954.

Clematis 'Kasmu'. Photo by R. Savill.

Clematis 'Kasugayama'. Photo by C. Chesshire.

Habit: Hardy, moderately vigorous, compact, deciduous climber.

Height: 1.8–2.4 m (6–8 ft.).

Description: The single, bright lavender-blue flowers, 6–8 cm (2.25–3.25 in.) wide, are composed of six to eight tepals. Striking stamens are made of white filaments and dark red anthers.

Pruning group: 2.

Flowering period: Late spring to early summer and late summer.

Cultivation: Tolerates most garden soils and any aspect.

Recommended use: Ideal for container-culture. Use to cover bare lower stems of wall-trained shrubs. May also be grown on a small obelisk or short trellis. Zones 4–9.

Clematis 'Kathleen Dunford'

Origin: Found in Kathleen Dunford's garden in Hampshire, England, and introduced in 1962 by Fisk's Clematis Nursery, Suffolk, England.

Parentage and year: Chance seedling. Late 1940s.

Habit: Hardy, moderately vigorous, compact, deciduous climber.

Height: 2–2.5 m (6.5–8 ft.).

Description: The rosy purple, semi-double flowers, produced on the previous season's old wood, are 15–20 cm (6–8 in.) in diameter. The overlapping base tepals are broad yet pointed, with one or two subsequent layers of tepals of similar size and colour. As the flowers mature, the tepals become mottled and mauvish blue at the margins. Single flowers are produced later in the

Clematis 'Kathleen Dunford'. Photo by C. Chesshire.

season on new growth. The filaments are yellow with dark red anthers.

Pruning group: 2.

Flowering period: Late spring to early summer (semi-double) and late summer (single).

Cultivation: Tolerates most garden soils. Best grown in full sun or partial shade. Requires a sheltered position to prevent wind damage to the large flowers.

Recommended use: Grow on a medium-sized obelisk or trellis, or with other wall-trained plants which do not require pruning. Suitable for a display on an arch. Zones 4–9.

Clematis 'Kathleen Wheeler'

Origin: Raised by Walter Pennell of Pennell and Sons nursery and named in 1967 after the wife of the company's Doncaster shop manager.

Parentage and year: Open-pollinated seedling of *C.* 'Mrs. Spencer Castle'. ca. 1952.

Habit: Hardy, moderately vigorous, deciduous climber.

Height: 1.8–2.4 m (6–8 ft.).

Description: The single, large, plum-mauve flowers, 18–23 cm (7–9 in.) across, are composed of six to eight overlapping tepals, each boasting a deeper colouring in grooves along the centre. The flowers of the second flush are slightly smaller in size and sometimes have fewer tepals. The central boss of stamens is large, consisting of filaments with lilac shading and golden yellow anthers.

Pruning group: 2.

Flowering period: Late spring to early summer and late summer.

Cultivation: Tolerates most garden soils and any aspect. Requires a sheltered position to prevent wind damage to the large flowers.

Recommended use: Grow with other wall-trained shrubs and roses. Suitable for a large container, pergola, obelisk, or trellis. Zones 4–9.

Clematis 'Keith Richardson'

Origin: Raised by Walter Pennell of Pennell and Sons nursery and named in 1975 after the company's chief propagator.

Parentage and year: *C.* 'Barbara Dibley' × *C.* 'Bracebridge Star'. Hybridized in 1961. Seed sown in 1962.

Habit: Hardy, moderately vigorous, compact, deciduous climber.

Height: 1.8–2.4 m (6–8 ft.).

Description: The single, petunia-red flowers, 15–20 cm (6–8 in.) across, are composed of six to eight broad, overlapping tepals, each with slightly bluish margins and deeper purplish red coloured bars along the centre. Prominent pinky white filaments and dark red anthers make up the stamens.

Pruning group: 2.

Flowering period: Late spring and early summer and late summer.

Cultivation: Tolerates most garden soils and any aspect.

Recommended use: Suitable for a small obelisk or trellis. May be grown with wall-trained shrubs which do not require annual pruning. Useful for container-culture. Zones 4–9.

Clematis 'Kathleen Wheeler'. Photo by C. Chesshire.

Clematis 'Keith Richardson'. Photo by C. Chesshire.

Clematis 'Ken Donson'

Origin: Raised by Walter Pennell of Pennell and Sons nursery and named in 1976 after a long-serving employee. Awarded RHS Award of Garden Merit.

Parentage and year: *C.* 'Barbara Jackman' × *C.* 'Daniel Deronda'. Hybridized in 1961. Seed sown in 1962.

Habit: Hardy, not-so-vigorous, deciduous climber.

Height: 2.5–3 m (8–10 ft.).

Description: A good all round cultivar noted for its single, well-formed flowers, seedheads, and beautiful leaves. The purple-blue flowers, 15–18 cm (6–7 in.) wide, are composed of six broad but pointed tepals. The reverse of each tepal carries a whitish bar fading into blue at the margins. White filaments and bright yellow anthers make up the stamens.

Pruning group: 2.

Flowering period: Early summer to early autumn.

Cultivation: Tolerates most garden soils and any aspect.

Recommended use: Ideal for a medium-sized trellis or obelisk. May be grown with other wall-trained shrubs which do not require annual pruning. Zones 4–9.

Clematis 'Kermesina'

VITICELLA GROUP

Synonyms: *C. viticella* 'Kermesina', *C. viticella* 'Rubra'

Origin: Raised by Victor Lemoine of Nancy, France.

Parentage and year: Unknown. 1883.

Habit: Hardy, vigorous, deciduous climber.

Height: 3–4 m (10–13 ft.).

Description: A very floriferous cultivar. The single, semi-nodding, deep crimson flowers, 6 cm (2.25 in.) across, are normally composed of four blunt tepals, each recurving at the margins, and carrying a white blotch at the base surrounding the almost black stamens. Early in the season, the tips of the tepals may have green markings on them.

Pruning group: 3.

Flowering period: Midsummer to early autumn.

Cultivation: Tolerates most garden soils and any aspect.

Recommended use: Shows up well against a lightish background. Ideal growing through medium-sized trees, conifers, and large shrubs, or as a specimen on a free-standing obelisk, trellis, or pergola. Zones 3–9.

Clematis 'Ken Donson'. Photo by C. Chesshire.

Clematis 'Kermesina'. Photo by J. Lindmark.

Clematis 'King Edward VII'

Origin: Raised by George Jackman and Son, England.
Parentage and year: *C.* 'Fairy Queen' × *C.* 'Sir Trevor Lawrence'. 1902.
Habit: Hardy, moderately vigorous, compact, deciduous climber.
Height: 1.8–2.4 m (6–8 ft.).
Description: The single, rather large, rose-pink flowers, 17–21 cm (7–8.5 in.) wide, are composed of six to eight overlapping, textured, pointed tepals. The unique colouring of the tepals gives them a mottled effect, fading outwards to deep mauve at the margins and sometimes to white at the tips. Each tepal carries a pink central bar. White filaments and light reddish brown anthers make up the stamens.
Pruning group: 2.
Flowering period: Early summer to late summer.
Cultivation: Tolerates most garden soils and any aspect. Requires a sheltered position to prevent wind damage to the large flowers.
Recommended use: Best grown with dark-leaved shrubs which do not require annual pruning, or conifers. Ideal for container-culture. Suitable for a small obelisk or trellis. Zones 4–9.

Clematis 'King George V'

Origin: Raised by George Jackman and Son, England.
Parentage and year: Unknown.
Habit: Hardy, moderately vigorous, compact, deciduous climber.
Height: 1.8–2.4 m (6–8 ft.).
Description: The single, somewhat small, pale pink flowers, 15 cm (6 in.) in diameter, are composed of five or six tepals, each with a wide raspberry-pink bar along the centre. The edges are slightly notched, and the tepals taper to a red-tipped point. The stamens carry creamy white filaments and reddish brown anthers.
Pruning group: 2.
Flowering period: Midsummer to late summer.
Cultivation: Tolerates most garden soils. Best grown in partial shade to prevent premature fading of flower colour. Flowers may not be freely produced, as the plant is somewhat shy to flower.
Recommended use: Useful for container-culture or growing on a small obelisk or trellis. Ideal against a dark background, such as a wall or shaded area, to give bright colour. Zones 4–9.

Clematis 'Kiri Te Kanawa'

Origin: Raised by Barry Fretwell of Peveril Clematis Nursery, England. Named in honour of the New Zealand singer.
Parentage and year: *C.* 'Chalcedony' × *C.* 'Beauty of Worcester'. 1986.
Habit: Hardy, compact, deciduous climber.
Height: 1.8–2.4 m (6–8 ft.).
Description: The deep purplish blue, sumptuous, double flowers, measuring 12.5–15 cm (5–6 in.) in diameter, are composed of many layers of broad, yet pointed, overlapping tepals. Yellow filaments and anthers contrast well with the tepal colour. Double flowers are produced on the previous season's old wood and the current season's new wood, although the flowers tend to get smaller as the season progresses.

Clematis 'King Edward VII'. Photo by C. Chesshire.

Clematis 'King George V'. Photo by Y. Aihara.

Pruning group: 2.

Flowering period: Late spring to early summer and late summer.

Cultivation: Tolerates most garden soils. Best grown in full sun or partial shade. Requires a sheltered position to prevent wind damage to the flowers.

Recommended use: Grow on a small to medium-sized obelisk or trellis. Ideal for container-culture. May be grown with medium-sized shrubs which have softly coloured foliage and which do not require pruning. Zones 4–9.

Clematis 'Kiri Te Kanawa' growing through *Pittosporum tenuifolium* 'Silver Magic'. Photo by C. Chesshire.

Clematis 'Kirimäe'

Origin: Raised by Uno Kivistik of Harjumaa, Estonia.

Parentage and year: *C.* 'Ramona' × pollen mixture. 1980.

Habit: Hardy, moderately vigorous, compact, deciduous climber.

Height: 1.8–2.4 m (6–8 ft.).

Description: The single, very light pink flowers, measuring 10–12 cm (4–4.75 in.) across, are composed of six tepals, each with a reddish pink bar. The anthers are purple.

Pruning group: 2.

Flowering period: Late spring to early summer and late summer.

Cultivation: Tolerates most garden soils. Plant out of full sun to preserve flower colour.

Recommended use: Ideal for container-culture or for covering bare stems of other wall-trained shrubs and roses. Suitable for a small obelisk or trellis. Zones 4–9.

Clematis 'Königskind'

Origin: Raised by Friedrich Manfred Westphal of Prisdorf, Germany

Parentage and year: Open-pollinated seedling of *C.* 'The President'. 1982.

Habit: Hardy, very compact, deciduous climber.

Height: 1.2–1.8 m (4–6 ft.).

Description: The single, upward-facing, mauvish blue flowers, 10–12 cm (4–4.75 in.) across, are composed of six to eight broad yet pointed, overlapping tepals. Mauvish white filaments and dark red anthers constitute the central boss of stamens.

Clematis 'Kirimäe'. Photo by R. Savill.

Clematis 'Königskind'. Photo by J. Lindmark.

Pruning group: 2.

Flowering period: Late spring to early summer and late summer.

Cultivation: Tolerates most garden soils and any aspect.

Recommended use: Ideal for container-culture or for covering the bare stems of other wall-trained shrubs and roses. Suitable for a small obelisk or trellis. Zones 4–9.

Clematis koreana
ATRAGENE GROUP

Origin: Korea and adjacent northeastern China.

Parentage and year: Species. 1901.

Habit: Hardy, moderately vigorous, deciduous climber.

Height: 2–3 m (6.5–10 ft.).

Description: Reddish purple flowers appear solitarily from the previous season's ripened old stems or in clusters from new stems. The four nodding, pointed tepals are up to 7.5 cm (3 in.) long. The light green leaves are composed of three leaflets divided further into three parts or may even be three lobed, slightly hairy, and coarsely toothed. Flower colour varies in degrees of suffusion to dull yellow. Stems tend to become bare at the base.

Pruning group: 1.

Flowering period: Late spring to early summer, with intermittent flowering during later months.

Cultivation: Requires sharp drainage, especially in container-culture. Best grown in full sun or partial shade.

Recommended use: Ideal for the small garden, container, obelisk, or trellis. Grow through a low-growing shrub to cover the bare lower clematis stems. Zones 6–9.

Clematis koreana var. *fragrans*
ATRAGENE GROUP

Origin: Raised from seed collected in Korea by members of the Nordic Arboretum.

Parentage and year: A variant of *C. koreana*. 1976.

Habit: Hardy, moderately vigorous, deciduous climber.

Height: 2–3 m (6.5–10 ft.).

Description: The single, slightly scented, nodding, bell-shaped, reddish mauve flowers are composed of four narrow, pointed tepals, each 9 cm (3.5 in.) long, and curving outwards at their tips. There are slight spurs at the base of each tepal, which continue along the length of the tepal in the form of low ridges. Flowers are produced on the previous season's old wood and the current season's new wood.

Pruning group: 1.

Flowering period: Late spring to early summer, with sporadic flowering to late summer.

Cultivation: Tolerates most well-drained garden soils enriched with humus. Suitable for any aspect.

Recommended use: Grow through medium-sized,

Clematis koreana. Photo by J. Lindmark.

Clematis koreana var. *fragrans*. Photo by J. Lindmark.

open shrubs which do not require annual pruning. Can be grown with other wall-trained shrubs or on its own over a small or medium-sized obelisk or trellis. Zones 5–9.

Clematis koreana var. *lutea*
ATRAGENE GROUP

Origin: Korea.

Parentage and year: A variant of *C. koreana*. 1934.

Habit: Hardy, moderately vigorous, deciduous climber.

Height: 2.5–3 m (6.5–10 ft.).

Description: The single, nodding, bell-shaped, pale yellow flowers are composed of four narrow tepals which are deeply ridged from the base to the tip. The tepals are overlaid with a mauve shading, which is more pronounced at the base, and the tips gently curve outwards. Pale yellow staminodes are slightly tinged with mauve. Flowers are produced on old and new wood.

Pruning group: 1.

Flowering period: Late spring to early summer, with sporadic flowering to late summer.

Cultivation: Tolerates most well-drained garden soils enriched with humus. Suitable for any aspect.

Recommended use: Grow through medium-sized shrubs which do not require annual pruning. May be grown with other wall-trained shrubs or trained over a medium-sized obelisk or trellis. Allow it to tumble over a low wall or fence. Zones 5–9.

Clematis 'Kuba'

Origin: Raised by Maria F. Sharonova of Moscow.

Parentage and year: *C.* 'Ernest Markham' × pollen mixture. 1972.

Habit: Hardy, not very vigorous, compact, deciduous climber.

Height: 1.5–2.1 m (5–7 ft.).

Description: The single, flat pinkish purple flowers, 15–18 cm (6–7 in.) across, are composed of six spear-shaped, pointed tepals, each overlapping at a point midway along its length. There is a cerise bar along the central grooves running from base to tip, and the stamens carry white filaments and pinkish brown anthers.

Pruning group: 3.

Flowering period: Early summer to late summer.

Cultivation: Tolerates most garden soils enriched with humus. Suitable for any aspect.

Recommended use: Ideal for container-culture or for growing over prostrate conifers and small to medium-sized, moderately vigorous shrubs. Zones 4–9.

Clematis 'Kugotia'
TANGUTICA GROUP

Trade name: GOLDEN TIARA

Origin: Raised by Henk J. M. Kuijf of the Netherlands. Awarded British Clematis Society Certificate of Merit (1999). Plant Breeders' Rights.

Parentage and year: Chance seedling of *C.* 'Golden Harvest'. 1994.

Habit: Hardy, compact, not-so-vigorous, deciduous climber.

Height: 2–3 m (6.5–10 ft.).

Description: The single, nodding, bright yellow flowers, 5–7 cm (2–2.75 in.) across, are composed of four thick tepals that open wide and spreading, with the tips turning upwards and the margins turning slightly back on themselves. Prominent, dark mauvish brown stamens contrast well with the flower colour. The plant carries buds, flowers, and fluffy seedheads at the same time.

Pruning group: 3.

Flowering period: Midsummer to early autumn, with main display reserved for late summer to early autumn.

Cultivation: Tolerates most well-drained garden soils and any aspect.

Clematis 'Kugotia' (GOLDEN TIARA™). Photo by E. Leeds.

Clematis koreana var. *lutea*. Photo by J. Lindmark.

Clematis 'Kuba'. Photo by J. Lindmark.

Recommended use: Suitable for a pergola, obelisk, or free-standing trellis. Grow through large shrubs. Zones 4–9.

Clematis ladakhiana
TANGUTICA GROUP

Origin: China, India, and Kashmir. Named after the district Ladakh in northern India.

Parentage and year: Species. 1875.

Habit: Hardy, moderately vigorous, deciduous climber.

Height: To 3 m (10 ft.).

Description: The single flowers with four tepals, each 15–25 mm (0.5–1 in.) long, are borne in clusters of three to seven in the leaf axils. The upper sides of the tepals are yellowish bronze mottled with dark red, and the undersides are paler. As they mature, the tepals open and twist, revealing the reddish brown anthers. The bluish green leaves are 12–15 cm (4.75–6 in.) long and are divided into five to seven narrow leaflets, some with one or both sides notched.

Pruning group: 3.

Flowering period: Midsummer to early autumn.

Cultivation: Needs sharp drainage. Best grown in sun or partial shade.

Recommended use: Grow through small to medium-sized trees, conifers, and large shrubs. Suitable for a large container but must have sharp drainage. Zones 6–9.

Clematis 'Lady Betty Balfour'

Origin: Raised by George Jackman and Son, England, and named after a patron of the nursery. Awarded RHS Award of Merit.

Parentage and year: *C.* 'Gipsy Queen' × *C.* 'Beauty of Worcester'. 1910.

Habit: Hardy, very vigorous, deciduous climber. Produces numerous new shoots annually.

Height: 3–3.6 m (10–12 ft.).

Description: The single, deep rich blue flowers, 15–20 cm (6–8 in.) wide, are composed of six broad and overlapping tepals surrounding a central boss of contrasting creamy yellow stamens. The young flowers tend to boast a dash of red near the base of the tepals, disappearing with age. Attractive leaves with three leaflets do not smother the flowers.

Pruning group: 3.

Flowering period: Late summer to late autumn.

Cultivation: Tolerates most garden soils. Best grown in full sun since it flowers late.

Recommended use: Allow to grow naturally through medium-sized shrubs, trees, and conifers, especially those with light foliage. Suitable for a medium-sized obelisk, trellis, arbour, arch, or pergola. Zones 4–9.

Clematis 'Lady Bird Johnson'
TEXENSIS-VIORNA GROUP

Synonyms: *C. texensis* 'Ladybird Johnson', *C. texensis* 'Lady Bird Johnson'

Clematis ladakhiana. Photo by C. Chesshire.

Clematis 'Lady Betty Balfour'. Photo by J. Lindmark.

Origin: Raised by Barry Fretwell of Peveril Clematis Nursery, England. Named after the wife of U.S. president Lyndon Johnson.

Parentage and year: *C.* 'Bees Jubilee' × *C. texensis*. 1984.

Habit: Hardy, deciduous, slender climber. Normally of herbaceous habit with new shoots emerging from below ground level.

Height: 2.5–3 m (8–10 ft.).

Description: Single, dusky red, tuliplike flowers, 4–5 cm (1.5–2 in.) across, are composed of four tepals, each with a slightly brighter crimson central bar, recurving on maturity. The stamens are creamy yellow in colour.

Pruning group: 3.

Flowering period: Midsummer to early autumn.

Cultivation: Tolerates most garden soils. Best grown in full sun or partial shade. Prone to mildew. Take early precaution by spraying with a fungicide monthly from early summer. New shoots at soil level need protection from slugs and snails.

Recommended use: Ideal for growing with climbing roses. Flowers look exceptionally well when grown over prostrate conifers, low-growing shrubs, and other groundcover plants. Zones 4–9.

Clematis 'Lady Caroline Nevill'

Origin: Raised by Thomas Cripps and Son of Tunbridge Wells, England.

Parentage and year: Unknown. ca. 1866.

Habit: Hardy, moderately vigorous, deciduous climber.

Height: 2.4–3 m (8–10 ft.).

Description: The first flush of semi-double flowers, 12.5–15 cm (5–6 in.) across, produced on wood made the previous year, carries a base layer of pale whitish mauve tepals, each with a deeper mauve bar running from the base to the tip. These are overlaid with a varying number of narrower and shorter tepals, which surround the brown stamens. The secondary flush of single flowers produced on the current season's growth later in the summer is slightly smaller, paler in colour, and is composed of overlapping, pointed tepals.

Pruning group: 2.

Flowering period: Early summer and midsummer to late summer.

Cultivation: Tolerates most garden soils. Best placed in full or partial sun.

Recommended use: Suitable for a pergola, trellis, or obelisk. Grow with other wall-trained plants which do not require severe annual pruning. Zones 4–9.

Clematis 'Lady Bird Johnson'. Photo by C. Chesshire.

Clematis 'Lady Caroline Nevill'. Photo by C. Chesshire.

Clematis 'Lady Londesborough'

Origin: Raised by Charles Noble of Sunningdale, England. Introduced in 1869. Awarded RHS First Class Certificate.

Parentage and year: *C.* 'Standishii' × *C.* 'Fortunei'.

Habit: Hardy, not-so-vigorous, deciduous climber.

Height: 1.8–2.4 m (6–8 ft.).

Description: The single, small, pale pinkish mauve flowers fading to silver-mauve with age, measuring 12.5–15 cm (5–6 in.) in diameter, are normally composed of eight wide, overlapping tepals with slightly notched or wavy edges. They have a textured surface with a satin sheen, and a hint of a pale mauve central bar. The white filaments with dark reddish anthers making up the stamens contrast well with the flower colour. The neat, attractive leaves have three leaflets.

Pruning group: 2.

Flowering period: Late spring to early summer or midsummer.

Cultivation: Tolerates most garden soils. Requires protection from cold and winds.

Recommended use: Shows up well against a dark background. Suitable for an arch, small pergola, or obelisk. Grow with other wall-trained, moderately vigorous shrubs and small to medium-sized roses. Ideal for container-culture. Zones 4–9.

Clematis 'Lady Northcliffe'

Origin: Raised by George Jackman and Son, England. Awarded RHS Award of Merit.

Parentage and year: *C.* 'Beauty of Worcester' × *C.* 'Otto Froebel'. 1906.

Habit: Hardy, quite vigorous but compact, deciduous climber.

Height: 1.8–2.4 m (6–8 ft.).

Description: The single, somewhat small, deep royal blue flowers, fading to lavender-blue with age and measuring 13–15 cm (5–6 in.) across, are composed of six to eight tepals. The more or less half-upright tepals, which do not lie flat, are wide, overlapping, and pointed with wavy and gently notched edges. The stamens carry creamy white filaments and pale greenish yellow anthers. Some outer stamens take on the colour of the tepals.

Pruning group: 2.

Flowering period: Early summer to early autumn.

Cultivation: Tolerates most garden soils. Needs a warm, sheltered position.

Clematis 'Lady Londesborough'. Photo by R. Surman.

Clematis 'Lady Northcliffe'. Photo by J. Lindmark.

Recommended use: Suitable for a pergola, trellis, or small obelisk. Ideal for container-culture. Zones 4–9.

Clematis 'Lagoon'
ATRAGENE GROUP

Synonyms: *C. macropetala* 'Lagoon', *C.* 'Blue Lagoon'
Origin: Raised by George Jackman and Son, England.
Parentage and year: Selected form of *C. macropetala*. 1958.
Habit: Hardy, moderately vigorous, deciduous climber.
Height: 2–3 m (6.5–10 ft.).
Description: The nodding, bell-shaped, dark blue flowers are composed of four somewhat elongated, pointed tepals, each 5–6 cm (2–2.25 in.) deep, with an inner row of petal-like staminodes resembling the tepal colour. These in turn surround a cluster of creamy white staminodes encasing the innermost fertile stamens.
Pruning group: 1.
Flowering period: Spring. One of the latest cultivars of *C. macropetala* to flower.
Cultivation: Requires sharp-draining garden soils enriched with humus. Suitable for any aspect.
Recommended use: Ideal for small gardens. Suitable for a pergola or trellis, or roaming into small trees. Shows up well against a white or light background. Zones 3–9.

Clematis 'Lambton Park'
TANGUTICA GROUP

Synonym: *C. tangutica* 'Lambton Park'
Origin: Found growing at the Lambton Park Garden Centre, England, by Tom Bennett.

Parentage and year: Selected form of *C. tangutica*. Late 1980s.
Habit: Hardy, moderately vigorous, deciduous climber.
Height: 3–4 m (10–13 ft.).
Description: The bright yellow, nodding, lanternlike, single flowers are composed of four broad and pointed tepals, each 5 cm (2 in.) long, and currently the largest flowers of any *C. tangutica* cultivar. Large silky seedheads develop as the earlier flowers wither and are carried on the plant as the flowering continues. Some clones exude a coconut scent.
Pruning group: 3.
Flowering period: Early summer to midautumn.
Cultivation: Tolerates most well-drained garden soils and any aspect.
Recommended use: Ideal for a pergola or free-standing trellis. Can be grown through large shrubs or medium-sized trees. Zones 4–9.

Clematis 'Lansdowne Gem'
EVERGREEN/CIRRHOSA GROUP

Synonym: *C. cirrhosa* 'Lansdowne Gem'
Origin: Discovered in 1995 by Michael Jerard of Christchurch, New Zealand. Plant Breeders' Rights.
Parentage and year: Sport of *C.* 'Freckles'. Introduced 1997.
Habit: Half-hardy to hardy, vigorous, evergreen climber.
Height: To 6 m (20 ft.).

Clematis 'Lagoon'. Photo by J. Lindmark.

Clematis 'Lambton Park' flower detail. Photo by J. Lindmark.

Clematis 'Lambton Park' in the garden. Photo courtesy Thorncroft Clematis Nursery.

Description: The single, small, nodding, bell-shaped, dull claret-coloured flowers, 7 cm (2.75 in.) across, are composed of four broad but somewhat pointed tepals, each 3.5 cm (1.25 in.) long, with slightly recurved tips. The outside of the tepals boasts a hairy silver shading, and the stamens are made of creamy lime-green filaments and creamy anthers. The midgreen leaves are oval in outline with toothed margins.

Pruning group: 1. Any pruning to keep the plant in check should be carried out immediately after the main flowering period by cutting back to 1 m (3.25 ft.) from the ground once the plant is well established.

Flowering period: In the Southern Hemisphere, March to August; in the Northern Hemisphere, midautumn to late autumn.

Cultivation: Tolerates most well-drained and somewhat gritty garden soils. Requires a frost-free, sunny position.

Recommended use: Not for the small garden. Grow on a warm wall or fence or over a pergola or unsightly garden building. Zones 7–9.

Clematis lanuginosa

Origin: Eastern China. First discovered by plant hunter Robert Fortune.

Parentage and year: Species. 1850.

Habit: Hardy, not-so-vigorous, deciduous climber.

Height: To 2 m (6.5 ft.).

Description: The single, upward-facing, pale-lilac or purplish to white flowers, 8–15 cm (3.25–6 in.) across—to 20 cm (8 in.) in cultivation—are composed of six to eight overlapping, broad yet pointed tepals. The stamens consist of creamy white filaments and purple anthers.

Pruning group: 2.

Flowering period: Late spring to early summer and late summer.

Cultivation: Tolerates most well-drained garden soils and any aspect.

Recommended use: Ideal for container-culture. Grow naturally through small to medium-sized shrubs or conifers. Zones 4–9.

Clematis lasiandra

Origin: Central and southern China, southern Japan, and Taiwan.

Parentage and year: Species. 1866. Introduced into cultivation by Ernest Wilson in 1900.

Habit: Hardy, moderately vigorous, deciduous, semi-herbaceous climber.

Height: 3–6 m (10–20 ft.).

Clematis 'Lansdowne Gem'. Photo by M. Jerard.

Clematis lanuginosa. Photo by J. Lindmark.

Description: The off-white or pale rose-purple, nodding, bell-shaped flowers, 1–2 cm (0.5–0.75 in.) wide, are borne in small clusters of three or occasionally up to nine. Each flower is made of four tepals, 1.5–2 cm (0.5–0.75 in.) long, which roll back at the tips. There is a distinct deep purple ring at the point where the flower stalk joins the flower. The stamens consist of pale yellow tinged with mauve filaments and yellow anthers. The stems are ridged and sticky when young and, where the main stems are facing the light, they change colour from green to mauvish brown.

Pruning group: 3.

Flowering period: Early summer to midautumn.

Cultivation: Tolerates most garden soils with good drainage. Best grown in full sun to ripen the late-flowering wood.

Recommended use: Grow through medium-sized, open trees or over a pergola or trellis where the small flowers can be easily observed. Zones 6–9.

Clematis lasiantha

Common names: Chaparral clematis, pipestem clematis

Origin: United States (California).

Parentage and year: Species. 1838.

Habit: Tender, moderately vigorous, deciduous climber.

Height: 1.8–3 m (6–10 ft.).

Description: The white or cream, open, flat, flowers held on long stalks are composed of four tepals which are longer than broad, 2.5–4.5 cm (1–1.75 in.) long, and covered in fine silky hairs, more densely underneath. The stamens are made of creamy white filaments and anthers. Flowers are usually solitary or sometimes borne in groups of three to five. Male and bisexual flowers are carried on separate plants. In the wild, plants undergo a period of dormancy during summer before being revived by the rains.

Pruning group: 1.

Flowering period: Early autumn.

Cultivation: Does well in poor, well-drained soils in a warm location.

Recommended use: Grow in a warm conservatory or greenhouse. Zones 8–9.

Clematis 'Lasurstern'

Origin: Raised at the nursery of Goos and Koenemann of Germany. Awarded RHS Award of Garden Merit.

Parentage and year: Unknown. 1905.

Habit: Hardy, strong-growing, deciduous climber.

Height: 2.5–3 m (8–10 ft.).

Description: The single, large, deep lavender-blue flowers, 18–23 cm (7–9 in.) wide, are composed of six to eight tepals overlapping at the base and smartly tapering to acute points. The tepals with undulating edges open out fully and lie flat. With age the colour tends to fade along the centre of each tepal, but the flowers, whose large size and shape almost hide the leaves, are held well on the plant for a long time. The contrasting stamens are made of white filaments and yellow anthers. Flowers are produced from the previous season's old wood, and the large seedheads are spherical in shape.

Clematis lasiandra purple form. Photo by C. Chesshire.

Clematis lasiandra white form. Photo by E. Leeds.

Pruning group: 2.

Flowering period: Late spring to early summer and late summer.

Cultivation: Tolerates most garden soils and any aspect. Requires a sheltered position to prevent wind damage to the large flowers.

Recommended use: Grow with other wall-trained shrubs and roses which do not require annual pruning. Suitable for growing on a trellis, obelisk, or arch. Seed-heads may be used in flower arrangements. Zones 4–9.

Clematis 'Laura'

Origin: Raised by Brother Stefan Franczak of Warsaw, Poland.

Parentage and year: Unknown. 1980s.

Habit: Hardy, not-so-vigorous, compact, deciduous climber.

Height: 1.8–2.4 m (6–8 ft.).

Description: The single, large, bright lilac flowers, 20–25 cm (8–10 in.) across, are composed of six long, pointed, wavy-edged tepals, each carrying a pale mauve central bar. The prominent boss has crimson stamens.

Pruning group: 2.

Flowering period: Late spring to late summer.

Cultivation: Tolerates most garden soils and any aspect. Requires a sheltered position to prevent wind damage to the large flowers.

Recommended use: Useful for container-culture or for covering bare stems of wall-trained shrubs. Suitable for a small obelisk or trellis. Zones 4–9.

Clematis 'Lauren'

HERBACEOUS/INTEGRIFOLIA GROUP

Synonym: *C. integrifolia* 'Lauren'

Origin: Raised by nurseryman Robin Savill of Pleshey, England.

Parentage and year: Selected seedling of *C.* 'Olgae'. 1993.

Habit: Hardy, deciduous, non-clinging, herbaceous perennial.

Height: 0.6 m (2 ft.).

Description: The bell-shaped flowers, 5 cm (2 in.) wide, are composed of four pointed, bluish purple tepals with recurving tips and incurving margins. The colour near the base of each tepal is a deeper shade of blue-purple, becoming more pink towards the tip. The anthers are yellow, and the flowers are slightly scented.

Pruning group: 3.

Flowering period: Late spring to late summer.

Clematis 'Laura'. Photo by C. Chesshire.

Clematis 'Lasurstern'. Photo by D. Harding.

Clematis 'Lauren'. Photo by C. Chesshire.

Cultivation: Tolerates most garden soils enriched with humus. Suitable for any aspect but produces the strongest scent in a sunny position.

Recommended use: Ideal for the front of a herbaceous border. Zones 3–9.

Clematis 'Lawsoniana'

Origin: Raised by Isaac Anderson-Henry of Edinburgh, Scotland.

Parentage and year: *C. lanuginosa* × *C.* 'Fortunei'. 1870.

Habit: Hardy, moderately vigorous, compact, deciduous climber.

Height: 2.5–3 m (8–10 ft.).

Description: The single, mauvish blue flowers, measuring 18–23 cm (7–9 in.) across, and produced from the ends of long shoots, are formed of six to eight overlapping and tapering tepals. A hint of pink is very noticeable as the young flowers open, and with age the general colour fades to a pale lavender-blue. The large central boss of stamens is made of white filaments and beige anthers.

Pruning group: 2.

Flowering period: Early summer to early autumn.

Cultivation: Tolerates most garden soils. Requires a sheltered position to prevent wind damage to the large flowers.

Recommended use: Grow with other wall-trained shrubs which do not require annual pruning. Suitable for a trellis or pergola. Zones 4–9.

Clematis 'Lawsoniana'. Photo by J. Lindmark.

Clematis 'Lemon Bells'
ATRAGENE GROUP

Synonym: *C. chiisanensis* 'Lemon Bells'

Origin: A seedling selection made at the University of British Columbia Botanical Garden in 1992 from seed sent from South Korea. Introduced in 1999.

Parentage and year: Chance seedling of *C. chiisanensis*. 1988.

Habit: Hardy, moderately vigorous, deciduous, woody climber.

Height: 2–3 m (6.5–10 ft.) at maturity.

Description: Most flowers are produced on the previous season's growth, but a few are produced on new growth throughout the summer. In full sun, the pre-

Clematis 'Lemon Bells'. Photo by L. Beutler.

dominantly pale yellow, pendulous flowers are darker wine red at the base of the four tepals while in the shade the wine-red flush is reduced. The tepals are very thick, spongy, and predominantly ridged, and curve outward toward their wavy tips. There is a ring of flattened spoon-shaped staminodes about half the length of the tepals, between the fertile stamens and tepals. The seedheads, about 4 cm (1.5 in.) across, are very attractive when they are young and silky green as well as when they mature and become fluffy and off-white. Young stems, leaf stalks, and flower stalks are a shiny dark purple. Bright green leaves remain clean throughout the summer. Leaves are in threes with large marginal teeth. They are dull on the upper surface and shiny below.

Pruning group: 1. Any pruning to keep the plant tidy should be carried out immediately after the main flowering period.

Flowering period: Late spring to early summer

Cultivation: Tolerates most garden soils with some humus and good drainage. Best grown in partial shade to full sun.

Recommended use: Ideal for small gardens. Suitable for an obelisk, trellis, or small arch. May be grown with large shrubs which do not require annual pruning. Zones 6–8.

Clematis 'Lemon Chiffon'

Synonym: *C.* 'Yellow Chiffon'
Origin: Raised by Ed Philips of Busheyfields Nursery, Herne, Kent, England.

Parentage and year: Unknown. 1993.
Habit: Hardy, not-so-vigorous, compact, deciduous climber. Shy to flower.
Height: 1.8–2.4 m (6–8 ft.).
Description: The single, large, pale yellow-cream flowers, 10–15 cm (4–6 in.) in diameter, are formed of eight rounded, wide, overlapping, slightly recurving tepals and yellow stamens. The seedheads are large.
Pruning group: 2.
Flowering period: Late spring to early summer and late summer.
Cultivation: Tolerates most garden soils. Best grown out of direct sun to preserve flower colour.
Recommended use: Suitable for a small obelisk or trellis. Useful for container-culture. Shows up well against a dark background. Zones 4–9.

Clematis ligusticifolia

Common name: Western virgin's bower
Origin: Canada, United States, and northern Mexico.
Parentage and year: Species. 1838.
Habit: Hardy, vigorous, deciduous climber.
Height: 4–7 m (13–23 ft.) or more, to 20 m (66 ft.).
Description: Not very floriferous in British gardens. The single, white flowers with long, slender pedicels are borne in loose clusters along the upper lengths of the stems. Each flower is composed of four narrow,

Clematis 'Lemon Chiffon'. Photo by M. Toomey.

Clematis ligusticifolia. Photo by J. Lindmark.

egg-shaped tepals, 1.3 cm (0.5 in.) long, spreading widely apart and covered with fine soft hairs on both surfaces. Filaments and anthers are white. The stems are ridged and often shaded dark purple on mature vines and becoming woody with age. Leaves are a bright, glossy green and resemble those of Scots lovage (*Ligusticum scothicum*) in texture, gloss, and lobing of the leaflets—hence the specific epithet.

Pruning group: 3.

Flowering period: Midsummer to early autumn.

Cultivation: Tolerates most well-drained garden soils and is very drought tolerant. Best grown in sun or partial shade.

Recommended use: Suitable for a large pergola. Grow through large trees or along a wall or fence. Zones 5–9.

Clematis 'Lilacina'
MONTANA GROUP

Synonym: *C. montana* 'Lilacina'

Origin: Raised by Victor Lemoine of Nancy, France.

Parentage and year: *C.* 'Grandiflora' × *C. montana* var. *rubens*. 1910.

Habit: Vigorous, deciduous climber.

Height: 6–9 m (20–39 ft.).

Description: The single, saucer-shaped, pink flowers, 5–7 cm (2–2.75 in.) across, are composed of four broad, round-edged tepals, which are flushed with lilac-blue.

Pruning group: 1. Any pruning to keep the plant in check should be carried out immediately after the main flowering period by removing some of the old, flowered stems.

Flowering period: Late spring to early summer.

Cultivation: Prefers well-drained soil. Suitable for any aspect. Hardy in temperate gardens.

Recommended use: Grow through large trees and conifers, or on a wall, fence, and strong pergola. Not for a small garden or container. Zones 7–9.

Clematis 'Lilactime'

Origin: Raised by Ken Pyne of Chingford, London, in 1983. Named in 1990. Awarded RHS Certificate of Preliminary Commendation (1990).

Parentage and year: Selected seedling of *C.* 'Alice Fisk'. Unknown.

Habit: Hardy, compact, deciduous climber.

Height: 1.8–2.4 m (6–8 ft.).

Description: The semi-double, wisteria-blue flowers produced on the previous season's old wood and measuring 15–20 cm (6–8 in.) in diameter, are formed of six to eight main basal tepals followed by usually six shorter segments, which are petaloid stamens. These sepals may have red-tinted edges. The white filaments carry magenta anthers. Single flowers are produced on the current season's new wood.

Pruning group: 2.

Flowering period: Late spring to early summer (semi-double) and late summer (single).

Cultivation: Tolerates most garden soils. Best grown in full or partial sun. Requires a sheltered position to prevent wind damage to the flowers.

Recommended use: Grow on a small to medium-sized obelisk or trellis. Suitable for container-culture. Zones 4–9.

Clematis 'Lilacina'. Photo by C. Chesshire.

Clematis 'Lilactime'. Photo by K. Pyne.

Clematis 'Lincoln Star'

Origin: Raised by Walter Pennell of Pennell and Sons nursery. Named in 1954.

Parentage and year: Open-pollinated seedling of *C.* 'Nelly Moser'. 1950.

Habit: Hardy, moderately vigorous, deciduous climber.

Height: 2.4–3 m (8–10 ft.).

Description: The single, gappy, raspberry pink flowers, 15 cm (6 in.) in diameter, are composed of six to eight pointed tepals, each with a deeper pink central bar. White filaments carrying reddish maroon anthers make up the prominent stamens.

Pruning group: 2.

Flowering period: Late spring to early summer and late summer.

Cultivation: Tolerates most garden soils. Best grown out of direct sun to preserve flower colour.

Recommended use: Shows up well against a dark background. Ideal for a pergola, arbour, or trellis. Zones 4–9.

Clematis 'Lisboa'
VITICELLA GROUP

Synonym: *C. campaniflora* 'Lisboa'

Origin: Raised from *C. campaniflora* seed collected at the University of Lisbon botanic gardens by Magnus Johnson of Södertälje, Sweden, in 1956. Seedling selected and named by Johnson in 1993.

Parentage and year: Believed to be *C. campaniflora* × *C. viticella*.

Habit: Hardy, moderately vigorous, deciduous climber.

Height: 2.4–3.6 m (8–12 ft.).

Description: The mauvish blue, bell-shaped flowers are larger than those of *C. campaniflora*, measuring 5 cm (2 in.) across. Each flower is composed of four tepals which are longer than broad and pointed, with wavy margins. These open wide and recurve at the tips. The stamens are greenish yellow.

Pruning group: 3.

Flowering period: Midsummer to late summer.

Cultivation: Tolerates most garden soils and any aspect.

Recommended use: A handsome climber for a large pergola, obelisk, or trellis. May be grown up and over large shrubs or medium-sized trees. Zones 3–9.

Clematis 'Little Nell'
VITICELLA GROUP

Synonym: *C. viticella* 'Little Nell'

Origin: Raised by Ernest Markham, head gardener at Gravetye Manor, and named after a local child.

Parentage and year: Unknown. Before 1935.

Habit: Hardy, moderately vigorous, deciduous climber.

Height: 2.5–3 m (8–10 ft.).

Description: A very floriferous cultivar. The single, semi-nodding, pale creamy white flowers are 5–6.5 cm (2–2.5 in.) across with mauvish pink margins. The tepals usually number four, occasionally five, and are

Clematis 'Lincoln Star'. Photo by C. Chesshire.

Clematis 'Lisboa'. Photo by J. Lindmark.

gently recurved at the somewhat broad tips. The mauvish pink veins are very distinct. The stamens are greenish yellow, and the leaves have five to seven leaflets.

Pruning group: 3.

Flowering period: Midsummer to early autumn.

Cultivation: Tolerates most garden soils and any aspect.

Recommended use: Grow through small to medium-sized trees and large shrubs, and over prostrate conifers and contrasting heathers. Zones 3–9.

Clematis 'Lord Herschell'
HERBACEOUS GROUP

Origin: Introduced by Barry Fretwell of Peveril Clematis Nursery, England.

Parentage and year: Unknown. 1998.

Habit: Hardy, deciduous, non-clinging, herbaceous perennial.

Height: 46–61 cm (18–24 in.).

Clematis 'Little Nell'. Photo by J. Lindmark.

Description: The single, tulip-shaped flowers, borne on numerous stems and measuring 5 cm (2 in.) wide, are composed of four or five rich reddish purple, pointed tepals with a velvety sheen. The stamens are yellow.

Pruning group: 3.

Flowering period: Late spring to late summer.

Cultivation: Tolerates most garden soils and any aspect.

Recommended use: Ideal for container-culture or for placing towards the front of a herbaceous or mixed border to scramble over neighbouring plants. Zones 3–9.

Clematis 'Lord Nevill'

Origin: Raised by Thomas Cripps and Son of Tunbridge Wells, England, and named after a local patron. Awarded RHS First Class Certificate (1875).

Parentage and year: *C. patens* × *C.* 'Standishii'. Before 1875.

Habit: Hardy, moderately vigorous, deciduous climber.

Height: 2.4–3 m (8–10 ft.).

Description: The single, striking, deep blue flowers, 15–20 cm (6–8 in.) in diameter, are composed of six to eight tepals which are veined and which overlap at the base and smartly taper to fine points. The tepals boast

Clematis 'Lord Herschell'. Photo by C. Chesshire.

a textured surface and handsome wavy edges. White filaments tipped with purplish red anthers harmonize with the tepal colour.

Pruning group: 2.

Flowering period: Late spring to early summer and late summer.

Cultivation: Tolerates most garden soils. Best grown out of full sun to preserve flower colour.

Recommended use: Shows up well against a light background. Suitable for growing on a trellis, obelisk, or pergola. May also be grown with other wall-trained shrubs which require no annual pruning. Zones 4–9.

Clematis 'Louise Rowe'

Origin: Raised by Jean B. Rowe of Norfolk, England, and named after a younger member of the family.

Parentage and year: *C.* 'Marie Boisselot' × *C.* 'William Kennett'. Introduced in 1983.

Habit: Hardy, not-so-vigorous, compact, deciduous climber.

Height: 1.2–1.8 m (4–6 ft.).

Description: A unique cultivar in that double, semi-double, and single flowers are produced simultaneously on the previous season's old wood. They measure 12.5–15 cm (5–6 in.) across. The rounded, yet pointed tepals are pale lilac, and this colour varies slightly, depending on the level of light and the maturity of the flower, from pale shades of mauve to almost greyish white. In semi-double and double flowers, the smaller, secondary rows of tepals have scalloped margins, and some are twisted, giving the flower a frilly appearance. Single flowers, somewhat paler in colour and with six tepals, are borne on the current season's wood. The central boss of stamens is primrose-yellow.

Pruning group: 2.

Flowering period: Early summer to midsummer and early autumn.

Cultivation: Tolerates most garden soils.

Recommended use: Ideal for container-culture or for growing on a small obelisk or trellis. Zones 4–9.

Clematis 'Love Child'
ATRAGENE GROUP

Synonym: *C. chiisanensis* 'Love Child'

Origin: A selected seedling collected from the wild by Thomas Largerstrom, a member of the Nordic Arboretum expedition to South Korea.

Parentage and year: *C. chiisanensis*. 1976.

Habit: Hardy, moderately vigorous, deciduous climber.

Height: 2.4–3 m (8–10 ft.).

Description: The single, nodding, bell-shaped, pale lemon flowers are composed of four tepals, each 5–6.5

Clematis 'Lord Nevill'. Photo by J. Lindmark.

Clematis 'Louise Rowe'. Photo by E. Leeds.

cm (2–2.5 in.) long and curving outwards at their tips, and have spurs at their base which carry on down to the tips in the form of deep ridges. These ridges are speckled with reddish brown blotches and spots. Flower stalks and main stems are a reddish dark brown colour. The central tuft of spoon-shaped staminodes (sterile stamens) mirrors a similar colour to the tepals. Flowers are produced on old wood from the previous season and new shoots from the current one, thus giving this plant a long flowering period.

Pruning group: 1. Any pruning to keep the plant tidy should be carried out immediately after the main flowering period.

Flowering period: Late spring to early summer, with sporadic flowering to late summer.

Cultivation: Tolerates most garden soils with some humus and good drainage. Suitable for any aspect.

Recommended use: Grow through open, medium-sized shrubs which do not require annual pruning. Suitable as a companion for other clematis with similar pruning requirements. Zones 5–9.

Clematis 'Lucey'

Origin: Raised by John Lucey of Surrey, England. Introduced into cultivation by Fisk's Clematis Nursery, Suffolk, England.

Parentage and year: Unknown, but believed to be an open-pollinated seedling. 1989.

Habit: Hardy, not-so-vigorous, compact, deciduous climber.

Height: 1.8–2.4 m (6–8 ft.).

Description: The single, mauvish pink flowers,

12.5–18 cm (5–7 in.) wide, are normally composed of six rounded and cup-shaped tepals with deeply veined central bars. The prominent stamens are yellow.

Pruning group: 3.

Flowering period: Late spring to late summer.

Cultivation: Tolerates most garden soils and any aspect.

Recommended use: Grow naturally through small trees and medium-sized shrubs or over prostrate conifers. Ideal for container-culture. Zones 4–9.

Clematis 'Lunar Lass'
EVERGREEN GROUP

Origin: Raised by Graham Hutchins of County Park Nursery, Essex, England.

Parentage and year: *C. marata* × *C. marmoraria*. 1986.

Habit: Half-hardy to hardy, evergreen, non-clinging, trailing shrub.

Height: 30–50 cm (12–20 in.).

Description: Single, pale green, female flowers are composed of four or five, occasionally six, tepals, each 1–1.8 cm (0.5–0.75 in.) long. Six staminodes surround the pistils made of ovaries, styles, and stigmas. Seedheads are distinctly hairy. The leaves are small, dark green, leathery, and firm.

Pruning group: 1.

Flowering period: Midspring to late spring.

Cultivation: Requires good drainage in a warm position.

Recommended use: Best for container-culture in a cold greenhouse or conservatory, or plunged in an alpine bed under glass. Zones 8–9.

Clematis 'Love Child'. Photo by C. Chesshire.

Clematis 'Lucey'. Photo by C. Chesshire.

Clematis 'Luther Burbank'

Origin: Raised by A. N. Volosenko-Valenis of the State Nikitsky Botanic Gardens, Ukraine. Named after a North American clematis enthusiast (1849–1926).

Parentage and year: *C.* 'Jackmanii' × pollen mixture of *C.* 'Lanuginosa Candida', *C. texensis*, and *C. montana*. 1962.

Habit: Hardy, vigorous, strong-growing, deciduous climber.

Height: 3–4 m (8–13 ft.).

Description: The single, large, violet-purple flowers, 13–20 cm (5–8 in.) in diameter, are composed of six rounded tepals with undulating margins and white downy surface on the reverse. A prominent contrasting boss of stamens made of whitish filaments and large pale yellow anthers enlivens the flowers.

Pruning group: 3.

Flowering period: Early summer to late summer.

Cultivation: Tolerates most garden soils and any aspect.

Recommended use: Shows up well against a light background. Grow naturally through small trees or shrubs, or with moderately vigorous climbing roses. Suitable for growing as a specimen plant on a medium-sized obelisk or free-standing trellis in a mixed border. May also be grown in a large container for a short term only. Zones 4–9.

Clematis macropetala
ATRAGENE GROUP

Origin: Northern China, eastern Mongolia, and eastern Siberia.

Parentage and year: Species. 1829.

Habit: Very hardy, moderately vigorous, deciduous climber or scrambler.

Height: 2–3 m (6.5–10 ft.).

Clematis 'Lunar Lass'. Photo courtesy Thorncroft Clematis Nursery.

Clematis 'Luther Burbank'. Photo by J. Lindmark.

Clematis macropetala, wild form collected by Reginald Farrer in China. Photo by J. Lindmark.

Clematis macropetala in an Irish garden. Photo by J. Lindmark.

Description: The flowers are pale blue to purple-blue with four tepals 3–4.5 cm (1.25–1.75 in.) long. The tepals enclose numerous petal-like staminodes (sterile stamens), ranging from the blue outer set to the inner cluster of bluish white, and giving the appearance of a double flower. These staminodes enclose a set of fertile stamens, which are slightly shorter in length. Leaves are divided into nine leaflets, with sharply serrated margins. The seedheads are numerous.

Pruning group: 1.

Flowering period: Spring, with some blooms in late summer.

Cultivation: Requires sharp-draining garden soils enriched with humus. Suitable for any aspect.

Recommended use: Ideal for container-culture. Withstands cold and windy aspects such as a north- or northeast-facing wall. Grow on a pergola or through small trees. Zones 3–9.

Clematis 'Madame Baron Veillard'

Origin: Raised at the nursery of Baron Veillard of Orléans, France.

Parentage and year: Unknown. 1885.

Habit: Hardy, vigorous, deciduous climber.

Height: 3–4 m (10–13 ft.).

Description: The single, dusky midmauvish pink flowers, 10–13 cm (4–5 in.) in diameter, are made of six to eight blunt, overlapping tepals, each with textured margins and grooves running along the centre. With age the tepals recurve slightly at their tips. Creamy filaments tipped with greenish anthers constitute the stamens.

Clematis 'Madame Baron Veillard'. Photo by C. Chesshire.

Pruning group: 3.

Flowering period: Early autumn to midautumn.

Cultivation: Tolerates most garden soils. Best grown in full sun where the vines can ripen to produce the exceptionally late flowers.

Recommended use: Ideal to grow naturally through medium-sized shrubs or trees or with other wall-trained climbers. Suitable for an arbour, pergola, or large trellis. Zones 4–9.

Clematis 'Madame Édouard André'

Origin: Raised at the nursery of Baron Veillard of Orléans, France. Awarded RHS Award of Garden Merit.

Parentage and year: Unknown. ca. 1892.

Habit: Hardy, not-so-vigorous, compact, deciduous climber.

Height: 1.8–2.4 m (6–8 ft.).

Description: The single, wine-red flowers, 10–12.5 cm (4–5 in.) across, remaining slightly cupped on opening and ultimately becoming flat, are made of four to six rounded but pointed tepals slightly flecked with white, and incurving margins. As the flower matures the colour fades to a more mauvish red. Creamy yellow stamens set off the flowers.

Pruning group: 3.

Flowering period: Late spring to late summer.

Cultivation: Tolerates most garden soils and any aspect.

Recommended use: Ideal for container-culture or for growing through prostrate conifers and other medium-sized shrubs. Suitable for a small to medium-sized obelisk or trellis. Zones 4–9.

Clematis 'Madame Grangé'

Origin: Raised by Th. L. Grangé of Orléans, France. Awarded RHS Award of Garden Merit.

Parentage and year: *C. lanuginosa* × *C. viticella* (possibly 'Rubra Grandiflora'). 1875.

Habit: Hardy, moderately vigorous, deciduous climber.

Height: 2.4–3 m (8–10 ft.).

Description: The single, rich velvety, dusky-purple flowers, 12.5–15 cm (5–6 in.) across, are composed of four to six tepals, each with incurving margins and a concentration of red along the middle. The reverse of each tepal is distinguished by a silvery purple colouring. With age the tepals open out fully rendering the flowers flat. The somewhat insignificant stamens are made of light reddish purple filaments and coffee-coloured anthers.

Pruning group: 3.

Flowering period: Midsummer to late summer.

Cultivation: Tolerates most garden soils. Best grown in sun or partial shade.

Clematis 'Madame Édouard André'. Photo by C. Chesshire.

Clematis 'Madame Grangé'. Photo by J. Lindmark.

Recommended use: Shows up well against a light background or with plants which have light-coloured foliage. Suitable for a medium-sized trellis or obelisk, or for training through small trees or large shrubs. Zones 4–9.

Clematis 'Madame Julia Correvon'
VITICELLA GROUP

Synonym: *C. viticella* 'Madame Julia Correvon'

Origin: Raised by Francisque Morel of Lyon, France.

Parentage and year: Believed to be a hybrid of *C.* 'Ville de Lyon' × *C. viticella*. 1900.

Habit: Hardy, moderately vigorous, deciduous climber.

Height: 3–4 m (10–13 ft.).

Description: The single, semi-nodding, vibrant, rich claret red, 7- to 10-cm (2.25- to 4-in.) wide flowers, unfold from their slightly twisted buds with four to six narrow tepals, which are deeply veined down the midrib. The margins of the tepals are somewhat scalloped and recurving. As the flowers mature, they become gappy as a result of the tepals twisting, but this adds to their charm and beauty. The stamens are yellow and are not held tightly together. The midgreen to dark green leaves are usually made of five leaflets.

Pruning group: 3.

Flowering period: Midsummer to late summer.

Cultivation: Tolerates most garden soils and any aspect. Produces best flower colour in sun or semi-shade.

Recommended use: Suitable for large containers or

growing on an obelisk or medium-sized, free-standing trellis. Ideal for covering the bare lower stems of old climbing roses. May be allowed to climb into small trees, conifers, or medium-sized to large, open shrubs. Zones 3–9.

Clematis 'Madame van Houtte'

Origin: Raised by Thomas Cripps and Son of Tunbridge Wells, England. Awarded RHS First Class Certificate (1867).

Parentage and year: Seedling of *C. lanuginosa*. 1867.

Habit: Hardy, moderately vigorous, deciduous climber.

Height: 2.4–3 m (8–10 ft.).

Description: The single, rather large, fully rounded, white flowers, measuring up to 25 cm (10 in.) in diameter, are normally composed of six overlapping tepals. The stamens are reddish purple.

Pruning group: 2.

Flowering period: Late spring to late summer.

Cultivation: Tolerates most garden soils and any aspect. Requires a sheltered position to prevent wind damage to the large flowers.

Recommended use: Grow with other wall-trained plants or roses which do not require annual pruning. Suitable for a medium-sized obelisk or trellis, or for growing through medium-sized shrubs or small trees. Zones 4–9.

Clematis 'Madame Julia Correvon'. Photo by E. Leeds.

Clematis 'Madame van Houtte'. Photo by J. Lindmark.

Clematis 'Maidwell Hall'

ATRAGENE GROUP

Synonym: *C. macropetala* 'Maidwell Hall'

Origin: Raised by Oliver Wyatt of Maidwell Hall, Northamptonshire, England, and introduced by George Jackman and Son, England. Awarded RHS Award of Garden Merit.

Parentage and year: Seedling of *C. macropetala*. 1956.

Habit: Hardy, moderately vigorous, compact, deciduous climber.

Height: 2–2.5 m (6.5–8 ft.).

Description: The double, nodding and semi-nodding, bell-shaped, pale blue flowers are composed of four tepals, each 4.5–5 cm (1.75–2 in.) long and somewhat blunt with an inner skirt of numerous, similarly coloured, petal-like staminodes surrounding an inner core of bluish white fertile stamens. Leaves are divided into nine leaflets, the margins of which are sharply serrated.

Pruning group: 1.

Flowering period: Early spring to midspring.

Cultivation: Requires sharp-draining garden soils enriched with humus. Suitable for any aspect.

Recommended use: Ideal for covering bare lower stems of Montana Group, wisteria, or old climbing roses. Also ideal for container-culture. Allow to tumble over a low wall or fence. Zones 3–9.

Clematis mandschurica

HERBACEOUS GROUP

Origin: Northern China.

Parentage and year: Species. 1857.

Habit: Hardy, spreading, herbaceous perennial. Tall clones are climbers that make their way through other plants by intertwining their flexible stems, while the short ones are non-clinging and tend to lie on the ground.

Height: 0.9–1.5 m (3–5 ft.).

Description: The numerous, small, pure white, scented flowers, borne on terminal shoots and in leaf axils measuring 2–3 cm (0.75–1.25 in.) across, are composed of four or five narrow and pointed tepals. Greenish cream filaments and anthers constitute the stamens.

Pruning group: 3.

Flowering period: Midsummer to late summer.

Cultivation: Tolerates most garden soils. Suitable for any aspect but produces the strongest scent in full sun. If trained on an artificial support, the stems need tying-in.

Recommended use: Plant at the back of a mixed border where it can use other shrubs for support. Shorter growing clones can be brought closer to the front of borders and supported with pea-sticks or short branches. Zones 3–9.

Clematis marata

EVERGREEN GROUP

Origin: New Zealand.

Parentage and year: Species. 1880.

Clematis 'Maidwell Hall'. Photo by C. Chesshire.

Clematis mandschurica. Photo by J. Lindmark.

Habit: Half-hardy to hardy, low-growing, slender, evergreen climber.

Height: Up to 90 cm (3 ft.).

Description: The single, small, yellowish green flowers, about 2.5 cm (1 in.) across, are composed of four or five tepals, each with a slightly darker mark at its base. Flowers may be solitary or in groups of two to four, and they have a spicy cinnamon scent. The leaves are dull green and hairy, and divided into three very variable leaflets.

Pruning group: 1.

Flowering period: Early spring.

Cultivation: Requires a sharp-draining soil and a sunny position.

Recommended use: Ideal for container-culture in a sheltered position or in a cold greenhouse or conservatory. Suitable for an alpine house. Zones 8–9.

Clematis 'Margaret Hunt'

Origin: Raised by Margaret Hunt of Norwich, England, and introduced in 1969 by Fisk's Clematis Nursery, Suffolk, England.

Parentage and year: Unknown.

Habit: Hardy, quite vigorous, deciduous climber.

Height: 3–3.6 m (10–12 ft.).

Description: The single, star-shaped, lavender-pink flowers, which are medium-sized and measure 10–15 cm (4–6 in.) across, are made of four to six tepals hav-

ing a bluish tint when first opened that fades away as the flower matures. The stamens are dark brown purple.

Pruning group: 3.

Flowering period: Late spring to late summer.

Cultivation: Tolerates most garden soils and any aspect.

Recommended use: Grow naturally through large shrubs or on a pergola, arbour, or large obelisk. May be grown with other wall-trained shrubs. Zones 4–9.

Clematis 'Margaret Jones'
MONTANA GROUP

Synonym: *C. montana* 'Margaret Jones'

Origin: Found in the garden of Anne Smyth of Hoveton, Norfolk, England, and named after her mother. Introduced by Thorncroft Clematis Nursery.

Parentage and year: Chance seedling. 1991.

Habit: Vigorous, deciduous climber.

Height: To 6 m (20 ft.).

Description: The semi-double, white, starry flowers, 3 cm (1.25 in.) across, are composed of four base tepals and an inner layer of 6–12 shorter, narrower, greenish cream petal-like staminodes. There are no anthers. The centrally placed style is greenish white. The leaves are light green with leaflets in threes.

Pruning group: 1. Any pruning to keep the plant in check should be carried out immediately after the

Clematis marata. Photo by J. Hudson.

Clematis 'Margaret Hunt'. Photo by J. Lindmark.

main flowering period by removing some of the old, flowered stems.

Flowering period: Late spring.

Cultivation: Tolerates most well-drained garden soils. Hardy in temperate gardens. Produces best flowers in a sunny position. Slow to establish itself and flower well.

Recommended use: Grow on a pergola, large trellis, wall, or fence. Zones 7–9.

Clematis 'Margot Koster'
VITICELLA GROUP

Synonym: *C. viticella* 'Margot Koster'

Origin: Raised by Marinus Koster of Boskoop, Netherlands.

Parentage and year: Unknown, but possibly *C. viticella* × *C. patens*. 1890s.

Habit: Hardy, moderately vigorous, compact, deciduous climber.

Height: 2.5–3 m (8–10 ft.).

Description: The single, semi-nodding, deep mauvish pink flowers, up to 10 cm (4 in.) across, are borne freely. The four to six tepals recurve at the margins and tips, and with age literally roll back on themselves, giving the flowers a gappy, loose, untidy appearance. Nevertheless, the tepals retain their colour right to the end. The stamens are greenish yellow. The leaves are midgreen with five leaflets.

Pruning group: 3.

Flowering period: Midsummer to early autumn.

Cultivation: Tolerates most garden soils and any aspect.

Recommended use: For best colour, plant in sun or partial shade. Ideal for container-culture or for covering bare lower stems of old climbing roses and wisteria. Grow naturally through small trees, medium-sized to large, open shrubs or over prostrate conifers. Zones 3–9.

Clematis 'Maria Louise Jensen'

Origin: Raised by Friedrich Manfred Westphal of Prisdorf, Germany.

Parentage and year: Unknown. 1982.

Habit: Hardy, not-so-vigorous, deciduous climber.

Height: 1.8–2.4 m (6–8 ft.).

Clematis 'Margot Koster'. Photo by J. Lindmark.

Clematis 'Margaret Jones'. Photo by E. Leeds.

Clematis 'Maria Louise Jensen'. Photo by C. Chesshire.

Description: Normally single but occasional semi-double flowers are borne on old growths made during the previous years. The upward-facing, violet blue flowers, 14 cm (5.5 in.) wide, are composed of six to eight broad yet tapering and pointed, overlapping tepals, each with undulating edges and slightly paler central bar. Mauvish white filaments and reddish brown anthers form the central boss of stamens. A second flush of smaller flowers is produced on new shoots made later in the season.

Pruning group: 2.

Flowering period: Late spring to early summer and late summer.

Cultivation: Tolerates most garden soils and any aspect.

Recommended use: Ideal for container-culture. Grow with wall-trained shrubs or other climbing plants to cover bare lower stems or grow over medium-sized shrubs or a small obelisk. Zones 4–9.

Clematis 'Marie Boisselot'

Synonym: *C.* 'Madame Le Coultre'

Origin: Raised by Auguste Boisselot of Nantes, France. Awarded RHS Award of Garden Merit.

Parentage and year: Open-pollinated seedling of *C.* 'The President'. 1885.

Habit: Hardy, vigorous, deciduous climber.

Height: 2.4–3 m (8–10 ft.).

Description: The single, rather large, slightly creamy white flowers which open flat measure 15–20 cm (6–8 in.) in diameter and are composed of eight broad, rounded, overlapping tepals boasting a textured satiny surface. The tepals are deeply grooved along the middle. The small stamens are made of cream filaments and golden yellow anthers. This universally popular cultivar flowers on old wood and on the current season's new growth.

Pruning group: Optional, 2, or 3. A hard pruning (group 3) delays flowering.

Flowering period: Early summer to early autumn.

Cultivation: Tolerates most garden soils and any aspect. Train the flowering stems in a horizontal plane to enjoy the flowers at eye level.

Recommended use: Grow naturally through and over prostrate conifers or medium-sized shrubs. Also grow with climbing roses and other wall-trained shrubs or climbing plants which do not require annual pruning. Zones 4–9.

Clematis 'Marjorie'

MONTANA GROUP

Synonym: *C. montana* 'Marjorie'

Origin: Raised by Marjorie Free of Suffolk, England. Introduced into commerce by Jim Fisk of Fisk's Clematis Nursery, Suffolk, England.

Clematis 'Marie Boisselot'. Photo by M. Toomey.

Clematis 'Marjorie'. Photo by E. Leeds.

Parentage and year: Seedling of *C. montana* var. *wilsonii*. 1980.

Habit: Vigorous, deciduous climber.

Height: To 8 m (26 ft.).

Description: The semi-double flowers are creamy pink with salmony petal-like staminodes (sterile stamens). Early spring flowers may open with a green tinge due to insufficient sunlight, but the right colour is restored as the season progresses and more light becomes available.

Pruning group: 1. Any pruning to keep the plant in check should be carried out immediately after the main flowering period by removing some of the old, flowered stems.

Flowering period: Late spring to early summer.

Cultivation: Needs sharp drainage. Produces best flower colour in a warm position.

Recommended use: Grow on its own or through medium-sized to large trees or conifers. Suitable for a pergola or warm wall. Zones 7–9.

Clematis 'Markham's Pink'
ATRAGENE GROUP

Synonyms: *C. macropetala* 'Markham's Pink', *C. macropetala* var. *markhamii*

Origin: Raised by Ernest Markham, head gardener at Gravetye Manor. Awarded RHS Award of Garden Merit.

Parentage and year: Unknown. 1935.

Habit: Hardy, moderately vigorous, deciduous climber.

Height: 2–2.5 m (6.5–8 ft.).

Description: The nodding and semi-nodding, double, bell-shaped flowers are composed of four clear, deep pink base tepals, each 5 cm (2 in.) long. These enclose an inner skirt of similar but narrower, pointed staminodes, giving the flower a spiky appearance. The stamens are cream coloured, and the leaves are divided into nine leaflets which are sharply serrated.

Pruning group: 1.

Flowering period: Midspring.

Cultivation: Needs sharp drainage. Suitable for any aspect but produces best flower colour in full sun.

Recommended use: Good for small gardens or container-culture. May be allowed to roam into medium-sized shrubs or small trees. Zones 3–9.

Clematis marmoraria
EVERGREEN GROUP

Origin: New Zealand.

Parentage and year: Species. 1975.

Habit: Low mound-forming, non-clinging, dwarf, suckering, evergreen alpine.

Height: 8–10 cm (3.25–4 in.).

Description: Flower buds are distinctly greenish. The single, small, creamy white flowers, carried just above the foliage, are 2 cm (0.75 in.) across and are composed of six, sometimes five, seven, or eight, broad but not overlapping, rounded, yet pointed tepals. Leaves are dark glossy green, rigid, thick, and divided into three leaflets, which are further divided deeply and closely.

Pruning group: 1.

Flowering period: Early spring.

Clematis 'Markham's Pink'. Photo by R. Surman.

Cultivation: Requires sharp drainage in a sheltered position. Best grown in sun or semi-shade.

Recommended use: Best grown in a container in a cool greenhouse or conservatory. Also suitable for an alpine house or border. Zones 8–9.

Clematis 'Masquerade'

Origin: A wrongly labelled plant, which came into the possession of Raymond Evison of Guernsey Clematis Nursery, was recognized as a distinct cultivar and named and introduced by him.

Parentage and year: Unknown. 1993.

Habit: Hardy, moderately vigorous, compact, deciduous climber.

Height: 1.8–2.4 m (6–8 ft.).

Clematis marmoraria early flowers are green, fading to almost white. Photo by I. Holmåsen.

Description: The single, mauvish blue flowers, 18 cm (7 in.) across, are formed of six to eight gappy, pointed tepals, each of which narrows towards the base and has a pinky mauve central band and undulating margins. The stamens are made of cream filaments and chocolate-coloured anthers.

Pruning group: 2.

Flowering period: Late spring to early summer, and late summer to early autumn.

Cultivation: Tolerates most garden soils and any aspect.

Recommended use: Suitable for a small trellis or obelisk. Ideal for container-culture. Zones 4–9.

Clematis 'Matka Teresa'

Origin: Raised by Brother Stefan Franczak of Warsaw, Poland. Introduced into the British Isles in 1993 by Jim Fisk of Fisk's Clematis Nursery, Suffolk, England. The translation of the name is "Mother Teresa."

Parentage and year: Unknown. 1989.

Habit: Hardy, moderately vigorous, compact, deciduous climber.

Height: 1.8–2.4 m (6–8 ft.).

Description: The single, large, white flowers, 15–20 cm (6–8 in.) across, are composed of six to eight tepals with wavy edges. The tepals of young flowers carry a very pale mauve central band, which fades away with age. The cream filaments tipped with prominent deep red anthers constitute the stamens.

Pruning group: 2.

Flowering period: Late spring to late summer.

Clematis 'Masquerade'. Photo by C. Chesshire.

Cultivation: Tolerates most garden soils. Best grown in sun or partial shade. Requires a sheltered position to prevent wind damage to the large flowers.

Recommended use: Suitable for a small obelisk or trellis. Ideal for container-culture. Zones 4–9.

Clematis 'Maureen'

Origin: Raised by George Strudwick of Worth Park Nurseries, England, and named after his granddaughter. Awarded RHS Award of Merit (1956).

Parentage and year: Unknown. ca. 1950.

Habit: Hardy, not very vigorous, compact, deciduous climber.

Height: 1.8–2.4 m (6–8 ft.).

Description: The single, velvety purple-red flowers, which lose their lustre with age and which measure 12–15 cm (4.75–6 in.) in diameter, are formed of six overlapping, broad, slightly recurving tepals, each with a dash of red along the middle and gently undulating margins. Creamy white filaments and pale pinky reddish anthers make up the stamens. The attractive, rounded leaves are not plentiful.

Pruning group: 3.

Flowering period: Early summer to early autumn.

Cultivation: Tolerates most garden soils and any aspect.

Recommended use: Shows up well against a light background. Suitable for a small trellis or obelisk, or for growing through medium-sized shrubs. Ideal for container-culture or for cascading over a low wall. Zones 4–9.

Clematis mauritiana

EVERGREEN GROUP

Origin: Mauritius and Madagascar.

Parentage and year: Species. 1786.

Habit: Tender, climbing or sprawling evergreen.

Height: 3–3.6 m (10–12 ft.).

Description: The white, nodding flowers on long stalks, 3–4 cm (1.2–1.5 in.) across, are composed of four, occasionally five, somewhat broad, egg-shaped tepals, 1.5–2.5 cm (0.5–1 in.) long and downy on both sides. Juvenile flowers are edged in pale lilac. The leaves are glossy and finely net-veined, with toothed margins. Young stems and undersides of leaves are densely woolly.

Pruning group: 1.

Flowering period: Midwinter to early spring.

Cultivation: Requires well-drained soil and a warm, sunny position to flower well.

Recommended use: Suitable for a warm conservatory or greenhouse. Zones 8–9.

Clematis 'Mayleen'

MONTANA GROUP

Synonym: *C. montana* 'Mayleen'

Origin: Given to Jim Fisk of Fisk's Clematis Nursery, Suffolk, England, by a customer.

Parentage and year: Possibly a selected seedling. 1984.

Habit: Vigorous, deciduous climber.

Height: 6–8 m (20–26 ft.).

Description: The single, deep pink, vanilla-scented,

Clematis 'Matka Teresa'. Photo by R. Savill.

Clematis 'Maureen'. Photo by C. Chesshire.

saucer-shaped flowers, 7.5 cm (3 in.) in diameter, are composed of four somewhat rounded tepals. The stamens are gold coloured, and the leaves tinted bronze.

Pruning group: 1. Any pruning to keep the plant in check should be carried out immediately after the main flowering period by removing some of the old, flowered stems.

Flowering period: Late spring to early summer, with occasional flowers in late summer.

Cultivation: Needs sharp drainage. Hardy in temperate gardens. Produces the strongest scent and best flower colour in full sun, but can also be grown in partial shade.

Recommended use: Ideal growing through medium-sized to large trees and conifers. Too vigorous for container-culture. Zones 7–9.

Clematis meyeniana
EVERGREEN/ARMANDII GROUP

Origin: Macao and Hong Kong. Named after Franz T. J. Meyen (1804–1840) of Germany.

Parentage and year: Species. Close relative of *C. armandii*. 1820.

Habit: Half-hardy to hardy, vigorous, evergreen climber or scrambler.

Height: 4.5 m (14.5 ft.).

Description: The single, fragrant, pure white flowers are 2.5 cm (1 in.) across and have four or five tepals borne in racemes from the leaf axils. The leaves are composed of three leaflets, and are broad at the base, tapering like a lance towards the tip, and thick in texture.

Pruning group: 1. Any pruning should be carried out immediately after the main flowering period.

Flowering period: Early spring to midspring.

Cultivation: More tender than *C. armandii*. Suitable for very sheltered south-facing wall.

Recommended use: Best in a large conservatory, except in mild or maritime gardens. Zones 7–9.

Clematis microphylla
EVERGREEN GROUP

Common name: Small-leaved clematis
Origin: Australia (northern Tasmania).
Parentage and year: Species. 1818.
Habit: Half-hardy, slender, evergreen climber.
Height: 2.1–2.7 m (7–8 ft.).
Description: The greenish cream flowers, 2.5–4 cm (1–1.5 in.) across, are borne in short clusters at the upper nodes. Each flower is composed of four tepals, which are narrow, oblong, twisted, and spidery looking. The small narrow leaves are greyish to matt green with either three or nine leaflets. Male and female flowers are borne on separate plants.

Pruning group: 1.
Flowering period: Early spring to midspring.
Cultivation: Tolerates heavy or light soils. Requires a warm position.
Recommended use: Grow as a container plant in a warm conservatory or heated greenhouse. Zones 8–9.

Clematis 'Mayleen'. Photo by C. Chesshire.

Clematis meyeniana. Photo by S. Kuriyama.

Clematis 'Midnight'

Origin: Raised by Keith and Carol Fair of Valley Clematis Nursery.

Parentage and year: Unknown. 1980s.

Habit: Hardy, moderately vigorous, deciduous climber.

Height: 2.4–3 m (8–10 ft.).

Description: The single, deep blue flowers, 15 cm (6 in.) across, are composed of eight overlapping, rounded, yet pointed tepals, each with a lighter coloured stripe running from the base to the tip. The anthers are red. The reverse of the tepals boasts an interesting greenish bar on immature flowers that turns creamy on maturity. The leaves are large, simple to trifoliate.

Pruning group: Optional, 2, or 3. For late flowers, choose group 3.

Flowering period: Early summer to late summer.

Cultivation: Tolerates most garden soils and any aspect.

Recommended use: Suitable for a medium-sized obelisk or trellis. May be grown with other wall-trained plants. If pruning group 3 is used, grow naturally through shrubs or over conifers. Zones 4–9.

Clematis 'Mikelite'

Origin: Raised by Uno Kivistik of Harjumaa, Estonia. Mikelite is a Lithuanian girl's name.

Parentage and year: *C.* 'Madame Julia Correvon' × *C.* 'Valge Daam'. 1987.

Habit: Hardy, moderately vigorous, compact, deciduous climber.

Height: 1.8 2.4 m (6–8 ft.).

Description: The single, rich reddish purple flowers, 11–14 cm (4.5–5.5 in.) across, are composed of four to six broad yet pointed, non-overlapping tepals, each with a slight rosy red bar along the centre. The bar is widest at the base and tapers towards the tip. The filaments and anthers are golden yellow.

Pruning group: 3.

Flowering period: Midsummer to late summer.

Cultivation: Tolerates most garden soils enriched with humus. Suitable for any aspect.

Recommended use: Suitable for container-culture, or for a medium-sized obelisk or trellis. Grow to cover bare lower stems of other wall-trained shrubs. May be grown with another clematis having similar pruning requirements and vigour. Zones 3–9.

Clematis microphylla. Photo by E. Leeds.

Clematis 'Midnight'. Photo by J. Lindmark.

Clematis 'Mikelite'. Photo by J. Lindmark.

Clematis 'Miniseelik'

Origin: Raised by Uno Kivistik of Harjumaa, Estonia. The name means "miniskirt."

Parentage and year: *C.* 'Jubileijnyj-70' × pollen mixture. 1982.

Habit: Hardy, compact, deciduous climber.

Height: 1.5–1.8 m (5–6 ft.).

Description: The single, rather small, deep reddish purple flowers, 6–7 cm (2.25–2.75 in.) across, are composed of tepals, each with a central white stripe. Mature flowers fade to purplish red, and the white stripe takes on a pronounced red veining.

Pruning group: 3.

Flowering period: Midsummer to late summer.

Cultivation: Tolerates most garden soils and any aspect.

Recommended use: Ideal for container-culture or for growing over a low wall. May also be trained through low shrubs or prostrate conifers. Zones 4–9.

Clematis 'Minister'

Origin: Raised by Uno Kivistik of Harjumaa, Estonia.

Parentage and year: *C.* 'Hagley Hybrid' × *C.* 'Bal Tzvetov'. 1982.

Habit: Hardy, compact, deciduous climber.

Height: 1.5–1.8 m (5–6 ft.).

Description: The single, lavender blue flowers, with a shading of purple and measuring 18–20 cm (7–8 in.) across, are composed of four to six tepals. Cream filaments and reddish purple anthers make up the contrasting stamens.

Pruning group: 2.

Flowering period: Late spring to early summer and late summer.

Cultivation: Tolerates most garden soils and any aspect.

Recommended use: Ideal for container-culture or for growing over small shrubs and prostrate conifers. Suitable for a small obelisk. Zones 4–9.

Clematis 'Miniseelik'. Photo by J. Lindmark.

Clematis 'Minister'. Photo courtesy Thorncroft Clematis Nursery.

Clematis 'Minuet'
VITICELLA GROUP

Synonym: *C. viticella* 'Minuet'

Origin: Believed to have been raised by Francisque Morel of Lyon, France, and given to William Robinson of Gravetye Manor. Named by Robinson's head gardener, Ernest Markham, and brought into commerce by George Jackman and Son, England. Awarded RHS Award of Garden Merit.

Parentage and year: Unknown. ca. 1900.

Habit: Hardy, moderately vigorous, compact, deciduous climber.

Height: 2.5–3 m (8–10 ft.).

Description: Handsome, single, semi-nodding flowers, 6 cm (2.25 in.) across, are made of four pale white, blunt-tipped tepals carrying pale purplish red, deeply veined margins. Stamens are greenish yellow.

Pruning group: 3.

Flowering period: Midsummer to midautumn.

Cultivation: Tolerates most garden soils and any aspect.

Recommended use: Ideal for growing through dark leaves of medium-sized trees or conifers. May also be grown over heathers and prostrate conifers or up a trellis or obelisk. Zones 3–9.

Clematis 'Miriam Markham'

Origin: Raised by Ernest Markham, head gardener at Gravetye Manor. Following his death in December 1937, the plant was named after Markham's wife and introduced by George Jackman and Son, England.

Parentage and year: Unknown. ca. 1930s.

Habit: Hardy, moderately vigorous, compact, deciduous climber.

Height: 1.8–2.4 m (6–8 ft.).

Description: The pale lilac, double flowers, 15–20 cm (6–8 in.) wide, are formed of one or sometimes two basal rows of overlapping, tapering, pointed tepals.

Clematis 'Minuet'. Photo by J. Lindmark.

Four or five additional, loose layers of smaller, rosy lilac tepals with silky texture complete the flower. Pale green filaments and rosy beige anthers collectively form the central boss of stamens.

Pruning group: 2.

Flowering period: Late spring to early summer and late summer to early autumn.

Cultivation: Tolerates most garden soils. Best grown in full or partial sun. Requires a sheltered position to prevent wind damage to the flowers.

Recommended use: Grow on a small to medium-sized trellis or obelisk. May be planted in containers and trained on a support. Zones 4–9.

Clematis 'Miss Bateman'

Origin: Raised by Charles Noble of Sunningdale, England. Named after Catharine Bateman, daughter of the orchid specialist James Bateman (1837–1874). Awarded RHS First Class Certificate (1869).

Parentage and year: *C.* 'Fortunei' × *C.* 'Standishii'. Mid-1860s.

Habit: Hardy, moderately vigorous, compact, deciduous climber.

Height: 1.8–2.4 m (6–8 ft.).

Description: The freely produced, single, rounded, satin-white flowers, 14–15 cm (5.5–6 in.) across, are made of six to eight wide, translucent tepals, which overlap, taper, and terminate at blunt tips. A central green stripe distinctly displayed on the reverse of each tepal is characteristic of early flowers and those grown in the shade. Conspicuous, contrasting stamens are made of white filaments and dark red anthers.

Pruning group: 2.

Flowering period: Late spring to early summer.

Cultivation: Tolerates most garden soils and any aspect.

Recommended use: Ideal for container-culture or for growing with other wall-trained or free-standing shrubs and roses not pruned annually. Suitable for a small obelisk or trellis. Zones 4–9.

Clematis 'Miss Crawshay'

Origin: Raised by George Jackman and Son, England.

Parentage and year: *C. patens* × *C. lanuginosa*. Before 1873.

Habit: Hardy, moderately vigorous, compact, deciduous climber.

Height: 1.8–2.4 m (6–8 ft.).

Description: The early, semi-double flowers, produced on the previous season's wood and measuring

Clematis 'Miriam Markham'. Photo by C. Chesshire.

Clematis 'Miss Bateman'. Photo by J. Lindmark.

12.5–18 cm (5–7 in.) across, are composed of a basal row of six to eight overlapping, broad yet pointed, mauvish pink tepals, each with slightly deeper linear markings along the centre. There are further layers of shorter, narrower, similar coloured tepals. The stamens are made of white filaments and pale brown anthers. Single flowers composed of eight tepals, with round tips and narrowing at the base, are produced on the current season's new wood.

Pruning group: 2.

Flowering period: Late spring to early summer (semi-double) and late summer (single).

Cultivation: Tolerates most garden soils. Best grown in full or partial sun. Requires a sheltered position to prevent wind damage to flowers.

Recommended use: Grow on a medium-sized obelisk or trellis, or with other wall-trained shrubs which do not require pruning. May be grown in containers. Zones 4–9.

Clematis montana
MONTANA GROUP

Synonym: *C. montana* 'Alba'

Origin: Himalaya, central and western China. Introduced by Lady Amherst in 1831.

Parentage and year: Species. 1818.

Habit: Vigorous, deciduous climber.

Height: To 8 m (26 ft.).

Description: Single, somewhat flat, white flowers in groups of one to five are borne from the leaf axils of the previous season's ripened wood. The four, rarely

five, tepals are 3–4 cm (1.25–1.5 in.) long. The leaves are dark to midgreen, divided into three leaflets, and have leaf margins notched with forward-pointing teeth.

Pruning group: 1. Any pruning to keep the plant in check should be carried out immediately after the main flowering period by removing some of the old, flowered stems.

Flowering period: Late spring to early summer, with occasional summer flowers.

Cultivation: Needs sharp drainage. Not fully hardy in very cold areas and therefore should not be planted in known frost pockets.

Recommended use: Grow through tall trees and conifers, along a boundary wall and fence, and over a pergola. Also grow as a ground cover. Zones 7–9.

Clematis montana var. *rubens*
MONTANA GROUP

Synonym: *C. montana* 'Rubens'

Origin: Found in China by Augustine Henry. Rediscovered by Ernest Wilson who sent seed to Veitch and Son of England, ca. 1900. Awarded RHS Award of Garden Merit and First Class Certificate (1905).

Parentage and year: Pink form of *C. montana*. 1886.

Habit: Vigorous, deciduous climber.

Height: 8–10 m (26–30 ft.).

Description: When first described this plant had large pinkish red flowers, but this form does not seem to be in cultivation any more. The plant which is available to gardeners under this name carries smaller,

Clematis 'Miss Crawshay'. Photo by C. Chesshire.

Clematis montana. Photo by J. Lindmark.

scented, midpink to pale pink flowers, 5 6 cm (2–2.25 in.) across. The young leaves are tinged bronze and change to dark green with age.

Pruning group: 1. Any pruning to keep the plant in check should be carried out immediately after the main flowering period by removing some of the old, flowered stems.

Flowering period: Late spring to early summer, with a few flowers in late summer.

Cultivation: Can be planted in sun or partial shade. Not fully hardy in very cold areas.

Recommended use: Ideal for growing through large trees and conifers, or along a boundary wall or fence. Not suitable for container-culture. Zones 7–9.

Clematis montana var. *wilsonii*
MONTANA GROUP

Origin: Western and southwestern China. First collected from Hubei and introduced into cultivation by Ernest Wilson.

Parentage and year: Selected form of *C. montana*. 1907.

Habit: Vigorous, deciduous climber.

Height: 6–9 m (20–29 ft.).

Description: The single flowers carried on long stalks are creamy white, 5–7.5 cm (2–3 in.) in diame-

Clematis montana var. *wilsonii*. Photo by R. Kirkman.

Clematis montana var. *rubens*. Photo by E. Leeds.

ter, with a large central boss of stamens, and boast a strong scent. The four tepals are twisted. Some modern clones flower earlier or later, either with or without scent. The leaves are slightly thicker than those of other members of the Montana Group, have three leaflets and leaf margins notched with forward-pointing teeth, and are midgreen.

Pruning group: 1. Any pruning to keep the plant in check should be carried out immediately after the main flowering period by removing some of the old, flowered stems.

Flowering period: Midsummer to late summer.

Cultivation: Needs sharp-draining soil enriched with humus. Suitable for sun or partial shade but produces the strongest scent in a sunny position.

Recommended use: Grow through large trees and conifers, along a wall or fence, or up and over a pergola. Zones 6–9.

Clematis 'Monte Cassino'

Origin: Raised by Brother Stefan Franczak of Warsaw, Poland. Named after the battle of Monte Cassino in the Second World War, when a Polish regiment overcame stout resistance by the Germans who were occupying the Benedictine monastery of that name. Introduced to the British Isles by Fisk's Clematis Nursery, Suffolk, England.

Parentage and year: Unknown. 1990.

Habit: Hardy, vigorous, strong-growing, deciduous climber.

Height: 2.4–3 m (8–10 ft.).

Description: The single, well-rounded, velvety reddish purple flowers, 15–20 cm (6–8 in.) across, are

composed of six wide, overlapping tepals with irregularly notched edges. The contrasting stamens are made of cream filaments and golden yellow anthers.

Pruning group: Optional, 2, or 3. A hard pruning (group 3) results in the loss of early flowers.

Flowering period: Late spring to early summer or midsummer to late summer.

Cultivation: Tolerates most garden soils. Best grown in fairly high light but not in strong sunlight.

Recommended use: Grow through medium-sized shrubs or small trees. Shows up well against a light background. Suitable for a medium-sized obelisk, arch, or pergola. May be grown in a very large container but not recommended for long-term container-culture. Zones 4–9.

Clematis 'Moonbeam'
EVERGREEN GROUP

Origin: Raised by Graham Hutchins of County Park Nursery, Essex, England.

Parentage and year: *C.* 'Fairy' × *C. foetida*. 1990.

Habit: Half-hardy to hardy, compact, evergreen climber or scrambler.

Height: 2 m (6.5 ft.).

Description: Male selection. Single flowers are borne in compound panicles of 5 to 15, each flower about 2 cm (0.75 in.) across, drooping at first, but soon upward facing, and slightly hairy underneath. The six tepals are 10–12 mm (ca. 0.5 in.) long, bluntly pointed, and greenish yellow in colour, becoming creamy white

Clematis 'Monte Cassino'. Photo by C. Chesshire.

Clematis 'Moonbeam'. Photo by J. Hudson.

when fully mature. The spreading stamens are green at first, becoming yellowish with cream anthers.

Pruning group: 1.

Flowering period: Late spring to early summer.

Cultivation: Requires a sunny, sheltered position.

Recommended use: Grow in a container in cold greenhouse or conservatory, or in an alpine bed. Zones 8–9.

Clematis 'Moonlight'

Origin: Given to Magnus Johnson of Södertälje, Sweden, by the head gardener of Copenhagen University in 1947. Named and introduced to the British Isles by Fisk's Clematis Nursery, Suffolk, England.

Parentage and year: Believed to be a seedling of either *C.* 'Lawsoniana' or *C.* 'Henryi'. Before 1947.

Habit: Hardy, weak-growing, deciduous climber.

Height: 2.4–3 m (8–10 ft.).

Description: The single, pale cream-yellow flowers, 15–20 cm (6–8 in.) in diameter, are composed of six to eight overlapping tepals which tend to twist on maturity. Yellow filaments and anthers which constitute the large stamens harmonize with the flower colour. Occasionally a dash of green is noticeable in the tepal colouring.

Pruning group: 2.

Flowering period: Late spring and early summer and late summer.

Cultivation: Tolerates most garden soils. Requires a sheltered position to prevent wind damage to the flowers. Best grown in partial shade to prevent premature fading of flower colour.

Recommended use: Shows up well against a dark background. Grow on a trellis, pergola, or arch. May be carefully trained through moderately vigorous shrubs which do not require annual pruning. Zones 4–9.

Clematis 'Mrs. Bush'

Origin: Unknown.

Parentage and year: Unknown. Before 1935.

Habit: Hardy, moderately vigorous, deciduous climber.

Height: 2.4–3 m (8–10 ft.).

Description: The single, lavender-blue flowers, 15–20 or 25 cm (6–8 or 10 in.) across, are composed of six, sometimes seven, tepals. The stamens are made of white filaments and beige anthers.

Pruning group: 2.

Flowering period: Late spring to early summer and late summer.

Cultivation: Tolerates most garden soils and any aspect. Requires a sheltered position to prevent wind damage to the large flowers.

Recommended use: Grow on an arbour, pergola, or trellis or through large shrubs and medium-sized trees. Zones 4–9.

Clematis 'Mrs. Cholmondeley'

Origin: Raised by Charles Noble of Sunningdale, England. Awarded RHS Award of Garden Merit.

Parentage and year: *C.* 'Fortunei' × *C.* 'Jackmanii'. Introduced in 1873.

Habit: Hardy, vigorous, deciduous climber.

Height: 3–3.6 m (10–12 ft.).

Description: The single, quite large, gappy, light

Clematis 'Moonlight'. Photo by Y. Aihara.

Clematis 'Mrs. Bush'. Photo by Y. Aihara.

Clematis 'Mrs. Cholmondeley' Photo by R. Surman.

blue-mauve flowers, 15–20 cm (6–8 in.) across, are composed of six to eight wide tepals which do not overlap but taper towards the base. The tepals are deeply veined along the midribs, which are also slightly paler in colour. White filaments tinged with blue carrying pale chocolate-coloured anthers constitute the stamens.

Pruning group: Optional, 2, or 3. A hard pruning (group 3) results in the loss of early flowers.

Flowering period: Late spring to late summer.

Cultivation: Tolerates most garden soils and any aspect. Requires a sheltered position to prevent wind damage to the flowers.

Recommended use: Grow on a large trellis, obelisk, pergola, or arch. Zones 4–9.

Clematis 'Mrs. George Jackman'

Origin: Raised by George Jackman and Son, England. Awarded RHS Award of Garden Merit.

Parentage and year: *C.* 'Lanuginosa Candida' × *C.* 'Fortunei'. Introduced in 1873.

Habit: Hardy, fairly vigorous, deciduous climber.

Height: 1.8–2.4 m (6–8 ft.).

Description: The creamy white, semi-double flowers, 15–18 cm (6–7 in.) across, are produced on the previous season's old wood. The six to eight overlapping basal tepals are broad yet pointed, with a satin sheen on the textured surface. Further layers of shorter tepals surmount those at the base. Single flowers with six to eight tepals are borne on the current season's new wood. The stamens are conspicuous with creamy white filaments and light pinky brown anthers.

Pruning group: 2.

Flowering period: Late spring to early summer (semi-double) and late summer to early autumn (single).

Cultivation: Tolerates most garden soils and any aspect.

Recommended use: Grow on a small to medium-sized obelisk or trellis. Suitable for container-culture. Zones 4–9.

Clematis 'Mrs. Hope'

Origin: Raised by George Jackman and Son, England.

Parentage and year: *C.* 'Standishii' × *C. lanuginosa*. Before 1875.

Habit: Hardy, vigorous, deciduous climber.

Height: 3–3.6 m (10–12 ft.).

Description: The single, large, satiny light blue flowers, 15–20 cm (6–8 in.) in diameter, are normally composed of six to eight overlapping, broad and blunt tepals, each with deeper blue grooves running from base to tip. White filaments and dark red anthers make up the stamens.

Clematis 'Mrs. George Jackman'. Photo by R. Surman.

Clematis 'Mrs. Hope'. Photo by C. Chesshire.

Pruning group: Optional, 2, or 3. A hard pruning (group 3) results in the loss of early flowers.

Flowering period: Late spring to late summer.

Cultivation: Tolerates most garden soils and any aspect.

Recommended use: Grow on a large obelisk, pergola, or trellis. Zones 4–9.

Clematis 'Mrs. James Mason'

Origin: Raised by Barry Fretwell of Peveril Clematis Nursery, England.

Parentage and year: *C.* 'Vyvyan Pennell' × *C.* 'Doctor Ruppel'. 1984.

Habit: Hardy, fairly vigorous, compact, deciduous climber.

Height: 1.8–2.4 m (6–8 ft.).

Description: The large, semi-double, violet-blue flowers, 15–18 cm (6–7 in.) across, borne on the previous year's old wood, are made of eight, somewhat overlapping, basal tepals, each with a velvety dark red bar along the centre. The tepals are broad yet pointed, boat-shaped, with undulating and almost frilly margins. Several shorter inner rows of lilac-blue tepals tower above the basal row of vibrantly coloured tepals, almost eclipsing them. A central mass of rich, creamy yellow stamens distinguishes the flowers. Single flowers are borne profusely on the current season's new wood.

Pruning group: 2.

Flowering period: Late spring to early summer (semi-double flowers) and early autumn (single flowers).

Cultivation: Tolerates most garden soils and any aspect. Requires a sheltered position to prevent wind damage to the flowers.

Recommended use: Grow on a small to medium-sized pergola or trellis. Ideal for container-culture or for covering the bare lower stems of other wall-trained plants. Zones 4–9.

Clematis 'Mrs. N. Thompson'

Origin: Raised by Walter Pennell of Pennell and Sons nursery from seed probably sown in 1954, and named after the wife of the nursery office manager in 1961.

Parentage and year: Unknown. Introduced in 1961.

Habit: Hardy, weak-growing, compact, deciduous climber.

Height: 1.8–2.4 m (6–8 ft.).

Description: The single, striking, rich purple-blue flowers, measuring 12.5–15 cm (5–6 in.) in diameter, have six to eight broad yet tapering tepals, each of which boasts a vivid scarlet central bar. The tepal edges are slightly scalloped, and the reverse has a greenish cream bar fading to pinkish purple at the margins. The stamens are made of pale pink filaments and dark red anthers.

Pruning group: 2.

Flowering period: Late spring to early summer and early autumn.

Cultivation: Tolerates most garden soils. Best grown in full sun or partial shade. Can be slow to establish itself.

Recommended use: Suitable for container-culture. Grow on a small to medium-sized obelisk or trellis. Zones 4–9.

Clematis 'Mrs. James Mason'. Photo by E. Leeds.

Clematis 'Mrs. N. Thompson'. Photo by C. Chesshire.

Clematis 'Mrs. P. B. Truax'

Origin: Believed to have been raised by George Jackman and Son, England.

Parentage and year: Unknown. Before 1939.

Habit: Hardy, moderately vigorous, compact, deciduous climber.

Height: 1.8–2.4 m (6–8 ft.).

Description: The medium-sized, single flowers, 12.5–15 cm (5–6 in.) across, boast six to eight rounded but pointed, periwinkle blue tepals, fading to a light blue as they age. The stamens are composed of white filaments and cream anthers. The seedheads are small and globular.

Pruning group: 2.

Flowering period: Late spring to early summer and early autumn.

Cultivation: Tolerates most garden soils. Best grown in sun or partial shade.

Recommended use: Grow in a container, as a cover for bare stems of moderately vigorous, wall-trained shrubs, or as a specimen plant on a medium-sized obelisk or trellis. Zones 4–9.

Clematis 'Mrs. P. T. James'

Origin: Raised by the Wayside Gardens Company of Mentor, Ohio. Plant Breeders' Rights.

Parentage and year: Unknown. 1965.

Habit: Hardy, not very vigorous, compact, deciduous climber.

Height: 1.8–2.4 m (6–8 ft.).

Description: The single, open flowers, 12–18 cm (4.75–7 in.) across, are composed of six to eight overlapping, broad yet pointed, violet blue tepals, with a silvery blue sheen along their centres and with prominent veining and texturing. The stamens comprise pinkish filaments and pinkish chocolate anthers surrounding contrasting yellow stigmas.

Pruning group: 2.

Flowering period: Early summer to late summer.

Cultivation: Tolerates most garden soils enriched with humus. Suitable for any aspect.

Recommended use: Grow on a small to medium-sized obelisk or trellis and as a companion for other wall-trained shrubs which do not require a heavy, annual pruning. Zones 4–9.

Clematis 'Mrs. Robert Brydon'
HERBACEOUS/HERACLEIFOLIA GROUP

Origin: Found growing in the garden of Elizabeth Prentiss of Cleveland, Ohio, and named after the wife of the gardener, Robert Brydon.

Parentage and year: *C. heracleifolia* var. *davidiana* × *C. virginiana*. ca. 1935.

Habit: Hardy, deciduous, non-clinging, herbaceous perennial.

Height: 1.8–2.4 m (6–8 ft.).

Description: The bluish white flowers, 3 cm (1.25 in.) wide, are composed of four or five narrow tepals which roll back on themselves, exposing the prominent white filaments and cream anthers. Coarse, large, dark green leaves are produced on vigorous woody stems.

Pruning group: 3.

Flowering period: Midsummer to early autumn.

Cultivation: Tolerates most garden soils but appreci-

Clematis 'Mrs. P. B. Truax'. Photo by C. Chesshire.

Clematis 'Mrs. P. T. James'. Photo by J. Lindmark.

ates moist yet free-draining conditions. If trained on an artificial support, the stems need tying-in.

Recommended use: Ideal to cover old tree stumps or as a ground cover. Zones 4–9.

Clematis 'Mrs. Spencer Castle'

Origin: Raised by George Jackman and Son, England.

Parentage and year: Unknown. Introduced in 1913.

Habit: Hardy, moderately vigorous, deciduous climber.

Height: 1.8–2.4 m (6–8 ft.).

Description: The pinky mauve, semi-double flowers, 10–15 cm (4–6 in.) in diameter, are produced on the previous season's old wood. The six base tepals slightly overlap at their base, are pointed, and each carries a deeper pink central bar. A secondary irregular row of shorter tepals surmounts those at the base of the flowers produced early in the season. Single blooms on the current year's new wood appear later in the season. White filaments and yellow anthers form the central stamens.

Pruning group: 2.

Flowering period: Late spring to early summer (semi-double) and late summer (single).

Cultivation: Tolerates most garden soils and any aspect. Requires a sheltered position to prevent wind damage to the flowers.

Recommended use: Grow on a small to medium-sized arch or trellis. May also be planted in containers. Zones 4–9.

Clematis 'Mrs. Robert Brydon' growing through a picket fence with buddleias. Photo by C. Chesshire.

Clematis 'Mrs. T. Lundell'
VITICELLA GROUP

Synonyms: *C.* 'Mrs. Tage Lundell', *C. viticella* 'Mrs. T. Lundell'

Origin: Found growing in Tage Lundell's garden in Helsingborg, Sweden, and named after his wife. Introduced by Cedergren and Company, Råå, Sweden.

Parentage and year: Unknown. 1985.

Habit: Hardy, moderately vigorous, deciduous climber.

Height: 2.5–3 m (8–10 ft.).

Description: The single, pale bluish violet flowers, 7.5–9 cm (3–3.5 in.) across, consist generally of four slightly recurving blunt tepals, and are semi-nodding at first, opening flat, and are cross-shaped with maturity. The anthers are creamy yellow. The leaves are midgreen with three to five leaflets.

Pruning group: 3.

Flowering period: Midsummer to early autumn.

Cultivation: Tolerates most garden soils and any aspect.

Recommended use: Ideal for growing over heathers or prostrate conifers. May be allowed to climb into small to medium-sized trees or open shrubs. Suitable on a low trellis or obelisk. Zones 3–9.

Clematis 'Multi Blue'

Origin: Raised in the nursery of J. Bouter and Zoon, Boskoop, Netherlands.

Parentage and year: Sport of *C.* 'The President'. 1983.

Habit: Hardy, fairly vigorous, deciduous climber.

Height: 1.8–2.4 m (6–8 ft.).

Clematis 'Mrs. T. Lundell'. Photo by J. Lindmark.

Clematis 'Multi Blue' boasts much deeper colour in an English climate. Photo by R. Surman.

Clematis 'Mrs. Spencer Castle'. Photo by C. Chesshire.

Description: The early, well-rounded, fully double flowers, 10–12.5 cm (4–5 in.) in diameter, are borne on the previous season's old wood. These are formed of an outer, base row of six to eight, somewhat broad, rich navy blue tepals, topped with many inner layers of shorter, narrower and more pointed, reddish purple-blue tepals with white tips conferring a spiky appearance on the central crown of the flower. Each tepal boasts a light green central bar on the reverse. The inner tepals remain after the outer row of tepals wither and fall away. Semi-double flowers, similar in shape and form to the early double flowers, are produced on the current season's new wood later in the season. There are no stamens.

Pruning group: 2.

Flowering period: Late spring to early summer (double) and late summer to early autumn (semi-double).

Cultivation: Tolerates most garden soils. Best grown in sun or semi-shade. Requires a sheltered position to prevent wind damage to the flowers.

Recommended use: Grow on a small obelisk or trellis. Ideal for container-culture. Zones 4–9.

Clematis 'Myōjō'

Origin: Raised by Seijūrō Arai of Japan and named after the planet Venus.

Parentage and year: Unknown. Early 1980s.

Habit: Hardy, moderately vigorous, deciduous climber.

Height: 1.8–2.4 m (6–8 ft.).

Description: The single flowers, 12.5–15 cm (5–6

in.) wide, carry six to eight broad, overlapping violet-purple tepals, and a prominent central boss of golden stamens.

Pruning group: 2.

Flowering period: Late spring to early summer and late summer.

Cultivation: Tolerates most garden soils and any aspect.

Recommended use: Ideal for container-culture. Grow on a small to medium-sized obelisk, trellis, or other such support. Zones 4–9.

Clematis napaulensis
EVERGREEN GROUP

Synonym: *C. forrestii*

Origin: Himalaya, southeastern Tibet, and southwestern China. Introduced into cultivation by George Forrest in 1912. Awarded RHS Award of Merit (1957).

Parentage and year: Species. 1818.

Habit: Vigorous, semi-evergreen climber.

Height: To 7.7 m (25 ft.).

Description: The unusual, small, solitary, creamy yellow to greenish white, nodding, bell-shaped flowers, 1.6–1.8 cm (0.5–0.75 in.) across, are borne in short-stemmed clusters of up to 10 in a pair of leaf nodes. Each flower, carried on a hairy stalk with a pair of fused, hairy, greenish, cupped, leaflike growths (bracts) midway along the stalk, is composed of four tepals, 1.5–2.5 cm (0.5–1 in.) long. The tepals roll back or recurve at the tips. The stamens consist of prominent purple filaments and anthers which protrude from the flower by almost the length of the tepals. Young shoots

Clematis 'Myōjō'. Photo by C. Chesshire.

Clematis napaulensis. Photo by E. Leeds.

are greyish, and the grooved stems become woody with age. Leaves are bright green and congested. During its period of dormancy in midsummer the plant may lose its leaves.

Pruning group: 1.

Flowering period: Winter to early spring.

Cultivation: Tolerates most garden soils with good drainage. Also tolerates light frost but is best in a frost-free position. Requires a warm, sheltered, south-facing wall or similar location in the garden.

Recommended use: Can look drab in summer, so choose the planting position carefully. Best grown in a conservatory or cool glasshouse. Zones 7–9.

Clematis 'Natacha'

Origin: Raised by Krister Cedergren of Råå, Sweden.

Parentage and year: Unknown. 1985.

Habit: Hardy, moderately vigorous, compact, deciduous climber.

Height: 1.8–2.4 m (6–8 ft.).

Description: The single, lavender-violet flowers, 10–14 cm (4–5.5 in.) across, are composed of six to eight broad, oval-shaped, overlapping tepals with gently undulating margins. As the flower matures the central bar running from the base to the tip in each tepal takes on a lighter shade. The stamens are made of creamy white filaments and brownish purple anthers.

Pruning group: 2.

Flowering period: Late spring to early summer and late summer.

Cultivation: Tolerates most garden soils enriched with humus.

Recommended use: Suitable for a medium-sized obelisk or trellis. Ideal for container-culture. Grows well with other wall-trained plants which do not require severe annual pruning. Zones 3–9.

Clematis 'Natascha'

Origin: Raised by Friedrich Manfred Westphal of Prisdorf, Germany.

Parentage and year: Open-pollinated seedling of *C.* 'Nelly Moser'. 1989.

Habit: Hardy, moderately vigorous, compact, deciduous climber.

Height: 1.8–2.4 m (6–8 ft.).

Description: The single flowers, 10–15 cm (4–6 in.) wide, are made of six to eight lilac-pink tapering tepals, each with deeper mauve grooves running from base to tip. The reverse of the tepals boasts a white central band and, with age, the pointed tepals recurve. Reddish mauve anthers are carried on pinkish red filaments. Very attractive flowers, which fade gradually, are borne on a neat and compact plant.

Pruning group: 2.

Flowering period: Late spring to early summer and late summer.

Cultivation: Tolerates most garden soils and any aspect.

Recommended use: Grow in a container or to cover the bare lower stems of other moderately vigorous, wall-trained shrubs. Zones 4–9.

Clematis 'Natacha'. Photo by R. Savill.

Clematis 'Natascha'. Photo by J. Lindmark.

Clematis 'Negritjanka'

Origin: Raised by M. Orlov, Central Republic Botanical Garden of the Ukrainian Academy of Sciences, Kiev, Russia. The name means "African girl."

Parentage and year: *C.* 'Gipsy Queen' × *C. viticella*. 1964.

Habit: Hardy, moderately vigorous, deciduous climber.

Height: 2.4–3 m (8–10 ft.).

Description: The plant carries a profusion of rich plum-purple, single flowers, 10–13 cm (4–5 in.) in diameter. The five or six tepals are well formed and rounded. Anthers are reddish purple and complement the vibrant tepal colour.

Pruning group: 3.

Flowering period: Midsummer to late summer.

Cultivation: Tolerates most garden soils and any aspect.

Recommended use: Shows up well against a light background. Grow through medium-sized shrubs and small trees, preferably with silver or golden leaves. Ideal for a trellis, obelisk, or pergola. Zones 4–9.

Clematis 'Negus'

Origin: Raised by Maria F. Sharonova of Moscow.

Parentage and year: Open-pollinated seedling of *C.* 'Luther Burbank'. 1972.

Habit: Hardy, moderately vigorous, compact, deciduous climber.

Height: 1.8 m (6 ft.).

Description: The single, deep violet blue flowers, 10–15 cm (4–6 in.) across, are composed of six to eight tepals, which are broadest at their midpoint, and tapering at both ends. The tepals boast slightly deeper coloured grooves and wavy margins. Greenish white filaments and reddish brown anthers make up the central boss of stamens.

Pruning group: 3.

Flowering period: Midsummer to late summer.

Cultivation: Tolerates most garden soils and any aspect.

Recommended use: Ideal for container-culture. Grow through prostrate conifers or small to medium-sized, open, moderately vigorous shrubs. Suitable for a small obelisk or trellis. Zones 4–9.

Clematis 'Nelly Moser'

Origin: Raised by Moser of Versailles, France. Awarded RHS Award of Garden Merit.

Parentage and year: *C.* 'Belisaire' × *C.* 'Marcel Moser'. 1897

Habit: Hardy, vigorous, deciduous climber. Floriferous once established.

Height: 2.4–3 m (8–10 ft.).

Description: An excellent tried and tested, early and late-flowering cultivar. The single flowers, 15–20 cm (6–8 in.) wide, are composed of six to eight pointed, overlapping pale mauvish pink tepals, each with a distinct deeper pink central bar. White filaments carrying dark red anthers bring vibrancy to the well-held, fully open, flattish flowers. Large, globular seedheads are an added bonus.

Pruning group: 2.

Clematis 'Negritjanka'. Photo by J. Lindmark.

Clematis 'Negus'. Photo by C. Chesshire.

Flowering period: Late spring to early summer and early autumn.

Cultivation: Tolerates most garden soils. Best grown in partial or full shade, preferably a north-facing aspect, as flower colour fades badly in full sun.

Recommended use: Grows well with other wall-trained shrubs which do not require annual pruning, especially early flowering climbing roses. Ideal for a medium-sized obelisk, arch, or trellis. Zones 4–9.

Clematis 'New Dawn'
MONTANA GROUP

Synonym: *C. montana* 'New Dawn'
Origin: Unknown.
Parentage and year: Unknown.
Habit: Vigorous, deciduous climber.
Height: To 9 m (29 ft.).
Description: A very floriferous cultivar. The single, saucer-shaped, bright pink flowers are composed of four broad, rounded tepals surrounding yellow stamens.

Pruning group: 1. Any pruning to keep the plant in check should be carried out immediately after the

main flowering period by removing some of the old, flowered stems.

Flowering period: Midspring to late spring.

Cultivation: Tolerates most well-drained garden soils and any aspect. Hardy in temperate gardens.

Recommended use: Ideal for a large pergola, wall, or boundary fence. Allow it to roam into large trees or conifers. Zones 7–9.

Clematis 'New Love'
HERBACEOUS/HERACLEIFOLIA GROUP

Synonym: *C. heracleifolia* 'New Love'
Origin: Found in the clematis collection of Jan Fopma, Boskoop, Netherlands.
Parentage and year: Chance seedling. ca. 1994.
Habit: Hardy, non-clinging, woody-based, deciduous subshrub.

Clematis 'New Dawn'. Photo by C. Chesshire.

Clematis 'New Love'. Photo by C. Chesshire.

Clematis 'Nelly Moser'. Photo by M. Toomey.

Height: 0.6–0.8 m (2–2.75 ft.).

Description: The single, tubular, hyacinth-like, fragrant, pale violet-blue flowers, each 2–2.5 cm (0.75–1 in.) long, are made of four tepals with spreading and recurving tips. The outside of the flower is a darker shade of violet blue. White filaments and yellow anthers make up the stamens. The plant has a compact, round habit, and the flowers are held above the foliage.

Pruning group: 3.

Flowering period: Midsummer to early autumn.

Cultivation: Prefers well-drained but moist garden soils. Can be planted in sun or shade.

Recommended use: Plant at the front of mixed or herbaceous borders. Suitable for container-culture. Zones 5–9.

Clematis 'Nikolaj Rubtzov'

Synonym: *C.* 'Nikolai Rubtzov'

Origin: Raised by A. N. Volosenko-Valenis and M. A. Beskaravainaja of the State Nikitsky Botanic Gardens, Ukraine.

Parentage and year: *C.* 'Jackmanii' (F$_1$ hybrid) × *C.* 'Nelly Moser'. 1967.

Habit: Hardy, moderately vigorous, deciduous climber.

Height: 2.4–3 m (8–10 ft.).

Description: The single, reddish lilac flowers, borne profusely or sometimes moderately, measure 10–14 cm (4–5.5 in.) across. The four to six tepals are distinguished by paler lilac central bars. The anthers are yellow or light yellow. Compound leaves are somewhat thick, and carry three to five leaflets.

Pruning group: 3.

Flowering period: Midsummer to late summer.

Cultivation: Tolerates most garden soils and any aspect.

Recommended use: Suitable for a medium-sized obelisk or trellis. Grow with small to medium-sized shrubs and trees. Zones 4–9.

Clematis 'Niobe'

Origin: Raised by Vladyslaw Noll of Warsaw, Poland. Introduced to the British Isles in 1975 by Jim Fisk of Fisk's Clematis Nursery, Suffolk, England. Awarded RHS Award of Garden Merit.

Parentage and year: Unknown. 1970.

Habit: Hardy, not-so-vigorous, deciduous climber.

Height: 1.8–2.4 m (6–8 ft.).

Description: A universally popular cultivar. The buds unfurl gradually to expose the juvenile flowers, composed of six to eight velvety, ruby reddish black tepals. As the flowers open wide with age, they measure 12.5–15 cm (5–6 in.) in diameter, and the colour gradually fades to deep wine red. The tepals are broad at the base and taper towards the tips. The central boss of stamens, consisting of white filaments with shadings of reddish purple, and butter-yellow anthers, contrasts well with the tepal colour.

Pruning group: 2 or 3. A hard pruning (group 3) results in the loss of early flowers.

Flowering period: Late spring to early autumn.

Clematis 'Nikolaj Rubtzov'. Photo by C. Chesshire.

Clematis 'Niobe' flower is rich-coloured when young. Photo by M. Toomey.

Cultivation: Tolerates most garden soils. Flower colour is best in sunlight, although it tends to fade quickly in full sun.

Recommended use: Suitable as a specimen plant in the garden or in a container. Grow with medium-sized shrubs, prostrate conifers, and moderately vigorous roses. Zones 4–9.

Clematis 'Nunn's Gift'
EVERGREEN GROUP

Origin: Raised by Roy Nunn of Cambridge, England.

Parentage and year: Hybrid of two seedlings of *C. petriei* × *C. marmoraria*. 1995.

Habit: Half-hardy, compact, evergreen scrambler.

Height: To 1.2 m (4 ft.).

Description: An extremely floriferous cultivar. The single, pale cream male flowers, 4–6.5 cm (1.5–2.5 in.) across, are composed of six to eight narrow, pointed tepals, which overlap only at the base and are textured with faint green veining. The stamens are made of greenish filaments and pale cream anthers.

Pruning group: 1.

Clematis 'Niobe' flower colour fades with age.
Photo by R. Surman.

Flowering period: Early spring to midspring.

Cultivation: Requires free-draining soil and a warm, semi-shaded aspect. Needs protection from winter rain and frost.

Recommended use: Ideal for container-culture in a conservatory or cold greenhouse. Zones 7–9.

Clematis obvallata

Synonym: *C. japonica* var. *obvallata*

Origin: Shikoku Island, Japan.

Parentage and year: Species. 1938.

Habit: Half-hardy to hardy, not-so-vigorous, compact, deciduous climber.

Height: 1.8–2.4 m (6–8 ft.).

Description: The small, single, rosy red, shiny, slightly hairy, pendulous, bell-shaped flowers, borne in axillary clusters, are composed of four thick tepals which are longer than wide and which open at the tips

Clematis 'Nunn's Gift'. Photo by R. Nunn.

Clematis obvallata. Photo by S. Kuriyama.

and gently recurve, exposing the whitish lips. A distinguishing feature is the pair of wing-shaped, leaflike outgrowths (bracts) at the base of the flower; these are pinkish cream streaked with pink at the margins. The leaves are oval in shape and the margins are punctuated with forward-pointing teeth.

Pruning group: 2.

Flowering period: Late spring to early summer.

Cultivation: Tolerates most well-drained garden soils. Best grown in sun or partial shade.

Recommended use: Grow on a warm wall in maritime gardens or under glass in very cold gardens. Zones 5–9.

Clematis occidentalis
ATRAGENE GROUP

Origin: Canada and United States.

Parentage and year: Species. 1824.

Habit: Hardy, not-so-vigorous, compact, deciduous climber or scrambler.

Height: To 2 m (6.5 ft.).

Description: The blue to violet or rose-violet, solitary, nodding flowers have four tepals, each 4 cm (1.5 in.) long, spreading, and prominently veined. The veins and margins are downy, and young stems are furrowed or grooved. Leaves are divided into three leaflets and are somewhat downy beneath when young.

Pruning group: 1.

Flowering period: Late spring to early summer.

Cultivation: Needs sharp drainage. Suitable for any aspect.

Recommended use: Good for a small garden, container-culture, tumbling over a low wall, in an alpine bed, or growing through small, open shrubs. Zones 3–9.

Clematis occidentalis var. *dissecta*
ATRAGENE GROUP

Origin: Wenatchee Mountains of Washington, United States.

Parentage and year: A variant of *C. occidentalis*. 1964.

Habit: Hardy, deciduous climbing or sprawling shrub.

Height: To 1 m (3.25 ft.).

Description: The nodding, bell-shaped, single, reddish violet (occasionally bluish violet) flowers are composed of four pointed tepals, each 4 cm (1.5 in.) long. The leaves are prominently toothed, and the central one is often deeply three lobed.

Pruning group: 1.

Flowering period: Late spring to early summer.

Cultivation: In the wild grows in thin, fast-draining rocky soils. Suitable for any aspect.

Recommended use: Grow in an alpine scree garden or container. Zones 3–9.

Clematis occidentalis var. *grosseserrata*
ATRAGENE GROUP

Origin: Rocky Mountains from Colorado to northern British Columbia.

Parentage and year: A variant of *C. occidentalis*. 1829.

Habit: Hardy, deciduous, climbing or sprawling shrub.

Height: 1 m (3.25 ft.).

Description: The nodding, bell-shaped, single, violet-blue (rarely white) flowers are composed of four pointed tepals, each 6 cm (2.5 in.) long, sometimes more or less fluted. The leaflets are normally entire, rarely two or three lobed.

Pruning group: 1.

Flowering period: Late spring.

Cultivation: In the wild grows on thin, fast-draining rocky soils. Suitable for any aspect.

Recommended use: Grow in an alpine scree garden or container. Zones 3–9.

Clematis ochotensis
ATRAGENE GROUP

Origin: China, Korea, and Japan.

Parentage and year: Species. 1812.

Clematis occidentalis var. *dissecta*. Photo by R. Ratko.

Clematis occidentalis var. *grosseserrata*. Photo by J. Lindmark.

Habit: Hardy, moderately vigorous, deciduous climber or scrambler.

Height: To 3 m (10 ft.).

Description: The single, nodding, bell-shaped, violet blue flowers are composed of four spear-shaped tepals, each 4–5.5 cm (1.5–2.25 in.) long, with ridged veining towards the pointed tip. The stamens are made of thick, hairy, pale white filaments and yellow anthers. Leaves are midgreen.

Pruning group: 1.

Flowering period: Midspring to late spring.

Cultivation: Needs sharp drainage. Suitable for any aspect. Tolerates exposed conditions.

Recommended use: Suitable for a large or small garden, or in a container. Grow through medium-sized trees or large shrubs. Zones 3–9.

Clematis ochroleuca
HERBACEOUS/INTEGRIFOLIA GROUP

Origin: United States.

Parentage and year: Species. 1767.

Habit: Hardy, deciduous, non-clinging, clump-forming, herbaceous perennial.

Height: 46–61 cm (18–24 in.).

Description: The long, bell-shaped, greenish yellow flowers, 2.5–4 cm (1–1.5 in.) wide, are composed of four tepals, which recurve at the tips, forming a complete roll. The outside of the tepals and the stems are hairy. There is a trace of purple where the stem joins the flower head, and mature flowers fade to a creamy yellow. Stamens are yellow.

Pruning group: 3.

Flowering period: Late spring to early summer.

Cultivation: Tolerates most garden soils and any aspect. Prefers sharp drainage.

Recommended use: Plant at the front of a herbaceous border or use in a scree garden. Zones 4–9.

Clematis 'Odorata'
ATRAGENE GROUP

Synonym: *C. alpina* 'Odorata'

Origin: Raised by Magnus Johnson of Södertälje, Sweden.

Parentage and year: Selected form of *C. alpina*. 1980.

Habit: Hardy, neat-growing and not-so-vigorous, deciduous climber.

Height: 2.4–3 m (8–10 ft.).

Description: The small, single, nodding, midblue to light blue flowers are composed of four somewhat elongated and pointed tepals, each 2.5–5 cm (1–2 in.) long, and a central, tight tuft of creamy white staminodes. There is a very faint scent. Plants come into flower very early in the spring and remain in flower for a long period. Leaves are composed of three leaflets, and the leaf margins are serrated, resembling the teeth of a saw.

Pruning group: 1. Any pruning to keep the plant tidy should be carried out immediately after the main flowering period.

Flowering period: Early spring to midspring.

Cultivation: Tolerates most well-drained garden soils. Produces the strongest scent in a sunny position.

Clematis ochotensis. Photo by J. Lindmark.

Clematis ochroleuca. Photo by Y. Aihara.

Recommended use: Associate with other wall-trained plants. Grow on a free-standing, medium-sized obelisk or trellis. Allow to tumble over a low wall or fence. Suitable for container-culture. Zones 3–9.

Clematis 'Odorata'
MONTANA GROUP

Synonyms: *C. montana* 'Odorata', *C. montana* 'Odorata Trelleborg'

Origin: Found in a yard in Trelleborg, Sweden, by Göran Johnson. Propagated from cuttings and distributed by Magnus Johnson of Södertälje, Sweden.

Parentage and year: Selected form of *C. montana*. 1970.

Habit: Vigorous, deciduous climber.

Height: 7–10 m (23–30 ft.).

Description: The single, sweetly scented, saucer-shaped, pale pink flowers, 5–8 cm (2–3.25 in.) across, are composed of four broad, rounded, and dark-veined tepals.

Pruning group: 1. Any pruning to keep the plant in check should be carried out immediately after the main flowering period by removing some of the old, flowered stems.

Flowering period: Midspring to late spring.

Cultivation: Tolerates most well-drained garden soils. Hardy in temperate gardens. Produces the strongest scent in full or partial sun.

Recommended use: Grow over a large pergola or let it roam into a large tree. Ideal for a boundary fence. Zones 7–9.

Clematis 'Olgae'
HERBACEOUS/INTEGRIFOLIA GROUP

Origin: Russia.

Parentage and year: *C. integrifolia* × *C. viticella*. 1950s.

Habit: Hardy, deciduous, non-clinging, scraggy, herbaceous perennial or subshrub.

Height: 1 m (3.25 ft.).

Description: The bell-shaped, single flowers are composed of four midblue, pointed tepals, each 4–4.5 cm (1.5–1.75 in.) long, opening wide with the tips curling backwards and twisting. The stamens are made of thick, greenish yellow filaments and yellow anthers.

Clematis 'Odorata' (Atragene Group). Photo by E. Leeds.

Clematis 'Odorata' (Montana Group). Photo by C. Chesshire.

The outside of each tepal has ridges running from the base to the tip. Flowers are borne in clusters of 10–12 to a stem and are slightly scented.

Pruning group: 3.

Flowering period: Early summer to late summer.

Cultivation: Tolerates most garden soils with good drainage and some moisture. Needs suitable supports to prevent the slender stems from flopping around too much.

Recommended use: Grow in the front half of a herbaceous or mixed border. Zones 4–9.

Clematis 'Olimpiada-80'

Origin: Raised by M. A. Beskaravainaja of the State Nikitsky Botanic Gardens, Ukraine, and named to celebrate the Moscow Olympics.

Clematis 'Olgae'. Photo by C. Chesshire.

Clematis 'Olimpiada-80'. Photo by M. A. Beskaravainaja.

Parentage and year: *C.* 'Madame van Houtte' × *C.* 'Madame Édouard André'. 1973.

Habit: Hardy, moderately vigorous, deciduous climber.

Height: 2.4–3 m (8–10 ft.).

Description: The single, bright crimson-red flowers, 16–18 cm (6.25–7 in.) across, are composed of six tepals. The anthers are yellow. The leaves may be simple or compound, consisting of three to five leaflets. This attractive plant flowers profusely early in the season on old wood and again from midsummer.

Pruning group: 2.

Flowering period: Late spring and midsummer to late summer.

Cultivation: Tolerates most garden soils and any aspect.

Recommended use: Suitable for a medium-sized trellis, obelisk, arbour, or pergola. Grow with other wall-trained, moderately vigorous shrubs. Zones 4–9.

Clematis orientalis
TANGUTICA GROUP

Origin: Western China and westwards through Russia, Afghanistan, Iran, Turkey, and eastern Europe.

Parentage and year: Species. 1753.

Habit: Moderately vigorous deciduous climber or scrambler.

Height: To 3–3.4 m (10–12 ft.).

Description: The single, nodding flowers are composed of four small greenish yellow tepals, which are sometimes tinged with purple-brown mottling on the outside. The tepals recurve at the tips when the flower

Clematis orientalis. Photo by C. Chesshire.

is fully open, which also exposes the central boss of pinky mauve anthers and dark reddish brown filaments. Because of its wide distribution, this species can be variable in colour from yellow to greenish yellow. Prominent seedheads are produced after flowering. Stems have fine longitudinal lines or ridges. Leaves are grey-green to bluish green and compound, with five to seven leaflets arranged on either side of the main leaf stalk.

Pruning group: 3.

Flowering period: Midsummer to early autumn.

Cultivation: Needs sharp drainage. Suitable for sun or partial shade.

Recommended use: Grow through medium-sized trees, conifers, and large, open shrubs. Suitable for a pergola or trellis. Zones 6–9.

Clematis 'Paddington'

Origin: Raised by Frank Watkinson of Doncaster, England. Named after the nearby factory making toy bears of that name.

Parentage and year: Unknown. Introduced in 1991.

Habit: Hardy, moderately vigorous, compact, deciduous climber.

Height: 1.8–2.4 m (6–8 ft.).

Description: The single, reddish purple flowers, 10–15 cm (4–6 in.) across, are composed of six tepals with central bars which are a deeper shade. As the flower matures, the wavy margins become more plum red. The stamens are made of pale pink filaments and deep red anthers.

Pruning group: 3.

Flowering period: Early summer to late summer.

Cultivation: Tolerates most garden soils and any aspect.

Recommended use: Suitable for container-culture. Grow through prostrate conifers and moderately vigorous, small to medium-sized shrubs or on a medium-sized obelisk or trellis. Zones 4–9.

Clematis 'Pafar'

Trade name: PATRICIA ANN FRETWELL

Origin: Raised by Barry Fretwell of Peveril Clematis Nursery, England. Plant Breeders' Rights.

Parentage and year: Unknown. Before 1994.

Habit: Hardy, not-so-vigorous, weak-growing, deciduous climber.

Clematis 'Paddington'. Photo courtesy Thorncroft Clematis Nursery.

Clematis 'Pafar' (PATRICIA ANN FRETWELL™).
Photo by C. Chesshire.

Height: 1.8–2.4 m (6–8 ft.).

Description: The early double flowers are produced on the previous season's old wood. The eight rich-red base tepals are broad, mostly with rounded tips, and as they mature, their colouring changes to deep pink. The subsequent layers of inner tepals are a soft shell-pink, each with a deeper colour along the centre. Cream filaments and yellow anthers make up the stamens. The second flush of flowers is produced on the current season's new wood and consists of single flowers with pale pink tepals, each with a deeper colour along the centre.

Pruning group: 2.

Flowering period: Late spring to early summer (double) and late summer (single).

Cultivation: Tolerates most garden soils. Prefers full or partial sun. Requires a sheltered position to prevent wind damage.

Recommended use: Suitable for a small to medium-sized obelisk or trellis. Grow with small to medium-sized shrubs which have soft-coloured foliage and which do not require pruning. Ideal for container-culture. Zones 4–9.

Clematis 'Pagoda'
VITICELLA GROUP

Synonyms: *C. viticella* 'Pagoda', *C. texensis* 'Pagoda'

Origin: Raised by John Treasure, Treasures of Tenbury, England.

Clematis 'Pagoda'. Photo by J. Lindmark.

Parentage and year: Hybrid of *C. viticella* × *C.* 'Etoile Rose'. ca. 1980.

Habit: Hardy, not-too-vigorous, neat-growing and compact, deciduous climber.

Height: 1.8–2.5 m (6–8 ft.).

Description: The single, gently nodding, bell-shaped flowers are generally made of four pale white tepals, each 4–5 cm (1.5–2 in.) long, with mauvish pink margins, and distinct veining. A prominent purple-pink central bar is on the reverse of each tepal. Tepals recurve generously, curl and twist at the tips with age. The yellow stamens form a tight bundle. Leaves are midgreen with seven leaflets.

Pruning group: 3.

Flowering period: Midsummer to early autumn.

Cultivation: Tolerates most garden soils and any aspect.

Recommended use: Grow over heathers, prostrate conifers, and medium-sized shrubs. Good for a short obelisk or for covering bare stems of climbing roses. Ideal for short-term container-culture. Zones 3–9.

Clematis 'Pamela'
HERBACEOUS GROUP

Origin: Raised by Frank L. Skinner of Dropmore, Manitoba, Canada.

Parentage and year: *C. recta* × *C. terniflora*. 1962.

Habit: Hardy, non-clinging, deciduous, herbaceous perennial.

Height: 2 m (6.5 ft.).

Description: The single, pure white, scented flowers,

Clematis 'Pamela'. Photo by C. Chesshire.

3–4 cm (1.25–1.5 in.) wide, made of four tepals, are borne on terminal shoots and in leaf axils. The tepals are broader than long and wider at the tips, which are blunt. The margins are smooth and the surface textured, and on mature flowers the tepals tend to droop. Cream filaments and greenish yellow anthers make up the stamens, which harmonize with the tepal colour.

Pruning group: 3.

Flowering period: Midsummer to late summer.

Cultivation: Tolerates most garden soils. Produces the strongest scent in a sunny position.

Recommended use: Grow with other herbaceous plants and support it by sticks or allow it to scramble at will. Zones 5–9.

Clematis 'Pamela Jackman'
ATRAGENE GROUP

Synonym: *C. alpina* 'Pamela Jackman'

Origin: Raised by Rowland Jackman of George Jackman and Son, England, and named after his daughter.

Parentage and year: Unknown. 1960.

Habit: Hardy, not-so-vigorous, deciduous climber.

Height: 2–3 m (6.5–10 ft.).

Description: The small, nodding, deep blue single

Clematis 'Pamela Jackman'. Photo by C. Chesshire.

flowers are composed of four short, pointed tepals, each 4 cm (1.5 in.) long, surrounding a central tuft of staminodes, the outer ones being pale bluish and the inner being a creamy colour. The leaves are made of three leaflets with coarsely toothed margins.

Pruning group: 1. Any pruning to keep the plant in check should be carried out immediately after the main flowering period by removing some of the old, flowered stems.

Flowering period: Midspring to late spring, with occasional flowers in late summer.

Cultivation: Tolerates most free-draining garden soils and any aspect.

Recommended use: Grow with other wall-trained shrubs which require little or no annual pruning. Suitable for a free-standing trellis, obelisk, or similar artificial support. Ideal for container-culture. Zones 3–9.

Clematis 'Pamiat Serdtsa'
HERBACEOUS GROUP

Synonyms: *C.* 'Pamjat Serdtsa', *C.* 'Pamjatj Serdtza', *C.* 'Pamjatj Sertsa'

Origin: Raised by M. A. Beskaravainaja of the State Nikitsky Botanic Gardens, Ukraine. The name means "memory of the heart."

Parentage and year: *C. integrifolia* var. *bergeronii* × *C.* 'Lanuginosa Candida'. 1967.

Habit: Hardy, semi-herbaceous, normally non-clinging, semi-shrub.

Height: 1.5–2 m (5–6.5 ft.).

Description: The single, nodding, broadly bell-shaped, delicate, satiny, pale lilac-mauve flowers, 5–8 cm (2–3.25 in.) wide, are made of four, sometimes up to six, wide, twisting, and slightly recurving tepals. The filaments are white with pale mauve at the base and the anthers light yellow. The flowers are borne in groups of one to three on the current year's shoots. Stems are hairy and brownish or reddish when young. Leaves are simple or with three or five leaflets.

Pruning group: 3.

Flowering period: Midsummer to late summer.

Cultivation: Tolerates most garden soils and any aspect. If trained on an artificial support, the stems need tying-in.

Recommended use: Allow to scramble through medium-sized shrubs in a mixed border or plant in herbaceous borders and provide support. Zones 3–9.

Clematis 'Pamiat Serdtsa'. Photo by J. Lindmark.

Clematis 'Pangbourne Pink'. Photo by J. Lindmark.

Clematis paniculata flower (female) detail.
Photo by J. Sterndale-Bennett.

Clematis 'Pangbourne Pink'
HERBACEOUS/INTEGRIFOLIA GROUP

Synonym: *C. integrifolia* 'Pangbourne Pink'

Origin: Raised in the late 1980s by Bill Baker of Tidmarsh, Herne, England. Introduced by Denis Bradshaw of Busheyfields Nursery, Herne, Kent, England.

Parentage and year: Selected form of *C.* 'Rosea'. 1992.

Habit: Hardy, deciduous, non-clinging, woody-based, herbaceous perennial or subshrub.

Height: 0.6 m (2 ft.).

Description: The single, open, bell-shaped, nodding flowers, 5 cm (2 in.) wide, are composed of four deep pinkish mauve tepals which have a brighter colour with slight ribbing on the inside and a more smoky shade with deep ribbing on the outside. The margins of the top half of each tepal tend to recurve. Leaves are much larger than those of the species, *C. integrifolia*.

Pruning group: 3.

Cultivation: Best grown in well-drained but moisture-retentive soil and any aspect. May require some support such as unobtrusive pea-sticks.

Recommended use: Grow at the front of a herbaceous or mixed border. Zones 3–9.

Clematis paniculata
EVERGREEN GROUP

Origin: New Zealand. Known as the sacred flower (*puawhananga*) in Maori folklore, it was considered one of the firstborn children of the two stars, Rehua and Puanga, its first flowers indicating the coming of spring.

Parentage and year: Species. 1791.

Habit: Half-hardy to hardy, moderately vigorous, evergreen climber.

Height: 3–4.5 m (10–14.5 ft.).

Description: Male and female flowers are borne profusely on separate plants. The single, semi-nodding, starry, fragrant, pure white flowers, 5 cm (2 in.) across, are composed of six to eight smooth tepals. On male plants these are set off by fertile stamens with creamy yellow filaments and large salmony pink anthers, and the flowers are slightly larger. The female flowers are

Clematis paniculata (male flowers) in an Irish garden. Photo by M. Toomey.

smaller and carry infertile stamens with much smaller anthers and a prominent central bundle of styles and stigmas. The seedheads produced in abundance in the autumn on the female plant are silvery and fluffy. The leaves are made of three dark green, somewhat leathery and shiny leaflets, each with a brownish central bar.

Pruning group: 1. The plant benefits from a light trim after the main flowering period.

Flowering period: Early spring to midspring.

Cultivation: Needs sharp drainage and a warm position in front of a south-facing wall or support in frost-free gardens. Slow to establish itself in the open garden.

Recommended use: Best grown in a cool greenhouse or conservatory where the exquisite flowers can be enjoyed without damage from the weather. An excellent plant for a sheltered maritime garden. Zones 7–9.

Clematis paniculata var. *lobata*
EVERGREEN GROUP

Synonym: *C. paniculata* var. *lobulata*

Origin: New Zealand.

Parentage and year: A variant of *C. paniculata*. 1791.

Habit: Half-hardy to hardy, moderately vigorous, evergreen climber.

Height: 2–3 m (6.5–10 ft.).

Description: Male and female flowers are borne on separate plants. Female flowers are smaller. The pure, glistening white, saucer-shaped, single flowers, 4 cm (1.5 in.) across, are composed of seven, sometimes six or eight, narrow spear-shaped tepals which are longer than broad. Creamy yellow filaments with contrasting

and pretty pink anthers make up the stamens in the male flowers. The leaves differ from those of the species, *C. paniculata*, in being deeply lobed.

Pruning group: 2.

Flowering period: Early spring to midspring.

Cultivation: Needs sharp drainage in soil enriched with humus. Requires a warm, sheltered, frost-free position in front of a south-facing wall in mild or maritime gardens.

Recommended use: Best grown in a cool greenhouse or conservatory where the exquisite flowers can be enjoyed without damage from the weather. Zones 7–9.

Clematis 'Pastel Blue'
HERBACEOUS/INTEGRIFOLIA GROUP

Synonym: *C. integrifolia* 'Pastel Blue'

Origin: Raised by Barry Fretwell of Peveril Clematis Nursery, England.

Parentage and year: Unknown. Introduced 1986.

Habit: Hardy, deciduous, non-clinging, herbaceous perennial.

Height: 0.6 m (2 ft.).

Description: The single, bell-shaped, slightly scented, light-blue flowers, borne in clusters of up to 12 flowers on a stem, are composed of four pointed tepals, each 5–6 cm (2–2.25 in.) long, with crimped edges. Anthers are yellow.

Pruning group: 3.

Flowering period: Early spring to late summer.

Cultivation: Tolerates most garden soils enriched with humus. Suitable for any aspect but produces the

Clematis paniculata var. *lobata*.
Photo by C. Chesshire.

Clematis 'Pastel Blue'.
Photo by C. Chesshire.

Clematis 'Pastel Pink'.
Photo by C. Chesshire.

strongest scent in a sunny position. May require some support.

Recommended use: Ideal for the front half of a herbaceous border. Zones 3–9.

Clematis 'Pastel Pink'

HERBACEOUS/INTEGRIFOLIA GROUP

Synonym: *C. integrifolia* 'Pastel Pink'

Origin: Raised by Barry Fretwell of Peveril Clematis Nursery, England.

Parentage and year: Unknown. Introduced 1986.

Habit: Hardy, deciduous, non-clinging, herbaceous perennial.

Height: 0.6 m (2 ft.).

Description: The single, nodding, scented, bell-shaped flowers, borne in clusters, are composed of four pale pink tepals, each 4.5–5 cm (1.75–2 in.) long with slightly scalloped margins. Anthers are yellow.

Pruning group: 3.

Flowering period: Early summer to late summer.

Cultivation: Tolerates most garden soils enriched with humus. Suitable for any aspect but produces the strongest scent in a sunny position. May need some support—pea-sticks are ideal and unobtrusive.

Recommended use: Ideal for the front of a herbaceous border. Zones 3–9.

Clematis 'Pat Coleman'

Origin: Raised by Pat Coleman of Higham, Norfolk, England.

Parentage and year: Chance seedling found growing at the base of *C.* 'Lasurstern' with *C.* 'Miss Bateman' growing nearby. ca. 1990.

Habit: Hardy, moderately vigorous, deciduous climber.

Height: 2.4–3 m (8–10 ft.).

Description: The single flowers, 15–18 cm (6–7 in.) across, are composed of six pinky white tepals, each with a faint rose-pink central bar running from the base to the tip along the length of two or three grooves. The tepals boast translucent, undulating, and frilly margins. The centre of the flower is set off by stamens made of white filaments and wine-red anthers.

Pruning group: 2.

Flowering period: Late spring to early summer and early autumn.

Cultivation: Tolerates most garden soils. Best grown in partial shade to prevent fading of flower colour.

Recommended use: Suitable for a pergola, medium-sized trellis, or obelisk. Grow with moderately vigorous trees or flowering shrubs which do not require heavy annual pruning. Zones 4–9.

Clematis patens

Origin: Northeastern China, Korea, and Japan, where it may have become naturalized.

Parentage and year: Species. Introduced into European gardens by Philipp von Siebold in 1836.

Habit: Hardy, slender, deciduous climber.

Height: 1.8–2.4 m (6–8 ft.).

Clematis 'Pat Coleman'.
Photo courtesy Thorncroft Clematis Nursery.

Clematis 'Paul Farges' (SUMMER SNOW™). Photo by J. Lindmark.

Description: The solitary, upright flowers, 10–13 cm (4–5 in.) across, are borne terminally on short lateral shoots. Flower stalks are hairy. Flower colour variable, from pure white to pink and to shades of blue. Each flower is composed of six to eight pointed, non-overlapping tepals which are oval in outline but wider towards the base. The stamens consist of white filaments and reddish violet anthers in most forms but can also be yellow.

Pruning group: 2.

Flowering period: Midspring to early summer and late summer.

Cultivation: Tolerates most garden soils with good drainage. Prefers sun or semi-shade.

Recommended use: Ideal for container-culture. Suitable for a small obelisk or trellis. Grow through medium-sized shrubs and prostrate conifers which do not require annual pruning. Zones 4–9.

Clematis 'Paul Farges'

Trade name: SUMMER SNOW
Synonym: *C.* 'Fargesioides'
Origin: Raised by A. N. Volosenko-Valenis and M. A. Beskaravainaja of the State Nikitsky Botanic Gardens, Ukraine. Awarded RHS Award of Garden Merit.

Parentage and year: *C. potaninii* subsp. *fargesii* × *C. vitalba*. 1964.

Habit: Hardy, vigorous, deciduous climber.
Height: 4.6–6 m (14.5–20 ft.).

Description: The open, gappy, creamy white flowers, 4–5 cm (1.5–2 in.) across, are composed of four to six narrow, blunt-tipped tepals, which are held proud above the main stems on long stalks in clusters from the leaf axils. The prominent central boss has creamy white stamens. Some clones are scented. Mature stems are ridged and purplish brown.

Pruning group: 3.

Flowering period: Midsummer to early autumn.

Cultivation: Tolerates most garden soils and any aspect.

Recommended use: Ideal for covering large areas of a fence or a wall. May be trained over a pergola. Grow through medium-sized to large, open trees and conifers with dark foliage. Attractive when grown as a ground cover in large gardens. Zones 3–9.

Clematis 'Pauline'
ATRAGENE GROUP

Origin: Raised by Washfield Nursery of Hawkhurst, England.

Parentage and year: Chance seedling of *C.* 'Frances Rivis' (English form). 1966.

Habit: Hardy, moderately vigorous, deciduous climber.

Heights: 2.4–3 m (8–10 ft.).

Description: The semi-double, nodding, bell-shaped, midblue to dark blue flowers, 5–7 cm (2–2.75 in.) long, are composed of four tepals, with an inner ring of similarly coloured but narrower petal-like staminodes almost as long as the tepals. The light green leaves are finely cut.

Clematis patens. Photo by J. Lindmark.

Clematis 'Pauline'. Photo by C. Chesshire.

Pruning group: 1.
Flowering period: Midspring to late spring.
Cultivation: Tolerates most well-drained garden soils and any aspect.
Recommended use: Suitable for a medium-sized obelisk or trellis, or for a large container. Grow through medium-sized, open shrubs or trees which do not require annual pruning. Allow it to tumble over a low wall. Zones 3–9.

Clematis 'Perle d'Azur'
Origin: Raised by Francisque Morel of Lyon, France. Awarded RHS Award of Garden Merit.
Parentage and year: *C. viticella* 'Coerulea Grandiflora' × *C.* 'Modesta'. 1885.
Habit: Hardy, vigorous, deciduous climber.
Height: 3–3.6 m (10–12 ft.).
Description: A first-class, extremely floriferous plant. The slightly nodding buds unfurl to show off the 10- to 12.5-cm (4- to 5-in.) wide, somewhat rounded flowers with four to six broad, translucent tepals of a good midblue, boasting a hint of pink on the central bars, and recurving gently along the edges and at the tips. Mature flowers fade slightly to a pinky azure-blue. The creamy white filaments carrying pale yellow anthers collectively form a handsome central boss of stamens. The lower parts of the vines tend to become naked as they lose the old, withered, and brown leaves.
Pruning group: 3.

Flowering period: Midsummer to late summer.
Cultivation: Tolerates most garden soils and any aspect. Slightly difficult to establish itself and prone to wilt as a young plant. Quite vibrant in sunshine. Prone to mildew.
Recommended use: Ideal for a pergola, arbour, or large obelisk. Grow through large shrubs, medium-sized trees, or conifers. Associates splendidly with wall-trained climbing roses. Zones 4–9.

Clematis 'Perrin's Pride'
Origin: Raised by Arthur H. Steffen of Fairport, New York, and introduced by Fisk's Clematis Nursery, Suffolk, England.
Parentage and year: *C.* 'Jackmanii' × *C.* 'Ville de Lyon'. 1991.
Habit: Hardy, moderately vigorous, deciduous climber.
Height: 2.4–3 m (8–10 ft.).
Description: A good cultivar flowering on old and new wood, although the flowers are more abundant on the new shoots. The 10- to 15-cm (4- to 6-in.) wide, well-formed, single, and somewhat rounded flowers, carry four to six broad, soft purple, overlapping, and gently recurved tepals, with slightly darker shaded central bars. Creamy green filaments and dark pinkish anthers confer added beauty to the flowers.
Pruning group: 3. If early large flowers are required, leave a few old vines unpruned.
Flowering period: Early summer to late summer.

Clematis 'Perle d'Azur'. Photo by J. Lindmark.

Clematis 'Perrin's Pride'. Photo by R. Savill.

Cultivation: Thrives in most garden soils and any aspect.

Recommended use: Grow naturally up and over large shrubs and medium-sized trees, or on a trellis, pergola, or arch. Suitable with other wall-trained shrubs. Zones 4–9.

Clematis petriei
EVERGREEN GROUP

Origin: New Zealand (northwestern South Island). Named after the Scottish botanist Donald Petrie (1846–1925).

Parentage and year: Species. 1961.

Habit: Half-hardy to hardy, moderately vigorous, evergreen climber.

Height: To 2 m (6.5 ft.).

Description: The single, small, nodding, scented, greenish yellow flowers, borne in the axils solitarily or in a few-flowered cluster, measure 2.5–3.5 cm (1–1.25 in.) across and are composed of five to eight oval tepals which are longer than broad and hairy beneath. The stamens are cream coloured in the male flowers. Male and female flowers are borne on separate plants. Male flowers slightly larger and showier than the female ones, which give rise to attractive and fluffy seedheads. Leaves are pale green, thin, and somewhat leathery. Leaf margin may be smooth and uninterrupted or with one or two lobes.

Pruning group: 1.

Flowering period: Early spring to late spring.

Cultivation: Requires well-drained soil and a warm location. Generally known to be slightly more hardy than most New Zealand species.

Recommended use: Best grown as a specimen plant in a conservatory or cold greenhouse. Zones 7–9.

Clematis 'Peveril'
MONTANA GROUP

Synonym: *C. montana* 'Peveril'

Origin: Raised by Barry Fretwell of Peveril Clematis Nursery, England, from seed sent to his nursery from China.

Parentage and year: Selected form of *C. montana*. 1979.

Habit: Moderately vigorous, deciduous climber.

Height: 4.5–6 m (14.5–20 ft.).

Description: The single, pure white flowers are 7.5 cm (3 in.) across, with an outstanding central boss of long thin filaments carrying yellow anthers. The four tepals have broad tips and are somewhat gappy. The

Clematis petriei. Photo by J. Elliott.

Clematis 'Peveril'. Photo by E. Leeds.

flowers, which are not scented, are held well away from the blunt-toothed leaflets, on leaf stalks up to 15 cm (6 in.) long.

Pruning group: 1. Any pruning to keep the plant in check should be carried out immediately after the main flowering period by removing some of the old, flowered stems.

Flowering period: Early summer to midsummer.

Cultivation: Best grown in sun or partial shade. Hardy in temperate gardens, but not suitable for very cold gardens.

Recommended use: Grow through medium-sized trees, conifers, and large shrubs, on a wall, or along a fence. Suitable for a large trellis or pergola. Too vigorous for container-culture. Zones 6–9.

Clematis 'Peveril Pearl'

Origin: Raised by Barry Fretwell of Peveril Clematis Nursery, England.

Parentage and year: Unknown. 1979.

Habit: Hardy, moderately vigorous, deciduous climber.

Height: 1.8–2.4 m (6–8 ft.).

Description: The single flowers, 15–20 cm (6–8 in.) in diameter, carry eight overlapping and pointed pale lilac-pink tepals, with a deeper colouring and grooved texture along the centre. Creamy white filaments and coffee-coloured anthers form the large and generous, central boss of stamens.

Pruning group: 2.

Flowering period: Late spring to early and late summer.

Cultivation: Tolerates most garden soils. Best grown out of full sun to retain the flower colour.

Recommended use: Suitable for container-culture and for covering bare lower stems of other wall-trained climbers and roses which do not require severe pruning. Grow through prostrate shrubs and conifers. Zones 4–9.

Clematis 'Phil Mason'
TEXENSIS-VIORNA GROUP

Origin: Raised by John McLellan-Scott of Scott's Clematis Nursery, Devon, England, and named in memory of a friend of a customer, in 1996.

Parentage and year: *C. pitcheri* × *C. viorna*. 1994.

Habit: Hardy, moderately vigorous, deciduous climber.

Height: 1.8–2.4 m (6–8 ft.).

Description: The single, nodding, pitcher-shaped flowers, 2.5 cm (1 in.) long and 1 cm (0.5 in.) wide, are composed of four pale lilac-pink, thick, and fleshy tepals fading to cream. The tips recurve gently, exposing cream filaments and anthers. Leaflets are irregularly toothed.

Pruning group: 3.

Flowering period: Midsummer to late summer.

Clematis 'Peveril Pearl'. Photo by J. Lindmark.

Clematis 'Phil Mason'. Photo by T. Bowran.

Cultivation: Tolerates most well-drained soils enriched with humus. Suitable for any aspect.

Recommended use: Ideal for container-culture or for growing naturally through medium-sized shrubs and conifers. Zones 5–9.

Clematis phlebantha

Origin: West Nepal. First discovered in 1952 by the Polunin, Sykes, and Williams botanical expedition to Nepal. Seed introduced under the number PSW 3436 from which all examples known to be in cultivation have originated. Awarded RHS Award of Merit (1968).

Parentage and year: Species. 1952.

Habit: Half-hardy, sprawling or scandent shrub or an upright bush.

Height: 1.8–2.4 m (6–8 ft.). In cultivation it is known to have reached a height of 9.25 m (30 ft.).

Description: Not very floriferous. The solitary and rather flattish, white to creamy white flowers, 2.5–4.5 cm (1–1.75 in.) across, are borne on terminal or short lateral shoots. Each flower is composed of five to seven non-overlapping, broad yet pointed tepals with reddish brown or reddish purple delicate veining (*phlebos*, Greek word meaning "vein") running the length of and down the centre of each tepal. The stamens are yellow. The dissected potentilla-like leaves are small, deeply veined, and dark silky green above and silvery silky beneath. Young stems are ribbed and covered in white down, later turning brown and woody.

Pruning group: 1.

Flowering period: Late spring to early summer.

Cultivation: Tolerates well-drained garden soils enriched with humus. Requires a warm, sheltered, frost free position. If trained on an artificial support, the stems need tying-in.

Recommended use: Ideal for a south-facing wall. An extremely worthwhile specimen plant for container-culture in a conservatory due to its glittering, silvery, silky leaves. Zones 8–9.

Clematis 'Picton's Variety'
MONTANA GROUP

Synonym: *C. montana* 'Picton's Variety'

Origin: Raised by Percy Picton of Old Court Nurseries, Colwall, England.

Parentage and year: Unknown. Mid-1960s.

Habit: Moderately vigorous, deciduous climber.

Height: To 4.5 m (14.5 ft.).

Description: The single, bowl-shaped, mauvish pink flowers, up to 7.5 cm (3 in.) across, are composed of four to six broad tepals with slightly undulating margins and a prominent central boss of stamens made of white filaments and yellow anthers. Leaves are an attractive, bronzy colour.

Pruning group: 1. Any pruning to keep the plant in check should be carried out immediately after the main flowering period by removing some of the old, flowered stems.

Flowering period: Late spring to early summer.

Cultivation: Tolerates most well-drained soils. Hardy in temperate gardens. Suitable for any aspect

Clematis phlebantha.
Photo courtesy British Clematis Society Slide Library.

Clematis 'Picton's Variety'.
Photo courtesy British Clematis Society Slide Library.

but produces the best flower colour in a sunny position. Not as rampant as most cultivars of *C. montana*.

Recommended use: Suitable for a pergola, or along a wall or fence. Zones 7–9.

Clematis pierotii

Origin: Japan

Parentage and year: Species. 1867.

Habit: Slender, scrambling or climbing, deciduous perennial.

Height: 3–3.6 m (10–12 ft.), often less in cultivation.

Description: The small, rather flat, cream to creamy white flowers, 2.5–3.5 cm (1–1.25 in.) across, are borne from lateral shoots in groups of one to three. Each flower is composed of four spear-shaped, pointed tepals covered with dense, short, fine white hairs on the outside. The creamy stamens are somewhat shorter than the tepals. Stems are thin and wiry. Leaves are divided into three or nine leaflets with irregularly toothed margins and are small, deep green, and somewhat glossy.

Pruning group: 3.

Flowering period: Late summer to late autumn.

Cultivation: Tolerates most garden soils with good drainage. Best grown in full sun where flowering stems can ripen.

Recommended use: Grow against a warm wall or through medium-sized open shrubs. Suitable for a large container. Zones 4–9.

Clematis 'Piilu'

Origin: Raised by Uno Kivistik of Harjumaa, Estonia. The name means "little duckling."

Clematis pierotii. Photo by J. Hudson.

Parentage and year: *C.* 'Hagley Hybrid' × *C.* 'Mahrovyi'. 1984.

Habit: Hardy, very compact, deciduous climber.

Height: 1.2–1.5 m (4–5 ft.).

Description: A cultivar of medium vigour. Leaves are dark green, early flowers are double, and later ones are single, upright, open, spreading, and 9–11 cm (3.5–4.5 in.) across. Overlapping, oval tepals vary in number from four to six and are pale mauvish pink inside, distinctly paler towards the scalloped margins, with deeper pink central bars. Numerous tepal-like structures, which are modified spoon-shaped staminodes (sterile stamens), confer the double appearance on the handsome flowers. White filaments and cream anthers constitute the inner fertile stamens. The seedheads are an attractive golden brown.

Pruning group: 1 or 2.

Flowering period: Late spring to early summer and late summer.

Cultivation: Tolerates most garden soils. Best grown in full sun.

Recommended use: Ideal for container-culture. Grow over medium-sized, moderately vigorous shrubs which do not require pruning. Suitable for a small trellis or obelisk. Zones 4–9.

Clematis 'Pink Fantasy'

Origin: Raised by a Canadian nursery, details not known. Introduced to the British Isles by Fisk's Clematis Nursery, Suffolk, England.

Parentage and year: Unknown. 1975.

Habit: Hardy, moderately vigorous, compact, deciduous climber.

Height: 1.8–2.4 m (6–8 ft.).

Description: A floriferous cultivar. The single flowers, 11.5–14 cm (4.5–5.5 in.) wide, are made of six to eight scalloped, pointed, shell-pink tepals with deeper pink central bars, more prominent towards the base. The tepals are inclined to twist, giving rise to a rather irregular shaped flower, and as the tepals age, the colour fades to a pale pink or even whitish pink. Filaments are deeper reddish pink with dusky red anthers.

Pruning group: 2 or 3. A hard pruning (group 3) results in the loss of early flowers.

Flowering period: Early summer to early autumn.

Cultivation: Tolerates most garden soils and any aspect. Best grown in partial shade to prevent premature fading of flower colour.

Recommended use: A superb plant for containers or raised beds. May be grown horizontally by pegging down the vines to hold them in place and show off the blooms. Grow on a small trellis or an obelisk or over prostrate conifers and low shrubs that do not require severe pruning. Zones 4–9.

Clematis 'Pink Flamingo'
ATRAGENE GROUP

Synonym: *C. alpina* 'Pink Flamingo'

Origin: Raised by Elizabeth Jones in Brecon, Wales, and introduced by Raymond Evison of Guernsey Clematis Nursery.

Parentage and year: Seedling of *C. alpina*. Early 1990s.

Habit: Hardy, moderately vigorous, deciduous climber.

Height: 2.5–3 m (8–10 ft.).

Description: Flowers are pale pink, semi-double, semi-nodding, and 4 cm (1.5 in.) long. They are distinguished by deeper pink veining on the tepals. Leaves are composed of three leaflets, and the leaf margins are serrated, resembling the teeth of a saw.

Clematis 'Pink Fantasy'. Photo by C. Chesshire.

Clematis 'Piilu'. Photo by V. Miettinen.

Pruning group: 1. Any pruning to keep the plant tidy should be carried out immediately after the main flowering period.

Flowering period: Midspring to late spring, with occasional flowers in late summer.

Cultivation: Needs sharp drainage. Suitable for any aspect, especially north- or east-facing aspects.

Recommended use: Ideal for a small garden or container-culture. Zones 3–9.

Clematis 'Pink Pearl'

Origin: Raised by Nihon Kaki of Japan.

Parentage and year: Unknown.

Habit: Hardy, not-too-vigorous, compact, deciduous climber.

Height: 1.8–2.4 m (6–8 ft.).

Description: The single, pearly pink flowers, 10–15 cm (4–6 in.) across, are composed of six to eight broad, rounded, overlapping tepals, each with mauvish pink central veining. Pale greenish yellow filaments and yellow anthers constitute the central boss of stamens.

Pruning group: 2.

Flowering period: Midspring to late spring and late summer.

Cultivation: Tolerates most garden soils enriched with humus. Suitable for any aspect.

Recommended use: Ideal for container-culture or for a medium-sized trellis or obelisk. Zones 4–9.

Clematis 'Pink Perfection'
MONTANA GROUP

Synonym: *C. montana* 'Pink Perfection'

Origin: Raised by George Jackman and Son, England.

Parentage and year: Chance seedling. Early 1950s.

Habit: Vigorous, deciduous climber.

Height: To 9 m (29 ft.).

Description: The well-formed, single, vanilla-scented, pinky rose flowers, 5–7.5 cm (2–3 in.) across, are made of four broad, rounded tepals with a centre of yellow anthers. The young leaves are bronze coloured.

Pruning group: 1. Any pruning to keep the plant in check should be carried out immediately after the main flowering period by removing some of the old, flowered stems.

Flowering period: Late spring to early summer.

Cultivation: Tolerates most well-drained garden soils. Hardy in temperate gardens. Produces the strongest scent in sun or partial shade.

Recommended use: Suitable for a large pergola, or along a wall or fence. Grow naturally through large trees. Zones 7–9.

Clematis pitcheri
TEXENSIS-VIORNA GROUP

Synonym: *C. simsii*

Origin: Southeastern United States from Indiana to eastern Nebraska and south to Texas.

Parentage and year: Species. 1838.

Habit: Moderately vigorous, deciduous climber, almost herbaceous in habit.

Height: 2.5–3 m (8–10 ft.).

Description: The single, small, nodding, deeply grooved, pitcher-shaped, dull purple to brick-red or

Clematis 'Pink Flamingo'. Photo by J. Lindmark.

Clematis 'Pink Pearl'. Photo by J. Lindmark.

brownish purple flowers, up to 4 cm (1.5 in.) long, are composed of four tepals, which on the outside are downy with short hairs closely pressed together. The inside of the tepals can be green to yellow or purple. The tepals, slightly exceeding the stamens almost to twice their length, spread and recurve at the tips, exposing the central tuft of yellow stamens. Young stems are hairy, and leaves are compound with three to seven leaflets, slightly or deeply two to five lobed, rounded at base, thick, and hairy beneath. The terminal leaflet is reduced to a tendril-like structure.

Pruning group: 3.

Flowering period: Early summer to late summer.

Cultivation: Needs sharp drainage. Suitable for sun or partial shade. Root crown must be protected in winter.

Recommended use: Grow through other wall-trained plants. Shows up well against a light background, such as light-coloured, prostrate conifers, near pathways where the flowers can be easily viewed. Suitable for a large container. Zones 4–9.

Clematis 'Pixie'
EVERGREEN GROUP

Origin: Raised by Graham Hutchins of County Park Nursery, Essex, England.

Parentage and year: *C.* 'Princess' × *C. marmoraria*. 1986.

Habit: Half-hardy to hardy, evergreen, trailing shrub.

Height: 46–61 cm (18–24 in.).

Description: The single, pale yellow-green flowers, borne in small clusters of five or more from the leaf axils, are at first bell shaped but open flat as they

Clematis pitcheri. Photo by J. Pringle.

Clematis 'Pixie'. Photo courtesy Thorncroft Clematis Nursery.

Clematis 'Pink Perfection'. Photo by D. Bradshaw.

mature and are 30–35 mm (ca. 1.25 in.) across. The six, sometimes as few as five or as many as eight, tepals are oval to somewhat longer than broad, have rounded tips, and are smooth above and hairy beneath. The filaments are pale green with cream anthers. Only male flowers are produced. Much-divided leaves are thick and firm. Leaflets are deeply lobed with each lobe terminating in a short, blunt point.

Pruning group: 1.

Flowering period: In the garden, early spring to midspring; under glass, sometimes earlier.

Cultivation: Requires sharp-draining compost. Can be planted in sun or partial shade.

Recommended use: Grow in a cold greenhouse or conservatory, or in an alpine garden if sheltered from frost. Zones 7–9.

Clematis 'Plena'

Synonyms: *C. florida* 'Alba Plena', *C. florida* 'Flore Pleno'

Origin: Japan.

Parentage and year: Sport of *C.* 'Sieboldii'. In cultivation in Europe since 1835.

Habit: Half-hardy, slender, mostly deciduous climber.

Height: 1.8–2.5 m (6–8 ft.).

Description: The long-lasting, rosette-like, sumptuous double flowers, 8–10 cm (3.25–4 in.) across, are sterile. All the stamens have been modified into layers of numerous petal-like sterile stamens, forming the central tight rosette, and are greenish cream, wide at the base and narrowing towards pointed tips. Six outer protective basal tepals, which overlap and taper to

points, unfold first to reveal the rosette of petal-like sterile stamens. The central rosette opens over a period of days, and at the end of the flower's life the layers of petal-like sterile stamens drop gradually over a long time too, thereby extending the flowering period.

Pruning group: 2.

Flowering period: In the garden, early summer to early autumn; under glass, to late autumn.

Cultivation: If planted outside, requires a moisture-retentive soil in a sheltered, warm location.

Recommended use: Best for container-culture in a conservatory or cold greenhouse. May be grown outside through prostrate conifers or small evergreen shrubs. Zones 7–9.

Clematis 'Pleniflora'

MONTANA GROUP

Synonym: *C. montana* 'Pleniflora'

Origin: Raised by Hans R. Horn-Gfeller of Merligen, Switzerland.

Clematis 'Plena'. Photo by C. Chesshire.

Clematis 'Pleniflora'. Photo by C. Chesshire.

Parentage and year: Chance seedling of *C. montana*. Early 1980s.

Habit: Moderately vigorous, deciduous climber.

Height: To 6 m (20 ft.).

Description: The semi-double, white flowers are made of four narrow, base tepals with an inner layer of narrower, pointed, petaloid staminodes. Leaves are midgreen.

Pruning group: 1. Any pruning to keep the plant in check should be carried out immediately after the main flowering period by removing some of the old, flowered stems.

Flowering period: Midspring to late spring.

Cultivation: Tolerates most well-drained soils and any aspect. Hardy in temperate gardens.

Recommended use: Suitable for a pergola or large trellis, or along a warm wall or boundary fence. Zones 7–9.

Clematis 'Pöhjanael'

Origin: Raised by Uno Kivistik of Harjumaa, Estonia. The name means "north star."

Parentage and year: *C.* 'Ernest Markham' × pollen mixture. 1981.

Habit: Hardy, moderately vigorous, compact, deciduous climber.

Height: 1.2–1.8 m (4–6 ft.).

Description: The single flowers, 15–18 cm (6–7 in.) in diameter, are composed of six light purple-violet tepals, with darker purple central bars. White filaments carrying dark purple anthers form a generous central boss of stamens.

Pruning group: 3.

Flowering period: Midsummer to late summer.

Cultivation: Tolerates most garden soils and any aspect.

Recommended use: Good for container-culture. Grow through moderately vigorous, prostrate conifers and shrubs. Suitable for a small obelisk or trellis. Zones 4–9.

Clematis 'Polish Spirit'

Origin: Raised by Brother Stefan Franczak of Warsaw, Poland, and introduced into commerce by Raymond Evison of Guernsey Clematis Nursery. Awarded RHS Award of Garden Merit.

Parentage and year: Unknown. 1984.

Habit: Hardy, strong-growing, compact, deciduous climber.

Height: 2.5–3 m (8–10 ft.).

Description: Single, open, dark purple, velvety flowers are generously produced throughout the flowering season. The four or five tepals are up to 9 cm (3.5 in.) across and are blunt with a lighter bar along the mid-

Clematis 'Pöhjanael'. Photo by C. Chesshire.

Clematis 'Polish Spirit'. Photo by J. Lindmark.

rib. Greenish white filaments carry pinkish purple anthers and complement the tepal colour.

Pruning group: 3.

Flowering period: Midsummer to early autumn.

Cultivation: Tolerates most garden soils and any aspect.

Recommended use: Grow as a covering for bare lower stems of climbing roses or through small trees and medium-sized shrubs with silver or gold foliage. Suitable against a pillar or in a large container. Shows up well against a light background. Zones 3–9.

Clematis potaninii

Synonym: *C. fargesii* var. *souliei*

Origin: Western and southwestern China. Attributed to the Russian explorer G. H. Potanin and collected during an expedition. Introduced into cultivation by Ernest Wilson in 1911.

Parentage and year: Species. 1885.

Habit: Hardy, vigorous, deciduous climber.

Height: 3–5 m (10–16 ft.).

Description: The flattish, white or creamy white flowers, borne laterally and numbering from one to three in a small flowerhead, are 4.5–7 cm (1.75–2.75 in.) across and normally composed of six, sometimes five or seven, broad, rounded, widely spreading tepals with three to five longitudinal veins and gently undulating margins. The prominent crown of stamens is pale yellow. Stems are very strongly ribbed, green, sometimes shaded with purple or violet. Leaves are large, divided into a number of leaflets with toothed or serrated margins, broadest below the middle, and arranged along the main leaf stalk in two rows.

Pruning group: 3.

Flowering period: Early summer to early autumn.

Cultivation: Tolerates most garden soils with good drainage. Suitable for any aspect.

Recommended use: Very effective with medium-

Clematis potaninii. Photo by J. Lindmark.

sized conifers, evergreen shrubs, or late-flowering, deep-coloured roses. Suitable for a large pergola or trellis. Zones 3–9.

Clematis 'Poulala'

Trade name: ALABAST

Origin: Raised by Mogens Olesen of Poulsen Roser International, Denmark. Plant Breeders' Rights.

Parentage and year: Unknown. Late 1980s.

Habit: Hardy, moderately vigorous, deciduous climber.

Height: 2.5–3 m (8–10 ft.).

Description: The well-formed, single, greenish cream flowers, 12–15 cm (4.75–6 in.) in diameter, are composed of six to eight tepals and are produced from late spring to early summer. The stamens are creamy yellow. The second flush of flowers, appearing in mid-summer and late summer, are smaller at 9 cm (3.5 in.). The leaves are slightly bluish green.

Pruning group: 2.

Flowering period: Late spring to early summer and late summer.

Cultivation: Tolerates most garden soils. Produces best flower colour in partial shade.

Recommended use: Shows up well against a dark background. Ideal for a small to medium-sized obelisk, trellis, or arbour. Grow with other clematis in pruning group 2 which have a contrasting flower colour. Zones 4–9.

Clematis 'Poulvo'

Trade name: VINO

Origin: Raised by D. T. Poulsen of Denmark. Plant Breeders' Rights.

Parentage and year: *C.* 'Lasurstern' × *C.* 'Daniel Deronda'. 1970.

Habit: Hardy, moderately vigorous, deciduous climber.

Height: 2.4–3 m (8–10 ft.).

Description: The single, rather large, petunia-red flowers, 10–18 cm (4–7 in.) wide, are composed of six to eight broad, overlapping, tapering tepals, each with

Clematis 'Poulala' (ALABAST™). Photo by C. Chesshire.

Clematis 'Poulvo' (VINO™). Photo by R. Surman.

a deeper colour along the centre, fading with maturity. The stamens carry creamy yellow filaments and yellow anthers, which contrast with the tepal colour.

Pruning group: 2.

Flowering period: Late spring to early summer and early autumn. Flowers produced later in the season may not be as wide as the early flowers and also have a tendency to demonstrate some variation in colour, bordering onto mauvish red.

Cultivation: Tolerates most garden soils and any aspect.

Recommended use: Grow with large shrubs which require little or no pruning and small trees. Ideal for an obelisk, pergola, or arch. Zones 4–9.

Clematis 'Prairie River'
ATRAGENE GROUP

Synonym: *C. alpina* 'Prairie River'

Origin: Raised by Stanley J. Zubrowski of Prairie River, Saskatchewan, Canada.

Parentage and year: Unknown.

Habit: Hardy, moderately vigorous, deciduous climber.

Height: 2.4–3 m (8–10 ft.).

Description: The single, nodding, bell-shaped, violet-blue flowers are composed of four somewhat broad tepals, with the colour fading to a lighter blue at the tips. An inner skirt of cream staminodes tinged with blue surrounds the fertile stamens. Leaves are composed of three leaflets, and leaf margins are serrated, resembling the teeth of a saw.

Pruning group: 1. Any pruning to keep the plant tidy

should be carried out immediately after the main flowering period.

Flowering period: Midspring.

Cultivation: Tolerates most well-drained garden soils and any aspect.

Recommended use: Grow with other wall-trained plants. Suitable for a free-standing medium-sized obelisk or trellis. Allow to tumble over a low wall. Ideal for container-culture. Zones 3–9.

Clematis 'Prince Charles'

Origin: Raised from a seedling given to Alister Keay of New Zealand Clematis Nurseries, Christchurch. Introduced to the British Isles in 1986 by Jim Fisk of Fisk's Clematis Nursery, Suffolk, England.

Parentage and year: Unknown. 1975.

Habit: Hardy, moderately vigorous, deciduous climber.

Height: 1.8–2.4 m (6–8 ft.).

Description: A very floriferous, compact cultivar. The semi-nodding flowers measure 10 cm (4 in.)

Clematis 'Prince Charles'. Photo by C. Chesshire.

Clematis 'Prairie River'. Photo by C. Chesshire.

across and carry four to six broad but tapering, slightly twisting, deeply ribbed, midblue tepals with a satin sheen. Filaments are greenish yellow, and anthers are deep yellow.

Pruning group: 3.

Flowering period: Early summer to early autumn.

Cultivation: Tolerates most garden soils and any aspect except north. Prone to mildew.

Recommended use: Ideal for container-culture. Grow on an obelisk or trellis, or with climbing roses. Zones 4–9.

Clematis 'Prince Philip'

Origin: Raised in the United States. Reintroduced to England by Raymond Evison of Guernsey Clematis Nursery in the 1980s.

Parentage and year: *C.* 'Atrorubens' × *C. lanuginosa*. Before the 1980s.

Habit: Hardy, moderately vigorous, deciduous climber.

Height: 2.4–3 m (8–10 ft.).

Description: The single flowers, 15 cm (6 in.) in diameter, are composed of seven or eight rosy mauve tapering tepals, crimped at the margins and each with a reddish plum pink central bar. The attractive tepals tend to overlap at the base of the juvenile flowers, but with age they twist and lose their lustre. Anthers are pale brown. Leaves are made of three long and pointed leaflets.

Pruning group: 2.

Flowering period: Late spring to early summer and late summer.

Cultivation: Tolerates most garden soils and any aspect.

Recommended use: Grow on a pergola, trellis, or medium-sized obelisk. Zones 4–9.

Clematis 'Princess Diana'
TEXENSIS-VIORNA GROUP

Synonyms: *C. texensis* 'Princess Diana', *C. texensis* 'The Princess of Wales'

Origin: Raised by Barry Fretwell of Peveril Clematis Nursery, England.

Clematis 'Princess Diana'. Photo by M. Toomey.

Clematis 'Prince Philip'. Photo by E. Leeds.

Parentage and year: *C.* 'Bees Jubilee' × *C. texensis*. 1984.

Habit: Hardy, deciduous climber. Normally of herbaceous habit with new shoots emerging from below ground level. Strong growing and very floriferous once established.

Height: 1.8–2.4 m (6–8 ft.).

Description: The single, 6-cm (2.25-in.) long, tulip-like flowers are composed of four luminous pink tepals,

Clematis 'Princess of Wales'. Photo by C. Chesshire.

Clematis 'Prins Hendrik' (Prince Hendrik™).
Photo by R. Savill.

each with a deeper pink central bar and pointed tip, which recurves gently to make a trumpetlike shape as the flower matures. The outside of the tepals boasts a distinctive bright pink colour at the margins. The stamens are made of cream filaments and maroon anthers, and the leaves are light green.

Pruning group: 3.

Flowering period: Midsummer to early autumn.

Cultivation: Tolerates most garden soils. Can be planted in sun or partial shade. Not prone to mildew. New shoots at soil level need protection from slugs and snails.

Recommended use: Grow naturally through and over low shrubs, prostrate conifers, and heathers where the flowers will face upward. Suitable for a large container. Zones 4–9.

Clematis 'Princess of Wales'

Origin: Raised by George Jackman and Son, England, and named after Princess, later Queen, Alexandra.

Parentage and year: Believed to be a seedling of *C.* 'Lanuginosa Violacea'. 1875.

Habit: Hardy, moderately vigorous, deciduous climber.

Height: 2.4–3 m (8–10 ft.).

Description: The single, large, flat, satiny, pale mauve flowers, 15–20 cm (6–8 in.) across, are composed of six to eight somewhat overlapping tepals, which are wide at the middle but slightly taper towards both ends. Each tepal carries central grooves shaded darker towards the basal half. The tepal tips are drawn to points. Creamy filaments carrying reddish brown anthers constitute the attractive stamens.

Pruning group: 2.

Flowering period: Early summer to late summer.

Cultivation: Tolerates most garden soils and any aspect.

Recommended use: Suitable for a pergola, trellis, or medium-sized obelisk. Zones 4–9.

Clematis 'Prins Hendrik'

Trade name: Prince Hendrik

Origin: Raised by P. Goedt of Boskoop, Netherlands.

Parentage and year: Unknown. 1908.

Habit: Hardy, moderately vigorous, compact, deciduous climber.

Height: 1.8–2.4 m (6–8 ft.).

Description: The single flowers, 15–20 cm (6–8 in.) in diameter, are made of six, sometimes seven, overlapping, lavender-blue tepals with indented or notched margins and deeply grooved central bars. The stamens boast greenish cream filaments and purple anthers.

Pruning group: 2.

Flowering period: Late spring to midsummer.

Cultivation: Tolerates most garden soils. Prefers sun or partial shade.

Recommended use: Ideal for container-culture. Suitable for a small to medium-sized obelisk or trellis. Grow with other wall-trained plants which do not require severe pruning. Zones 4–9.

Clematis 'Propertius'
ATRAGENE GROUP

Origin: Raised by Magnus Johnson of Södertälje, Sweden.

Parentage and year: *C. koreana* var. *fragrans* × *C.* 'Rosy O'Grady'. 1979.

Habit: Hardy, moderately vigorous, deciduous climber.

Height: 2.4–3 m (8–10 ft.).

Description: The double, slightly scented, nodding, pinkish mauve flowers, 7.5–9 cm (3–3.5 in.) across, are composed of four broad, spear-shaped tepals, each with three or four prominent ridges running from the base to the tip, which are a darker shade similar to that which surrounds the flower stalk where it joins the base. There is much veining and crinkled texturing, and the colouring fades to silvery white at the margins. As the flower matures, the tip and its nearby margins recurve slightly. Inside there are two layers of long, paler and narrower petal-like staminodes of similar length to the outer ones and these in turn surround an inner skirt of short pale cream staminodes tipped with green, which cover the pale green filaments and anthers. The flower has a very full appearance.

Pruning group: 1.

Flowering period: Early spring to midspring.

Cultivation: Tolerates most well-drained garden soils. Produces the strongest scent in a sunny position.

Recommended use: Suitable for a medium-sized obelisk or trellis. Grow with other early flowering clematis which belong to pruning group 1 or with wall-trained shrubs which do not require heavy annual pruning. Zones 3–9.

Clematis 'Proteus'

Origin: Raised by Charles Noble of Sunningdale, England.

Parentage and year: *C.* 'Grandiflora' × *C.* 'Fortunei'. Introduced in 1876.

Habit: Hardy, quite vigorous, deciduous climber.

Height: 1.8–2.4 m (6–8 ft.).

Description: The early, fully double flowers, measuring 12.5–15 cm (5–6 in.) in diameter, are produced on the previous season's old wood. The outermost base layer is composed of at least six purple-pink broad yet pointed tepals, each with shades of pale green along

Clematis 'Propertius'. Photo by J. Lindmark.

Clematis 'Proteus' double flowers are carried early in the eason. Photo by C. Chesshire.

the centre and a deeply textured surface. There are successive inner layers of paler mauvish pink tepals, many of which are twisted with incurving margins and tips. Single flowers are produced later in the season on new wood. White filaments and pale yellow anthers form the central mass of stamens.

Pruning group: 2.

Flowering period: Late spring to early summer (double) and late summer (single).

Cultivation: Tolerates most garden soils. Best grown in full or partial sun. Requires protection from strong winds.

Recommended use: Suitable for a small to medium-sized obelisk or trellis. Ideal for container-culture. Grow with other wall-trained plants which do not require pruning. Zones 4–9.

Clematis 'Proteus' single flowers are carried later in the season or in cold climates. Photo by J. Lindmark.

Clematis 'Pruinina'

ATRAGENE GROUP

Synonym: *C. barbellata* 'Pruinina'

Origin: Raised by Magnus Johnson of Södertälje, Sweden.

Parentage and year: *C. fauriei* × *C. sibirica* (F_2 hybrid). 1972.

Habit: Hardy, moderately vigorous, deciduous climber.

Height: 2.4–3 m (8–10 ft.).

Description: The single, nodding, deep plum-purple flowers are composed of four broad tepals, each 5 cm (2 in.) long, and a central mass of pale silvery mauve staminodes (sterile stamens). Leaves are dark green and finely divided.

Pruning group: 1.

Flowering period: Midspring to late spring.

Cultivation: Tolerates most well-drained soils and any aspect.

Recommended use: Grow with other wall-trained plants or on a medium-sized obelisk or trellis. Allow to tumble over a low wall or fence. Ideal for container-culture. Zones 3–9.

Clematis 'Purple Spider'

ATRAGENE GROUP

Synonym: *C. macropetala* 'Purple Spider'

Origin: Found by Wim Snoeijer at the nursery of Jan Fopma, Boskoop, Netherlands. Named in 1992.

Parentage and year: Open-pollinated seedling of *C. macropetala*.

Habit: Hardy, moderately vigorous, compact, deciduous climber.

Height: 1.8–2.4 m (6–8 ft.).

Description: The nodding, dark purple, almost purplish black, semi-double, compact flowers are composed of four broad but pointed tepals, each 4–5 cm (1.5–2 in.) long, with an inner skirt of similar coloured petal-like staminodes surrounding the innermost central tuft of fertile stamens. Seedheads are large and attractive.

Pruning group: 1.

Flowering period: Midspring to late spring, with sporadic flowering in summer.

Cultivation: Tolerates most well-drained garden soils and any aspect.

Recommended use: Ideal for container-culture.

Clematis 'Purple Spider'. Photo by C. Chesshire.

Clematis 'Pruinina'. Photo by J. Lindmark.

Shows up well against a light background or up and over shrubs which have silver or gold foliage and which do not require annual pruning. Allow to tumble over a low wall or fence. Train as a specimen plant on a small obelisk or free-standing trellis in a mixed border. Zones 3–9.

Clematis 'Purpurea' young foliage early in the year. Photo by C. Chesshire.

Clematis 'Purpurea'
HERBACEOUS GROUP

Synonym: *C. recta* 'Purpurea'

Origin: Central and southern Europe.

Parentage and year: Form of *C. recta*.

Habit: Hardy, deciduous, clump-forming, herbaceous perennial.

Height: 0.9–1.8 m (3–6 ft.).

Description: The single, strongly scented, white flowers, 2–3 cm (0.75–1.25 in.) across, are normally composed of four narrow tepals, which open fully and slightly recurve, bringing the creamy white stamens into prominence. Although this form is similar in many respects to *C. recta*, its distinguishing feature is the purple leaves, which are distinctly dark and almost purple-bronze when young, turning green with age. The white flowers contrast exceptionally well with the rich, dark foliage.

Pruning group: 3.

Flowering period: Early summer to late summer.

Clematis 'Purpurea' in full flower. Photo by R. Kirkman.

Cultivation: Tolerates most garden soils. Prefers a sunny aspect. If trained on an artificial support, the stems need tying-in.

Recommended use: Place tall clones at the back of a herbaceous or mixed border and provide artificial support. Place lower-growing clones in the middle or at the front of the border and allow them to rest on other nearby plants or provide pea-sticks for support. If space permits, allow the flowering stems to flop on the ground, where they make an effective display. Zones 3–9.

Clematis 'Purpurea Plena Elegans'
VITICELLA GROUP

Synonym: *C. viticella* 'Purpurea Plena Elegans'

Origin: Obscure but possibly a sixteenth-century cultivar, or one raised and introduced by Francisque Morel of Lyon, France, almost 300 years later. Awarded RHS Award of Garden Merit.

Parentage and year: Possibly a sport of *C. viticella*. Either prior to 1600 or ca. 1900.

Habit: Hardy, deciduous climber. Quite vigorous once it is established.

Height: 3–4 m (10–13 ft.).

Description: The sterile, dark magenta flowers, carried on long stalks, are fully double multitepalled rosettes, 4.5–6 cm (1.75–2.25 in.) across, and each

Clematis 'Purpurea Plena Elegans' flower detail. Photo by J. Lindmark.

Clematis 'Purpurea Plena Elegans' in bloom. Photo by J. Lindmark.

tepal recurves elegantly towards the tip. The reverse has a greyish tinge. Occasionally the outer tepals may show green tips as the flowers open. With age the outer tepals wither and fall off, leaving the inner rows of tepals to open gradually over a period of time.

Pruning group: 3.

Flowering period: Midsummer to early autumn.

Cultivation: Tolerates most garden soils and any aspect.

Recommended use: Shows up well against a light background. Grow through medium-sized trees, large shrubs, and early flowering climbing roses. Ideal against a wall or over an arch or pergola. Zones 3–9.

Clematis 'Rahvarinne'

Origin: Raised by Uno Kivistik of Harjumaa, Estonia.

Parentage and year: *C.* 'Ernest Markham' × *C.* 'Bal Tzvetov'. 1985.

Habit: Hardy, not very vigorous, compact, deciduous climber.

Height: 1.5–1.8 m (5–6 ft.).

Description: The single, purple flowers 10–13 cm (4–5 in.) across, are composed of four to six wide, overlapping, and rounded tepals, each heavily textured and veined with central grooves running from base to tip. The margins are gently wavy, and the tips tend to recurve. The stamens are made of pinky white filaments and pinky brown anthers.

Pruning group: 3.

Flowering period: Midsummer to late summer.

Cultivation: Tolerates most garden soils enriched with humus. Suitable for any aspect.

Recommended use: Ideal for container-culture or for growing over moderately vigorous, prostrate conifers or small to medium-sized shrubs. Zones 3–9.

Clematis ranunculoides

Origin: Southwestern China. Introduced into cultivation by George Forrest in the early 1900s.

Parentage and year: Species. 1886.

Habit: Moderately hardy, erect, perennial herb or clambering, deciduous climber.

Height: 0.5–1.5 m (1.5–5 ft.).

Description: The solitary and axillary, or sometimes grouped in small, terminal clusters, nodding, bell-shaped, rose-pink to pink-purple flowers, 1–2 cm (0.5–0.75 in.) across, are held on short, hairy stalks and are composed of four tepals, 0.7–1.5 cm (0.25–0.5 in.) long, which are broadly spreading, acutely reflexed, and deeply ribbed on the upper surface. The central tuft consists of prominent stamens which are pinkish and almost as long as the tepals. The flower stalks, leaf stalks, and stems are ridged and are a reddish purple in colour. Leaves are midgreen, coarsely toothed, and with very curled or coiled leaf stalks.

Pruning group: 3.

Flowering period: Early to late autumn.

Cultivation: Requires very well drained soil. Resents winter wet. Flowers well in a sunny position.

Recommended use: Best grown as a specimen for container-culture in a conservatory or cool greenhouse. If grown in a container in the open, it can be moved to a frost-free environment before winter. Effective in a herbaceous border in frost-free gardens. Zones 7–9.

Clematis 'Rahvarinne'. Photo by J. Lindmark.

Clematis ranunculoides. Photo by Y. Aihara.

Clematis recta
HERBACEOUS GROUP

Origin: Central and southern Europe, western and central Russia.

Parentage and year: Species. 1597.

Habit: Hardy, deciduous, clump-forming, herbaceous perennial.

Height: 1–2 m (3.25–6.5 ft.).

Description: The numerous star-shaped, white flowers are borne in large terminal panicles or flowerheads usually covering the upper half of the plant. They are 2–3 cm (0.75–1.25 in.) wide and are composed of normally four narrow tepals, which open wide and slightly recurve, exposing the creamy white filaments and anthers. Some forms exude a strong hawthorn scent. Leaves carry five or seven leaflets and are deep green or bluish green.

Pruning group: 3.

Flowering period: Early summer to late summer.

Cultivation: Tolerates most garden soils. Best grown in a sunny aspect. If trained on an artificial support, the stems need tying-in.

Recommended use: Tall clones to the rear of herbaceous or mixed borders where they require some artificial support. Lower growing clones can be placed near to the middle or to the front and be allowed to rest on other nearby plants for support, or pea-sticks can be utilized for the purpose. If space permits, allow the flowering stems to flop on the ground, where they make an effective display. Zones 3–9.

Clematis 'Red Beetroot Beauty'
ATRAGENE GROUP

Synonym: *C.* 'Betina'

Origin: Raised by Magnus Johnson of Södertälje, Sweden.

Parentage and year: *C. fauriei* × *C. sibirica* (F$_2$ hybrid). 1980.

Habit: Hardy, not-so-vigorous, compact, deciduous climber.

Height: 1.8–2.4 m (6–8 ft.).

Description: The small, bell-shaped, nodding, beetroot-purple flowers are composed of four wide spear-shaped tepals 3.2 cm (1.25 in.) long, with textured surfaces. There is an inner skirt of purple-tipped, pale white staminodes. The bright green leaves are divided into leaflets with serrated margins.

Pruning group: 1.

Flowering period: Early spring to midspring.

Cultivation: Tolerates most well-drained garden soils enriched with humus. Suitable for any aspect.

Recommended use: Ideal for container-culture. Suitable for a small to medium-sized obelisk or trellis. Allow to tumble over a low wall. Zones 3–9.

Clematis 'Red Cooler'

Origin: Raised by Nihon Kaki of Japan.

Parentage and year: Unknown. 1985.

Habit: Hardy, moderately vigorous, compact, deciduous climber.

Height: 1.8–2.4 m (6–8 ft.).

Description: The single flowers, 15–20 cm (6–8 in.) across, are composed of six to eight broad yet pointed, overlapping, crimson tepals when young, and fading to

Clematis 'Red Beetroot Beauty'. Photo by J. Lindmark.

Clematis 'Red Cooler'. Photo by C. Chesshire.

Clematis recta. Photo by J. Lindmark.

reddish purple when mature but leaving a reddish central bar. Greenish cream filaments carry deep-red anthers. Occasionally the first flowering period has semi-double flowers.

Pruning group: 2.

Flowering period: Late spring to early and late summer.

Cultivation: Tolerates most garden soils. Best grown in sun or semi-shade.

Recommended use: Ideal for container-culture. Suitable for a small obelisk or trellis. Grow as a covering for the bare lower stems of taller wall-trained shrubs. Zones 4–9.

Clematis rehderiana

Origin: Western China. Named after Alfred Rehder (1863–1949), a German botanist, but first introduced to France by Père George Aubert. Awarded RHS Award of Garden Merit.

Parentage and year: Species. 1898.

Habit: Hardy, quite vigorous, scandent, woody, deciduous climber.

Height: Up to 7.7 m (25 ft.).

Description: Several small, pendulous, bell-shaped, and cowslip-scented flowers are borne on erect axillary and terminal clusters up to 23 cm (9 in.) long. Each flower, 1.5–1.8 cm (0.5–0.75 in.) long, is composed of four pale yellow tepals which are longer than broad and which are velvety hairy on the outer surface and smooth and hairless on the inner. The tepals reflex at the blunt tips just enough to expose the pale brownish yellow anthers carried on hairy, greenish cream fila-

ments. Leaflike bracts, which are similar in colour to that of the tepals, often three lobed, and about 20 mm (0.75 in.) long, are a characteristic feature. Mature stems are ribbed and change from green to mauvish brown. Leaves are divided into five, seven, or nine leaflets and are quite roughly veined above but smoother with prominent veining beneath.

Pruning group: 3.

Flowering period: Midsummer to early autumn.

Cultivation: Tolerates most well-drained garden soils. Produces the strongest scent in a sunny position.

Recommended use: Suitable for a spacious wall or fence. Grow through medium-sized trees or large shrubs. Ideal for a large pergola, arch, or free-standing trellis. A good groundcover plant for large gardens. Zones 6–9.

Clematis 'Rhapsody'

Origin: Attributed variously to Frank Watkinson of Doncaster and to Barry Fretwell of Peveril Clematis Nursery, England.

Parentage and year: Unknown. Introduced in 1991 (Watkinson) or in 1992 (Fretwell).

Habit: Hardy, moderately vigorous, deciduous climber.

Height: 2.4–3 m (8–10 ft.).

Clematis rehderiana. Photo by C. Chesshire.

Clematis 'Rhapsody'. Photo by R. Kirkman.

Description: A free-flowering cultivar with beautiful, single flowers which are 10–12.5 cm (4–5 in.) across and which are composed of four to six broad but pointed indigo-blue tepals. The colour becomes intense as the flowers mature. Creamy yellow stamens with anthers spread out are an attractive feature.

Pruning group: 3.

Flowering period: Midsummer to late summer.

Cultivation: Tolerates most garden soils. Best grown in sun or semi-shade. Avoid north-facing aspects.

Recommended use: Grow with other climbing plants and roses or through conifers, large shrubs, and small trees. Train on a medium-sized obelisk or trellis. Suitable for short-term container-culture. Zones 4–9.

Clematis 'Richard Pennell'

Origin: Raised by Walter Pennell of Pennell and Sons nursery and named after his son in 1974. Awarded RHS Award of Garden Merit.

Parentage and year: *C.* 'Vyvyan Pennell' × *C.* 'Daniel Deronda'. 1962.

Habit: Hardy, moderately vigorous, deciduous climber.

Height: 2.4–3 m (8–10 ft.).

Description: A graceful cultivar. The 15- to 20-cm (6- to 8-in.) wide, well-formed single, full flowers are composed of six to eight warm, rosy purple-blue, saucer-shaped, overlapping tepals. Tepal colour tends to lose its lustre gradually with age. The stamens are made of unusual whorled rose-pink filaments and golden yellow anthers.

Pruning group: 2.

Clematis 'Richard Pennell'. Photo by C. Chesshire.

Flowering period: Late spring to early and late summer.

Cultivation: Tolerates most garden soils and any aspect.

Recommended use: Grow with climbing roses and other wall-trained shrubs which do not require severe pruning. Suitable for a medium-sized obelisk or trellis. Zones 4–9.

Clematis 'Riga'
ATRAGENE GROUP

Synonyms: *C. sibirica* 'Riga', *C. alpina* subsp. *sibirica* 'Riga'

Origin: Raised by Magnus Johnson of Södertälje, Sweden, who received seed gathered at the University Botanic Garden, Riga, Latvia.

Parentage and year: Seedling of *C. sibirica*. 1994.

Habit: Hardy, moderately vigorous, deciduous climber.

Height: 1.5–2 m (5–6.5 ft.).

Description: The single, pure white flowers, 4–6 cm (1.5–2.25 in.) across, are composed of four pointed tepals which open wider than do those of most other forms. The petal-like staminodes are pale greenish yellow.

Pruning group: 1.

Flowering period: Early spring to midspring.

Cultivation: Tolerates most garden soils with good drainage. Suitable for any aspect, especially cold, windy situations.

Recommended use: Ideal for a small garden. Grow through medium-sized shrubs which do not require annual pruning. Zones 3–9.

Clematis 'Robusta'
EVERGREEN GROUP

Synonyms: *C. terniflora* 'Robusta', *C. terniflora* var. *robusta*

Origin: China, Taiwan, Korea, and Japan.

Parentage and year: Species. Selected form. 1953.

Habit: Very vigorous, deciduous (sometimes semi-evergreen) climber.

Height: 7.7 m (25 ft.) or more.

Description: The scented, starlike, white flowers are somewhat larger than those of *C. terniflora*, measuring 5 cm (2 in.) across. Each flower is composed of four tepals, which are narrow, longer than broad, and hairy

Clematis 'Riga'. Photo by J. Lindmark.

on the outside. The stamens are made of greenish cream filaments and yellow anthers. The leaves are also larger than those of *C. terniflora*, up to 35 cm (14 in.) long, and the leaflets often boast a silvery stripe along the midrib. This cultivar is much more robust than the typical plant.

Pruning group: 3.

Flowering period: Late summer to midautumn.

Cultivation: Prefers a dry, sunny, warm location.

Recommended use: Not for cold, wet gardens. Suitable for covering a warm, south-facing wall or fence. Allow it to scramble into medium-sized to large trees or shrubs. Zones 5–9.

Clematis 'Romantika'

Origin: Raised by Uno Kivistik of Harjumaa, Estonia.

Parentage and year: Open-pollinated seedling of *C.* 'Devjatyj Val'. 1983.

Habit: Hardy, moderately vigorous, deciduous climber.

Height: 1.8–2.4 m (6–8 ft.).

Description: The 10- to 15-cm (4- to 6-in.) wide, well-formed, firm and handsome, single flowers are composed of four very rich, almost blackish purple tepals, which are heavily grooved along the centre. As the flowers mature, a faint sign of a lighter purple bar in each tepal becomes evident. The stamens are greenish yellow.

Pruning group: 3.

Flowering period: Early summer to late summer.

Cultivation: Tolerates most garden soils and any aspect. Prone to mildew.

Recommended use: Shows up well against a light background. Grow through golden, prostrate conifers or up and over moderately vigorous shrubs with either silver or golden leaves to show off the deep rich colour. Suitable for a large container plant or trained on a small obelisk or trellis. Zones 3–9.

Clematis 'Rosea'
HERBACEOUS / INTEGRIFOLIA GROUP

Synonym: *C. integrifolia* 'Rosea'

Origin: Raised by Magnus Johnson of Södertälje, Sweden.

Parentage and year: Seedling of *C. integrifolia*. 1952.

Habit: Hardy, deciduous, non-clinging, herbaceous perennial.

Height: 0.7–1.2 m (2–4 ft.).

Description: The single, bell-shaped, nodding, slightly scented flowers, borne on terminal shoots and in upper leaf axils, are composed of four pointed, prominently ribbed tepals, each 4–5 cm (1.5–2 in.) long, variable in colour from light pink to a darker shade of mauve pink. Deep colouring of pink is concentrated at the base of each tepal. The tepal margins of some forms are slightly twisted, wavy, and covered in dense, short, and fine hairs. The filaments are white with yellow anthers. This variable cultivar is often propagated from seed. Beware of inferior seedlings. Best acquired from a reputable source.

Pruning group: 3.

Flowering period: Early summer to late summer.

Clematis 'Robusta'. Photo by E. Leeds.

Clematis 'Romantika'. Photo by J. Lindmark.

Cultivation: Tolerates most gardens soils enriched with humus. Suitable for any aspect but produces the strongest scent in a sunny position.

Recommended use: Place in the middle of a herbaceous border. Zones 3–9.

Clematis 'Rosy O'Grady'
ATRAGENE GROUP

Origin: Raised by Frank L. Skinner of Dropmore, Manitoba, Canada.

Parentage and year: *C. macropetala* × *C. alpina*. 1964.

Habit: Hardy, vigorous, deciduous climber.

Height: 3–4 m (10–13 ft.).

Description: The nodding, semi-double, pinkish mauve flowers, 10–12 cm (4–4.75 in.) across, are composed of four narrow tepals which are much longer than broad, each 5–7 cm (2–2.75 in.) long, with margins which tend to curve back upon themselves at a midpoint, giving a slightly twisted appearance. The outside of the tepal is darker than the inside and has dark pink veining running from the base to the tip. The inner skirt of petaloid staminodes is pale pinkish mauve colour and surrounds the pale yellow centre of fertile stamens. The leaves are pale green and have nine leaflets. The stems are dark reddish brown.

Pruning group: 1.

Flowering period: Midspring to late spring, with sporadic flowering in summer.

Cultivation: Tolerates most well-drained garden soils and any aspect.

Recommended use: Useful for a small garden. Ideal for container-culture or for growing through medium-sized, open shrubs which do not require annual pruning. Suitable for a pergola, medium-sized obelisk, or trellis. Zones 3–9.

Clematis 'Rosy Pagoda'
ATRAGENE GROUP

Synonym: *C. alpina* 'Rosy Pagoda'

Origin: Raised by Magnus Johnson of Södertälje, Sweden.

Parentage and year: Seedling of *C.* 'Ruby'. 1974.

Habit: Hardy, moderately vigorous, deciduous climber.

Height: 2.4–3 m (8–10 ft.).

Description: The single, small, bell-shaped, nodding, cerise flowers are composed of four tepals, 4.5 cm (1.75 in.) long, broadening in the middle and tapering to gently recurving, pointed tips. Each tepal is distinguished by a blush-pink edge. The tepals spread and open wide with age to expose an inner tuft of pinkish white staminodes. The fertile stamens in the heart of the flower are made of cream filaments and butter yellow anthers.

Pruning group: 1.

Flowering period: Early spring to midspring.

Clematis 'Rosea'. Photo by R. Surman.

Clematis 'Rosy O'Grady'. Photo by C. Chesshire.

Cultivation: Tolerates most well-drained garden soils enriched with humus. Suitable for any aspect.

Recommended use: Ideal for a colder pocket in the garden. Train on a medium-sized obelisk, trellis, or pergola. Grow with other clematis from pruning group 1. Zones 3–9.

Clematis 'Rouge Cardinal'

Origin: Raised by A. Girault of Orléans, France.

Parentage and year: *C.* 'Ville de Lyon' × *C.* 'Pourpre Mat'. 1968.

Habit: Hardy, strong-growing, deciduous climber.

Height: 1.8–2.4 m (6–8 ft.).

Description: The single flowers, 10–13 cm (4–5 in.) wide, normally carry six velvety red tepals, which are rounded yet pointed and slightly recurved, giving the flower a very full and rounded appearance. Creamy white filaments and dark brown anthers which consti-

Clematis 'Rosy Pagoda'. Photo by R. Surman.

Clematis 'Rouge Cardinal'. Photo by J. Lindmark.

tute the stamens contrast beautifully with the tepal colour.

Pruning group: 3.

Flowering period: Early summer to late summer.

Cultivation: Tolerates most garden soils and any aspect.

Recommended use: Shows up well against a light background. Grow naturally through prostrate or medium-sized conifers and shrubs. Suitable for container-culture or in the garden as a covering for the bare lower stems of other wall-trained plants. Zones 4–9.

Clematis 'Royal Velours'
VITICELLA GROUP

Synonym: *C. viticella* 'Royal Velours'

Origin: Raised by Francisque Morel of Lyon, France, and brought into cultivation by William Robinson of Gravetye Manor and his head gardener, Ernest Markham. Awarded RHS Award of Garden Merit.

Parentage and year: Unknown. Early 1900s.

Habit: Hardy, moderately vigorous, deciduous climber.

Height: 2.5–3 m (8–10 ft.).

Description: The single, semi-nodding flowers, 6–8 cm (2.25–3.25 in.) wide, are composed of four to six velvety, dark reddish purple to reddish black overlapping tepals, which are deeply veined with lighter midribs. The anthers are reddish purple.

Pruning group: 3.

Flowering period: Midsummer to early autumn.

Clematis 'Royal Velours'. Photo by J. Lindmark.

Cultivation: Tolerates most garden soils and any aspect.

Recommended use: Shows up well against a light background or in sunlight. Most effective when grown through shrubs with silver, grey, or golden foliage, and climbing roses. Zones 3–9.

Clematis 'Royalty'

Origin: Raised by John Treasure, Treasures of Tenbury, England.

Parentage and year: Unknown. Introduced in 1987.

Habit: Hardy, moderately vigorous, compact, deciduous climber.

Height: 1.8–2.4 m (6–8 ft.).

Description: The rich blue mauve, double flowers, 10–15 cm (4–6 in.) wide, are produced on the previous season's old wood and consist of an outer basal row of eight or nine overlapping, rounded, tepals, each with a pale mauve bar overlaid with dark purple veins, along the centre. Subsequent inner layers of shorter tepals boast similar colouring. Purple filaments and yellow anthers forming the central tuft of stamens complement the tepal colour. Single flowers are produced on the current season's new growth.

Pruning group: 2.

Flowering period: Late spring to early summer (double) and early autumn (single).

Cultivation: Tolerates most garden soils. Can be planted in full or partial sun. Requires protection from strong winds.

Recommended use: Suitable on a small obelisk or trellis. Ideal for container-culture. Grow with other wall-trained plants which do not require pruning. Zones 4–9.

Clematis 'Ruby'
ATRAGENE GROUP

Synonym: *C. alpina* 'Ruby'

Origin: Raised by Ernest Markham, head gardener at Gravetye Manor.

Parentage and year: Seedling of *C. alpina*. 1937.

Habit: Hardy, quite vigorous, deciduous climber.

Height: 2.5–3 m (8–10 ft.).

Clematis 'Royalty'. Photo by R. Surman.

Clematis 'Ruby'. Photo by R. Surman.

Description: An extremely floriferous cultivar. The single, slightly nodding, dusky mauvish red flowers are composed of four tepals, each 4–5 cm (1.5–2 in.) long. The central tuft of staminodes is off-white and shaded pink. The leaves are midgreen and composed of nine leaflets. The leaf margins are serrated, resembling the teeth of a saw.

Pruning group: 1. Any pruning to keep the plant in check should be carried out immediately after the main flowering period by removing some of the old, flowered stems.

Flowering period: Midspring to late spring. If planted in a sunny position will give some flowers in late summer.

Cultivation: Needs sharp drainage. Suitable for any aspect but produces vibrant flower colour in a sunny position. Useful for north- or east-facing aspects but always better in full sun.

Recommended use: Suitable for a pergola, wall, or container. Grow through a medium-sized tree or large shrub. Zones 3–9.

Clematis 'Rüütel'

Origin: Raised by Uno Kivistik of Harjumaa, Estonia. The name means "knight."

Parentage and year: *C.* 'Ernest Markham' × *C.* 'Valge Daam'. 1980.

Habit: Hardy, moderately vigorous, compact, deciduous climber.

Height: 1.8 m (6 ft.).

Description: A neat and floriferous cultivar. The single flowers, 13–15 cm (5–6 in.) in diameter, carry six to eight crimson tepals, deeply grooved in the middle. Reddish filaments and brown anthers form the central mass of stamens.

Pruning group: 3.

Flowering period: Midsummer to late summer.

Cultivation: Tolerates most garden soils and any aspect.

Recommended use: Allow to grow up and over medium-sized shrubs and conifers. Use as a covering for bare stems of other wall-trained shrubs. Suitable for a small obelisk or a large container. Zones 4–9.

Clematis 'Sander'
HERBACEOUS GROUP

Origin: Raised by Rinus Zwijnenburg of Boskoop, Netherlands.

Parentage and year: Believed to be an open-pollinated seedling of *C. potaninii*, the possible pollen parent being *C. heracleifolia*. 1991.

Habit: Hardy, deciduous, woody, non-clinging, herbaceous subshrub.

Height: 1.8–2.4 m (6–8 ft.). Approximately 0.9 m (3 ft.) if used as ground cover.

Description: The pale white flowers, 3–4 cm (1.25–1.5 in.) wide, are composed of four to six narrow, 5-mm (0.25-in.) long spoon-shaped tepals with a slight blue tinge to the frilly margins. The blunt tips are fully recurved on maturity. White filaments carry pale yellow anthers. The mauvish green stems are ribbed along their length, and the leaves are bluish green.

Pruning group: 3.

Flowering period: Early summer to late summer.

Clematis 'Rüütel'. Photo by J. Lindmark.

Clematis 'Sander'. Photo by C. Chesshire.

Cultivation: Tolerates most garden soils with good drainage. Suitable for any aspect. If trained on an artificial support, the stems need tying-in.

Recommended use: Grow in an island bed over a tripod or allow to scramble at ground level. Zones 4–9.

Clematis 'Sandra Denny'

Origin: Raised by Vince and Sylvia Denny of Denny's Clematis Nursery, Broughton, England.

Parentage and year: *C.* 'Lasurstern' × *C.* 'Twilight'. 1983.

Habit: Hardy, not-too-vigorous, compact, deciduous climber.

Height: 1.8–2.4 m (6–8 ft.).

Description: The large, open, pale lilac flowers, 15–20 cm (6–8 in.) across, are composed of six to eight broad yet pointed tepals which overlap from the base to about halfway along the gently undulating margins. There is a prominent central boss of yellow stamens.

Pruning group: 2.

Flowering period: Late spring to early summer and late summer.

Cultivation: Tolerates most garden soils and any aspect.

Recommended use: Suitable for a medium-sized obelisk or trellis. Grow with other moderately vigorous, wall-trained plants which do not require heavy annual pruning. Zones 4–9.

Clematis 'Satsukibare'

Origin: Raised by Sakuzi Uchida of Japan. The name means "fine weather in May."

Parentage and year: Unknown.

Habit: Hardy, moderately vigorous, deciduous climber.

Height: 2.4–3 m (8–10 ft.).

Description: The single, large, velvety, reddish mauve flowers, 13–18 cm (5–7 in.) across, are composed of six broad, blunt yet pointed tepals, each heavily textured with darker veining radiating from the central three grooves, which run from the base to the tip. The margins carry irregular creasing and possess a crimped appearance. A central boss of stamens comprising pinkish cream filaments and wine-red anthers complements the tepal colouring.

Pruning group: 2.

Flowering period: Midspring to late spring and late summer.

Cultivation: Tolerates most garden soils and any aspect.

Recommended use: Suitable for a pergola, medium-sized trellis, or obelisk. Grow with other wall-trained plants which do not require heavy annual pruning. Zones 4–9.

Clematis 'Saturn'

Origin: Raised by Walter Pennell of Pennell and Sons nursery. Named in 1978 after his death in honour of one of the subjects of his hobby, astronomy.

Parentage and year: *C.* 'Lord Nevill' × *C.* 'Nelly Moser'. 1962.

Habit: Hardy, moderately vigorous, deciduous climber.

Height: 2.4–3 m (8–10 ft.).

Clematis 'Sandra Denny'. Photo by V. Denny.

Clematis 'Satsukibare'. Photo by C. Chesshire.

Description: The single, lavender-blue, large flowers, measuring 13–15 cm (5–6 in.) across, are composed of six to eight tepals, each with a light mauve bar along the centre. The colour of the tepals is set off by stamens with white filaments tipped by dark purple anthers.

Pruning group: 2.

Flowering period: Midspring to late spring and late summer.

Cultivation: Tolerates most garden soils and any aspect.

Recommended use: Suitable for a medium-sized obelisk or trellis. Grow with other wall-trained plants which do not require severe pruning. Zones 4–9.

Clematis 'Scartho Gem'

Origin: Raised by Walter Pennell of Pennell and Sons nursery. Named in 1973 after the nursery where most of the seedlings were grown and selected.

Clematis 'Saturn'. Photo by C. Chesshire.

Parentage and year: *C.* 'Lincoln Star' × *C.* 'Mrs. N. Thompson'. 1962.

Habit: Hardy, moderately vigorous, compact, deciduous climber.

Height: 1.8–2.4 m (6–8 ft.).

Description: A good cultivar bearing two flushes of handsome, single flowers. The somewhat larger, late spring to early summer flowers measure 15–20 cm (6–8 in.) in diameter and are composed of six to eight broad, overlapping, bright pink-cochineal tepals, each with a deeper coloured band along the centre, and gently scalloped edges. Pinkish red anthers and filaments, which form the central mass of stamens, harmonize well with the tepal colour. Spring flowers may be semi-double. Late summer flowers are normally smaller, being 15 cm (6 in.), and paler in colour.

Pruning group: 2.

Flowering period: Late spring to early and late summer.

Cultivation: Tolerates most garden soils and any aspect.

Recommended use: Suitable for a medium-sized obelisk or trellis. Grow with other wall-trained plants which do not require severe pruning. Also grow for container-culture. Zones 4–9.

Clematis 'Sealand Gem'

Origin: Raised by Bees of Chester, England.

Parentage and year: Unknown. 1957.

Habit: Hardy, not-so-vigorous, deciduous climber.

Height: 2.4–3 m (8–10 ft.).

Description: Neither very strong growing nor very

Clematis 'Scartho Gem'. Photo by C. Chesshire.

Clematis 'Sealand Gem'. Photo by Anne Green-Armytage.

floriferous, this cultivar bears single flowers which give the appearance of being semi-double. The flowers, which do not open out fully or flat, measure 13 cm (5 in.) wide and carry six to eight blunt, overlapping, twisted, satiny mauvish blue tepals with irregularly wavy edges and reddish pink central bars. Cream filaments and reddish brown anthers making up the central boss of stamens blend well with the tepal colour.

Pruning group: 2.

Flowering period: Late spring to early summer and early autumn.

Cultivation: Tolerates most garden soils and any aspect.

Recommended use: Suitable for a medium-sized obelisk, trellis, arch, or pergola. Grow with small to medium-sized, moderately vigorous shrubs which do not require pruning. Zones 4–9.

Clematis 'Serenata'

Origin: Raised by Tage Lundell of Helsingborg, Sweden.

Parentage and year: Open-pollinated seedling of *C.* 'Madame Édouard André'. 1960.

Habit: Hardy, moderately vigorous, deciduous climber.

Height: 2.4–3 m (8–10 ft.).

Description: The single flowers, 10–13 cm (4–5 in.) in diameter, carry four to six rich reddish purple tepals, each with a violet-purple central band. They are broad yet tapered at each end, giving the flower an open appearance. White filaments and bright yellow anthers constitute the central mass of prominent stamens, which contrasts well with the tepal colour.

Pruning group: Optional, 2, or 3. For early flowers, do not prune the plant.

Flowering period: Early summer to early autumn.

Cultivation: Tolerates most garden soils and any aspect.

Recommended use: Suitable for a medium-sized pergola, obelisk, or arch. Grow with other moderately vigorous wall-trained shrubs and climbing roses which have similar pruning requirements. Zones 4–9.

Clematis serratifolia
TANGUTICA GROUP

Origin: Korea and northeastern China.

Parentage and year: Species. 1910.

Habit: Hardy, vigorous, deciduous climber or scrambler.

Height: 3–4.6 m (10–14.5 ft.).

Description: The flowers are single, pale yellow, nodding, and 3–4 cm (1.25–1.5 in.) wide. Each of the four tepals opens out fully to expose the central boss of dark purple-violet anthers. The compound leaves consist of nine leaflets and are light green, and the leaf margins are toothed like a saw. Attractive seedheads are produced from autumn through winter.

Pruning group: 3.

Flowering period: Midsummer. Limited to a few weeks only.

Clematis 'Serenata'. Photo by J. Lindmark.

Clematis serratifolia. Photo by C. Chesshire.

Cultivation: Needs sharp drainage. Suitable for sun or partial shade.

Recommended use: Grow through medium-sized trees, conifers, or shrubs. Suitable for a pergola or free-standing trellis. Train along a wall or fence. Zones 3–9.

Clematis 'Sheila Thacker'

Origin: Raised by Charles Thacker of Norfolk, England, and named after his wife.

Parentage and year: Chance seedling of *C.* 'Marie Boisselot'. ca. 1975.

Habit: Hardy, moderately vigorous, compact, deciduous climber.

Height: 2.8–3 m (8–10 ft.).

Description: The single, pale blue flowers, 15–18 cm (6–7 in.) across, are composed of six spear-shaped tepals, which are broadest at the midway point and overlap only near the base. Gently undulating margins and a very faint mauvish tint along the centre of each tepal running from base to tip are complemented by prominent stamens comprising white filaments and midbrown anthers.

Pruning group: 2.

Flowering period: Late spring to early summer and late summer to early autumn.

Cultivation: Tolerates most garden soils and any aspect.

Recommended use: Grow with other wall-trained shrubs and roses which do not require severe pruning.

Suitable for an obelisk, medium-sized trellis, or pergola. Zones 4–9.

Clematis 'Sho-un'

Origin: Raised by Gen Sakurai of Japan. The name means "auspicious clouds."

Parentage and year: Unknown. Mid-1970s.

Habit: Hardy, strong-growing, deciduous climber.

Height: 1.8–2.4 m (6–8 ft.).

Description: A robust cultivar. The large flowers, measuring 20–25 cm (8–10 in.) in diameter, are composed of six to eight overlapping, pointed, pale lavender-blue tepals with deeper blue veining. White filaments and ivory white anthers collectively contrast well with the tepal colour.

Pruning group: Optional, 2, or 3. If flowers are required in late spring, do not prune the plant.

Flowering period: Late spring to late summer.

Cultivation: Tolerates most garden soils and any aspect. Requires protection from strong winds to prevent damage to the large flowers.

Recommended use: Suitable for a medium-sized obelisk or a trellis. Grow as a covering for the bare lower stems of other wall-trained plants. Ideal for container-culture. Zones 4–9.

Clematis sibirica
ATRAGENE GROUP

Origin: North Europe to Siberia.

Parentage and year: Variant of *C. alpina*. 1768.

Habit: Hardy, moderately vigorous, deciduous climber or scrambler.

Clematis 'Sheila Thacker'.
Photo courtesy Thorncroft Clematis Nursery.

Clematis 'Sho-un'. Photo by C. Chesshire.

Height: 1.8–2.4 m (6–8 ft.).

Description: The single, nodding, yellow-white flowers are composed of four tepals, each 5 cm (2 in.) long. The central tuft of staminodes is pale cream. The leaves are lighter green than those of *C. alpina*, and the leaflets are more irregularly toothed.

Pruning group: 1. Any pruning to keep the plant tidy should be carried out immediately after the main flowering period.

Flowering period: Midspring to late spring.

Cultivation: Requires soils with sharp drainage. Suitable for any aspect, especially north- or east-facing aspects.

Recommended use: Grow in a small garden or patio. Ideal in the garden or for container-culture. Zones 3–9.

Clematis 'Sieboldii'

Synonyms: *C. florida* 'Sieboldiana', *C. florida* 'Bicolor'

Origin: Japan.

Parentage and year: Believed to be a sport of *C.* 'Plena'. Introduced by Philipp von Siebold to the Leiden Botanic Garden and arrived in Britain in 1837.

Habit: Half-hardy, slender, normally deciduous climber; under glass may remain semi-evergreen.

Height: 1.2–2.4 m (4–8 ft.).

Description: The handsome flowers, 8–10 cm (3.25–4 in.) across, consist of six basal overlapping tepals, which are creamy white during the summer and creamy green during the autumn. Superimposed over these is a large central boss of purple, streaked with white, petal-like sterile stamens, which stay on the plant for a few days after the main tepals have dropped off. Generally the flowers are sterile, but there have been recorded instances of seed being produced. The flowers are held on long stalks with leaflike bracts halfway along, between the main stems and the flowers. The flowers look somewhat like those of the passion flower (*Passiflora caerulea*) and are produced from old and new wood.

Pruning group: Optional, 2, or 3. A hard pruning (group 3) delays flowering until midsummer.

Flowering period: In the garden, early summer to early autumn; under glass, to late autumn.

Cultivation: Requires a free-draining but moist soil. Best grown in a warm, sheltered position to prevent wind damage to the outer, delicate tepals.

Recommended use: Best grown in a container that can be moved to a frost-free site during the winter months. Looks exceptionally well growing through low to medium-sized shrubs in a well-sheltered garden. Excellent plant for a conservatory. Zones 7–9.

Clematis 'Signe'

Origin: Raised by A. Antonsen of Denmark.

Parentage and year: Unknown. ca. 1983.

Habit: Hardy, moderately vigorous, deciduous climber.

Height: 2.4–3 m (8–10 ft.).

Description: The single, large, flat flowers, 15–20 cm (6–8 in.) across, are composed of six to eight overlapping, pale violet-blue, broad, spear-shaped tepals with central grooving shaded rosy pink running from the base and fading towards the tips. The edges of the tepals

Clematis sibirica. Photo by J. Lindmark.

Clematis 'Sieboldii'. Photo by C. Chesshire.

are also scalloped with textured veining. The stamens are made of whitish pink filaments and pink anthers.

Pruning group: 2.

Flowering period: Midspring to late spring and late summer.

Cultivation: Tolerates most garden soils enriched with humus. Suitable for sun or semi-shade.

Recommended use: Grow on a medium-sized trellis, obelisk, pergola, or arbour. Zones 4–9.

Clematis 'Silver Moon'

Origin: Raised by Percy Picton of Old Court Nurseries, Colwall, England. Introduced by Fisk's Clematis Nursery, Suffolk, England. Awarded RHS Award of Garden Merit.

Parentage and year: Unknown. 1971.

Habit: Hardy, quite vigorous, deciduous climber.

Height: 2.4–3 m (8–10 ft.).

Clematis 'Signe'. Photo courtesy Thorncroft Clematis Nursery.

Clematis 'Silver Moon'. Photo by C. Chesshire.

Description: A strong growing cultivar with a long flowering season. The single flowers, 10–15 cm (4–6 in.) wide, with white filaments and yellow anthers, carry six to eight overlapping, blunt, mother-of-pearl grey tepals, with a satiny sheen.

Pruning group: Optional, 2, or 3. A hard pruning (group 3) results in the loss of early flowers.

Flowering period: Late spring to early autumn.

Cultivation: Tolerates most garden soils and any aspect. For best flower effect, grow in semi-shade or north-facing aspect.

Recommended use: Grow on a medium-sized trellis, obelisk, pergola, or arbour. Zones 4–9.

Clematis 'Sinij Dozhdj'
HERBACEOUS GROUP

Trade name: BLUE RAIN

Origin: Raised by M. A. Beskaravainaja of the State Nikitsky Botanic Gardens, Ukraine. The name means "blue rain."

Parentage and year: Unknown. 1979.

Habit: Hardy, semi-herbaceous, non-clinging, shrubby perennial.

Height: 1.2–1.8 m (4–6 ft.).

Description: The single, violet-blue, bell-shaped, nodding, slightly fragrant flowers, produced in abundance and measuring 5 cm (2 in.) across, are composed

Clematis 'Sinij Dozhdj' (BLUE RAIN™). Photo by C. Chesshire.

of four tepals, each boasting some purple colouring along the middle and pale blue along the margin. The undulating tepals are 3.5 cm (1.25 in.) long and 1.5 cm (0.5 in.) wide, broad at and above the midpoint, tapering towards the base. Greenish filaments and pale yellow anthers make up the stamens. Leaves with five simple leaflets are dark green and somewhat leathery.

Pruning group: 3.

Flowering period: Early summer to late summer.

Cultivation: Tolerates most garden soils and any aspect. If trained on an artificial support, the stems need tying-in.

Recommended use: Grow naturally through medium-sized shrubs with golden foliage or in a herbaceous border. Zones 4–9.

Clematis 'Sir Garnet Wolseley'

Origin: Raised by George Jackman and Son, England.

Parentage and year: Unknown. 1874.

Habit: Hardy, moderately vigorous, compact, deciduous climber.

Height: 1.8–2.4 m (6–8 ft.).

Description: A very early and free-flowering cultivar. The flowers may fail to colour up well if spring is dull, without much sunshine. They are 12.5–15 cm (5–6 in.) in diameter, mauvish blue, and single, with a mass of reddish purple anthers, and are composed of six to eight overlapping tepals, each with a purple band along the centre.

Pruning group: 2.

Flowering period: Late spring to early summer and late summer.

Cultivation: Tolerates most garden soils and any aspect.

Recommended use: Suitable for a small garden. Grow on a small to medium-sized obelisk or trellis. Ideal for container-culture. Zones 4–9.

Clematis 'Sir Trevor Lawrence'
TEXENSIS-VIORNA GROUP

Synonym: *C. texensis* 'Sir Trevor Lawrence'

Origin: Raised by George Jackman and Son, England, and named after a former president (1885–1913) of the Royal Horticultural Society.

Parentage and year: *C. texensis* × *C.* 'Star of India'. 1890.

Habit: Hardy, deciduous climber. Normally of herbaceous habit with shoots emerging from below ground level.

Height: 2.5–3 m (8–10 ft.).

Description: The single, 5-cm (2-in.) long, tuliplike flowers are composed of four dark purple-red, pointed tepals with scarlet central bars. The outer surface of the tepals ranges in colour from whitish pink to reddish pink dictated by the amount of exposure to sunshine. Deep pink veins extend along the length of the tepals. As the flower matures, the tips of the tepals recurve to expose the yellow anthers.

Pruning group: 3.

Flowering period: Midsummer to early autumn.

Clematis 'Sir Garnet Wolseley'. Photo by E. Leeds.

Clematis 'Sir Trevor Lawrence'. Photo by E. Leeds.

Cultivation: Tolerates most garden soils. Can be planted in sun or partial shade. Prone to mildew. Take early precaution by spraying with a fungicide monthly from late spring. New shoots at soil level need protection from slugs and snails.

Recommended use: Grow naturally over ground-cover shrubs, prostrate conifers, and a low wall where the upright, well-held flowers can be appreciated. Train as specimen plant on a small to medium-sized obelisk or trellis. Shows up well against a light background. Zones 4–9.

Clematis 'Snow Queen'

Origin: Raised by W. S. Callick. Named and introduced into commerce by Alister Keay of New Zealand Clematis Nurseries, Christchurch, in 1958.

Parentage and year: Unknown, chance seedling. 1956.

Habit: Hardy, moderately vigorous, compact, deciduous climber.

Height: 1.8–2.4 m (6–8 ft.).

Description: The single flowers, 15–18 cm (6–7 in.) in diameter, carry six to eight overlapping, pointed, blue white tepals, which fade to pure white as the flower matures. The tepals boast a textured, deeply ribbed surface, with a rippling effect, and taper to blunt tips. Upon second flowering, the tepals are a pinky white, later fading to pure white. The stamens are made of pale pink filaments and dark red anthers.

Pruning group: 2.

Flowering period: Late spring to early summer and late summer.

Clematis 'Snow Queen'. Photo by M. Toomey.

Cultivation: Tolerates most garden soils and any aspect.

Recommended use: Excellent against a dark background. Suitable for a medium-sized obelisk or trellis. Ideal for container-culture. Grow with other wall-trained shrubs and roses. Zones 4–9.

Clematis 'Snowbird'
ATRAGENE GROUP

Synonym: *C. macropetala* 'Snowbird'

Origin: Raised by Barry Fretwell of Peveril Clematis Nursery, England.

Parentage and year: Unknown. 1969.

Habit: Hardy, not-so-vigorous, compact, deciduous climber.

Height: To 2 m (6.5 ft.).

Description: The double, nodding and semi-nodding, pure white flowers are composed of four broad yet pointed, base tepals, each 4.5–5 cm (1.75–2 in.) long. Inside these are approximately 14–16 narrower and more pointed staminodes, which surround an inner tuft of fertile stamens tinged with green. Leaves are pale green, and new growths and stems are yellow green.

Pruning group: 1.

Flowering period: Late spring, with some flowers in late summer.

Cultivation: Needs sharp drainage. Suitable for any aspect.

Recommended use: Good for a small garden. Ideal against a dark background. Suitable for container-culture and growing over a low wall. Zones 3–9.

Clematis 'Snowdrift'
EVERGREEN/ARMANDII GROUP

Synonym: *C. armandii* 'Snowdrift'

Origin: Raised by George Jackman and Son, England. Awarded RHS Award of Garden Merit.

Parentage and year: Selected form of *C. armandii*.

Habit: Half-hardy to hardy, vigorous, evergreen climber.

Height: To 6 m (20 ft.) or more.

Description: The single, flat, pure white flowers, 6–7.5 cm (2.25–3 in.) across, are composed of four to six overlapping tepals with pointed tips. The anthers are creamy white. The leaves are bright, dark green, and glossy.

Clematis 'Snowbird'. Photo courtesy Thorncroft Clematis Nursery.

Pruning group: 1.

Flowering period: Early spring to midspring.

Cultivation: Tolerates most garden soils with good drainage. Requires a warm, frost-free location with protection from cold winds.

Recommended use: Grow against a sheltered, warm, south- or southwest-facing wall or fence. Place it carefully in the garden, as it loses some of its leaves in summer. Zones 7–9.

Clematis socialis
HERBACEOUS GROUP

Origin: Southeastern United States (Alabama).

Parentage and year: Species. 1982.

Habit: Slender, erect, non-climbing, herbaceous perennial.

Height: 30–60 cm (12–24 in.).

Description: The solitary, rounded, bell-shaped, vio-let-blue flowers on long, hairy stalks are composed of four distinctly ribbed tepals, each 2–2.5 cm (0.75–1 in.) long, with a gently recurving pointed tip and yellowish green on the inner surface. The stamens are yellowish, and the outer ones are somewhat longer. The leaves are pale green, long and narrow, simple or divided into leaflets arranged in pairs on either side of the main stalk. An extensive system of creeping underground rhizomes gives rise to aerial stems at intervals, forming patches of plants rather than clumps.

Pruning group: 3.

Flowering period: Midspring to late spring.

Cultivation: Rare in cultivation. Prefers sharp drainage and moderately dry conditions. Drought-resistant.

Recommended use: Grow as a specimen plant in an alpine bed or cool greenhouse. Zones 5–9.

Clematis 'Södertälje'
VITICELLA GROUP

Synonym: *C. viticella* 'Södertälje'

Origin: Raised by Magnus Johnson of Södertälje, Sweden.

Parentage and year: Selected seedling of *C.* 'Grandiflora Sanguinea' (Viticella Group). 1952.

Habit: Hardy, strong-growing, deciduous climber.

Height: 3–4 m (10–13 ft.).

Description: The single, semi-nodding, gappy, pinkish red flowers, 5–7.5 cm (2–3 in.) across, are composed of four to six tepals with recurving tips. The anthers are yellowish green.

Pruning group: 3.

Flowering period: Midsummer to early autumn.

Clematis 'Snowdrift'. Photo by C. Chesshire.

Clematis socialis. Photo by J. Pringle.

Clematis 'Södertälje'. Photo by J. Lindmark.

Cultivation: Tolerates most garden soils and any aspect, but best colour is achieved in sun or semi-shade.

Recommended use: Ideal for growing through medium-sized trees, prostrate conifers, and large, open shrubs such as rhododendron. Zones 3–9.

Clematis songarica
HERBACEOUS GROUP

Origin: Russia, Mongolia, southern Siberia, Turkistan, Korea, and northwestern China. Named after the region of Dzungaria (Songaria) in northwestern China.

Parentage and year: Species. 1839.

Habit: Hardy, non-clinging, deciduous subshrub.

Height: 0.9–1.2 m (3–4 ft.).

Description: The single, starlike, scented, cream or pure white flowers, 2.5–3.5 cm (1–1.25 in.) across, are borne on terminal shoots and in leaf axils. Each flower consists of four to six narrow, widely spreading tepals, which are downy on the outside, smooth or slightly hairy on the inside, and open flat on reaching maturity. The leaves are grey or blue green and lance shaped, with margins coarsely toothed or sometimes smooth. White filaments and cream anthers make up the stamens.

Pruning group: 3.

Flowering period: Midsummer to late summer.

Cultivation: Tolerates most garden soils but prefers sharp drainage and some sun. If trained on an artificial support, the stems need tying-in.

Recommended use: Grow against a wall or over a low artificial support. If space permits, allow it to ramble. Zones 6–9.

Clematis 'Special Occasion'

Origin: Raised by Ken Pyne of Chingford, London.

Parentage and year: Open-pollinated seedling of *C.* 'Mrs. Cholmondeley'. Introduced in 1995.

Habit: Hardy, not very vigorous, compact, deciduous climber.

Height: 1.5–1.8 m (5–6 ft.).

Description: A free-flowering cultivar. The single flowers, 10–15 cm (4–6 in.) in diameter, are composed of six to eight rounded, pale bluish pink tepals, each with lighter colouring along the centre. The tepals are distinguished by a pronounced ribbing. The dark

Clematis songarica, growing through *Fuchsia magellanica* 'Riccartonii'. Photo by C. Chesshire.

Clematis 'Special Occasion'. Photo by E. Leeds.

brown anthers carried on white filaments contrast elegantly with the tepal colour.

Pruning group: 2. Since this cultivar flowers on short growths produced from the previous season's stems, it should be pruned immediately after the main flowering period, to encourage young fresh growths from lower down the plant.

Flowering period: Late spring to late summer.

Cultivation: Tolerates most garden soils and any aspect.

Recommended use: Ideal for container-culture or for covering the bare lower stems of wall-trained, moderately vigorous climbers or shrubs. Grow up and over small to medium-size, prostrate shrubs which do not require severe pruning. Also grow with low-growing conifers. Zones 4–9.

Clematis spooneri
MONTANA GROUP

Synonym: *C. montana* var. *sericea*

Origin: Southwestern China and neighbouring parts of Tibet. Awarded RHS Award of Garden Merit.

Parentage and year: Species. 1890s.

Habit: Vigorous, deciduous climber.

Height: 6–9 m (20–29 ft.).

Description: The single, sparkling white flowers, 7–9

Clematis spooneri. Photo by R. Surman.

cm (2.75–3.5 in.) across, are borne in profusion and on long flower stalks up to 19 cm (7.5 in.) long. The four tepals, which are longer than broad, occasionally boast a slight pink flush along the centre. The stamens are creamy white, and the young stems and buds are clothed in golden down. The leaves and leaflets are somewhat hairier than those of *C. montana*.

Pruning group: 1.

Flowering period: Late spring to early summer.

Cultivation: Needs sharp drainage. Suitable for sun or partial shade.

Recommended use: Grow along a wall or fence. May be allowed to roam into trees or large, robust shrubs which do not require annual pruning. Zones 7–9.

Clematis 'Sputnik'

Origin: Raised by M. Orlov, Central Republic Botanical Garden of the Ukrainian Academy of Sciences, Kiev, Russia.

Parentage and year: *C.* 'Gipsy Queen' × *C.* 'Durandii'. 1964.

Habit: Hardy, vigorous, deciduous climber.

Height: 2.4–3 m (8–10 ft.).

Description: The single, 10- to 12.5-cm (4- to 5-in.) diameter flowers of many shades of blue, are composed of four to six, non-overlapping, spear-shaped tepals, each with two or three central ridges running from base to tip, and heavily textured, crinkled margins. Pale greenish filaments and dark mauve anthers make up the stamens.

Pruning group: 2.

Flowering period: Early summer to early autumn.

Clematis 'Sputnik'. Photo by C. Chesshire.

Cultivation: Tolerates most garden soils. Prefers sun or partial shade.

Recommended use: Suitable for a medium-sized obelisk, trellis, arbour, or pergola. Zones 4–9.

Clematis stans

HERBACEOUS GROUP

Origin: Japan. Introduced by Phillip von Siebold, director of the Leiden Botanic Garden.

Parentage and year: Species. ca. 1860.

Habit: Hardy, deciduous, non-clinging, woody-based, herbaceous subshrub.

Height: 0.9–1.2 m (3–4 ft.).

Description: The single, long, tubular, hyacinth-like flowers are borne in abundance on branched stalks, each 2–2.5 cm (0.75–1 in.) long, with four pointed tepals which strongly recurve with age. The colour can vary from plant to plant, being very pale blue, almost white, to pale lavender-blue with a paler centre. The flowers are somewhat hairy on the outside. The stamens, about half the length of the tepals, boast white filaments and yellow anthers. Some clones have very congested flower heads, others more open, and some forms are scented. Male or female flowers may be on the same or different plants.

Pruning group: 3.

Flowering period: Midsummer to early autumn.

Cultivation: Tolerates most garden soils with good drainage and some moisture. Young plants may require staking.

Recommended use: Plant towards the back of a mixed or herbaceous border. Zones 4–9.

Clematis 'Star of India'

Origin: Raised by Thomas Cripps and Son of Tunbridge Wells, England. The cultivar by this name in Japan is believed to be different from the 'Star of India' that is grown and sold elsewhere. Awarded RHS Award of Garden Merit.

Parentage and year: *C. lanuginosa* × *C.* 'Jackmanii'. Introduced in 1867.

Habit: Hardy, vigorous, deciduous climber.

Height: 3–3.6 m (10–12 ft.).

Description: The single, blue-purple flowers, measuring 10–12.5 cm (4–5 in.) across, are composed of four to six tepals, each with a cerise central bar. The tepals have rounded edges, which taper to blunt tips, and have a textured surface with reddish veins radiating from the central bars. The stamens are made of creamy white filaments and dark brown anthers.

Pruning group: 3.

Clematis stans. Photo by J. Lindmark.

Clematis 'Star of India'. Photo by J. Lindmark.

Flowering period: Midsummer to early autumn.

Cultivation: Tolerates most garden soils and any aspect. Prone to mildew. Take early precaution by spraying with a fungicide monthly.

Recommended use: Grow through medium-sized to large shrubs and conifers. Ideal for a pergola, obelisk, or arbour. Zones 4–9.

Clematis 'Strawberry Roan'

Origin: Unknown.

Parentage and year: Unknown.

Habit: Hardy, moderately vigorous, deciduous climber.

Height: 1.8–2.4 m (6–8 ft.).

Description: The single flowers, 12.5–15 cm (5–6 in.) in diameter, are composed of six to eight mauvish pink overlapping tepals, each with a deeper pink colouring along the centre. The stamens are made of cream filaments and pink anthers.

Pruning group: Optional, 2, or 3. A hard pruning (group 3) results in the loss of early flowers.

Flowering period: Midspring to late spring and late summer.

Cultivation: Tolerates most garden soils. Best grown out of full sun to preserve flower colour.

Recommended use: Ideal for container-culture. Suitable for a medium-sized obelisk or trellis. Zone: 4–9.

Clematis 'Sunset'

Origin: Raised by Arthur H. Steffen of Fairport, New York.

Parentage and year: Unknown.

Habit: Hardy, moderately vigorous, compact, deciduous climber.

Height: 1.8–2.4 m (6–8 ft.).

Description: The very freely borne deep reddish purple-pink, single flowers, 10–12.5 cm (4–5 in.) wide, are composed of six to eight lightly textured tepals, which taper towards the tips. Each tepal boasts a satin, cerise central bar. The butter-yellow anthers contrast neatly with the tepal colour.

Pruning group: 2.

Flowering period: Early summer to late summer.

Cultivation: Tolerates most garden soils and any aspect.

Recommended use: Ideal for a small to medium-sized obelisk or trellis. Grow through medium-sized shrubs which require little or no pruning. Suitable for short-term container-culture. Zones 4–9.

Clematis 'Susan Allsop'

Origin: Raised by Walter Pennell of Pennell and Sons nursery. Named in 1973 after a nursery employee who was closely involved in carrying out pollination work with Walter Pennell.

Parentage and year: *C.* 'Beauty of Worcester' × *C.* 'King Edward VII'. 1962.

Habit: Hardy, moderately vigorous, deciduous climber.

Height: 1.8–2.4 m (6–8 ft.).

Description: The single, rosy purple flowers, 15–20 cm (6–8 in.) in diameter, are composed of six to eight tepals, each with a red central bar. The flowers are set off by contrasting golden anthers.

Clematis 'Strawberry Roan'. Photo by R. Savill.

Clematis 'Sunset'. Photo by C. Chesshire.

Pruning group: Optional, 2, or 3. A hard pruning (group 3) results in the loss of early flowers.

Flowering period: Late spring to late summer.

Cultivation: Tolerates most garden soils and any aspect.

Recommended use: Suitable for growing on a small obelisk or trellis. Ideal for container-culture. If pruning group 3 is chosen, grow up and over medium-sized shrubs and prostrate conifers. Zones 4–9.

Clematis 'Sylvia Denny'

Origin: Raised by Vince and Sylvia Denny of Denny's Clematis Nursery, Broughton, England.

Parentage and year: *C.* 'Marie Boisselot' × *C.* 'Duchess of Edinburgh'. Introduced in 1983.

Habit: Hardy, moderately vigorous, compact, deciduous climber.

Height: 1.8–2.4 m (6–8 ft.).

Description: The neatly formed, camellia-like, 10- to 12.5-cm (4- to 5-in.) wide, semi-double flowers are produced on the previous season's old wood. A distinguishing feature of this white-flowered cultivar is the absence of any greening in the tepals. The central boss of stamens is creamy yellow. Single flowers are produced on the current season's new wood.

Pruning group: 2.

Flowering period: Late spring to early summer (semi-double) and late summer to early autumn (single).

Cultivation: Tolerates most garden soils. Suitable for full or partial sun. Requires protection from strong winds.

Recommended use: Grow on a small to medium-sized obelisk or trellis. Ideal for container-culture. Shows up best against a dark background. Zones 4–9.

Clematis 'Sympatia'

Synonym: *C.* 'Sympathia'

Origin: Raised by Brother Stefan Franczak of Warsaw, Poland.

Parentage and year: Unknown. 1990.

Habit: Hardy, moderately vigorous, compact, deciduous climber.

Height: 1.8–2.4 m (6–8 ft.).

Description: The single, rosy lilac flowers, 15–20 cm

Clematis 'Sylvia Denny'. Photo by V. Denny.

Clematis 'Susan Allsop'. Photo by C. Chesshire.

Clematis 'Sympatia'. Photo by J. Lindmark.

(6–8 in.) wide, are composed of six to eight tepals and a central boss of reddish brown stamens.

Pruning group: 2.

Flowering period: Early summer to late summer.

Cultivation: Tolerates most garden soils and any aspect.

Recommended use: Ideal for container-culture and growing on a small to medium-sized trellis or obelisk. Zones 4–9.

Clematis 'Tage Lundell'
ATRAGENE GROUP

Origin: Raised by Tage Lundell of Helsingborg, Sweden.

Parentage and year: *C. ochotensis* × *C. alpina*. 1970.

Habit: Hardy, moderately vigorous, deciduous climber.

Clematis 'Tage Lundell'. Photo by R. Surman.

Height: 2.5–3 m (8–10 ft.).

Description: The dark plum purple flowers are composed of four tepals, each 4–5 cm (1.5–2 in.) long. There is an inner skirt of mauvish pink petal-like staminodes, which confer a double appearance on the flower. The leaves are an attractive midgreen.

Pruning group: 1.

Flowering period: Midspring to late spring.

Cultivation: Needs sharp drainage. Suitable for any aspect. Tolerates cold, windy situations.

Recommended use: Ideal for a small garden. Suitable for a pergola or trellis. May be allowed to roam in medium-sized trees or large shrubs which can support the top growth. Zones 3–9.

Clematis 'Tango'
VITICELLA GROUP

Synonym: *C. viticella* 'Tango'

Origin: Raised by Barry Fretwell of Peveril Clematis Nursery, England.

Parentage and year: Unknown. 1986.

Habit: Hardy, vigorous, deciduous climber.

Height: 3–4 m (10–13 ft.).

Description: The single, somewhat rounded flowers, 5 cm (2 in.) across, are composed of four or five white tepals, each with wide crimson margins and deep pink veining towards the centre from the sides, and down the midrib. Green filaments carry brown anthers. Handsome midgreen leaves are composed of five to seven leaflets.

Pruning group: 3.

Flowering period: Midsummer to early autumn.

Clematis 'Tango'. Photo by E. Leeds.

Cultivation: Tolerates most garden soils and any aspect.

Recommended use: Grow naturally through medium-sized trees, large shrubs, climbing roses and conifers. Suitable for a large pergola, obelisk, or trellis. Ideal for growing with spring-flowering plants, thus bringing later flowering interest and colour. Zones 3–9.

Clematis tangutica
TANGUTICA GROUP

Synonym: *C. orientalis* var. *tangutica*

Origin: Northwestern China, the Tangut region of Tibet (hence its name), northern India, and Mongolia.

Parentage and year: Species. 1898.

Habit: Hardy, vigorous, deciduous climber.

Height: To 6 m (20 ft.).

Description: The single, solitary, pendulous, bell- to lantern-shaped, golden yellow flowers with a silky sheen are not fully open. They consist of four tepals, each 2.5–4 cm (1–1.5 in.) long, pointed, very slightly spreading, with small hairs on the outside, and smooth and shiny inside. The leaves are bright green and compound; the leaflets have margins coarsely toothed and teeth pointing outward. The attractive seedheads are produced from autumn through winter.

Pruning group: 3.

Flowering period: Early summer to late summer.

Cultivation: Needs sharp drainage. Suitable for sun or partial shade.

Recommended use: Grow through medium-sized to large shrubs, trees, or conifers. Useful for covering expansive wall spaces. May be grown to form mounds of foliage, flowers, and seedheads at ground level, in large gardens. Suitable for a large pergola or free-standing trellis. Zones 4–9.

Clematis tangutica subsp. *obtusiuscula*
TANGUTICA GROUP

Origin: China.

Parentage and year: A subspecies of *C. tangutica*. Introduced by Ernest Wilson in 1908.

Habit: Hardy, moderately vigorous, deciduous climber.

Height: 3–4 m (10–13 ft.).

Clematis tangutica. Photo by J. Lindmark.

Clematis tangutica. Photo by C. Sanders.

Description: The single, solitary, rich yellow flowers, somewhat tight and globular at first but spreading and opening widely with age, are composed of four tepals, each 3 cm (1. 25 in.) long. Young shoots are downy. The leaflets are smaller and the leaf margins not as heavily toothed as those of the species. The seedheads are attractive. In the absence of similar species in the vicinity, seed of this subspecies will come true.

Pruning group: 3.

Flowering period: Midsummer to midautumn.

Cultivation: Requires well-drained soil. Suitable for any aspect.

Recommended use: Ideal for a small garden. Suitable for a large obelisk, free-standing trellis, or a low wall or fence. Zones 4–9.

Clematis 'Tapestry'
HERBACEOUS/INTEGRIFOLIA GROUP

Synonym: *C. integrifolia* 'Tapestry'

Origin: Raised by Barry Fretwell of Peveril Clematis Nursery, England.

Parentage and year: Unknown. Mid-1980s.

Habit: Hardy, deciduous, non-clinging, herbaceous perennial.

Height: 0.6–0.9 m (2–3 ft.).

Description: The nodding, single, bell-shaped flowers, 6 cm (2.25 in.) across, are composed of four mid-mauve tepals, each with a brighter colour on the inside and shallow ribbing from the base to the tip. The outside of the tepal is more red, the deepest colouring being on the raised ribbing. The margins are lighter in colour and are delicately notched. Thick pale creamy white filaments and yellow anthers distinguish the flower.

Pruning group: 3.

Flowering period: Early summer to late summer.

Cultivation: Tolerates most garden soils enriched with humus. May need some support—pea-sticks are ideal and unobtrusive. Suitable for any aspect.

Recommended use: Ideal at the front of or in the middle of a herbaceous border. Zones 3–9.

Clematis 'Tartu'

Origin: Raised by Uno Kivistik of Harjumaa, Estonia, and named after an Estonian town.

Parentage and year: Open-pollinated seedling of *C.* 'Devjatyj Val'. 1983.

Habit: Hardy, moderately vigorous, compact, deciduous climber.

Height: 1.5–1.8 m (5–6 ft.).

Description: The single, bluish purple flowers, 10–15 cm (4–6 in.) wide, are composed of four to six tepals. Cream filaments and pale yellow anthers make up the contrasting stamens.

Pruning group: 2.

Flowering period: Late spring to early summer and late summer.

Clematis tangutica subsp. *obtusiuscula*. Photo by C. Chesshire.

Clematis 'Tapestry'. Photo by C. Chesshire.

Cultivation: Tolerates most garden soils and any aspect.

Recommended use: Ideal for container-culture. Grow over prostrate conifers and shrubs. Suitable for a small obelisk or trellis. Zones 4–9.

Clematis 'Teksa'

Origin: Raised by Uno Kivistik of Harjumaa, Estonia. The name is Estonian for "denim."

Parentage and year: Chance seedling of *C.* 'Ernest Markham'. 1981.

Habit: Hardy, not very vigorous, compact, deciduous climber.

Height: 1.5–1.8 m (5–6 ft.).

Description: The single, pale bluish mauve flowers, 10–14 cm (4–5.5 in.) across, are composed of six broad tepals with gently undulating margins. The tepals are heavily textured, with streaks of mauve running down the centre from base to tip, and the whole is overlaid with paler blue and whitish spots. The stamens are made of greenish cream filaments and pink anthers.

Pruning group: 3.

Flowering period: Midsummer to late summer.

Cultivation: Tolerates most garden soils and any aspect.

Recommended use: Ideal for container-culture or for growing over low, open shrubs and conifers. Suitable for a small obelisk or trellis. Zones 3–9.

Clematis 'Tentel'

Origin: Raised by Uno Kivistik of Harjumaa, Estonia. The name comes from a children's nursery rhyme.

Parentage and year: Chance seedling of *C.* 'Jubileijnyj-70'. 1984.

Habit: Hardy, not very vigorous, compact, deciduous climber.

Height: 1.8–2.4 m (6–8 ft.).

Description: The single, rosy lavender flowers, 5–8 cm (2–3.25 in.) across, are composed of six overlapping and pointed tepals, each with frilly and serrated margins, with a lighter shaded bar running from the

Clematis 'Teksa'. Photo by E. Leeds.

Clematis 'Tartu'. Photo by V. Miettinen.

Clematis 'Tentel'.
Photo courtesy British Clematis Society Slide Library.

base to the tip. The reverse has a pronounced ribbed rose bar, and the stamens are yellow.

Pruning group: 3.

Flowering period: Midsummer to late summer.

Cultivation: Tolerates most garden soils enriched with humus. Any aspect.

Recommended use: Ideal for container-culture or for covering the bare stems of other wall-trained climbers. Grow through medium-sized prostrate conifers or shrubs. Allow to tumble over a low wall. Zones 3–9.

Clematis terniflora
EVERGREEN GROUP

Common name: Sweet autumn clematis

Synonym: *C. maximowicziana*

Origin: China, Taiwan, Korea, and Japan.

Parentage and year: Species. 1818.

Habit: Hardy, strong-growing, vigorous, deciduous (sometimes semi-evergreen) climber.

Height: 10 m (30 ft.) or more.

Description: Large clusters of hawthorn-scented, single, starlike, white flowers, 1.5–3 cm (0.5–1.25 in.) across, are borne in leaf axils on the current year's new growth. Each flower is composed of four tepals, which are narrow, spreading widely apart, longer than broad, and hairy on the outside. The stamens carry greenish cream filaments and yellow anthers. The stems are grooved, hairy when young, and becoming semi-woody with age. The leaves are dark green, divided into leaflets arranged in pairs on either side of the leaf axis or, occasionally, trifoliate carrying three leaflets on long leaf stalks.

Pruning group: 3.

Flowering period: Late summer to midautumn.

Cultivation: Tolerates most well-drained garden soils. Prefers dry sites. Must have a warm to hot location with plenty of sunshine to flower well or at all. Does exceptionally well in the gardens of eastern United States.

Recommended use: Not for very cold and exposed gardens. Suitable for covering a warm, south-facing

Clematis terniflora. Photo by E. Leeds.

wall or fence. Allow it to scramble into medium-sized to large trees or shrubs. Zones 5–9.

Clematis 'Teshio'

Origin: Raised by Tasuku Taneko of Japan. Named after an area of Hokkaido Island in the northernmost part of Japan.

Parentage and year: Unknown.

Habit: Hardy, moderately vigorous, compact, deciduous climber.

Height: 1.8–2.4 m (6–8 ft.).

Description: The unusual spiderlike buds unfurl to expose fully double flowers, which are 7–10 cm (2.75–4 in.) across, and composed of layers of slim, pear-shaped, lavender-blue tepals giving the flower a spiky appearance The stamens are made of white filaments and dark purple anthers.

Pruning group: 2.

Flowering period: Late spring to early summer and late summer.

Cultivation: Tolerates most garden soils. Best grown in full sun or semi-shade. Requires protection from strong winds.

Recommended use: Suitable for a small obelisk or trellis. Ideal for container-culture. Zones 4–9.

Clematis 'Tetrarose'

MONTANA GROUP

Synonym: *C. montana* 'Tetrarose'

Origin: Raised at the Boskoop Research Station, Netherlands.

Parentage and year: Selected tetraploid form of *C. montana* var. *rubens*. 1960.

Habit: Vigorous, deciduous climber.

Height: To 8 m (26 ft.).

Description: The single, large flowers, to 7.5 cm (3 in.) across, are a rich, deep mauve pink and have a spicy scent. The four tepals are thick, with a satin sheen, and keep a slightly cupped shape even when mature. The stamens are golden yellow. The leaves are large and divided into three bronzy green leaflets. The stems are reddish brown.

Pruning group: 1. Any pruning to keep the plant in check should be carried out immediately after the main flowering period by removing some of the old, flowered stems.

Flowering period: Late spring to early summer.

Cultivation: Prefers sun or semi-shade. Keep clear of frost pockets.

Recommended use: Grow through medium-sized to large trees and conifers, along a boundary wall or fence, over a pergola or trellis. Zones 7–9.

Clematis 'Teshio'. Photo by M. Humphries.

Clematis 'Tetrarose'. Photo by R. Surman.

Clematis texensis
TEXENSIS-VIORNA GROUP

Origin: United States (northeastern Texas).

Parentage and year: Species. First mentioned in 1862.

Habit: Slender, herbaceous climber.

Height: 2 m (6.5 ft.).

Description: The single, 3- to 4-cm (1.25- to 1.5-in.) long, solitary, semi-nodding flowers are urn shaped and distinctly narrowed towards the mouth. They are carried on long, ribbed stalks. The four thick, almost fused tepals are scarlet red with recurving tips. The colour may vary through crimson to scarlet orange. The undersides of the tepals can be pink or cream, and the stamens are yellow. The margins of the tepals are white and densely covered in short fine hairs. The sea-green stems are slender, ribbed, and smooth. The compound, grey-green leaves are made of four or five pairs of leaflets with rounded to heart-shaped bases, short, sharp-pointed tips, and a fine network of veins. The terminal leaflet is reduced to a tendril-like structure. The seedheads are large; the achene bodies are disc-shaped and prominently rimmed.

Pruning group: 3.

Flowering period: Midsummer to early autumn.

Cultivation: Requires an alkaline or neutral soil with sharp drainage. Prefers sun or partial shade. Container-grown plants in a conservatory or cold greenhouse retain some top growth throughout winter. Prone to mildew attack. Take early precaution by spraying with a fungicide monthly from the end of spring to the end of the flowering period. Best to protect the root crown with light mulch during severe cold weather. New shoots at soil level need protection from slugs and snails.

Recommended use: Ideal for container-culture or a small obelisk. Once the plant is well established in a container, it may be planted out to grow naturally over low shrubs and conifers or to tumble over a low retaining wall. Zones 4–9.

Clematis 'The Bride'

Origin: Raised by George Jackman and Son, England.

Parentage and year: Unknown.

Habit: Hardy, moderately vigorous, deciduous climber.

Height: 1.8–2.4 m (6–8 ft.).

Description: The single, somewhat small, elegant, cup-shaped, ivory white flowers, measuring 7.5–10 cm (3–4 in.) in diameter, are composed of six to eight overlapping, rounded but pointed tepals. The stamens are made of creamy yellow filaments and anthers.

Pruning group: 2.

Flowering period: Late spring to late summer.

Cultivation: Tolerates most garden soils. Best grown out of full sun.

Recommended use: Ideal for container-culture. Grow through medium-sized shrubs which require ittle or no pruning. Suitable for an obelisk or trellis. Zones 4–9.

Clematis 'The First Lady'

Origin: Raised by Arthur H. Steffen of Fairport, New York.

Parentage and year: Unknown (chance seedling). Mid-1970s.

Clematis texensis. Photo by J. Pringle.

Clematis 'The Bride'. Photo by C. Chesshire.

Habit: Hardy, moderately vigorous, deciduous climber.

Height: 2.1–2.7 m (7–8 ft.).

Description: The single, very large, silvery lavender-blue flowers, measuring 20–25 cm (8–10 in.) across, are composed of six to eight pointed, overlapping tepals with deeply notched margins. In juvenile flowers there is a shading of pink along the centre of each tepal, which fades to a lighter shade of lavender blue on maturity. Prominent stamens carry reddish purple filaments and anthers.

Pruning group: 2.

Flowering period: Late spring to early summer and late summer.

Cultivation: Tolerates most garden soils and any aspect. Requires a sheltered position to prevent wind damage to the large flowers.

Recommended use: Suitable for a medium-sized to large obelisk, trellis, arbour, or pergola. Grow up and over large shrubs which require little or no pruning. Zones 4–9.

Clematis 'The President'

Origin: Raised by Charles Noble of Sunningdale, England.

Parentage and year: *C.* 'Jackmanii' × *C. lanuginosa*. Introduced 1876.

Habit: Hardy, moderately vigorous, deciduous climber.

Height: 2.4–3 m (8–10 ft.).

Description: The single, rich purple blue, and somewhat cupped flowers, 15–17 cm (6–7 in.) across, are composed of six to eight overlapping and pointed tepals with undulating edges and silvery undersides. The conspicuous and contrasting stamens are made of pinkish white filaments and deep red anthers. The juvenile leaves are bronzy, becoming dark green with age. This cultivar is extremely popular.

Pruning group: 2.

Flowering period: Late spring to early summer and late summer to early autumn.

Cultivation: Tolerates most garden soils and any aspect.

Recommended use: Ideal against a pillar or on a pergola, arch, large trellis, or obelisk. May be grown with

Clematis 'The President'.
Photo courtesy Thorncroft Clematis Nursery.

Clematis 'The First Lady'. Photo by C. Chesshire.

large shrubs or conifers which have light-coloured foliage and which do not require severe pruning or regular clipping, respectively. Zones 4–9.

Clematis 'The Vagabond'

Origin: Raised by Ken Pyne of Chingford, London. Introduced jointly in 1993 by Caddick's and Priorswood Nurseries.

Parentage and year: Seed of *C.* 'Rouge Cardinal' set in October 1984.

Habit: Hardy, moderately vigorous, compact, deciduous climber.

Height: 1.5–1.8 m (5–6 ft.).

Description: The single flowers, 13–15 cm (5–6 in.) in diameter, are composed of usually six, sometimes eight, pointed tepals with undulating margins. On initial opening they are very deep purple, almost black in colour. When fully open they are deep purple at the margins, shading to crimson at the centre. The stamens are made of white filaments and deep creamy yellow contrasting anthers.

Pruning group: 2.

Flowering period: Late spring to early summer and late summer to early autumn.

Cultivation: Tolerates most garden soils and any aspect.

Recommended use: Ideal for container-culture. Grow on a small obelisk or trellis. Zones 4–9.

Clematis 'Thyrislund'

Origin: Found growing unnamed in a Danish nursery by Flemming Hansen of Denmark. Possibly of British origin.

Parentage and year: Unknown.

Habit: Hardy, not-so-vigorous, compact, deciduous climber.

Height: 2.4–3 m (8–10 ft.).

Description: The pinkish mauve, double flowers, borne early in the season from the previous season's old wood, are 14–15 cm (5.5–6 in.) wide, and are composed of an outer row of eight incurving, slightly broad but pointed tepals upon which are arranged two or three more layers of shorter, narrower, incurving, and pointed tepals of a similar colour. All tepals are gently scalloped or deeply notched at the edges. The stamens carry yellow filaments and anthers. Single flowers are produced upon second flowering from the current season's new wood. Early flowers on old wood may be single.

Pruning group: 2.

Flowering period: Late spring to early summer (double) and late summer (single).

Cultivation: Tolerates most garden soils and any aspect.

Recommended use: Ideal for container-culture although regular feeding and annual top dressing are essential for the plant to grow and flower well. Grow also on a small to medium-sized obelisk, trellis, or arch. Zones 3–9.

Clematis tibetana subsp. *vernayi*
TANGUTICA GROUP

Origin: Tibet and Nepal.

Parentage and year: A subspecies of *C. tibetana*. 1937.

Habit: Hardy, moderately vigorous, deciduous climber.

Clematis 'The Vagabond'. Photo by C. Chesshire.

Clematis 'Thyrislund'. Photo by J. Lindmark.

Height: 2–3 m (6.5–10 ft.).

Description: The single, small, nodding, yellow to greenish yellow flowers, 4–5 cm (1.5–2 in.) across, are composed of four pointed, thick, and fleshy tepals, the outsides of which are covered with reddish bronze and purple-brown speckles. The stamens are dark purple. Attractive silvery and silky seedheads are produced. The leaves are bluish green and finely divided.

Pruning group: 3.

Flowering period: Midsummer or late summer to early autumn.

Cultivation: Tolerates most well-drained garden soils and any aspect. Best grown in sun to ripen the wood and flower profusely.

Recommended use: Grow naturally through robust and open, large shrubs or medium-sized trees. Suitable for short-term container-culture. Ideal for a small garden. Zones 6–9.

Clematis tibetana subsp. *vernayi*
Ludlow, Sherriff & Elliot
TANGUTICA GROUP

Synonym: *C.* 'Orange Peel'

Origin: Believed to be a selection from seed collected (LSE 13342) by Ludlow, Sherriff, and Elliot on an expedition to the Tsangpo valley of Tibet in 1947. It is likely the name 'Orange Peel' was given to it after it was awarded the RHS Award of Garden Merit in 1950. There are now several forms in cultivation, probably grown from seed, and their colour and form vary to some degree from lemon yellow to yellowish orange.

Parentage and year: Species. 1947.

Habit: Moderately vigorous, deciduous climber.

Height: To 5 m (16 ft.).

Description: The single, solitary, nodding flowers are greenish yellow to somewhat burnt orange in colour. The four tepals are thick, fleshy, slightly wrinkled, and pointed, and recurve fully as the flowers mature. A central tuft of yellow stigmas is surrounded by a mass of dark reddish brown stamens with beige anthers. The leaves are grey-greenish blue, and the leaf margins have forward-facing teeth. Prominent fluffy seedheads appear after flowering.

Pruning group: 3. Partial pruning is recommended. Prune half the vines down to just above the lowest pair of live buds. Prune back the remaining half to half their original height. Alternate the vines every successive year.

Flowering period: Midsummer to early autumn.

Cultivation: Needs sharp drainage. Suitable for sun or partial shade.

Recommended use: Grow through medium-sized trees, conifers, or large, open shrubs. Zones 6–9.

Clematis 'Titania'

Origin: Raised by Magnus Johnson of Södertälje, Sweden.

Parentage and year: Chance seedling of *C.* 'Nelly Moser'. 1952.

Habit: Hardy, vigorous, deciduous climber.

Height: 2.4–3 m (8–10 ft.).

Description: This cultivar is not floriferous. The single flowers, white tinged with violet, are up to 25 cm

Clematis tibetana subsp. *vernayi*. Photo by J. Lindmark.

Clematis tibetana subsp. *vernayi* Ludlow, Sherriff, & Elliot. Photo by C. Chesshire.

(10 in.) in diameter and comprise eight overlapping, broad yet pointed tepals, each with a wide pinkish violet central bar running from the base to the tip, which tends to fade as the flower matures. The stamens are composed of white filaments and maroon anthers.

Pruning group: 2.

Flowering period: Early summer to midsummer.

Cultivation: Tolerates most garden soils. Requires a sheltered position to prevent wind damage to the large flowers. Best grown in partial shade to prevent premature fading of flower colour.

Recommended use: Grow with other wall-trained shrubs which do not require annual pruning. Zones 4–9.

Clematis 'Titania'. Photo by J. Lindmark.

Clematis 'Torleif'

Origin: Raised by Magnus Johnson of Södertälje, Sweden.

Parentage and year: Chance seedling of *C*. 'Prins Hendrik'. 1955.

Habit: Hardy, moderately vigorous, deciduous climber.

Height: 2.4–3 m (8–10 ft.).

Description: The single, bluish mauve flowers, 18 cm (7 in.) across, are composed of six to eight tepals, each with a prominent double central rib, which occasionally can be more reddish in colour. As the flower matures, the tepals tend to twist. The prominent stamens consist of white filaments and red anthers.

Pruning group: Optional, 2, or 3. For late flowers, prune hard (group 3).

Flowering period: Early summer to late summer.

Cultivation: Tolerates most garden soils and any aspect.

Recommended use: Grow with other wall-trained plants. Suitable for a medium-sized obelisk or trellis. If pruning group 3 is employed, grow naturally through large shrubs or conifers. Zones 4–9.

Clematis 'Triternata Rubromarginata'
VITICELLA GROUP

Synonyms: *C.* ×*triternata* 'Rubromarginata', *C. flammula* 'Rubromarginata'

Origin: Believed to have been raised by Thomas Cripps and Son of Tunbridge Wells, England. Some

Clematis 'Torleif'. Photo by J. Lindmark.

Clematis 'Triternata Rubromarginata' flower detail. Photo by E. Leeds.

attribute the raising to George Jackman and Son, England. Awarded RHS Award of Garden Merit.

Parentage and year: *C. flammula* × *C.* 'Rubra'. ca. 1880.

Habit: Hardy, moderately vigorous, deciduous climber.

Height: 3–4 m (10–13 ft.).

Description: A popular, free-flowering hybrid. The numerous, single, small, strongly hawthorn-scented, mauvish pink tipped, white, star-shaped flowers, 3–5 cm (1.25–2 in.) across, are borne in large trusses from the current year's growth. Each flower is composed of four, or occasionally up to six, tepals, which are narrow with undulating, twisted margins and tips. Pale yellow stamens contrast well with the tepal colouring.

Pruning group: 3.

Flowering period: Midsummer to early autumn.

Cultivation: Requires well-drained garden soils. Prefers a sunny position with a west-facing aspect.

Recommended use: Place the plant where the scent can be enjoyed. Ideal for a pergola, large obelisk, or trellis. Grow with large shrubs or small trees. Zones 5–9.

Clematis 'Twilight'

Origin: Raised by Percy Picton of Old Court Nurseries, Colwall, England.

Parentage and year: Unknown. ca. 1970s.

Habit: Hardy, not-so-vigorous, compact, deciduous climber.

Height: 1.8–2.4 m (6–8 ft.).

Description: The single, deep mauvish pink, well-rounded flowers, 13–15 cm (5–6 in.) in diameter, are composed of six to eight overlapping, tapering but blunt-tipped tepals, each with brighter pink shading at its base towards the stamens. This colouring fades to mauvish pink as the flower matures.

Pruning group: 2.

Clematis 'Triternata Rubromarginata' covering a small maple. Photo by C. Chesshire.

Flowering period: Late spring to early summer and late summer.

Cultivation: Tolerates most garden soils and any aspect.

Recommended use: Ideal for container-culture. Suitable for a small to medium-sized obelisk or trellis. Grow with moderately vigorous, medium-sized shrubs or climbing roses which require little or no pruning. Zones 4–9.

Clematis 'Ulrique'

Origin: Raised by Magnus Johnson of Södertälje, Sweden.

Parentage and year: Open-pollinated seedling of *C.* 'Nelly Moser'. 1952.

Habit: Hardy, moderately vigorous, compact, deciduous climber.

Clematis 'Twilight'. Photo by C. Chesshire.

Clematis 'Ulrique'. Photo by J. Lindmark.

Height: 1.8–2.4 m (6–8 ft.).

Description: The single, pale lavender-blue flowers, 12–19 cm (4.75–7.5 in.) in diameter, are composed of six to eight tepals, each with deeply notched edges and pinkish red colouring along the centre. The stamens are made of pale green filaments and reddish purple anthers.

Pruning group: 2.

Flowering period: Late spring to midsummer.

Cultivation: Tolerates most garden soils and any aspect.

Recommended use: Ideal for container-culture. Suitable for a small to medium-sized obelisk or trellis. Zones 4–9.

Clematis uncinata

EVERGREEN GROUP

Origin: China, southern Japan, Taiwan, and North Vietnam.

Parentage and year: Species. 1851.

Habit: Half-hardy, evergreen climber.

Height: 4–8 m (13–26 ft.).

Description: The single, scented, star-shaped, creamy white flowers, 2–3 cm (0.75–1.25 in.) across, are composed of four narrow tepals with rounded to pointed tips borne in lateral and terminal clusters. The prominent anthers are yellow. The leaves are bluish green with a paler shade underneath.

Pruning group: 1.

Flowering period: Late summer to midautumn.

Clematis uncinata. Photo by V. Denny.

Cultivation: Tolerates well-drained soils of poor quality. Best grown against a warm, sunny wall in a sheltered position.

Recommended use: Grow as a covering for a warm brick wall or trellis. Allow to climb into medium-sized to large, open trees or conifers. Zones 7–9.

Clematis 'Valge Daam'

Origin: Raised by Uno Kivistik of Harjumaa, Estonia. The name means "white lady."

Parentage and year: *C.* 'Bal Tzvetov' × *C.* 'Madame Van Houtte'. 1980.

Habit: Hardy, moderately vigorous, compact, deciduous climber.

Height: 1.8–2.4 m (6–8 ft.).

Description: The single, small, white flowers, 10–12.5 cm (4–5 in.) across, are composed of six tepals. The stamens are made of white filaments and beige anthers.

Pruning group: 2.

Flowering period: Late spring to late summer.

Cultivation: Tolerates most garden soils and any aspect.

Recommended use: Ideal for container-culture. Suitable for a small obelisk or trellis. Zones 4–9.

Clematis 'Vanessa'

Origin: Raised by Vince Denny of Denny's Clematis Nursery, Broughton, England, and named after Vanessa Hulbert.

Parentage and year: *C.* 'Sandra Denny' × *C.* 'Perle d'Azur'. Mid-1990s.

Habit: Hardy, moderately vigorous, deciduous climber.

Height: 2.5–3 m (8–10 ft.).

Description: The single flowers, up to 7.5 cm (3 in.) across, are made of five or six pale blue tepals with a hint of pink. The tepals, although longer than wide, are wider towards the tips, with slightly undulating and occasionally twisting margins. The stamens are made of white filaments and light creamy yellow anthers.

Pruning group: 3.

Flowering period: Midsummer to early autumn.

Cultivation: Tolerates most garden soils and any aspect. Produces best flower colour in full sun or partial shade.

Recommended use: Ideal as a companion plant for climbing roses or to grow through small trees and large shrubs. Zones 3–9.

Clematis ×*vedrariensis*
MONTANA GROUP

Origin: Raised by Vilmorin of Vèrriere le Buisson, France.

Parentage and year: *C. chrysocoma* × *C. montana* var. *rubens*. 1914.

Habit: Moderately vigorous, deciduous climber.

Height: To 6 m (20 ft.).

Description: The single, solitary, rose-pink flowers, up to 6 cm (2.25 in.) wide, composed of four to six broad and somewhat oval tepals, are borne on slender hairy stalks, 10–12 cm (4–4.75 in.) long, in the leaf

Clematis 'Valge Daam'. Photo courtesy Thorncroft Clematis Nurs

Clematis 'Vanessa'. Photo by M. Humphries.

axils of the previous year's growth and sometimes also from the current year's shoots. The prominent, central boss is composed of yellow stamens. The leaves are purple-green with three leaflets, often three lobed with a wedge-shaped base, coarsely toothed, and downy. The young shoots are furrowed.

Pruning group: 1. Any pruning to keep the plant in check should be carried out immediately after the main flowering period by removing some of the old, flowered stems.

Flowering period: Late spring to early summer.

Cultivation: Requires soil with sharp drainage and humus. Suitable for sun or partial shade.

Recommended use: Grow through medium-sized to large trees and conifers. Suitable for a wall, pergola, or large trellis in a sheltered situation. Zones 7–9.

Clematis veitchiana

Origin: Southwestern China. Introduced into cultivation by Ernest Wilson.

Parentage and year: Species. 1904.

Habit: Hardy, vigorous, deciduous climber.

Height: 3–5 m (10–16 ft.).

Description: The small, scented, creamy white, bell-shaped flowers, 10–15 mm (ca. 0.5 in.) long, borne in clusters with characteristic awl-shaped, leaflike structures (bracts) and 10–15 cm (4–6 in.) long, are composed of four tepals which are much longer than broad and which recurve at the tips. The creamy filaments are tipped with brownish anthers. The leaves are deeply, irregularly, and sharply slashed, and composed of seven to nine leaflets, which are in turn divided into

20 or more smaller leaflets and arranged on both sides of a common leaf axis.

Pruning group: 3.

Flowering period: Early summer to early autumn.

Cultivation: Tolerates most garden soils with good drainage. Prefers a warm aspect.

Recommended use: Grow over a pergola, fence, or a trellis where the scent can be appreciated. Zones 6–9.

Clematis 'Venosa Violacea'
VITICELLA GROUP

Synonym: *C. viticella* 'Venosa Violacea'

Origin: Raised by Victor Lemoine of Nancy, France. Awarded RHS Award of Garden Merit.

Parentage and year: Unknown. 1883.

Habit: Hardy, moderately vigorous, deciduous climber.

Height: 2.5–3 m (8–10 ft.).

Description: This cultivar is not quite as floriferous as other cultivars of *C. viticella*. The single, open flowers, 10 cm (4 in.) wide, are composed of five or six tepals, the base colour of which is white with deep purple veining, becoming more intense towards the incurved margins. The veining is somewhat sparse towards the centre of the tepals. Creamy white filaments carry dark purple anthers.

Pruning group: 3.

Flowering period: Midsummer to early autumn.

Cultivation: Tolerates most garden soils and any aspect. Produces best flower colour in sun or partial shade.

Recommended use: Grow through large shrubs, with climbing roses, or on a trellis or obelisk. Effective

Clematis veitchiana. Photo by C. Chesshire.

Clematis 'Venosa Violacea' flower detail. Photo by E. Leeds.

when allowed to scramble over golden heathers and prostrate conifers. Extremely distinctive and pretty. Zones 3–9.

Clematis 'Vera'
MONTANA GROUP

Synonym: *C. montana* 'Vera'

Origin: Raised in Cornwall, England. Originator unknown.

Parentage and year: Unknown. Mid-1900s.

Habit: Vigorous, deciduous climber.

Height: To 9 m (29 ft.).

Description: The single, saucer-shaped, vanilla-scented, deep pink flowers, 5–7 cm (2–2.75 in.) across, are normally made of four broad tepals and a central mass of yellow stamens. The leaves are large, coarse, and slightly bronzy when young.

Pruning group: 1. Any pruning to keep the plant in check should be carried out immediately after the main flowering period by removing some of the old, flowered stems.

Flowering period: Late spring to early summer.

Cultivation: Tolerates most well-drained garden soils. Hardy in temperate gardens. Suitable for any aspect but produces the best scent in a sunny position.

Recommended use: Grow over a large pergola or allow to roam into large, open trees. Ideal for a boundary wall or fence. Zones 7–9.

Clematis 'Veronica's Choice'

Origin: Raised by Walter Pennell of Pennell and Sons nursery and named in 1973 after his second eldest daughter.

Parentage and year: *C.* 'Vyvyan Pennell' × *C.* 'Percy Lake'. 1962.

Habit: Hardy, quite vigorous, deciduous climber.

Height: 2.4–3 m (8–10 ft.).

Description: The fully double flowers, measuring 15–20 cm (6–8 in.) across and borne on the previous season's old wood, are composed of a basal row of normally eight, broad, overlapping, pale lavender tepals, with a glow of rose pink. The four or five further rows

Clematis 'Venosa Violacea' growing over *Caryopteris* ×*clandonensis* 'Worcester Gold'. Photo by C. Chesshire.

Clematis 'Vera'. Photo courtesy British Clematis Society Slide Library.

of tepals reduce in length progressively towards the centre, and almost cover the creamy yellow stamens. The outer ring of main and inner secondary tepals reflex as they mature and boast textured surfaces and frilled edges. Single flowers are produced on the current season's new wood.

Pruning group: 2.

Flowering period: Late spring to early summer (double) and late summer (single).

Cultivation: Tolerates most garden soils. Best grown in semi-shade for good flower colour. Requires protection from strong winds.

Recommended use: Suitable for a pergola, arbour, medium-sized obelisk, or trellis. Grow through large shrubs which do not require regular pruning. Zones 4–9.

Clematis versicolor
TEXENSIS-VIORNA GROUP

Origin: Central United States (Missouri, Arkansas).

Parentage and year: Species. 1901.

Habit: Woody, deciduous scrambler with herbaceous habit.

Height: 1.5–2 m (5–6.5 ft.).

Description: The single, solitary, nodding, small, 2-cm (0.75-in.) pitcherlike flowers are composed of four thin tepals, shaped like the head of a lance, much longer than broad, and wider below the middle. The tepals are pale lavender to reddish purple in colour, grading into pale green towards the tips, which are pointed, recurved, and densely hairy at the margins. The leathery leaves carried on slender leaf stalks are

divided into eight leaflets, roughly oval in shape, often two or three lobed, blue-green, smooth, and with a fine netlike arrangement of veins beneath. Achenes are rhomboid with white, feathery tails.

Pruning group: 3.

Flowering period: Midsummer to early autumn.

Cultivation: Tolerates most garden soils but requires sharp drainage and a sunny position to flower well.

Recommended use: Ideal for container-culture. Grow over moderately vigorous, prostrate shrubs in a warm, sheltered part of the garden. Zones 6–10.

Clematis 'Victoria'

Origin: Raised by Thomas Cripps and Son of Tunbridge Wells, England. Awarded RHS First Class Certificate (1870).

Parentage and year: *C. lanuginosa* × *C.* 'Jackmanii'. 1867.

Habit: Hardy, vigorous, strong-growing, deciduous climber.

Height: 3–3.6 m (10–12 ft.).

Description: A popular cultivar. The single, smart, well-formed, reddish mauve flowers, 14 cm (5.5 in.) across, are composed of four to six overlapping, pointed yet wide tepals, each with a shading of rose-pink along the centre. The tepals present a textured surface, are slightly notched along the edges, and fade to light mauve by tepal fall. The stamens are made of greenish white filaments and contrasting dark yellow anthers.

Pruning group: 3.

Flowering period: Midsummer to early autumn.

Clematis 'Veronica's Choice'. Photo by C. Chesshire.

Clematis versicolor. Photo by J. Lindmark.

Cultivation: Tolerates most garden soils and any aspect. May be prone to mildew in sheltered locations. If necessary, spray with a suitable fungicide as buds develop.

Recommended use: Ideal for growing naturally through other shrubs and climbers. Suitable for a pergola, arbour, or large obelisk. Shows up well against a light background. Zones 4–9.

Clematis 'Ville de Lyon'

Origin: Raised by Francisque Morel of Lyon, France.

Parentage and year: Believed to be *C.* 'Viviand Morel' × *C. coccinea* (synonym *C. texensis*). 1899.

Habit: Hardy, vigorous, strong-growing, deciduous climber.

Height: 3–3.6 m (10–12 ft.).

Description: A well-known, widely grown, and free-flowering cultivar. The single, cherry-red flowers with a velvety sheen, measuring 10–15 cm (4–6 in.) in diameter, are composed of six overlapping, neatly formed, rounded and blunt-tipped tepals, each with a wide, deepish pink central bar. The tepals boast pink veining, and the margins and tips recurve slightly. The stamens are made of creamy white filaments and yellow anthers, which contrast well with the tepal colour.

Pruning group: 3. If left unpruned, ripened old stems produce early flowers.

Flowering period: Early summer to early autumn.

Cultivation: Tolerates most garden soils and any aspect.

Recommended use: Grow through large shrubs or conifers as the older leaves at the base of this cultivar tend to go brown and are best hidden. Zones 4–9.

Clematis 'Viola'

Origin: Raised by Uno Kivistik of Harjumaa, Estonia.

Parentage and year: *C.* 'Lord Nevill' × pollen mixture. 1983.

Habit: Hardy, moderately vigorous, deciduous climber.

Height: 2.4–3 m (8–10 ft.).

Description: A very free flowering cultivar. The single, deep bluish violet flowers, 10–14 cm (4–5.5 in.) wide, are composed of five or six short, broad tepals with gently notched margins. The conspicuous tuft of stamens is made of greenish white filaments and greenish yellow anthers.

Pruning group: 3.

Flowering period: Midsummer to late summer.

Cultivation: Tolerates most garden soils and any aspect.

Recommended use: Grow naturally through large shrubs or small trees, or on a pergola, obelisk, or trellis. Zones 4–9.

Clematis 'Victoria'. Photo by J. Lindmark.

Clematis 'Ville de Lyon'. Photo by N. Hall.

Clematis 'Viola' in *Abies lasiocarpa* (alpine fir). Photo by J. Lindmark.

Clematis 'Violet Charm'

Origin: Raised by Mr. Maund of Solihull Nurseries, Birmingham, England.

Parentage and year: Chance seedling. 1966.

Habit: Hardy, moderately vigorous, compact, deciduous climber.

Height: 1.8–2.4 m (6–8 ft.).

Description: The single, pale violet-blue flowers, measuring 15–20 cm (6–8 in.) in diameter, are normally composed of six long, pointed, textured tepals with prominently grooved centres and gently curled or fluted edges. Reddish brown filaments and anthers constitute the central tuft of stamens, which contrasts well with the tepal colour. This free-flowering cultivar boasts exceptionally healthy and attractive leaves.

Pruning group: 2.

Flowering period: Late spring to late summer.

Cultivation: Tolerates most garden soils. Suitable for sun or partial shade.

Recommended use: Ideal for container-culture. Grow naturally through medium-sized shrubs which require little or no pruning or on a small to medium-sized obelisk or trellis. Zones 4–9.

Clematis 'Violet Elizabeth'

Origin: Raised by Walter Pennell of Pennell and Sons nursery and named in 1974 after an employee, Violet Smith.

Parentage and year: *C.* 'Vyvyan Pennell' × *C.* 'Mrs. Spencer Castle'. 1962.

Habit: Hardy, moderately vigorous, deciduous climber.

Height: 1.8–2.4 m (6–8 ft.).

Description: The fully double flowers, 15–18 cm (6–7 in.) in diameter, are produced on the previous season's old wood. The outer row of six basal tepals is a delicate mauve pink, and subsequent layers are shorter but of similar colour. The filaments and anthers are yellow. Smaller single flowers are borne on the current season's new growth, later in the season.

Pruning group: 2.

Flowering period: Late spring to early summer (double) and late summer (single).

Cultivation: Tolerates most garden soils. Best grown in full or partial sun. Requires protection from strong winds.

Recommended use: Suitable for a small to medium-sized obelisk or trellis. Grow with other moderately vigorous, wall-trained plants which do not require pruning. Zones 4–9.

Clematis 'Violet Purple'
ATRAGENE GROUP

Synonym: *C. alpina* 'Violet Purple'

Origin: Raised by Magnus Johnson of Södertälje, Sweden.

Parentage and year: Unknown. 1980.

Habit: Hardy, moderately vigorous, deciduous climber.

Height: 2.4–3 m (8–10 ft.).

Clematis 'Violet Charm'. Photo by J. Lindmark.

Clematis 'Violet Elizabeth'.
Photo courtesy Thorncroft Clematis Nursery.

Clematis 'Violet Purple' with *C. turkestanica*. Photo by J. Lindmark.

Description: The single, nodding, violet-purple flowers are composed of four narrow and somewhat elongated tepals, each 5–5.5 cm (2–2.25 in.) long, the margins curling back upon themselves at midpoint and gently at the tips. The short, central tuft of staminodes is pale mauvish purple with greenish tips. The leaves are not very crowded, narrow, midgreen, and made of nine leaflets.

Pruning group: 1. Any pruning to keep the plant tidy should be carried out immediately after the main flowering period.

Flowering period: Midspring to late spring.

Cultivation: Tolerates most well-drained garden soils and any aspect.

Recommended use: Grow through wall-trained or free-standing shrubs or on a medium-sized obelisk or trellis. Ideal for container-culture. Allow to tumble over a low wall. Zones 3–9.

Clematis viorna
TEXENSIS-VIORNA GROUP

Common names: Leather flower, vase vine

Origin: United States (southern Pennsylvania to northern Mississippi, and from Ohio west to southern Missouri).

Parentage and year: Species. 1753.

Habit: Woody-based, deciduous scrambler or sub-shrub of herbaceous habit.

Height: 1.8–2.4 m (6–8 ft.).

Description: The single, small, urn-shaped, strongly ribbed, nodding flowers are 2.5–4 cm (1–1.5 in.) long, consisting of four pointed, recurving, thick, leathery tepals, which can be variable in colour, pale lavender to reddish purple, and pale yellow towards the smooth woolly tips. Margins of the tepals are densely covered in short, fine, greyish white hairs, giving a cottony matted appearance. The seedheads are large and spectacular. The achene bodies are prominently rimmed, somewhat hairy, and the seedtails are feathery, light yellow or brownish, spreading or coiled loosely. The leaves are divided into five to seven leaflets, roughly oval in outline, heart shaped at base, entire or lobed, smooth and deep green. Terminal leaflets end in a slender tendril-like structure.

Pruning group: 3.

Flowering period: Midsummer to early autumn.

Cultivation: Tolerates most garden soils with sharp drainage. New shoots at soil level need protection from slugs and snails.

Recommended use: Grow naturally through low shrubs and over heathers and low walls, where the small flowers can be enjoyed at close quarters. Ideal as a specimen plant in a container. Zones 4–9.

Clematis viorna. Photo by E. Leeds.

Clematis virginiana. Photo by J. Lindmark.

Clematis virginiana

Common name: Eastern virgin's bower

Origin: Canada and United States, from Nova Scotia west to Manitoba, south to Florida and eastern Texas.

Parentage and year: Species. 1755.

Habit: Hardy, deciduous, herbaceous climber. In the British Isles tends to be woody.

Height: 1.5–7 m (5–23 ft.).

Description: Male and female flowers are borne on separate plants. The small, off-white to cream, starlike, scented flowers, 1.2–2.5 cm (0.5–1 in.) across, are composed of normally four, occasionally five, narrow tepals. The male flowers boast a prominent central boss of creamy white stamens. All the sterile stamens of the female flowers are much reduced and devoid of pollen. The stems are ribbed, and the leaves are rather thin textured, heart shaped to oval, and are mostly divided into three leaflets, which are coarsely and irregularly spring toothed and often lobed. The leaves may cause skin irritation. The plant is almost completely herbaceous in its native habitat, dying back in winter and replacing its stems each spring.

Pruning group: 3.

Flowering period: Midsummer to late summer.

Cultivation: Tolerates most garden soils and any aspect.

Recommended use: Allow to climb into open trees or large shrubs, or up and along open fences. Zones 3–9.

Clematis vitalba

Common name: Old man's beard

Origin: Central, southern, and southeastern Europe (central Britain and Germany southwards), eastwards to Turkey, Iran, and southwards to North Africa. Naturalized in Ireland.

Parentage and year: Species. 1753.

Habit: Very vigorous, deciduous climber.

Height: To 12 m (40 ft.) and more.

Description: The numerous, small, creamy white, star-shaped, faintly scented flowers, 1.5–2.5 cm (0.5–1 in.) across, are borne in clusters from the leaf axils. Each flower is composed of four, sometimes five or six, narrow tepals. The prominent stamens are cream coloured. Immature buds and flowers are tinged with green. Stems are ridged and become woody and thick in old plants. Prominent clusters of fluffy seedheads are produced from late autumn.

Pruning group: 3.

Flowering period: Midsummer to late summer.

Cultivation: Does well on chalky soil but tolerates most garden soils and any aspect.

Recommended use: Not for the small garden. Grow into tall, large trees and conifers or along open fences. Zones 3–9.

Clematis viticella

VITICELLA GROUP

Origin: Turkey and Italy.

Parentage and year: Species. Introduced to England in 1569.

Habit: Hardy, vigorous, deciduous climber.

Height: 3–5 m (10–16 ft.).

Description: The single, blue-violet, four-tepalled flowers, 3–5 cm (1.25–2 in.) wide, open to a pendulous bell shape, and are produced in abundance on the current season's stems. The inside margins of the tepals are a dark blue whilst there is a paler bar down the centre with darker veining. The outside of the tepals is paler and has a greyer appearance. The stamens are greenish yellow. The stems are ribbed, and the leaves divided into two or three parts, composed of five to seven leaflets arranged on both sides of the leaf axis in pairs. Leaflets are often two or three lobed.

Pruning group: 3.

Flowering period: Midsummer to late summer.

Cultivation: Thrives in most garden soils and any aspect.

Recommended use: Grow through small to

Clematis viticella. Photo by J. Lindmark.

Clematis vitalba. Photo by I. Holmåsen.

medium-sized trees and conifers and over large shrubs. Suitable for a trellis or pergola. Makes a good companion for early flowering climbing roses. Zones 3–9.

Clematis 'Vivienne Lawson'

Origin: Raised by Vince and Sylvia Denny of Denny's Clematis Nursery, Broughton, England.

Parentage and year: Unknown. 1988.

Habit: Hardy, moderately vigorous, deciduous climber.

Height: 2.4–3 m (8–10 ft.).

Description: The single, violet-purple flowers, 15–20 cm (6–8 in.) in diameter, are composed of six to eight tepals. The stamens are made of golden filaments and anthers.

Pruning group: 3.

Flowering period: Early to late summer.

Cultivation: Tolerates most garden soils and any aspect.

Recommended use: Grow with medium-sized shrubs and small trees. Suitable for an arch, pergola, obelisk, or trellis. Zones 4–6.

Clematis 'Vivienne Lawson'. Photo by C. Chesshire.

Clematis 'Voluceau'

Origin: Raised by A. Girault of Orléans, France.

Parentage and year: *C.* 'Ville de Lyon' × *C.* 'Pourpre Mat'. ca. 1970.

Habit: Hardy, strong-growing, deciduous climber.

Height: 2.4–3 m (8–10 ft.).

Description: The single, petunia-red flowers, 10–15 cm (4–6 in.) wide, are composed of six to eight gently twisted tepals, each with crimson-purple central veining. The stamens are of yellow filaments and anthers.

Pruning group: 3.

Flowering period: Midsummer to late summer.

Cultivation: Tolerates most garden soils and any aspect.

Recommended use: Ideal for growing through medium-sized to large shrubs and small trees. Suitable for an arch, pergola, or trellis. Zones 4–9.

Clematis 'Vostok'

Origin: Raised by M. Orlov, Central Republic Botanical Garden of the Ukrainian Academy of Sciences, Kiev, Russia. The name means "Orient." Awared RHS Certificate of Merit.

Parentage and year: Unknown. 1963.

Habit: Hardy, moderately vigorous, deciduous climber.

Height: 2.4–3 m (8–10 ft.).

Description: The single, reddish purple flowers, 10–15 cm (4–6 in.) in diameter, are composed of four to six

Clematis 'Voluceau'. Photo by J. Lindmark.

tepals, which are veined and deep red along the centres. The tepals tend to recurve at the margins and tips, and some are twisted. They do not overlap, conferring an open appearance on the flower. White filaments and yellow anthers constitute the tuft of stamens.

Pruning group: 3.

Flowering period: Midsummer to late summer.

Cultivation: Tolerates most garden soils and any aspect.

Recommended use: Ideal for growing through prostrate conifers, large shrubs, and wall-trained plants. Suitable for growing on a pergola, trellis, or large obelisk. Zones 4–9.

Clematis 'Vyvyan Pennell'

Origin: Raised by Walter Pennell of Pennell and Sons nursery and named in 1959 after his wife. Awarded RHS Award of Garden Merit.

Clematis 'Vostok'. Photo by C. Chesshire.

Clematis 'Vyvyan Pennell'. Photo by C. Chesshire.

Parentage and year: *C.* 'Daniel Deronda' × *C.* 'Beauty of Worcester'. ca. 1954.

Habit: Hardy, vigorous, deciduous climber. Quite strong growing once established.

Height: 1.8–3 m (6–10 ft.).

Description: The fully double flowers, 15–18 cm (6–7 in.) wide, are produced on the previous season's old wood. The 6–10 outer, somewhat broad and overlapping basal tepals are pinkish to mauvish purple, with hints of red. The subsequent layers of inner, shorter, pointed tepals form a rosette and are rosy lavender. The stamens are composed of white filaments and beige anthers. Single flowers are produced on the current season's new wood, and the tepals are deep lilac mauve.

Pruning group: 2.

Flowering period: Late spring to early summer (double) and early autumn (single).

Cultivation: Tolerates most garden soils. Best grown in full sun or partial shade, in a frost-free position. Requires protection from strong winds. Has a tendency to flower early. Can be susceptible to clematis wilt when young.

Recommended use: Suitable for a pergola, arbour, medium-sized to large obelisk, or trellis. Grow through large shrubs and wall-trained climbers which do not require regular pruning. Zones 4–9.

Clematis 'W. E. Gladstone'

Origin: Raised by Charles Noble of Sunningdale, England.

Parentage and year: Unknown. ca. 1881.

Habit: Hardy, strong-growing, deciduous climber.

Clematis 'W. E. Gladstone'. Photo by C. Chesshire.

Height: 3–3.6 m (10–12 ft.).

Description: The single, midblue to pale blue flowers, 20–25 cm (8–10 in.) wide, are composed of six or seven broad yet pointed tepals, each with rose pink shading along the centre in young flowers that fades away with age. The stamens are made of cream filaments and light reddish brown anthers.

Pruning group: Optional, 2, or 3. A hard pruning (group 3) results in the loss of early flowers.

Flowering period: Early summer to early autumn.

Cultivation: Tolerates most garden soils. Suitable for sun or partial shade. Requires a sheltered position to prevent wind damage to the large flowers.

Recommended use: Grow on an arbour, pergola, large obelisk, or trellis. Zones 4–9.

Clematis 'W. S. Callick'

Origin: Introduced by Fisk's Clematis Nursery, Suffolk, England.

Parentage and year: Unknown. 1983.

Habit: Hardy, moderately vigorous, deciduous climber.

Height: 2.4–3 m (8–10 ft.).

Description: The single, bright red flowers, 15–20 cm (6–8 in.) wide, are composed of six to eight overlapping, broad but pointed tepals, each grooved and textured along the centre. Gently incurving margins of the tepals open at the base and overlap halfway along the tepal length. Light pink filaments and dark red anthers constitute the stamens.

Pruning group: Optional, 2, or 3.

Flowering period: Without any major pruning (group 2), late spring to early summer and late summer. With hard pruning (group 3), midsummer to late summer.

Cultivation: Tolerates most garden soils and any aspect.

Recommended use: Grow through medium-sized to large shrubs which require little or no pruning. Suitable for a large obelisk or trellis. Zones 4–9.

Clematis 'Wada's Primrose'

Synonym: *C.* 'Manshu-Ki'

Origin: Acquired by Koichiro Wada of Japan from Manchuria. Possibly a form of *C. patens*.

Parentage and year: Unknown. Acquired in 1933.

Habit: Hardy, not-so-vigorous, compact, deciduous climber.

Height: 1.8–2.4 m (6–8 ft.).

Description: The somewhat thin and weak stems carry rather large, single, primrose-yellow flowers, measuring 15–17 cm (6–7 in.) in diameter, and are normally composed of eight tepals, which are broader in the middle, overlapping and tapering smartly to points, with the deepest colour concentrated along the centrally placed stripes. The prominent stamens carry yellow filaments and anthers which harmonize with the tepal colour. Attractive, spherical seedheads remain on the plant for a long period.

Pruning group: 2.

Clematis 'W. S. Callick'. Photo by C. Chesshire.

Clematis 'Wada's Primrose'. Photo by J. Lindmark.

Flowering period: Late spring to early summer and late summer.

Cultivation: Tolerates most garden soils. Prefers semi-shade that will preserve flower colour.

Recommended use: Ideal for container-culture. Grow on a small obelisk or trellis with another moderately vigorous, bushy climber which does not require severe annual pruning. Also grow through small to medium-sized open shrubs which do not require pruning. Zones 4–9.

Clematis 'Walenburg'
VITICELLA GROUP
Synonym: *C. viticella* 'Walenburg'

Clematis 'Walenburg'. Photo by R. Savill.

Origin: Found growing in the garden of the Walenburg Estate, Netherlands, by D. M. van Gelderen of Esveld Nurseries, Boskoop.

Parentage and year: Unknown (a chance seedling). ca. 1990.

Habit: Hardy, vigorous, deciduous climber.

Height: 2.4–3 m (8–10 ft.).

Description: The single, pinkish mauve flowers, 5–7 cm (2–2.75 in.) across, are normally made of four rounded but tipped tepals, each with a creamy white central bar, the widest part of which is at the base. The pink veining of each tepal is more pronounced towards the tip. Pale green filaments and purple-tipped anthers make up the central boss of stamens.

Pruning group: 3.

Flowering period: Midsummer to late summer.

Cultivation: Tolerates most garden soils and any aspect.

Recommended use: Grow through large, open shrubs, small trees, or prostrate conifers. Zones 3–9.

Clematis 'Walter Pennell'
Origin: Raised by Walter Pennell of Pennell and Sons nursery and named in 1974.

Parentage and year: *C.* 'Vyvyan Pennell' × *C.* 'Daniel Deronda'. 1961.

Habit: Hardy, vigorous, deciduous climber.

Height: 1.8–3 m (6–10 ft.).

Clematis 'Walter Pennell' double flowers appear early in the year. Photo by C. Chesshire.

Clematis 'Walter Pennell' single flowers appear later in the year. Photo by J. Lindmark.

Description: The greyish mauvish pink, semi-double flowers, 15–20 cm (6–8 in.) wide, are freely borne on the previous season's old wood. The rounded yet pointed tepals, each with a carmine-red bar along the centre, do not overlap, giving the flower an open appearance. The extreme edges of the tepal margins are also lined in carmine red. The filaments and anthers are cream in colour. The late single flowers produced on the current season's new wood are small, measuring 10–15 cm (4–6 in.) in diameter.

Pruning group: 2.

Flowering period: Late spring to early summer (semi-double) and late summer (single).

Cultivation: Tolerates most garden soils. Best grown in full or partial sun. Requires protection from strong winds.

Recommended use: Suitable for a pergola, arbour, medium-sized to large obelisk, or trellis. Grow with large shrubs or wall-trained plants which do not require regular pruning. Zones 4–9.

Clematis 'Warszawska Nike'

Synonym: *C.* 'Warsaw Nike'

Origin: Raised by Brother Stefan Franczak of Warsaw, Poland. Introduced to the British Isles by Jim Fisk of Fisk's Clematis Nursery, Suffolk, England.

Parentage and year: Unknown. 1986.

Habit: Hardy, moderately vigorous, compact, deciduous climber.

Height: 1.8–2.4 m (6–8 ft.).

Description: The single, rich, velvety, reddish purple flowers, 12.5–15 cm (5–6 in.) wide, are composed of six to eight overlapping tepals, each deeply grooved along the centre. The margins are gently scalloped and the reverse of the tepals carries a silvery shading. Bright yellow filaments and anthers constituting the central boss of stamens contrast well with the tepal colour.

Pruning group: 3.

Flowering period: Midsummer to early autumn.

Cultivation: Tolerates most garden soils and any aspect.

Recommended use: Shows up well against a light background, such as shrubs or medium-sized trees which have light-coloured leaves. Suitable for a medium-sized obelisk or trellis. Zones 4–9.

Clematis 'Warwickshire Rose'
MONTANA GROUP

Synonym: *C. montana* 'Warwickshire Rose'

Origin: Raised by John Williams of Warwickshire, England.

Parentage and year: Seedling of *C. montana* var. *rubens*. Early 1990s.

Habit: Vigorous, deciduous climber.

Clematis 'Warszawska Nike'. Photo by J. Lindmark.

Clematis 'Warwickshire Rose'. Photo by R. Surman.

Height: To 9 m (29 ft.).

Description: The single flowers, 5–6 cm (2–2.25 in.) across, are composed of four deep rose-pink tepals. The leaves are dark reddish bronze, darker than the leaves of any other cultivar of *C. montana*, and divided into three leaflets with their margins notched like a saw with forward-pointing teeth. The leaf colour makes this cultivar attractive even when it is not in flower.

Pruning group: 1. Any pruning to keep the plant in check should be carried out immediately after the main flowering period by removing some of the old, flowered stems.

Flowering period: Late spring to early summer.

Cultivation: Can be planted in sun or partial shade.

Recommended use: Grow through large trees and conifers or along a wall or fence. Too vigorous for a small garden or container. Zones 7–9.

Clematis 'Wesselton'

ATRAGENE GROUP

Synonym: *C. macropetala* 'Westleton'

Origin: Raised by Jim Fisk of Fisk's Clematis Nursery, Suffolk, England. The name honours the medieval spelling of the raiser's village.

Parentage and year: Selected form of *C. macropetala*. Mid-1990s.

Habit: Hardy, moderately vigorous, deciduous climber.

Height: 2.8–3 m (8–10 ft.).

Description: The nodding, bell-shaped, midblue, semi-double flowers are composed of four narrow, pointed, and slightly twisting tepals, each 6.5 cm (2.5 in.) long with paler coloured tips. Inside there is another cluster of narrower, more pointed staminodes of the same length and similar colouring, giving the flower a much fuller appearance.

Pruning group: 1.

Flowering period: Midspring to late spring.

Cultivation: Tolerates most well-drained garden soils and any aspect.

Recommended use: Grow through medium-sized shrubs and trees which do not require annual pruning. Suitable for a large container. Also grow with other wall-trained plants. Zones 3–9.

Clematis 'Western Virgin'

Origin: Raised by Frank L. Skinner of Dropmore, Manitoba, Canada.

Parentage and year: *C. virginiana* × *C. ligusticifolia*. 1962.

Habit: Hardy, vigorous, deciduous climber.

Height: To 10.7 m (35 ft.) or more.

Description: The small, star-shaped, open, white flowers, 2–2.5 cm (0.75–1 in.) across, are composed of four or five non-overlapping tepals and a central boss of prominent stamens almost as long as the tepals. The filaments are cream and the anthers are yellow. Three types of flowers are produced by this hybrid—male and bisexual flowers are borne on one plant, and female and bisexual flowers on a separate plant. Female plants carry enough functional stamens to set fruit plentifully

Clematis 'Wesselton'. Photo by E. Leeds.

Clematis 'Western Virgin'. Photo by E. Leeds.

in the absence of plants with male flowers. The leaves are mostly divided into three leaflets with the terminal one usually three lobed or occasionally completely divided into three secondary leaflets.

Pruning group: 3.

Flowering period: Midsummer to late summer.

Cultivation: Tolerates most garden soils and any aspect. Makes literally thousands of seedheads, which, if not required, are best removed before natural seed drop, as this clematis can become an invasive weed!

Recommended use: Grow naturally through large trees or conifers or along a lengthy fence. Zones 3–9.

Clematis 'Westerplatte'

Origin: Raised by Brother Stefan Franczak of Warsaw, Poland. Named after the peninsula that protects the port of Gdansk.

Parentage and year: Unknown. Before 1996.

Clematis 'Westerplatte'. Photo by C. Chesshire.

Habit: Hardy, compact, slender, deciduous climber.

Height: 1–1.8 m (3.25–6 ft.).

Description: The single, rich, dark velvet-red flowers, 10–12.5 cm (4–5 in.) wide, are composed of 8–10 tepals, which are broad, rounded, well-formed, and overlapping. The tips recurve and there are gaps between the tepals at the point of origination near the central boss. The stamens are made of deep-red filaments and yellow anthers.

Pruning group: Optional, 2, or 3. A hard pruning (group 3) results in the loss of early flowers.

Flowering period: Late spring to late summer.

Cultivation: Tolerates most garden soils and any aspect.

Recommended use: Ideal for container-culture. Grow up and over moderately vigorous shrubs with light green or golden leaves. Suitable for a small obelisk or trellis. Zones 4–9.

Clematis 'White Columbine'
ATRAGENE GROUP

Synonym: *C. alpina* 'White Columbine'

Origin: Raised by Treasures of Tenbury, England. Awarded RHS Award of Garden Merit.

Parentage and year: Open-pollinated seedling of *C.* 'Constance'. 1987.

Habit: Hardy, moderately vigorous, deciduous climber.

Height: 2–3 m (6.5–10 ft.).

Description: The single, nodding, white flowers, about 10 cm (4 in.) across, are composed of four pointed tepals, each 4–5 cm (1.5–2 in.) long. Young

Clematis 'White Columbine'. Photo by C. Chesshire.

flowers are normally creamy white changing to white on maturity. White petal-like staminodes boast greenish yellow tips. Leaves are composed of three leaflets, and the serrated leaf margins resemble the teeth of a saw.

Pruning group: 1. Any pruning to keep the plant tidy should be carried out immediately after the main flowering period.

Flowering period: Midspring to late spring and sometimes midsummer to late summer.

Cultivation: Tolerates most garden soils with good drainage. Suitable for any aspect.

Recommended use: Ideal for a small garden. Grow in a large container or with other climbing plants which do not require annual pruning. Zones 3–9.

Clematis 'White Moth'
ATRAGENE GROUP

Synonyms: *C. sibirica* 'White Moth', *C. alpina* subsp. *sibirica* 'White Moth'

Origin: Raised by George Jackman and Son, England.

Parentage and year: Unknown. ca. 1957.

Clematis 'White Moth'. Photo by J. Lindmark.

Habit: Hardy, not-too-vigorous, compact, deciduous climber.

Height: 1.8 m (6 ft.).

Description: The small, white, double flowers, 2.5–3 cm (1–1.25 in.) long, are composed of four broad, spear-shaped tepals, which surround another row of numerous narrower petal-like staminodes of a similar length. Creamy white filaments and pale yellow anthers make up the stamens at the heart of the flower.

Pruning group: 1.

Flowering period: Early spring to midspring.

Cultivation: Tolerates most well drained garden soils and any aspect.

Recommended use: Ideal for container-culture. Grow over a small trellis or allow to tumble over a low wall. Zones 3–9.

Clematis 'White Swan'
ATRAGENE GROUP

Origin: Raised by Frank L. Skinner of Dropmore, Manitoba, Canada.

Parentage and year: *C. macropetala* × *C. sibirica*. 1961.

Habit: Hardy, moderately vigorous, compact, deciduous climber.

Height: 1.8–2.4 m (6–8 ft.).

Description: The nodding, fully double, creamy white flowers are made of four broad yet pointed tepals, each 5–6 cm (2–2.25 in.) long with a full inner skirt of similar coloured petal-like staminodes. Pale

Clematis 'White Swan'. Photo by R. Surman.

green, finely cut leaves are an attractive feature of the plant.

Pruning group: 1.

Flowering period: Midspring to late spring.

Cultivation: Tolerates most well-drained garden soils and any aspect. May take some time to establish itself.

Recommended use: Ideal for container-culture. Suitable for a pergola or trellis. Zones 3–9.

Clematis 'White Wings'
ATRAGENE GROUP

Synonym: *C. macropetala* 'White Wings'

Origin: Found growing in Magus Johnson's nursery in Södertälje, Sweden.

Parentage and year: Unknown. 1970.

Habit: Hardy, moderately vigorous, compact, deciduous climber.

Height: 2–3 m (6.5–10 ft.).

Description: The nodding, creamy white, semi-double flowers, 6–9 cm (2.25–3.5 in.) wide, are composed of four narrow, pointed tepals which are longer than broad, 4–5 cm (1.5–2 in.) long, with margins often curving upwards midway. An inner, full skirt of similar coloured, narrow, petal-like staminodes, usually four, curve and spread outwards resembling wings. The petal-like staminodes surround another layer of spoon-shaped staminodes with green-tinged tips. Leaves made of nine leaflets with coarsely toothed margins are pale green.

Pruning group: 1.

Flowering period: Midspring to late spring.

Cultivation: Tolerates most well-drained garden soils and any aspect.

Recommended use: Ideal for container-culture. Grow with other moderately vigorous, wall-trained shrubs which do not require annual pruning. Zones 3–9.

Clematis 'Wilhelmina Tull'

Origin: Unknown.

Parentage and Year: Unknown. Before 1983.

Habit: Hardy, moderately vigorous, compact, deciduous climber.

Height: 1.8–2.4 m (6–8 ft.).

Description: The single, deep violet-purple flowers, 15–20 cm (6–8 in.) in diameter, are composed of six, sometimes eight, tepals with crimson midribs. The golden stamens enliven the flower colour.

Clematis 'White Wings'. Photo by J. Lindmark.

Clematis 'Wilhelmina Tull'. Photo by C. Chesshire.

Pruning group: 2.

Flowering period: Late spring to early summer and late summer.

Cultivation: Tolerates most garden soils. Can be grown in sun or partial shade.

Recommended use: Ideal for container-culture. Suitable for a small to medium-sized obelisk or trellis. Grow over shrubs which require little or no pruning. Zones 4–9.

Clematis 'Will Goodwin'

Origin: Raised by Walter Pennell of Pennell and Sons nursery. Named in 1961 after one of his employees. Awarded RHS Award of Garden Merit.

Parentage and year: Unknown. 1954.

Habit: Hardy, moderately vigorous, deciduous climber.

Height: 2.4–3 m (8–10 ft.).

Description: The single, lavender-blue flowers, 15–18 cm (6–7 in.) wide, are formed of six to eight overlapping but tapering tepals deeply notched at the edges. The colour fades to light blue as the flower matures. The stamens are composed of creamy white filaments and yellow anthers.

Pruning group: 2.

Flowering period: Early summer to early autumn.

Cultivation: Tolerates most garden soils and any aspect.

Recommended use: Ideal for a large obelisk or trellis. Suitable for a pergola or arbour. Grow with other wall-trained shrubs and roses which require little or no pruning. Zones 4–9.

Clematis 'William Kennett'

Origin: Raised by H. Cobbet of Horsell, Surrey, England.

Parentage and year: Unknown. ca. 1875.

Habit: Hardy, vigorous, strong-growing, deciduous climber.

Height: 3–3.6 m (10–12 ft.).

Description: An extremely free-flowering cultivar. The single, mauvish blue flowers, 15–20 cm (6–8 in.) in diameter, are composed of six to eight broad but tapering, overlapping, and ribbed tepals with a satiny textured surface and undulating edges. Rose-pink shadings diffuse from the centre of each tepal along each rib and fade gradually. White filaments and dark reddish maroon anthers make up the contrasting stamens.

Pruning group: 2.

Flowering period: Early summer to midsummer and early autumn.

Cultivation: Tolerates most garden soils and any aspect.

Recommended use: Grow on an arbour, arch, pergola, large obelisk, or trellis. Zones 4–9.

Clematis williamsii

Origin: Japan.

Parentage and year: Species. 1856.

Habit: Half-hardy, deciduous climber.

Height: To 3 m (10 ft.).

Description: The single, nodding, cream flowers, produced on the previous season's wood, are composed of four broad yet pointed tepals which are cup-shaped

Clematis 'Will Goodwin'. Photo by C. Chesshire.

Clematis 'William Kennett'.
Photo courtesy Thorncroft Clematis Nursery.

when young but which open and slightly recurve at the tips when they mature. Cream stamens harmonize with the flower colour. The leaves are made of three leaflets with deeply serrated margins.

Pruning group: 1.

Flowering period: Early spring to midspring.

Cultivation: Requires well-drained soil and a warm, sheltered aspect.

Recommended use: In temperate gardens plant against a south-facing wall or in a cold greenhouse or conservatory. Zones 7–9.

Clematis 'Willy'
ATRAGENE GROUP

Synonym: *C. alpina* 'Willy'

Origin: Raised by Pieter G. Zwijnenburg of Boskoop, Netherlands.

Parentage and year: Unknown. 1971.

Habit: Hardy, moderately vigorous, deciduous climber.

Height: 2–3 m (6.5–10 ft.).

Description: The single, nodding, pale rose-pink flowers, produced on short shoots from previous season's old wood, are about 10 cm (4 in.) wide, and are made of four tepals, each 4–5 cm (1.5–2 in.) long. The outside of the tepals is slightly darker and distinctly veined. Staminodes are white. The leaves are made of nine leaflets, and the margins are irregularly toothed.

Pruning group: 1. Any pruning to keep the plant in check should be carried out immediately after the main flowering period.

Flowering period: Midspring to late spring and some flowers during late summer.

Cultivation: Requires well-drained soil and any aspect.

Recommended use: Ideal for a small garden. Suitable for an arch or pergola. Grow with other climbers or medium-sized shrubs which do not require annual pruning. Zones 3–9.

Clematis 'Wyevale'
HERBACEOUS/HERACLEIFOLIA GROUP

Synonym: *C. heracleifolia* var. *davidiana* 'Wyevale'

Clematis williamsii. Photo by Y. Aihara.

Clematis 'Willy'. Photo by R. Surman.

Origin: Raised by Wyevale Nurseries of Hereford, England.

Parentage and year: A selected form of *C. heracleifolia* var. *davidiana*. ca. 1955.

Habit: Hardy, herbaceous subshrub.

Height: 0.9–1.2 m (3–4 ft.).

Description: The single, tubular, hyacinth-like, strongly scented flowers, 3.2 cm (1.25 in.) long, are composed of four deep midblue tepals, which broaden at the tips and recurve from about halfway along their length with frilly tips and margins. The stamens are yellow.

Pruning group: 3.

Clematis 'Wyevale'. Photo by J. Lindmark.

Clematis 'Yukikomachi'. Photo by M. Humphries.

Flowering period: Midsummer to early autumn.

Cultivation: Tolerates normal garden soils with good drainage. Produces the strongest scent in a sunny position.

Recommended use: Ideal for the middle or the back of a herbaceous border. Place where the scent can be enjoyed. Zones 5–9.

Clematis 'Yukikomachi'

Origin: Raised by Chieko Kurasawa of Japan.

Parentage and year: Unknown.

Habit: Hardy, moderately vigorous, compact, deciduous climber.

Height: 1.8–2.4 m (6–8 ft.).

Description: The single flowers, measuring 15–20 cm (6–8 in.) across, are composed of six broad yet pointed, slightly cupped, pale lavender tepals which overlap near to the base. Each has a central bar of white, which fades into the textured pale lavender surface. The tips of the tepals are frequently tinged yellowish brown. The prominent boss of stamens is greenish yellow.

Pruning group: 2.

Flowering period: Late spring to early summer and late summer.

Cultivation: Tolerates most garden soils. Best grown in partial shade to preserve flower colour.

Recommended use: Ideal for container-culture or on a small obelisk or trellis. Grow over medium, open shrubs which require little or no pruning. Zones 4–9.

Clematis 'Yvette Houry'

Origin: Raised by Houry of France.

Parentage and year: Unknown. ca. 1900.

Habit: Hardy, moderately vigorous, deciduous climber.

Height: 2.4–3 m (8–10 ft.).

Description: The early, double, pale blue flowers, 15–20 cm (6–8 in.) across, are borne on stems made the previous year and comprise a base layer of numerous tepals with successive layers on top surrounding stamens with creamy white filaments and anthers. Single smaller flowers are produced late in the current season on new wood.

Pruning group: 2.

Flowering period: Midspring to late spring (double) and in late summer (single).

Cultivation: Tolerates most garden soils enriched with humus. Best grown in full or partial sun. Requires a sheltered position to lessen wind damage to the large flowers.

Recommended use: Grow on a pergola, medium-sized obelisk, or trellis. Zones 4–9.

Clematis 'Yvette Houry'. Photo by J. Lindmark.

APPENDIX I

Clematis by Groups

To simplify a complex subject, the lists below have been compiled irrespective of botanical and or taxonomical boundaries. As a rule, plants with similar characteristics of growth and flowering habit are listed together.

Evergreen Group
C. afoliata
C. 'Aoife'
C. 'Apple Blossom'
C. armandii
C. armandii var. *biondiana*
C. australis
C. 'Blaaval' (AVALANCHE™)
C. 'Bowl of Beauty'
C. cirrhosa
C. cirrhosa var. *balearica*
C. 'Early Sensation'
C. fasciculiflora
C. finetiana
C. foetida
C. forsteri
C. 'Freckles'
C. gentianoides
C. glycinoides
C. 'Green Velvet'
C. 'Jeffries'
C. 'Jingle Bells'
C. 'Joe'
C. 'Lansdowne Gem'
C. 'Lunar Lass'
C. marata
C. marmoraria
C. mauritiana

C. meyeniana
C. microphylla
C. 'Moonbeam'
C. napaulensis
C. 'Nunn's Gift'
C. paniculata
C. paniculata var. *lobata*
C. petriei
C. 'Pixie'
C. 'Robusta'
C. 'Snowdrift'
C. terniflora
C. uncinata

Atragene Group
C. 'Albiflora'
C. 'Albina Plena'
C. 'Alborosea'
C. alpina
C. 'Ametistina'
C. 'Anders'
C. 'Ballet Skirt'
C. barbellata
C. 'Blue Bird'
C. 'Blue Dancer'
C. 'Broughton Bride'
C. 'Brunette'
C. 'Burford White'

C. 'Carmen Rose'
C. chiisanensis
C. 'Chili'
C. 'Claudius'
C. columbiana
C. columbiana var. *tenuiloba*
C. 'Columbine'
C. 'Columella'
C. 'Constance'
C. 'Cyanea'
C. fauriei
C. 'Floralia'
C. 'Foxy'
C. 'Frances Rivis' (Dutch form)
C. 'Frances Rivis' (English form)
C. 'Frankie'
C. 'G. Steffner'
C. 'Georg'
C. 'Helsingborg'
C. 'Jacqueline du Pré'
C. 'Jan Lindmark'
C. koreana
C. koreana var. *fragrans*
C. koreana var. *lutea*
C. 'Lagoon'
C. 'Lemon Bells'
C. 'Love Child'
C. macropetala
C. 'Maidwell Hall'
C. 'Markham's Pink'
C. occidentalis

C. occidentalis var. *dissecta*
C. occidentalis var. *grosseserrata*
C. ochotensis
C. 'Odorata' (Atragene Group)
C. 'Pamela Jackman'
C. 'Pauline'
C. 'Pink Flamingo'
C. 'Prairie River'
C. 'Propertius'
C. 'Pruinina'
C. 'Purple Spider'
C. 'Red Beetroot Beauty'
C. 'Riga'
C. 'Rosy O'Grady'
C. 'Rosy Pagoda'
C. 'Ruby'
C. sibirica
C. 'Snowbird'
C. 'Tage Lundell'
C. 'Violet Purple'
C. 'Wesselton'
C. 'White Columbine'
C. 'White Moth'
C. 'White Swan'
C. 'White Wings'
C. 'Willy'

Montana Group
C. 'Alexander'
C. 'Broughton Star'
C. chrysocoma
C. chrysocoma 'Hybrid'
C. 'Continuity'

C. 'Dovedale'
C. 'Elizabeth'
C. 'Fragrant Spring'
C. 'Freda'
C. 'Gothenburg'
C. gracilifolia
C. 'Grandiflora'
C. 'Highdown'
C. 'Jacqui'
C. 'Lilacina'
C. 'Margaret Jones'
C. 'Marjorie'
C. 'Mayleen'
C. montana
C. montana var. *rubens*
C. montana var. *wilsonii*
C. 'New Dawn'
C. 'Odorata' (Montana Group)
C. 'Peveril'
C. 'Picton's Variety'
C. 'Pink Perfection'
C. 'Pleniflora'
C. spooneri
C. 'Tetrarose'
C. ×*vedrariensis*
C. 'Vera'
C. 'Warwickshire Rose'

Double and Semi-double Cultivars

C. 'Andromeda'
C. 'Beauty of Worcester'
C. 'Belle of Woking'
C. 'Chalcedony'
C. 'Countess of Lovelace'
C. 'Daniel Deronda'
C. 'Denny's Double'
C. 'Duchess of Edinburgh'
C. 'Elgar'
C. 'Evijohill' (JOSEPHINE™)
C. 'Evitwo' (ARCTIC QUEEN™)
C. 'Glynderek'
C. 'Helen Cropper'
C. 'Jackmanii Alba'
C. 'Jackmanii Rubra'
C. 'John Gould Veitch'
C. 'Kathleen Dunford'
C. 'Kiri Te Kanawa'
C. 'Lady Caroline Nevill'
C. 'Lilactime'
C. 'Louise Rowe'
C. 'Miriam Markham'

C. 'Miss Crawshay'
C. 'Mrs. George Jackman'
C. 'Mrs. James Mason'
C. 'Mrs. Spencer Castle'
C. 'Multi Blue'
C. 'Pafar' (PATRICIA ANN FRETWELL™)
C. 'Piilu'
C. 'Plena'
C. 'Proteus'
C. 'Royalty'
C. 'Sandra Denny'
C. 'Sieboldii'
C. 'Sylvia Denny'
C. 'Teshio'
C. 'Thyrislund'
C. 'Veronica's Choice'
C. 'Violet Elizabeth'
C. 'Vyvyan Pennell'
C. 'Walter Pennell'

Large-flowered Cultivars

C. 'Akaishi'
C. 'Alice Fisk'
C. 'Allanah'
C. 'Alpinist'
C. 'Andrew'
C. 'Anna'
C. 'Aotearoa'
C. 'Asagasumi'
C. 'Asao'
C. 'Ascotiensis'
C. 'Barbara Dibley'
C. 'Barbara Jackman'
C. 'Beauty of Richmond'
C. 'Bees Jubilee'
C. 'Bella'
C. 'Belle Nantaise'
C. 'Benedictus'
C. 'Beth Currie' (VIVIENNE™)
C. 'Betty Risdon'
C. 'Blekitny Aniol' (BLUE ANGEL™)
C. 'Blue Boy'
C. 'Blue Gem'
C. 'Blue Ravine'
C. 'Boskoop Beauty'
C. 'Burma Star'
C. 'C. W. Dowman'
C. 'Captaine Thuilleaux'
C. 'Carnaby'
C. 'Caroline'

C. 'Charissima'
C. 'Christian Steven'
C. 'Colette Deville'
C. 'Comtesse de Bouchaud'
C. 'Corona'
C. 'Crimson King'
C. 'Dawn'
C. 'Doctor Le Bêle'
C. 'Doctor Ruppel'
C. 'Dorothy Tolver'
C. 'Dorothy Walton'
C. 'Duchess of Sutherland'
C. 'Edith'
C. 'Édomurasaki'
C. 'Édouard Desfossé'
C. 'Ekstra'
C. 'Eleanor of Guildford'
C. 'Elegija'
C. 'Elsa Späth' (BLUE BOY™ in Australia)
C. 'Emilia Plater'
C. 'Empress of India'
C. 'Entel'
C. 'Ernest Markham'
C. 'Etoile de Malicorne'
C. 'Etoile de Paris'
C. 'Evifive' (LIBERATION™)
C. 'Evifour' (ROYAL VELVET™)
C. 'Evione' (SUGAR CANDY™)
C. 'Evirida' (PISTACHIO™)
C. 'Evista' (EVENING STAR™)
C. 'Evithree' (ANNA LOUISE™)
C. 'Fair Rosamond'
C. 'Fairy Queen'
C. 'Fireworks'
C. florida
C. 'Fryderyk Chopin'
C. 'Fujimusume'
C. 'Gabriëlle'
C. 'George Ots'
C. 'Gillian Blades'
C. 'Gipsy Queen'
C. 'Gladys Picard'
C. 'Guernsey Cream'
C. 'Guiding Star'
C. 'H. F. Young'
C. 'Hagley Hybrid'
C. 'Hainton Ruby'
C. 'Hakuōkan'
C. 'Hanaguruma'
C. 'Henryi'

C. 'Herbert Johnson'
C. 'Honora'
C. 'Horn of Plenty'
C. 'Huldine'
C. 'Huvi'
C. 'Hybrida Sieboldii'
C. 'Imperial'
C. 'Iola Fair'
C. 'Ishobel'
C. 'Ivan Olsson'
C. 'Jackmanii'
C. 'Jackmanii Superba'
C. 'Jadwiga Teresa'
C. 'James Mason'
C. 'Jan Pawel II'
C. 'Jasper'
C. 'Joan Picton'
C. 'John Gudmundsson'
C. 'John Huxtable'
C. 'John Warren'
C. 'Jubileijnyj 70'
C. 'Kacper' (CASPAR™)
C. 'Kakio' (PINK CHAMPAGNE™)
C. 'Kardynal Wyszynski' (CARDINAL WYSZYNSKI™)
C. 'Karin'
C. 'Kasugayama'
C. 'Kathleen Wheeler'
C. 'Keith Richardson'
C. 'Ken Donson'
C. 'King Edward VII'
C. 'King George V'
C. 'Kirimäe'
C. 'Königskind'
C. 'Kuba'
C. 'Lady Betty Balfour'
C. 'Lady Londesborough'
C. 'Lady Northcliffe'
C. 'Lasurstern'
C. 'Laura'
C. 'Lawsoniana'
C. 'Lemon Chiffon'
C. 'Lincoln Star'
C. 'Lord Nevill'
C. 'Lucey'
C. 'Luther Burbank'
C. 'Madame Baron Veillard'
C. 'Madame Édouard André'
C. 'Madame Grangé'
C. 'Madame van Houtte'
C. 'Margaret Hunt'

C. 'Maria Louise Jensen'
C. 'Marie Boisselot'
C. 'Masquerade'
C. 'Matka Teresa'
C. 'Maureen'
C. 'Midnight'
C. 'Mikelite'
C. 'Miniseelik'
C. 'Minister'
C. 'Miss Bateman'
C. 'Monte Cassino'
C. 'Moonlight'
C. 'Mrs. Bush'
C. 'Mrs. Cholmondeley'
C. 'Mrs. Hope'
C. 'Mrs. N. Thompson'
C. 'Mrs. P. B. Truax'
C. 'Mrs. P. T. James'
C. 'Myōjō'
C. 'Natacha'
C. 'Natascha'
C. 'Negritjanka'
C. 'Negus'
C. 'Nelly Moser'
C. 'Nikolaj Rubtzov'
C. 'Niobe'
C. 'Olimpiada-80'
C. 'Paddington'
C. 'Pat Coleman'
C. patens
C. 'Perle d'Azur'
C. 'Perrin's Pride'
C. 'Peveril Pearl'
C. 'Pink Fantasy'
C. 'Pink Pearl'
C. 'Pöhjanael'
C. 'Polish Spirit'
C. 'Poulala' (ALABAST™)
C. 'Poulvo' (VINO™)
C. 'Prince Charles'
C. 'Prince Philip'
C. 'Princess of Wales'
C. 'Prins Hendrik' (PRINCE HENDRIK™)
C. 'Rahvarinne'
C. 'Red Cooler'
C. 'Rhapsody'
C. 'Richard Pennell'
C. 'Romantika'
C. 'Rouge Cardinal'
C. 'Rüütel'
C. 'Satsukibare'

C. 'Saturn'
C. 'Scartho Gem'
C. 'Sealand Gem'
C. 'Seranata'
C. 'Sheila Thacker'
C. 'Sho-un'
C. 'Signe'
C. 'Silver Moon'
C. 'Sir Garnet Wolseley'
C. 'Snow Queen'
C. 'Special Occasion'
C. 'Sputnik'
C. 'Star of India'
C. 'Strawberry Roan'
C. 'Sunset'
C. 'Susan Allsop'
C. 'Sympatia'
C. 'Tartu'
C. 'Teksa'
C. 'Tentel'
C. 'The Bride'
C. 'The First Lady'
C. 'The President'
C. 'The Vagabond'
C. 'Titania'
C. 'Torleif'
C. 'Twilight'
C. 'Ulrique'
C. 'Valge Daam'
C. 'Vanessa'
C. 'Victoria'
C. 'Ville de Lyon'
C. 'Viola'
C. 'Violet Charm'
C. 'Vivienne Lawson'
C. 'Voluceau'
C. 'Vostok'
C. 'W. E. Gladstone'
C. 'W. S. Callick'
C. 'Wada's Primrose'
C. 'Warszawska Nike'
C. 'Westerplatte'
C. 'Wilhelmina Tull'
C. 'Will Goodwin'
C. 'William Kennett'
C. 'Yukikomachi'
C. 'Yvette Houry'

Viticella Group
C. 'Abundance'
C. 'Alba Luxurians'
C. 'Betty Corning'

C. 'Black Prince'
C. 'Blue Belle'
C. campaniflora
C. 'Carmencita'
C. 'Cicciolina'
C. 'Elvan'
C. 'Etoile Violette'
C. 'Flore Pleno'
C. 'Foxtrot'
C. 'Joan Baker'
C. 'Kasmu'
C. 'Kermesina'
C. 'Lisboa'
C. 'Little Nell'
C. 'Madame Julia Correvon'
C. 'Margot Koster'
C. 'Minuet'
C. 'Mrs. T. Lundell'
C. 'Pagoda'
C. 'Purpurea Plena Elegans'
C. 'Royal Velours'
C. 'Södertälje'
C. 'Tango'
C. 'Triternata Rubromarginata'
C. 'Venosa Violacea'
C. viticella
C. 'Walenburg'

Texensis-Viorna Group
C. addisonii
C. 'Buckland Beauty'
C. 'Burford Bell'
C. crispa
C. 'Duchess of Albany'
C. 'Etoile Rose'
C. 'Gravetye Beauty'
C. hirsutissima
C. hirsutissima var. scottii
C. 'Kaiu'
C. 'Lady Bird Johnson'
C. 'Phil Mason'
C. pitcheri
C. 'Princess Diana'
C. 'Sir Trevor Lawrence'
C. texensis
C. versicolor
C. viorna

Tangutica Group
C. 'Anita'
C. 'Annemieke'
C. 'Aureolin'

C. 'Bill MacKenzie'
C. 'Bravo'
C. 'Burford Variety'
C. 'Corry'
C. 'Golden Harvest'
C. 'Grace'
C. 'Gravetye Variety'
C. 'Helios'
C. 'Kugotia' (GOLDEN TIARA™)
C. ladakhiana
C. 'Lambton Park'
C. orientalis
C. serratifolia
C. tangutica
C. tangutica subsp. obtusiuscula
C. tibetana subsp. vernayi
C. tibetana subsp. vernayi Ludlow, Sherriff & Elliot

Herbaceous Group
C. 'Alba'
C. albicoma
C. 'Alblo' (ALAN BLOOM™)
C. 'Alionushka'
C. 'Arabella'
C. 'Aromatica'
C. 'Blue Boy'
C. 'Bonstedtii'
C. 'Campanile'
C. coactilis
C. 'Côte d'Azur'
C. 'Crépuscule'
C. 'Cylindrica'
C. 'Durandii'
C. 'Edward Prichard'
C. 'Eriostemon'
C. 'Evisix' (PETIT FAUCON™)
C. fremontii
C. 'Heather Herschell'
C. 'Hendersoni'
C. heracleifolia
C. heracleifolia var. davidiana
C. hexapetala
C. integrifolia
C. integrifolia var. latifolia
C. 'Jouiniana'
C. 'Jouiniana Praecox'
C. 'Juuli'
C. 'Lauren'
C. 'Lord Herschell'
C. mandschurica
C. 'Mrs. Robert Brydon'

C. 'New Love'
C. ochroleuca
C. 'Olgae'
C. 'Pamela'
C. 'Pamiat Serdtsa'
C. 'Pangbourne Pink'
C. 'Pastel Blue'
C. 'Pastel Pink'
C. 'Purpurea'
C. recta
C. 'Rosea'
C. 'Sander'
C. 'Sinij Dozhdj' (BLUE RAIN™)
C. socialis
C. songarica

C. stans
C. 'Tapestry'
C. 'Wyevale'

Other Species and Cultivars
C. aethusifolia
C. apiifolia
C. aristata
C. brachiata
C. brachyura
C. brevicaudata
C. buchananiana
C. chinensis
C. connata
C. cunninghamii
C. denticulata

C. flammula
C. florida
C. fruticosa
C. fusca
C. fusca var. *violacea*
C. gouriana
C. grandiflora
C. grata
C. grewiiflora
C. intricata
C. ispahanica
C. japonica
C. lanuginosa
C. lasiandra
C. lasiantha

C. ligusticifolia
C. obvallata
C. 'Paul Farges' (SUMMER SNOW™)
C. peterae
C. phlebantha
C. pierotii
C. potanini
C. ranunculoides
C. rehderiana
C. veitchiana
C. virginiana
C. vitalba
C. 'Western Virgin'
C. williamsii

APPENDIX 2

Clematis by Flower Colour

RED
C. 'Abundance'
C. 'Allanah'
C. 'Barbara Dibley'
C. 'Black Prince'
C. 'Buckland Beauty'
C. 'Carmencita'
C. 'Carnaby'
C. 'Charissima'
C. 'Cicciolina'
C. 'Corona'
C. 'Crimson King'
C. 'Docteur Le Bêle'
C. 'Empress of India'
C. 'Ernest Markham'
C. 'Evifive' (LIBERATION™)
C. 'Gravetye Beauty'
C. 'Hainton Ruby'
C. 'Huvi'
C. 'Jackmanii Rubra'
C. 'Kardynal Wyszynski'
 (CARDINAL WYSZYNSKI™)
C. 'Keith Richardson'
C. 'Kermesina'
C. 'Lady Bird Johnson'
C. 'Lansdowne Gem'
C. 'Madame Édouard André'
C. 'Madame Julia Correvon'
C. 'Niobe'
C. 'Olimpiada-80'
C. 'Poulvo' (VINO™)
C. 'Purpurea Plena Elegans'
C. 'Red Cooler'

C. 'Rouge Cardinal'
C. 'Rüütel'
C. 'Sir Trevor Lawrence'
C. 'Södertälje'
C. texensis
C. versicolor
C. 'Ville de Lyon'
C. 'Voluceau'
C. 'W. S. Callick'
C. 'Westerplatte'

BLUE
C. 'Alblo' (ALAN BLOOM™)
C. 'Alice Fisk'
C. alpina
C. 'Alpinist'
C. 'Anders'
C. 'Andrew'
C. 'Aromatica'
C. 'Ascotiensis'
C. 'Beauty of Richmond'
C. 'Beauty of Worcester'
C. 'Belle Nantaise'
C. 'Blekitny Aniol' (BLUE
 ANGEL™)
C. 'Blue Belle'
C. 'Blue Bird'
C. 'Blue Boy'
C. 'Blue Dancer'
C. 'Blue Gem'
C. 'Blue Ravine'
C. 'Boskoop Beauty'
C. 'Campanile'

C. 'Chalcedony'
C. 'Chili'
C. 'Columbine'
C. 'Countess of Lovelace'
C. 'Crépuscule'
C. 'Cyanea'
C. 'Cylindrica'
C. 'Denny's Double'
C. 'Durandii'
C. 'Édouard Desfossé'
C. 'Ekstra'
C. 'Elsa Späth' (BLUE BOY™
 in Australia)
C. 'Elvan'
C. 'Emilia Plater'
C. 'Eriostemon'
C. 'Etoile de Malicorne'
C. 'Etoile de Paris'
C. 'Evisix' (PETIT FAUCON™)
C. 'Evithree' (ANNA LOUISE™)
C. 'Floralia'
C. 'Frances Rivis' (Dutch
 form)
C. 'Frances Rivis' (English
 form)
C. 'Frankie'
C. fremontii
C. 'Fujimusume'
C. 'Gabriëlle'
C. 'Georg Ots'
C. 'Glynderek'
C. 'Guiding Star'
C. 'H. F. Young'

C. 'Helsingborg'
C. 'Hendersoni'
C. heracleifolia
C. heracleifolia var. davidiana
C. 'Hybrida Sieboldii'
C. integrifolia
C. integrifolia var. latifolia
C. 'Ivan Olsson'
C. 'Jadwiga Teresa'
C. 'John Gould Veitch'
C. 'John Gudmundsson'
C. 'Juuli'
C. 'Kasugayama'
C. 'Ken Donson'
C. 'Kiri Te Kanawa'
C. 'Königskind'
C. 'Lady Betty Balfour'
C. 'Lady Northcliffe'
C. 'Lagoon'
C. 'Lasurstern'
C. 'Laura'
C. 'Lawsoniana'
C. 'Lilactime'
C. 'Lisboa'
C. 'Lord Nevill'
C. macropetala
C. 'Maidwell Hall'
C. 'Maria Louise Jensen'
C. 'Masquerade'
C. 'Midnight'
C. 'Minister'
C. 'Mrs. Bush'
C. 'Mrs. Cholmondeley'

C. 'Mrs. Hope'
C. 'Mrs. James Mason'
C. 'Mrs. P. B. Truax'
C. 'Mrs. P. T. James'
C. 'Mrs. Robert Brydon'
C. 'Multi Blue'
C. 'Natacha'
C. 'Negus'
C. 'New Love'
C. ochotensis
C. 'Odorata' (Atragene Group)
C. 'Olgae'
C. 'Pamela Jackman'
C. 'Pastel Blue'
C. 'Pauline'
C. 'Perle d'Azur'
C. 'Prairie River'
C. 'Prince Charles'
C. 'Prins Hendrik' (PRINCE HENDRIK™)
C. 'Rhapsody'
C. 'Sandra Denny'
C. 'Saturn'
C. 'Sealand Gem'
C. 'Sheila Thacker'
C. 'Sho-un'
C. 'Signe'
C. 'Sinij Dozhdj' (BLUE RAIN™)
C. 'Sir Garnet Wolseley'
C. socialis
C. 'Sputnik'
C. 'Teshio'
C. 'The First Lady'
C. 'The President'
C. 'Ulrique'
C. 'Vanessa'
C. 'Violet Charm'
C. 'W. E. Gladstone'
C. 'Wesselton'
C. 'Will Goodwin'
C. 'William Kennett'
C. 'Wyevale'
C. 'Yukikomachi'
C. 'Yvette Houry'

PINK

C. 'Alborosea'
C. 'Alionushka'
C. 'Ametistina'
C. 'Anna'
C. 'Asao'
C. 'Ballet Skirt'

C. 'Bees Jubilee'
C. 'Broughton Star'
C. 'Capitaine Thuilleaux'
C. 'Carmen Rose'
C. 'Caroline'
C. chrysocoma 'Hybrid'
C. 'Columella'
C. 'Comtesse de Bouchaud'
C. 'Constance'
C. 'Dawn'
C. 'Doctor Ruppel'
C. 'Dorothy Tolver'
C. 'Dorothy Walton'
C. 'Dovedale'
C. 'Duchess of Sutherland'
C. 'Edward Prichard'
C. 'Eleanor of Guildford'
C. 'Elizabeth'
C. 'Etoile Rose'
C. 'Evijohill' (JOSEPHINE™)
C. 'Fairy Queen'
C. 'Foxy'
C. 'Freda'
C. 'Gothenburg'
C. 'Hagley Hybrid'
C. 'Hanaguruma'
C. 'Heather Herschell'
C. 'Helen Cropper'
C. 'Highdown'
C. 'Imperial'
C. 'Jacqueline du Pré'
C. 'Jan Lindmark'
C. 'John Warren'
C. 'Kakio' (PINK CHAMPAGNE™)
C. 'King George V'
C. 'Kirimäe'
C. 'Lilacina'
C. 'Lincoln Star'
C. 'Lucey'
C. 'Margaret Hunt'
C. 'Margot Koster'
C. 'Markham's Pink'
C. 'Mayleen'
C. 'Miss Crawshay'
C. montana var. *rubens*
C. 'Natascha'
C. 'Nelly Moser'
C. 'New Dawn'
C. 'Odorata' (Montana Group)
C. 'Pafar' (PATRICIA ANN FRETWELL™)
C. 'Pangbourne Pink'

C. 'Pastel Pink'
C. 'Peveril Pearl'
C. 'Picton's Variety'
C. 'Piilu'
C. 'Pink Fantasy'
C. 'Pink Flamingo'
C. 'Pink Pearl'
C. 'Pink Perfection'
C. 'Princess Diana'
C. 'Propertius'
C. 'Proteus'
C. 'Rosea'
C. 'Rosy O'Grady'
C. 'Rosy Pagoda'
C. 'Ruby'
C. 'Scartho Gem'
C. 'Strawberry Roan'
C. 'Sunset'
C. 'Tango'
C. 'Tapestry'
C. 'Triternata Rubromarginata'
C. 'Twilight'
C. 'Vera'
C. 'Violet Elizabeth'
C. 'Walter Pennell'
C. 'Warwickshire Rose'
C. 'Willy'

PURPLE

C. 'Akaishi'
C. 'Alborosea'
C. 'Aotearoa'
C. 'Beth Currie' (VIVIENNE™)
C. 'Brunette'
C. 'Burford Bell'
C. 'Burma Star'
C. 'Christian Steven'
C. columbiana var. *tenuiloba*
C. 'Daniel Deronda'
C. 'Édomurasaki'
C. 'Elegija'
C. 'Etoile Violette'
C. 'Evifour' (ROYAL VELVET™)
C. fauriei
C. 'Fireworks'
C. 'Foxtrot'
C. 'G. Steffner'
C. 'Georg'
C. 'Gipsy Queen'
C. 'Hakuōkan'
C. 'Helsingborg'
C. 'Jackmanii'
C. 'Jackmanii Superba'

C. 'Jenny Caddick'
C. 'Jubilenyj-70'
C. 'Karin'
C. 'Kasmu'
C. 'Kathleen Dunford'
C. 'Kuba'
C. 'Lauren'
C. 'Luther Burbank'
C. 'Madame Grangé'
C. 'Maureen'
C. 'Mikelite'
C. 'Miniseelik'
C. 'Monte Cassino'
C. 'Mrs. N. Thompson'
C. 'Myōjō'
C. 'Paddington'
C. 'Perrin's Pride'
C. 'Pöhjanael'
C. 'Polish Spirit'
C. 'Pruinina'
C. 'Purple Spider'
C. 'Rahvarinne'
C. 'Red Beetroot Beauty'
C. 'Richard Pennell'
C. 'Romantika'
C. 'Serenata'
C. 'Star of India'
C. 'Susan Allsop'
C. 'Tage Lundell'
C. 'Tartu'
C. 'Tentel'
C. 'The Vagabond'
C. 'Venosa Violacea'
C. 'Viola'
C. 'Vivienne Lawson'
C. 'Vostok'
C. 'Warszawska Nike'
C. 'Wilhelmina Tull'

MAUVE

C. 'Arabella'
C. 'Barbara Jackman'
C. 'Belle of Woking'
C. 'Betty Corning'
C. 'Colette Deville'
C. 'Édouard Desfossé'
C. 'Elgar'
C. 'Entel'
C. 'Evione' (SUGAR CANDY™)
C. 'Evista' (EVENING STAR™)
C. 'Fragrant Spring'
C. 'Herbert Johnson'
C. 'Horn of Plenty'

C. 'Iola Fair'
C. 'Joan Baker'
C. 'Joan Picton'
C. 'Jouiniana'
C. 'Jouiniana Praecox'
C. 'Kathleen Wheeler'
C. 'Lady Caroline Nevill'
C. 'Lady Londesborough'
C. 'Laura'
C. 'Louise Rowe'
C. 'Madame Baron Veillard'
C. 'Miriam Markham'
C. 'Mrs. Spencer Castle'
C. 'Nikolaj Rubtzov'
C. 'Pamiat Serdtsa'
C. 'Prince Philip'
C. 'Royal Velours'
C. 'Royalty'
C. 'Satsukibare'
C. 'Silver Moon'
C. 'Sympatia'
C. 'Teksa'
C. 'Thyrislund'
C. 'Torleif'
C. 'Veronica's Choice'
C. 'Victoria'
C. viticella
C. 'Vyvyan Pennell'
C. 'Walenburg'

WHITE
C. 'Alba'
C. 'Alba Luxurians'
C. 'Albiflora'
C. 'Albina Plena'
C. 'Alexander'
C. 'Andromeda'
C. 'Anita'
C. 'Aoife'

C. apiifolia
C. 'Apple Blossom'
C. armandii
C. armandii var. *biondiana*
C. 'Asagasumi'
C. 'Bella'
C. 'Blaaval' (AVALANCHE™)
C. 'Bowl of Beauty'
C. brachiata
C. brevicaudata
C. 'Broughton Bride'
C. 'Burford White'
C. campaniflora
C. chrysocoma
C. denticulata
C. 'Duchess of Edinburgh'
C. 'Edith'
C. 'Evirida' (PISTACHIO™)
C. 'Evitwo' (ARCTIC QUEEN™)
C. 'Fair Rosamond'
C. fasciculiflora
C. flammula
C. 'Flore Pleno'
C. florida
C. gentianoides
C. 'Gillian Blades'
C. gouriana
C. 'Grace'
C. gracilifolia
C. grata
C. 'Henryi'
C. hexapetala
C. 'Huldine'
C. 'Ishobel'
C. ispahanica
C. 'Jackmanii Alba'
C. 'Jacqui'
C. 'James Mason'
C. 'Jan Pawel II'

C. 'Jasper'
C. 'Jeffries'
C. 'Jingle Bells'
C. 'Joe'
C. 'John Huxtable'
C. 'Kaiu'
C. ligusticifolia
C. 'Little Nell'
C. 'Madame van Houtte'
C. mandschurica
C. 'Margaret Jones'
C. 'Marie Boisselot'
C. marmoraria
C. 'Matka Teresa'
C. meyeniana
C. 'Miss Bateman'
C. montana
C. montana var. *wilsonii*
C. 'Mrs. George Jackman'
C. 'Nunn's Gift'
C. 'Pamela'
C. paniculata
C. 'Pat Coleman'
C. 'Paul Farges' (SUMMER SNOW™)
C. 'Peveril'
C. 'Plena'
C. potaninii
C. 'Poulala' (ALABAST™)
C. 'Purpurea'
C. recta
C. 'Riga'
C. 'Robusta'
C. sibirica
C. 'Sieboldii'
C. 'Snow Queen'
C. 'Snowbird'
C. 'Snowdrift'

C. songarica
C. spooneri
C. 'Sylvia Denny'
C. terniflora
C. 'The Bride'
C. 'Titania'
C. 'Valge Daam'
C. virginiana
C. vitalba
C. 'Western Virgin'
C. 'White Columbine'
C. 'White Moth'
C. 'White Swan'
C. 'White Wings'

YELLOW
C. 'Annemieke'
C. 'Aureolin'
C. australis
C. 'Bill MacKenzie'
C. 'Bravo'
C. chiisanensis
C. coactilis
C. 'Corry'
C. 'Golden Harvest'
C. 'Helios'
C. 'Kugotia' (GOLDEN TIARA™)
C. 'Lambton Park'
C. 'Lemon Bells'
C. 'Lemon Chiffon'
C. 'Moonlight'
C. rehderiana
C. serratifolia
C. tangutica
C. tangutica subsp. *obtusiuscula*
C. tibetana subsp. *vernayi*
C. 'Wada's Primrose'

APPENDIX 3

Trade and Cultivar Names

C. ALABAST™, see *C.* 'Poulala'
C. ALAN BLOOM™, see *C.* 'Alblo'
C. ANNA LOUISE™, see *C.* 'Evithree'
C. ARCTIC QUEEN™, see *C.* 'Evitwo'
C. AVALANCHE™, see *C.* 'Blaaval'
C. BLUE ANGEL™, see *C.* 'Blekitny Aniol'
C. BLUE BOY™ (in Australia only), see *C.* 'Elsa Späth'
C. BLUE RAIN™, see *C.* 'Sinij Dozhdj'
C. CARDINAL WYSZYNSKI™, see *C.* 'Kardynal Wyszynski'
C. CASPAR™, see *C.* 'Kacper'
C. EVENING STAR™, see *C.* 'Evista'
C. GOLDEN TIARA™, see *C.* 'Kugotia'

C. JOSEPHINE™, see *C.* 'Evijohill'
C. LIBERATION™, see *C.* 'Evifive'
C. PATRICIA ANN FRETWELL™, see *C.* 'Pafar'
C. PETIT FAUCON™, see *C.* 'Evisix'
C. PINK CHAMPAGNE™, see *C.* 'Kakio'
C. PISTACHIO™, see *C.* 'Evirida'
C. PRINCE HENDRIK™, see *C.* 'Prins Hendrik'
C. ROYAL VELVET™, see *C.* 'Evifour'
C. SUGAR CANDY™, see *C.* 'Evione'
C. SUMMER SNOW™, see *C.* 'Paul Farges'
C. VINO™, see *C.* 'Poulvo'
C. VIVIENNE™, see *C.* 'Beth Currie'

APPENDIX 4

Hybridizers and Nurseries
Mentioned in the Directory of Clematis

Anderson-Henry, Isaac, Hay Lodge, Edinburgh, Scotland.*
Baron Veillard of Orléans, France.*
Bees of Chester, England.*
Blooms of Bressingham, Diss, Norfolk, IP22 2AB, England.
Boisselot, Auguste, Nantes, France.*
Caddick's Clematis Nursery, Lymm Road, Thelwall, Warrington, Cheshire, WA4 2TG, England.
Cripps, Thomas, and Son, Tunbridge Wells, England.*
Denny's Clematis Nursery, Broughton, Lancashire, England.*
Desfossé, Orléans, France.*
Evison, Raymond J., The Guernsey Clematis Nursery, Domarie Vineries, Les Sauvagées, St. Sampson, Guernsey, GY2 4FD, Channel Islands.
Fisk, Jim, Fisk's Clematis Nursery, Suffolk, England.*
Fopma, Jan, Boskoop, Netherlands.*
Frères, Simon-Louis, France.*
Fretwell, Barry, Peveril Clematis Nursery, Christow, Nr. Exeter, Devon, EX6 7NG, England.
Goos and Koenemann of Germany.*
Hutchins, Graham, County Park Nursery, Essex Gardens, Hornchurch, Essex, RM11 3BU, England.
J. Bouter and Zoon, Boskoop, Netherlands.
Jackman, George, and Son, Woking, Surrey, England.*
Jerard, M. L., Potters Lane, Lansdowne Valley, R.D. 2, Christchurch, New Zealand 8021.
Johnson, Magnus, Södertälje, Sweden.*
Keay, Alister, New Zealand Clematis Nurseries, 67 Ngaio Street, St. Martins, Christchurch 2, New Zealand.
Kivistik, Uno, Roogoja Talu, Karlaküla, Kose 75101, Harjumaa, Estonia. (Now trading as Family Kivistik.)
Lemoine, Victor, Nancy, France.*

Morel, Francisque, Lyon, France.*
Noble, Charles, Sunningdale, Berkshire, England.*
Noll, Vladyslaw, Warsaw, Poland.*
Olesen, Mogens, Poulsen Roser International, Denmark.
Pennell, Walter, Pennell and Sons, Newark Road, South Hykeham, Lincoln, Lincolnshire, LN6 9NT, England.
Picton, Percy, The Old Court Nurseries, Colwall, Worcestershire, England.*
Pineapple Nursery, St. John's Wood, London, England.*
Savill, Robin, Clematis Specialist, 2 Bury Cottages, Bury Road, Pleshey, Chelmsford, Essex, CM3 1HB, England.
Scott's Clematis Nursery, Earlswood, Solihull, Birmingham, England.
Späth, L., Berlin, Germany.*
Standish, John, Ascot, Berkshire, England.*
Steffen, Arthur H., Fairport, New York, United States.*
Swadwick, George, Worth Park Nurseries, Horley, Surrey, England.*
Treasures of Tenbury, Burford House Gardens, Tenbury Wells, Worcestershire, WR15 8HQ, England.
Veitch and Son, Coombe Wood Nursery, Langley, Slough, England.*
Vilmorin, Vèrriere le Buisson, France.*
Watkinson, Frank, Doncaster, England.*
Westphal, Friedrich Manfred, Peiner Hof 7, 25497 Prisdorf, Germany.
White, Robin, Blackthorn Nursery, Kilmeston, Alresford, SO24 0NL, England.
Wyevale Nurseries, Hereford, England.
Zwijnenburg Jr., Pieter G., Halve Raak 18, 2771 AD Boskoop, Netherlands.
Zwijnenburg, Rinus, Boskoop, Netherlands.

* No longer trading

Nursery List

AUSTRALIA
Alameda Homestead Nursery
112-116, Homestead Road,
    Berwick
Victoria 3806
David and Judith Button
Wholesale

Clematis Cottage Nursery
41, Main Street
Sheffield 7306, Tasmania
Todd Miles
Retail; wholesale

AUSTRIA
Jungpflanzenbaumschule
    Alexander Mittermayr
Griesbach, A-4770 Andorf
Retail; wholesale

CANADA
Adera Nurseries
1971 Wain Road RR#4
Sidney, British Columbia V8L
    4R4
Retail; wholesale

Barrons Flowers
Box 250
2800 Hurricane Road
Fonthill, Ontario L0S 1E0
Wholesale

Clearview Horticultural Prod-
    ucts
5343-264th Street, RR#1
Aldergrove, British Columbia
    V4W 1K4
Wholesale

Connon Nurseries
1724 Concession IV
Rockton, Ontario L0R 1X0
Wholesale

Gardenimport
P.O. Box 760
Thornhill, Ontario L3T 4A5
Mail order; retail

Humber Nurseries
8386 Highway 50, RR#8
Brampton, Ontario L6T 3Y7
Retail

Linwell Gardens
344 Read Road, RR#36
St. Catherines, Ontario L2R
    7K6
Wholesale

Mason Hogue Gardens
2340 Durham Road #1, RR#4
Uxbridge, Ontario L9P 1R4
Mail order (in Canada); retail

Skinner Nurseries
Box 220
Roblin, Manitoba R0L 1P0
Retail

Zubrowski, Stanley
P.O. Box 26
Prairie River, Saskatchewan
    S0E 1J0
Mail order; retail; wholesale

DENMARK
Hansen, Flemming
Solbakken 22
Ugelbølle DK 8410 Rønde
Retail; wholesale

ENGLAND
Adams Plants of Cambridge
Rosewood, Taylors Lane,
    Buckden
Cambridge PE18 9TD
Carole and John Adams
Retail

Baines Paddock Nursery
Haverthwaite, Ulverston
Cumbria LA12 8PF
T. H. Barker and Son
Mail order; retail

Beamish Clematis Nursery
Burntwood Cottage, Stoney
    Lane, Beamish
Durham DH9 0SJ
Retail

Blooms of Bressingham
Diss, Norfolk IP22 2AB
Retail; wholesale

Bridgemere Nurseries
Bridgemere, Nantwich
Cheshire CW5 7QB
Retail; wholesale

Busheyfields Nursery
Herne, Herne Bay
Kent CT6 7LJ
J. Bradshaw and Son
Retail; wholesale

Caddick's Clematis Nursery
Lymm Road, Thelwall, War-
    rington
Cheshire WA4 2TG
Mail order; retail; export

Clematis Specialist
2 Bury Cottages, Bury Road,
Pleshey, Chelmsford
Essex CM3 1HB
Robin Savill
Mail order; retail; wholesale

Country Clematis
31, Sefton Lane, Maghull
Merseyside L31 8AE
Steve Gilsenan
Retail; wholesale

County Park Nursery
Essex Gardens, Hornchurch
Essex RM11 3BU
Graham Hutchins
Retail

Darby Nursery Stock
Old Feltwell Road, Meth-
    wold, Thetford
Norfolk IP26 4PW
Wholesale

Floyds Climbers and Clematis
77 Whittle Avenue, Compton
    Bassett, Calne
Wiltshire SN11 8QS
Wholesale

Glyndley Nurseries
Hailsham Road, Pevensey
East Sussex BN24 5BS
Wholesale

Goscote Nurseries
Systen Road, Cossington,
    Leicester
Leicestershire LE7 4UZ
Retail; wholesale; exports to
European Community countries

Great Dixter Nurseries
Northiam, Rye
East Sussex TN31 6PH
Retail; exports to European
Community countries

The Guernsey Clematis
    Nursery
Domarie Vineries, Les
    Sauvagées, St. Sampson
Guernsey GY2 4FD
Raymond J. Evison
Wholesale

The Hawthornes
Marsh Road, Hesketh Bank,
    Nr. Preston
Lancashire PR4 6XT
Retail

Haybridge Nurseries
Springacres, Dudnill,
    Cleobury Mortimer, Kid-
    derminster
Worcestershire DY14 0DH
Joe Link
Wholesale

Hollybrook Nursery
Exmouth Road, West Hill,
    Ottery St. Mary
Devon EX11 1JZ
Retail

John Richards Nurseries
Camp Hill, Malvern
Worcestershire WR14 4BZ
Wholesale

Liss Forest
Petersfield Road, Greatham
Hampshire GU33 6EX
Wholesale

Longstock Park Gardens
Longstock, Stockbridge
Hampshire SO20 6EH
Retail

M. Oviatt-Ham
Ely House, Green Street,
    Willingham
Cambridge CB4 5JA
Wholesale; exports

Notcutts Nursery
Woodbridge
Suffolk IP12 4AF
Retail; wholesale

Orchard Nurseries
Tow Lane, Foston, Nr.
    Grantham
Lincolnshire NG32 2IE
Retail

Oxney Clematis at Hanging
    Gardens Nurseries
Ongar Road West, (A414)
    Writtle-by-Pass, Writtle
Essex CM1 3NT
Retail

Paddocks Nursery
Sutton, Tenbury Wells
Worcestershire WR25 8RJ
Retail; wholesale

Pennell and Sons
Newark Road, South Hyke-
    ham, Lincoln
Lincolnshire LN6 9NT
Retail; wholesale

Peveril Clematis Nursery
Christow, Nr. Exeter
Devon EX6 7NG
Retail

Priorswood Clematis
Widbury Hill, Ware
Hertfordshire SG12 7QH
Retail; wholesale; exports

Quantock Climbing Plants
Bagborough, Taunton
Somerset TA4 3EP
Mike Cheadle
Retail; wholesale

Roseland House Nursery
Chacewater, Truro
Cornwall TR4 8QB
Charles Pridham
Retail

S. F. Hoddinott and Son
New Leaf Plants
Amberley Farm, Cheltenham
    Road
Evesham WR11 6LW
Wholesale

Scottclem
1 Huish Lodge, Instow
Devon EX39 4LT
Retail; exports

Sheila Chapman Clematis at
    Crowther Nurseries
Ongar Road, Abridge
Essex RM4 1AA
Retail

Sherston Parva Nursery
Malmesbury Road, Sherston
Wiltshire SN16 0NX
Retail; exports

Taylors Nurseries
Sutton Road, Sutton Askern,
    Doncaster
South Yorkshire DN6 9JZ
Retail

Thorncroft Clematis Nursery
The Lings, Reymerston, Nor-
    wich
Norfolk NR9 4QG
Ruth and Jonathon Gooch
Mail order; retail; exports

Top Plants
Broad Lane, North Curry,
    Taunton
Somerset TA3 6EE
Wholesale

Treasures of Tenbury
Burford House Gardens, Ten-
    bury Wells
Worcestershire WR15 8HQ
Mail order; retail; wholesale

Two Ways Nursery
Cleeve Road, Middle Little-
    ton, Evesham
Worcestershire WR11 5JT
Retail; wholesale

Woodcote Park Nursery
Ripley Road, Send, Woking
Surrey GU23 7LT
Retail; wholesale

Woodland Barn Nurseries
Lichfield Road, Abbots
    Bromley, Rugeley
Staffordshire WS15 3DN
Tony Slater
Wholesale

ESTONIA
Family Kivistik
Roogoja Talu, Karlaküla
Kose 75101, Harjumaa
Retail; wholesale

FINLAND
Puutarhakeskus Sofianletho
Sofianlehdonkatu 12
00610 Helsinki

FRANCE
ELLEBORE
La Chamotière
61360 St. Jouin de Blavou
Retail

La Vallée Blonde
L'Hôtellerie, RN 13
14100 Lisieux
Retail

Le Jardin des Clématites
5 bis allée du Fond du Val, BP
    172
76135 Mont St. Aignan
Retail

Pépinière Botanique
Jean Thoby
Château de Gaujacq
40330 Amou
Retail

Pépinière Rhône Alpes
3549 route de Paris
01440 Viriat
Retail

SNC N. Albouy Geoffroy
Jardin d'Acclimatation
Bois de Boulogne
75116 Paris
Retail

Travers
Cour Charette
45650 St. Jean Le Blanc
Retail

GERMANY
Baumschul-Center
    Schmidtlein
Oberer Bühl 18
91090 Effeltrich
Retail; wholesale

Kruse, Wilhelm Clematis-
    gärtnerei
Wallenbrückerstrasse 14
49328 Melle 7
Mail order; retail

Mayer, Robert
Gartenbau, An der Schleuse
96129 Strullendorf bei Bam-
    berg
Wholesale

Münster, Klaus
Baumschulen
Bullendorf 19-20
25335 Altenmoor
Retail; wholesale

Sachs, Lothar
Clematisgärtnerei
Großstückweg 10
01445 Radebeul
Retail

Straver, Adrian
Gartenbau, Zum Waldkreuz
    97
46446 Emmerich Elte
Retail; wholesale

Westphal, Friedrich Manfred
Peiner Hof 7
D-25497 Prisdorf
Mail order; retail

IRELAND
Woodtown Nurseries
Stocking Lane
Woodtown, Rathfarnham
Dublin 16
Wholesale

JAPAN
Chikuma Engei
1-19-27 Sugo Miyamae Ku
Kawasaki City 216-0015
Wholesale

Clema Corporation
270-17 Hachibudaira, Higa-
    shino
Nagaizumi Machi, Suntoo
    Gun
Shizuoka Ken 441-0931
Wholesale

Hayakawa Engei
65, Nakahongo Izumi Cho
Anjo City, Aicha Prefecture
    444-1221
Wholesale

Kasugai Engei
1709-120 Kakino Tsurusato
    Machi
Toki City, Gifu Prefecture
    509-5312
Kozo Sugimoto
Mail order (in Japan only);
wholesale

Ozawa Engei
951 Shimo-Asao Asao Ku
Kawasaki City, Kanagawa
    Prefecture 215-0022
Kazushige Ozawa
Wholesale

Shonan Clematis Nursery
3-7-24 Tsuzido-Motomachi
Fujisawa City, Kanagawa Pre-
    fecture 247-0043
Mail order (in Japan only);
wholesale

NETHERLANDS
Bulk, Rein en Mark
Rijneveld 115
2771 XV, Boskoop
Wholesale; exports

Bulkyard Plants
P.O. Box 56
2779 AB, Boskoop
Retail; wholesale

Kuijf, Henk J.M.
Mennonietenbuurt 116A
1427BC Uithoorn

Werf, Ruud van der
Goudserijweg 60
2771 AK Boskoop
Retail; wholesale; exports

Westerhoud, Ed
Boomwekerijen
Reijerskoop 305a
2771 BL Boskoop
Wholesale; exports

Zoest, Jan van
Azalealaan 29
2771 ZX Boskoop
Wholesale

Zoest, Peter van
Randenburgseweg 21
2811 PS Reeuwijk
Wholesale

Zwijnenburg Jr., Pieter G.
Halve Raak 18
2771 AD Boskoop
Retail; wholesale

NEW ZEALAND
Cadsonbury Plant Breeders
28 Vardon Crescent
Christchurch 8006
Robin and Lorna Mitchell
Retail

M. L. Jerard and Company
Potters Lane, Lansdowne Val-
    ley, R.D.2
Christchurch 8021
Michael Jerard
Wholesale

New Zealand Clematis Nurseries
67 Ngaio Street, St. Martins
Christchurch 2
Wholesale

POLAND
Szczepan Marczyñski
Szkolka Pojemnikowa
ul. Duchnicka 25
05-800 Pruszków
Retail; wholesale; trade exports

SWEDEN
Cedergren and Company
  Plantskola
Box 16016
250 16 Råå
Krister Cedergren
Mail order; retail; wholesale

SWITZERLAND
Forster, Alfred
CH-3207 Golaten
Retail

Lehmann Baumschulen AG
CH-3294 Büren an der Aare
Retail

Meier, Ernst AG
Garten-Center
CH-8630 Tann-Rüti
Retail

UNITED STATES
Chalk Hill Clematis Farm
P.O. Box 1847
11720 Chalk Hill Road
Healdsburg, California 95448
Mail order; retail

Collector's Nursery
16804 NE 102nd Avenue
Battle Ground, Washington
  98604
Mail order

Completely Clematis Specialty Nursery
217 Argilla Road
Ipswich, Massachusetts 01938
Mail order; retail

D. S. George Nurseries
2491 Penfield Road
Fairport, New York 14450
Mail order

Donahue's Clematis Specialists
P.O. Box 366
420 SW 10th Street
Faribault, Minnesota 55021
Mail order; retail; wholesale

Forestfarm
990 Tetherow Road
Williams, Oregon 97544
Mail order

Greer Gardens
1280 Goodpasture Island Road
Eugene, Oregon 97401
Mail order

Gutmann Nurseries
19131 NW Dairy Creek Road
Cornelius, Oregon 97113
Wholesale

Heronswood Nursery
7530 NE 288th Street
Kingston, Washington 98346
Mail order; retail

Joy Creek Nursery
20300 NW Watson Road
Scappoose, Oregon 97056
Mail order

New Life Nurseries
192 Starry Road
Sequim, Washington 98382
Frank Snow
Retail

Siskiyou Rare Plant Nursery
2825 Cummings Road
Medford, Oregon 97501
Mail order

Wayside Gardens
1, Garden Lane
Hodges, South Carolina
  29695
Mail order; retail

APPENDIX 6

National Clematis Collections and Display Gardens

NATIONAL CLEMATIS COLLECTIONS

The National Council for the Conservation of Plants and Gardens (NCCPG) in the United Kingdom administers a National Plant Collections scheme. Although all national collections are open to the public, some, due to location or size, may have restricted access; details of this kind are not listed. To view restricted-access collections, please write to the collection holder and make the appropriate arrangements. The following nurseries and individuals are holders of clematis collections.

Clematis—all groups
Raymond J. Evison
The Guernsey Clematis Nursery
Domarie Vineries, Les Sauvagées, St. Sampson
Guernsey GY2 4FD, Channel Islands

Atragene group
M. Oviatt-Ham
Ely House, Green Street, Willingham
Cambridgeshire CB4 5JA, England

Alpina group
Mrs. J. Floyd
39, Arundel Gardens, Winchmore Hill
London N21 3AG, England

Herbaceous group
M. Brown
Clematis Corner, 15, Plough Close
Shillingford, Wallingford
Oxfordshire OX10 7EX, England

C. texensis, C. viticella, and herbaceous group
Treasures of Tenbury
Burford House Gardens, Tenbury Wells
Worcestershire WR15 8HQ, England

C. texensis and cultivars
Mr. and Mrs. J. Hudson
The Mill, 21 Mill Lane
Cannington, Bridgewater
Somerset TA5 2HB, England

Orientalis group
Chris Sanders
Bridgemere Nurseries
Bridgemere, Nantwich
Cheshire CW5 7QB, England

Viticella group
Robin Savill
Clematis Specialist
2 Bury Cottages, Bury Road, Pleshey, Chelmsford
Essex CM3 1HB, England

D. Stuart
Longstock Park Gardens
Longstock, Stockbridge
Hampshire SO20 6EH, England

CLEMATIS DISPLAY GARDENS

Two gardens are operated in association with the British Clematis Society.

Bourne Hall Display Garden
Bourne Hall Park, Spring Street, Ewell
Surrey KT17 1UF, England

Helmsley Walled Garden
Cleveland Way, Helmsley
York YO6 5AH, England

APPENDIX 7

Useful Addresses

International Clematis Registrar
Victoria Matthews
Denver Botanic Gardens
909 York Street
Denver, Colorado 80206, USA

The British Clematis Society Trials Ground Coordinator
John Maskelyne
5 Brookside, Moulton, Newmarket
Suffolk CB8 8SG, England

Information on the Trials Ground may also be obtained from the administrator of the British Clematis Society.

Clematis Societies
The British Clematis Society
Richard Stothard, Administrator
4 Springfield, Lightwater
Surrey GU18 5XP, England

The International Clematis Society
Fiona Woolfenden, Honorary Secretary
3, Cuthbert's Close, Cheshunt
Waltham Cross EN7 5RB, England

American Clematis Society
P.O. Box 17085
Irvine, California 92623, USA

Pacific Northwest Clematis Society
Rosemary Torrence, Secretary
8007 SW Locust
Portland, Oregon 97223, USA

Japan Clematis Society
1548 Hikawa cho, Soka City
Saitama, 340-0034, Japan

Swedish Clematis Society
Ulf Svensson, Secretary
Laxholmsbacken 114
127 42 Skärholmen, Sweden

The Estonian Clematis Club
Mrs. Külvi Kaus
Mustamäe tee 60
01108 Tallinn, Estonia

The Finland Clematis Club
Timo Löfgren, Secretary
Hannika 32A 02360 ESPOO, Finland

Glossary

Achene. A small dry fruit enclosing a single seed, which does not split to scatter the seed. In *Clematis*, the receptacle bears a collection of achenes and is called a seedhead.

Anther. The swollen part (head) of a stamen which contains the pollen grains. The stalklike part of the stamen is the filament, and it supports the anther.

Apex. The extreme tip of a growing region such as a stem, shoot, or root. The word is also used to describe the leaf tip.

Axil. The angle between a leaf and the stem of a plant where the axillary bud develops.

Axillary. Developing in the axils. A bud, flower, or even a cluster of flowers that develops in the leaf axil is called axillary or lateral, as opposed to terminal.

Bipinnate. A term used to describe arrangement of leaflets. The leaflets are arranged in two series on either side of a main axis.

Bisexual. Having male and female parts in the same flower. This is also known as hermaphrodite.

Biternate. Description of a leaf divided into three leaflets, which are in turn again divided into three. This is often referred to as twice-ternate. A biternate leaf consists of nine leaflets.

Blade. Broad area (of a leaf, petal, or tepal) within the margin.

Bract. A leaflike structure found at the base of a flower or a cluster of flowers. Though usually green or brown, bracts sometimes become brightly coloured and look like petals.

Calyx. The outermost part or whorl of a flower enclosing a flower bud. The calyx is usually green in colour.

Campanulate. Bell-shaped.

Chlorosis. A term applied to leaves when they become pale green in colour or even yellow due to iron or magnesium deficiency.

Clone. A group of genetically identical plants propagated by vegetative methods.

Compound. A term used to describe a leaf consisting of separate leaflets.

Corolla. Inner whorl or part of the flower, composed of petals, which is usually brightly coloured.

Crenate. Leaf or tepal margins with scalloped or rounded teeth.

Crenulate. Leaf or tepal margins with tiny rounded teeth.

Crisped. Minutely wavy edged, as in the tepal margins of *Clematis crispa*.

Cross-pollination. Transfer of pollen from an anther in a flower on one plant to the stigma in a flower on another plant of the same species.

Cultivar. Cultivated variety—applied to a plant originating under cultivation. When discussing *Clematis* 'Niobe', for example, the cultivar 'Niobe' is set in roman letters within single quotation marks, while the generic name *Clematis* is set in italics.

Dentate. Coarsely toothed, regular indentations, as applied to leaf margins.

Denticulate. A term used to describe the leaf margin with minute teethlike indentations.

Dioecious. Sexes separated and carried in different plants. Plants in the same species are either male or female.

Downy. Normally applied to describe leaves that are covered with short, stiff hairs.

Elliptic. Normally applied to describe leaf or tepal shape— broadening in the centre and narrowing towards each end.

Entire. A term used to describe a smooth, uninterrupted, or untoothed margin of a leaf.

Evergreen. Leaves remaining green throughout the year, although some older leaves fall off at regular intervals.

F_1 hybrid. First generation of plants arising from a cross between two pure-bred strains.

F₂ hybrid. Second-generation plants obtained by crossing two F₁ hybrids.

Family. A group of related genera of plants. Clematis, buttercup, hellebore, larkspur, love-in-a-mist, monkshood, and anemone belong to the family Ranunculaceae.

Fasicle. A cluster or bundle of flowers, stems, or leaves— *Clematis fasciculiflora*, for example.

Fertilization. The union of the pollen (male unit) with the ovule (female unit) to result in a seed. Pollination is a prerequisite to the process of fertilization.

Fertilizer. Organic or inorganic material added to the soil or any other growing medium to improve its fertility.

Fibrous root. Fine thin roots, as opposed to thick bootlacelike roots.

Filament. The stalk of the stamen which carries the anther.

Flower. Specialized reproductive shoot of a plant concerned chiefly with the production of the seed. Main components of a typical flower include the calyx, corolla, stamens, and pistil. A flower may be single, semi-double, or double.

Flower stalk. The stem that supports the flower or the flower head. The flower stalk is also known as the pedicel.

Foliage. A collective term for the leaves of a plant.

Genus. A unit or category of botanic classification. A group of plant species which are closely related forms a genus. The species *patens*, *florida*, *marmoraria*, *viticella*, and so on, belong to the genus *Clematis*. The genus is the first component of a species' botanical name, such as *Clematis* in *Clematis patens*. The plural form of genus is genera.

Glaucous. Bluish or grey-green. The term is usually applied to leaf colour.

Habit. The general manner of a plant's growth, such as climbing, trailing, or erect.

Habitat. The natural home or environment in which a wild plant grows.

Hard prune. To cut back a plant to within a few buds from the base on shoots above the ground to promote vigorous growth.

Herbaceous. A term used to describe the habit of plants, mostly perennials, which die down at the end of a growing season and return to full growth above ground level the following spring. In botanical usage, the term also applies to annuals and biennials.

Hermaphrodite. Male and female sexes in the same flower. See bisexual.

Humus. A rich brownish black material resulting from the gradual breakdown of vegetable and other organic matter by bacterial activity.

Hybrid. A plant obtained by the crossing of two different varieties, species, or genera of plants. Hybrids seldom breed true and some are even sterile.

Hybridization. A method used by plant breeders to produce new hybrids. Hybridization is achieved through controlled cross-pollination, in which pollen from one plant is transferred to another plant with the aid of a camel-hair brush.

Inflorescence. Arrangement of flowers on a shoot, branch, or stem, meaning simply the grouping of the flowers or a definite flower cluster.

Internode. The part of the stem between two consecutive nodes (leaf joints).

Lanceolate. Of a leaf or tepal, the margins of which taper at both ends like a lance-head— much longer than wide, and wider below the mid-region.

Lanuginose. Woolly, covered in short, soft hairs.

Layering. A method of propagation carried out by bending down and burying a part of a stem in the ground, or in a compost-filled pot, while it is still attached to the parent plant.

Leaf margin. The outer edge of a leaf.

Leaflet. A leaflike subdivision of a compound leaf.

Node. A point where the leaf is attached to the stem, also known as the leaf joint.

Obovate. A term used to describe a leaf or tepal, more or less egg-shaped but broadest towards the top end away from the stalk.

Opposite. A term used to describe the leaf arrangement on a stem. Each node (leaf joint) has a pair of leaves arranged on opposite sides of the stem.

Ovary. Basal part of a pistil (of a flower) housing the ovules, which will become seeds after fertilization.

Ovate. A term used to describe the shape of a leaf or a tepal, more or less oval in outline but broadest at the base or toward the stalk.

Ovules. Contained inside the ovary. These structures will give rise to seeds on fertilization.

Pedicel. The stalk of a single or an individual flower.

Pendulous. Hanging, drooping, or suspended (of a flower).

Persistent. Not dropping or falling off, as in the case of the feathery style of a clematis seed (achene).

Petaloid. Petal-like. Sepals and staminodes, or sterile stamens, can look like petals.

Petiole. Leaf stalk.

pH. The measure of acidity or alkalinity of any substance.

Pistil. The female reproductive part of a flower, consisting of an ovary, style, and stigma.

Pollination. Transference of pollen grains from the anther to the stigma of the same or different flowers. Pollination is essential for fertilization and seed formation.

Pubescent. Hairy. The term is often used to describe leaves or buds covered with short, soft hairs.

Recurved. Curved backward or downward (of tepals).

Reflexed. Fully bent or turned back on itself (the tip of a tepal, for example).

Scalloped. Edges or margins having rounded teeth or notches (of tepals or leaves).

Sepal. A component of calyx, the outermost whorl of flower. Sepals are usually green and leaflike. Sometimes they may become brightly coloured like the petals or even replace the petals, as is the case in *Clematis*.

Sere. Dried or withered.

Serrated. Edges or margins toothed like a saw (of a leaf).

Sessile. A term used to describe leaves with no stalks or petioles.

Simple. A leaf with a continuous lamina (leaf blade) and a single expanse of tissue which is not divided into leaflets.

Solitary. A term used to describe flowers when they appear singly (one on its own), as opposed to appearing in clusters.

Species. Basic unit of biological classification which refers to a group of very closely related plants which can interbreed freely, and breed true, with one another but not usually with members of another species. If they do, the resulting hybrids will be infertile.

Stamen. The male reproductive part of a flower made up of a filament and anther.

Staminode. An infertile stamen—no pollen.

Stigma. Found at the tip of a pistil (female reproductive organ). The stigma serves as the receptive surface for pollen grains.

Subshrub. A shrublike plant in which only the basal part becomes woody.

Subspecies. Subdivision of a species. A subspecies usually differs in two or more characteristics from the typical plant and is geographically distinct.

Synonym. An alternate name or an earlier name that has been replaced.

Temperate. Mild, often used to describe climate.

Tepal. A term used when there is no clear differentiation between a sepal (calyx) and a petal (corolla), as is the case with *Clematis*.

Terminal. At the very end of a stem or shoot, ending it.

Ternate. A term used to describe a leaf which divides into three leaflets.

Tetraploid. Possessing four basic sets of chromosomes instead of the more usual two sets (diploid).

Tint. Hue of a colour.

Tip. See **apex**.

Trifoliate. In groups of three leaves.

Triternate. Three times ternate, where primary divisions of three leaflets are divided further, resulting in nine leaflets—which in turn proceed to divide again, giving rise to 27 leaflets.

Undulate. Wavy margins or edges (of tepals).

Variety. The subdivision of a species or subspecies. A variety differs from the typical plant in one or two characteristics but is usually found growing in the same geographical range, or at least in a part of it.

×. A sign used for hybridization.

Bibliography

Bean, W. J. 1919. *Trees and Shrubs Hardy in the British Isles*. 2nd ed. John Murray.

Buchan, U. 1992. *Wall Plants and Climbers: The National Trust Guide*. Pavilion.

Buczacki, S. 1998. *Best Clematis*. Hamlyn Publishers.

Burras, J. K., and M. Griffiths, eds. 1994. *Manual of Climbers and Wall Plants (New Royal Horticultural Society Dictionary)*. Macmillan.

Cedergren, K. 1986. The Swedish pioneers in raising *Clematis* hybrids. *Newsletter of the International Clematis Society* 3 (1): 15–16.

Clearview Horticultural Products, Ontario. Undated. *The Concise Guide to Clematis in North America*.

Erickson, R. O. 1943. Taxonomy of *Clematis* section *Viorna*. *Annals of the Missouri Botanical Garden* 30 (1): 1–62.

Evison, R. J. 1995. *Making the Most of Clematis*. 3rd ed. Burall Floraprint.

——. 1998. *The Gardener's Guide to Growing Clematis*. David and Charles.

Fair, K., and C. Fair. 1990. *Clematis for Colour and Versatility*. The Crowood Press.

Feltwell, J. 1998. Roll of honour. *The Garden* 123 (7): 480–483.

——. 1999. *Clematis for all Seasons*. Collins and Brown.

Fisk, J. 1962. *Success with Clematis*. Nelson.

——. 1975. *The Queen of Climbers*. Westleton, Suffolk: Fisk's Clematis Nursery.

——. 1984. Cultivars introduced by Jim Fisk. *Newsletter of the International Clematis Society* 2: 12–16.

——. 1989. *Clematis: The Queen of Climbers*. Cassell.

——. 1994. *Clematis: The Queen of Climbers*. Cassell.

Fretwell, B. 1989. *Clematis*. Collins.

——. 1994. *Clematis as Companion Plants*. Collins.

Gauntlett, P. 1995. *Jackmans of Woking*. Dolgellau, North Wales: Pamela Gauntlett.

Gooch, R. 1996. *Clematis: the Complete Guide*. Crowood Press.

Grey-Wilson, C. 1986. *Clematis orientalis*: a much confused species. *Plantsman* 7 (4): 193–205.

——. 2000. *Clematis, The Genus*. Batsford.

Hall, N., J. Newdick, and N. Sutherland. 1994. *Growing Clematis*. Aura Books.

Hawke, R. G. 1997. *Clematis for Northern Landscapes*. Plant Evaluation Notes, Chicago Botanic Garden. Chicago Horticultural Society Periodic Publications 10: 1–6.

Howells, J. 1996. *The Rose and the Clematis as Good Companions*. Garden Art Press.

——. 1998. *Trouble-free Clematis: The Viticellas*. Garden Art Press.

——, ed. 1991–1994. *The Clematis* (journal of the British Clematis Society).

——, ed. 1991–1995. *The Clematis* (spring supplement of the British Clematis Society).

Hutchins, G. 1990. New Zealand *Clematis*: hybrids and species in cultivation. *Plantsman* 11 (4): 193–209.

International Clematis Society. 1988–1990, 1998–2000. *Clematis International*.

Jackman, A. G. 1900. Hybrid *Clematis*. *Journal of the Royal Horticultural Society* 24: 315.

——. 1946. The *Clematis* as a garden plant. *Journal of the Royal Horticultural Society* 71: 350–358.

Johnson, M. 1984. Swedish clematis. *Newsletter of the International Clematis Society* 1: 6–30.

——. 1987. *C. integrifolia* × *C. viticella*. *Newsletter of the International Clematis Society* 4 (1): 13–15.

———. 1996. *Släktet Klematis (The Genus Clematis)*. Södertälje, Sweden: Magnus Johnson's Plantskola AB.

Lamb, J. G. D. 1990. The propagation of climbing *Clematis*. *Plantsman* 12 (3): 178–180.

Lloyd, C. 1977. *Clematis*. Collins.

Lloyd, C., and T. Bennett. 1989. *Clematis*. Rev. ed. Viking.

Lord, T., ed. 1999. *The RHS Plant Finder 1999–2000*. Dorling Kindersley.

Markham, E. 1935. *Clematis*. Country Life.

———. 1951. *Clematis*. 3rd ed. Country Life.

Mikolajski, A. 1997. *Clematis*. Lorenz.

Moore, T., and G. Jackman. 1872. *The Clematis as a Garden Flower*. Jackmans of Woking: John Murray.

Oviatt-Ham, M. 1996. Miniature belles. *The Garden* 121 (3): 140–145.

Pennell, R. 1984. Walter Pennell and the Pennell hybrids. *Newsletter of the International Clematis Society* 1: 31–40.

Pennell, W. E. 1966. Sense about *Clematis*. *Journal of the Royal Horticultural Society* 91: 27–36.

Pringle, J. S. 1971. Taxonomy and distribution of *Clematis*. Sect. Atragene in North America. *Brittonia* 23: 361–393.

———. 1973. The cultivated taxa of *Clematis*. Sect. Atragene. *Baileya* 19: 49–89.

Riekstina, I. 1986. *Clematis* 1986 in Latvia. *Newsletter of the International Clematis Society* 3 (2): 4.

Riekstina, W. 1985. The new clematis cutlivars and hybrids bred in the Soviet Union. *Newsletter of the International Clematis Society* 3: 5–15.

Robinson, W. 1912. *The Virgin's Bower*. John Murray.

Royal Horticultural Society. 1999. *Practical Guides: Clematis*.

Shiraishi, T. 1985a. *Clematis lasiandra* in Kumamoto. *Newsletter of the International Clematis Society* 4: 15.

———. 1985b. *Clematis japonica*. *Newsletter of the International Clematis Society* 4: 15.

Snoeijer, W. 1991. *Clematis Index*. Boskoop, Netherlands: J. Fopma.

Toomey, M. K. 1997. Notes on *Clematis ×aromatica*. *The New Plantsman* 4 (2): 79–82.

———. 1999. *Clematis: A Care Manual*. Hamlyn Publishers.

———, ed. 1995–1999. *The Clematis* (journal of the British Clematis Society).

———, ed. 1996–2000. *The Clematis* (spring supplement of the British Clematis Society).

Thurber, R. 1730. *Twelve Months of Flowers*. N.p.

Trehane, R. P., C. D. Brickell, B. R. Baum, W. L. A. Hetterscheid, A. C. Leslie, J. McNeill, S. A. Spongberg, and F. Vrugtman, eds. 1995. *The International Code of Nomenclature for Cultivated Plants*. Quarterjack Publishing.

Whitehead, S. B. 1959. *Garden Clematis*. The Trinity Press.

———. 1959. *Garden Clematis*. John Gifford.

Wild, R. C. 1984. Forty years with *Clematis* 'Down Under'. *Newsletter of the International Clematis Society* 2:17–18.

Catalogues

Bradshaw, J., and Son Catalogue 1998

Caddick's Clematis Nursery Catalogue 1998–1999, 2000

Denny's Clematis Nursery Catalogue 1998

Fisk's Clematis Nursery Catalogue 1962–1992

Peveril Clematis Nursery Catalogue 1981–1999

Priorswood Clematis Catalogue 1997, 2000

Robin Savill, Clematis Specialist Catalogue 1998–1999, 2000

Sheila Chapman, Clematis Catalogue 1996–1999, 2000

Thorncroft Clematis Nursery Catalogue 1989–2000

Treasures of Tenbury Catalogue 1976–1997

Valley Clematis Catalogue 1988–1996

Index of Plants

Plant Name Updates as of 2005

Clematis 'Alborosea' is now *Clematis* 'Blushing Ballerina'
Clematis 'Blue Boy' is now *Clematis* ×*diversifolia* 'Blue Boy'
Clematis 'Jadwiga Teresa' is now *Clematis* 'Général Sikorski'
Clematis 'Plena' is now *Clematis florida* var. *flor-pleno*
Clematis 'Purpurea' is now *Clematis recta* 'Purpurea'
Clematis 'Sieboldii' is now *Clematis florida* var. *sieboldiana*